THE NEW YORK STATE CONSTITUTION

**Reference Guides to the State Constitutions
of the United States**

This series includes a separate volume for each state constitution, analyzing
its history and current status, providing a text of the constitution with a
clause-by-clause commentary, a bibliography, a table of cases, and an index.
A volume describing common themes and variations in state constitutional
development and a final index volume to the preceding volumes are
forthcoming.

The New Jersey State Constitution: A Reference Guide
Robert F. Williams

The Tennessee State Constitution: A Reference Guide
Lewis L. Laska

THE NEW YORK STATE CONSTITUTION
A Reference Guide

Peter J. Galie

REFERENCE GUIDES TO THE STATE CONSTITUTIONS OF THE UNITED STATES,
NUMBER 3

G. Alan Tarr, *Series Editor*

GREENWOOD PRESS
New York • Westport, Connecticut • London

Library of Congress Cataloging-in-Publication Data

Galie, Peter J.
    The New York State Constitution : a reference guide / Peter J.
Galie
       p. cm. — (Reference guides to the state constitutions of the
United States : no. 3)
    Includes bibliographical references and index.
    ISBN 0–313–26156–3 (1ib. bdg. : a1k. paper)
    1. New York (State)—Constitution. 2. New York (State)—
Constitutional history. I. Title. II Series.
KFN5680 1777.A6G35 1991
342.747'02—dc20
[347.47022]   90–36627

British Library Cataloguing in Publication Data is available.

Library of Congress Catalog Card Number: 90–36627
ISBN: 0–313–26156–3

First published in 1991

Greenwood Press, 88 Post Road West, Westport, CT 06881
An imprint of Greenwood Publishing Group, Inc.

Printed in the United States of America

The paper used in this book complies with the
Permanent Paper Standard issued by the National
Information Standards Organization (Z39.48–1984).

10 9 8 7 6 5 4 3 2 1

To the three people most responsible for this book:
My Mother, My Father, and My Wife.

Contents

Article VII: State Finances   **165**

Abbreviations

Abb. N. Cas.	*Abbott's New Cases* (reporter of practice and code cases)
A.D.	Reporter for decisions of the appellate division of the Supreme Court
A.D.2d	Second series of A.D.
Barb.	*Barbour's Supreme Court Reports*
CLS	*Consolidated Legal Service Annotated Statutes* (unofficial set of consolidated laws of New York)
et seq.	"and following"
F.2d	*Federal Reporter* (reporter of U.S. Courts of Appeals decisions)
F. Supp.	*Federal Supplement Reporter* of U.S. District Court decisions
Hun.	*Hun's Supreme Court Reports*
Inf. Opin. A-G	Informal opinions of the Attorney-General of New York (cited by year and page, e.g. 83–76).
Johns.	*Johnson's Reports* (reports of court for the correction of errors)
McKinney	*McKinney's Consolidated Laws of New York Annotated*
Misc.	*Miscellaneous Reporter* (reporter for the decisions of New York courts of initial jurisdiction)
Misc. 2d	Second series of *Miscellaneous Reporter*

N.E.	*Northeastern Reporter* (regional reporter reporting court of appeals decisions)
N.E.2d	Second series of *Northeastern Reporter*
N.Y.	*New York Reports* (reporter for court of appeals decisions)
N.Y.2d	Second Series of *New York Reports*
N.Y. Jur.	*New York Jurisprudence* (multivolume encyclopedia of New York law)
N.Y. Jur. 2d	Revised edition of *New York Jurisprudence* (not yet completed)
Opin. A-G	*Opinions of the Attorney General of New York* (cited by year and page, e.g., 88–24).
Opin. St. Compt.	*Opinion of the State Comptroller* (cited by year and page)
Paige	*Paige's Chancery Reports*
Rev. Rec.	Revised records of the constitutional conventions held in 1894 and 1938, as specified in the text
S.D.N.Y.	Southern District of New York
Sheld.	*Sheldon's Reports*, Superior Court of Buffalo
U.S.	*U.S. Reports* (official reports of U.S. Supreme Court)
USCA	United States Code Annotated
Wend.	*Wendell's Reports* (reports of the court of correction and errors)

Series Foreword

In 1776, following the declaration of independence from England, the former colonies began to draft their own constitutions. Their handiwork attracted widespread interest, and draft constitutions circulated up and down the Atlantic seaboard, as constitution-makers sought to benefit from the insights of their counterparts in sister states. In Europe, the new constitutions found a ready audience seeking enlightenment from the American experiments in self-government. Even the delegates to the Constitutional Convention of 1787, despite their reservations about the course of political developments in the states during the decade after independence, found much that was useful in the newly adopted constitutions. And when James Madison, fulfilling a pledge given during the ratification debates, drafted the federal Bill of Rights, he found his model in the famous Declaration of Rights of the Virginia Constitution.

By the 1900s, however, few people would have looked to state constitutions for enlightenment. Instead, a familiar litany of complaints was heard whenever state constitutions were mentioned. State constitutions were too long and too detailed, combining basic principles with policy prescriptions and prohibitions that had no place in the fundamental law of a state. By including such provisions, it was argued, state constitutions deprived state governments of the flexibility they needed to respond effectively to changing circumstances. This—among other factors—encouraged political reformers to look to the federal government, which was not plagued by such constitutional constraints, thereby shifting the locus of political initiative away from the states. Meanwhile, civil libertarians concluded that state bills of rights, at least as interpreted by state courts, did not adequately protect rights and therefore looked to the federal courts and the federal Bill of Rights for redress. As power and responsibility shifted from the states

xxii   Series Foreword

to Washington, so too did the attention of scholars, the legal community, and the general public.

During the early 1970s, however, state constitutions were "rediscovered." The immediate impetus for this rediscovery was former President Richard Nixon's appointment of Warren Burger to succeed Earl Warren as Chief Justice of the United States Supreme Court. To civil libertarians, this appointment seemed to signal a decisive shift in the Supreme Court's jurisprudence, because Burger was expected to lead the Court away from the liberal activism that had characterized the Warren Court. They therefore sought ways to safeguard the gains they had achieved for defendants, racial minorities, and the poor during Warren's tenure from erosion by the Burger Court. In particular, they began to look to state bills of rights to secure the rights of defendants and to support other civil-liberties claims that they advanced in state courts.

The "new judicial federalism," as it came to be called, quite quickly advanced beyond its initial concern to evade the mandates of the Burger Court. Indeed, less than two decades after it originated, it has become a nationwide phenomenon. For when judges and scholars turned their attention to state constitutions, they discovered an unsuspected richness. They found not only provisions that paralleled the federal Bill of Rights but also constitutional guarantees of the right to privacy and of gender equality, for example, that had no analogue in the U.S. Constitution. Careful examination of the text and history of state guarantees revealed important differences between even those provisions that most resembled federal guarantees and their federal counterparts. Looking beyond state declarations of rights, jurists and scholars discovered affirmative constitutional mandates to state governments to address such important policy concerns as education and housing. Taken altogether, these discoveries underlined the importance for the legal community of developing a better understanding of state constitutions.

Yet the renewed interest in state constitutions has not been limited to judges and lawyers. State constitutional reformers have renewed their efforts with notable success: since 1960, ten states have adopted new constitutions and several others have undertaken major constitutional revisions. These changes have usually resulted in more streamlined constitutions and more effective state governments. Also, in recent years political activists on both the left and the right have pursued their goals through state constitutional amendments, often enacted through the initiative process, under which policy proposals can be placed directly on the ballot for voters to endorse or reject. Scholars too have begun to rediscover how state constitutional history can illuminate changes in political thought and practice, providing a basis for theories about the dynamics of political change in America.

Peter Galie's excellent study of the New York Constitution is the third volume in the series, Reference Guides to the State Constitutions of the United States, which reflects this renewed interest in state constitutions and will contribute to our knowledge about them. Because the constitutional tradition of each state is distinctive, the volume begins with the history and development of the New York Constitution. It then provides the complete text of New York's current constitution, with each section accompanied by commentary that explains the provision and traces its origins and its interpretation by the courts and by other governmental bodies. For readers with a particular interest in a specific aspect of New York's constitutional experience, the book offers a bibliography of the most important sources dealing with the constitutional history and constitutional law of the state. Finally, the book concludes with a table of cases cited in the history and the constitutional commentary, as well as a subject index.

G. Alan Tarr

Preface

It is a measure of the neglect of state constitutions that while numerous commentaries exist on our national document, there is no one volume commentary on the current constitution of New York. This is unfortunate for a number of reasons. The New York Legislature and State Board of Regents mandate that elementary and secondary school teachers introduce their students to the state constitution, a difficult task in light of the dearth of readily available materials. College instructors, students, and the general citizenry face the same problem. Even lawyers and judges, whose work requires a much more detailed analysis than could be provided in one volume, may have felt the need for a readily available reference work on the state constitution.

A one volume work of manageable proportions on a document that is nearly 50,000 words in length necessarily means that the treatment will be introductory in character: a variety of topics connected with each article and section had to be left out or given only cursory treatment. Within these limitations I have tried to provide the legislative intent for each section—why it was put there in the first place; some information about its evolution; and the interpretations by the judiciary and the attorney general which have shaped the contours of the section. Where relevant, I have noted statutory interpretations and/or implementations of the various clauses. I have tried to emphasize the basic principle or values embodied in each article. No attempt has been made to provide a complete doctrinal history of all aspects of each section. Such detailed commentary does not exist, though one can find commentary on various sections scattered throughout the multi-volumed legal encyclopedia, *New York Jurisprudence*. McKinney's and the Consolidated Legal Service both have volumes which provide case annotations for each section of the constitution, and the reader is referred to these for a more complete annotation of relevant cases.

The historical derivations in brackets after each section are not complete histories of the sections. They include only changes in renumbering, and amendments which form part of the sections as they currently stand. A list of sources on the current constitution organized by article is provided in the bibliography. As there is no such list currently available, I hope it will prove useful to those wishing to explore further.

Acknowledgments

For a work covering topics as diverse as civil liberties, taxes, conservation, social welfare, and canals, among others, of necessity I have relied on the research and support of others. I thank the Canisius College Faculty Research and Publications Committee for providing a research grant that enabled me to complete the bulk of the manuscript in the summer of 1989. G. Alan Tarr, the adviser to this series, devoted much of his free time to a careful reading of the entire manuscript, and it is much improved as a result. Gerald Benjamin of the State University of New York (SUNY), New Paltz, was kind enough to read the introductory chapter and provided me with numerous comments, many of which I have been able to incorporate. Buffalo is fortunate to have a number of lawyers who are both practitioners and students of constitutional law. I have drawn on some of this talent. James Magavern, a man who probably knows as much about Articles VII and VIII as anyone else, read my comments on both of these articles and spent much time enlightening me on the intricacies of state and local finance law. Mark Mahoney provided detailed and helpful comments on Article I. Milton Kaplan, for many years a teacher at SUNY Law School in Buffalo and now with the firm of Magavern & Magavern, gave me the benefit of his reading of Article IX. Ron Coan, a colleague now with the Planning Department of Erie County, helped make Article XVIII less obscure. Robert Klump, a former student of mine who is now a successful lawyer and teacher, gave me the benefit of careful and critical comments on Article XVI. Three student assistants have worked with me on the project. Karen Herzog, Paul D. McCormick, and John D'Amato, all aspiring lawyers, did a large part of the tedious but important cite checking and background research. I also express my gratitude to Paulette Kirsch, who fed the manuscript into the computer, formated the document, and patiently put up with my constant revisions with professionalism and patience. The assistance of all who helped me has measurably improved the document. Of course, they are not responsible for my decisions not to heed their advice.

I thank our department secretary, Francine Gray, who assisted with the table of cases and, more important, kept me from losing my place.

Part I

The Constitutional History of New York

> The State Constitutions are the oldest things in the political history of America for they are a continuation and representatives of the royal charters.
>
> James Bryce

New York's first constitution, that of 1777, was written and adopted in the midst of a revolutionary war by a government literally on the run. But the shape of that document reflected the state's peculiar history and geography more than the hazardous conditions under which it was hammered out. Three factors stand out in this respect: (1) the existence of wealthy, established families such as the Livingstons, Van Cortlands, Schuylers, Philipses, and Van Rensselaers; (2) the multiplicity of groups and regions vying for political power and social position; and (3) early colonial charters, the Duke's Laws (1665) and the Charter of Liberties and Privileges of 1683 and 1691.

The established families provided talented men who were to play a key role in the shaping of New York's first constitution. John Jay, Gouverneur Morris, and Robert Livingston were major actors at the state's 1777 Constitutional Convention who succeeded in moderating the more populist elements at the convention.

The second factor was the early development of diversified religious, economic, and ethnic interests. This pluralism created "A Factious People." Factions, the parties or groups formed around these interests, created a party spirit. Faction "was the instrument not simply of class or interest or ideology but all of this and something more—of politics, which contained and absorbed everything else".[1] This precocity in the politics of pluralism and self-interest was crucial in moving the constitutional structure of New York toward a new conception of the polity that was to triumph with the adoption of the national Constitution in 1787.

The third factor was the series of charters founding the colony of New York. These charters were the immediate source of a consensus in favor of a written constitution and government by fundamental law not to be altered except by extraordinary measures. Eventually they would be transformed into instruments of colonial self-government. The idea of inviolable rights, which also appeared in these charters, provided the basis for subsequent arguments about the expansion of those rights. The extent to which demands for more representative government, the rule of law, and liberty had developed is well illustrated by the following petition from a grand jury in 1681 begging for relief from

inexpressible burdens by having an arbitrary and absolute power used and exercised over us by which yearly revenue is extracted from us against our wills . . . our liberty and freedom intralled and the inhabitants wholly shut out or deprived of any share, vote or interest in the government . . . contrary to the laws, rights, liberties and privileges of the subjects.[2]

These demands persisted, and a new governor was appointed. In 1683, the Duke of York instructed that governor to call an assembly of people. The result was the Charter of Liberties and Privileges. The charter was a milestone in the development of constitutional liberty in New York; it was New York's first "experiment with representative government."[3]

By the opening of the eighteenth century, the constitutional structure of New York resembled the pattern that had developed in England after the Glorious Revolution of 1688. For the next seventy years constitutional disputes involved the question of ultimate authority: whether it was possessed by the governor or the legislature or shared by both. Though fundamental disputes reappeared after 1776 when the state's constitution makers had to decide how to distribute powers between the legislative and executive branches, the structure in place by the middle of the eighteenth century proved satisfactory enough to be adopted with only a few changes as the first constitution of the state of New York.

THE CONSTITUTION OF 1777

We have you know a government to form; and God only knows what it will resemble. Our politicians, like some guest at a feast, are perplexed and undetermined which dish to prefer.

John Jay

The Fourth Provincial Congress, or the "Convention of Representatives of the State of New York" as they renamed themselves on July 10, 1776, was not only the governing body of the newly independent state but also a body exercising constituent powers. Although the notion of an independent body chosen by the people for the specific purpose of drafting a constitution had not yet developed—

no state had entrusted the work of forming a new constitution to a specially elected constitutional convention—the members of the Third Provincial Congress of 1775 were troubled by the lack of any mandate to form a new government. For this reason, they called for a special election to obtain that mandate. This decision—to go to the electorate for a mandate to frame a new government— was a step in the direction of recognizing a distinction between a constitutional convention and a legislative body, and the notion of a state constitution as superior to legislative enactments.

The Provincial Congress's uneasiness about legislative adoption of a constitution was shared by the Committee of Mechanics of New York City, who demanded that any constitution drafted by the congress be submitted to the voters for ratification. For them it was a "God-given right for the people of New York to judge whether it be consistent with their interest to accept or reject a Constitution framed for the state of which they are members. That is the birth right of every man."[4]

The newly elected congress met, but no draft of a constitution was produced until March 1777, partly because the congress was repeatedly forced to move by the war and partly because conservatives in the congress wished to delay action until calmer conditions prevailed and the chance of radical triumph was less likely.[5] As two members of the congress expressed it: "We first ought to endeavor to secure the state to govern before we establish a form to govern it."[6]

Generally a broad division appeared in the convention between those who wished to keep change to a minimum, variously called traditionalists or Conservatives, and those who wished for extensive change, variously called majoritarians or Popular Whigs. Between these two were the moderates, who were less committed to any specific program. The central issues of the convention debates were how democratic the government should be, how far the consent of the people should be carried, and how power should be distributed among the various branches of government. The Popular Whigs favored minimal property qualifications and legislative supremacy; the Conservatives argued for large property requirements and some sharing of power among the branches of government. The result was a series of compromises tilted to the side of the traditionalists, under which roughly 60 percent of the adult white males and 70.7 percent of the heads of families could vote for the assembly but only 28.9 percent of the adult males could vote for senators and governor.

A related concern was whether voting should be by oral declaration or secret ballot. The Popular Whigs wanted the secret ballot, fearing the influence of landlords on their tenants. The congress compromised here as well, continuing voice voting during the war but authorizing the legislature to abolish it when the war ended.

The second major issue at the convention was the distribution of power among the branches of government. Again compromise occurred. The governor was directly elected by the voters for a term of three years, giving him an independence and stability not available to governors in other states. He was made commander in chief of the militia, given some pardoning powers, authorized to convene and adjourn the assembly, and empowered to make policy recommendations to the legislature. On the other hand, he shared the veto power with a council of revision (consisting of the governor, the chancellor, and judges of the supreme court), which could "revise all bills" which they deem to be unconstitutional or inconsistent with the public good (Art. 3). This council reflected the convention's concern to avoid both a governor with too much legislative power and the unsettling prospect of a veto-proof legislature. It may be that "hard political necessity" prevented the delegates from consistently following doctrines like the separation of powers,[7] but it is more likely that the council of revision was an anticipation of the Federalist view that the great danger in republican government was the tendency for all powers to be swept into the legislative vortex. Seen in this light, the council is an early attempt to mix the powers of government in order to keep the weaker branches (executives and judiciary) separate and independent.

The appointment power created as much difficulty as the question of suffrage. There was little support for lodging it in the governor's office alone, and the traditionalists feared that the assembly would use the power to appoint "lesser sorts" to numerous government positions. The compromise was the council of appointment, consisting of the governor and four senators, one from each senatorial district, with the assembly choosing the four senators annually. John Jay, who proposed the compromise, intended for the governor to make all nominations and the council could confirm or reject them but the article did not explicitly state this. This omission led to a constitutional crisis that precipitated a second convention in 1801.

The convention attempted to ensure an independent judiciary by giving judges tenure "during good behaviour." It also stripped the governor of his equity and probate jurisdiction, which had the effect of increasing the judiciary's separateness as well as its independence. A court of impeachment and errors consisting of the president of the senate, senators, the chancellor, and judges of the supreme court acted as a court of last resort hearing appeals from the supreme court. It is clear that the convention's understanding of the separation of powers did not prevent it from adopting structures that mixed the various powers for specific purposes.

Although the 1777 Constitution did not include a bill of rights, this did not indicate a lack of concern for rights. Rather, provisions protecting religious freedom, trial by jury, a due process of law clause, right to counsel, a conscientious objector clause for Quakers, and protection against bills of attainder are found in the body of the document. Moreover, the constitution provided for the continuation of most of the common law, which in itself afforded important protections. The religious liberty provisions ended the old struggle between the Church of England and the Dissenters for supremacy, defusing the potentially explosive issue of church and state.

The 1777 Constitution did not contain any provision for its amendment. Assuming this was not an oversight, the implication is that the legislature believed itself to be the body to initiate constitutional change and determine the process of amendment. This is consistent with the New York legislature's adoption of a bill of rights in 1787.

The 1777 Constitution: An Assessment

New York's first constitution stands out because it deviates from many of the assumptions and institutions that dominated state constitutional making from 1776 to 1780.

The New York Constitution of 1777 provided for the strongest executive in the American states, giving him the longest term with reeligibility, direct popular election, and a share with the judiciary in the veto power. In the council of revision and the court for the trial of impeachments and corrections of errors, the judiciary was given more power than any other comparable judiciary in its day. By requiring property qualifications for those voting for senators and governor, which disenfranchised 70 percent of the adult white males, and electing senators from the four "great" districts (the Southern, including Suffolk, Queens, New York, and Westchester counties; the Middle, including Dutchess, Elster, and Orange counties; the Eastern, including Charlotte, Gloucester, and Cumberland counties; and the Western, including Albany and Tyron counties), the convention distanced the representatives from the represented. The terms of office for the senate were the longest among the states, and there were no constitutional requirements for petitions to or instructions of legislators. The senate was to be more a filter than a mirror for popular sentiment. Moreover, much of the sentiment for doing so was similar to that which animated Madison and others at the federal convention: the need to put restraints on the "levelling spirit." Finally, where rights appear in the 1777 Constitution, these rights were written in the prescriptive *shall* and were clearly aimed at limiting legislative as well as executive actions. As such, they anticipated the movement to make rights legally binding on the legislature.

What we see in institutions like the councils of revision and appointment is a concern for institutional checks among the various branches of government rather than the relationship between government and the people. New York's long history of regional, religious, and group conflict made New York seem, in the eyes of one contemporary observer, "mad with politics."[8] As one student of colonial New York put it, at a time "when political factionalism was looked on as disruptive of public order, New Yorkers accepted it as legitimate."[9] Group conflict was a part of the political culture of New Yorkers almost from the beginning. It is this pluralism and interest group conflict that best explains the early appearance of politics in the modern sense and helps explain the character of New York's constitution as the bridge to the view embraced by the delegates at the Philadelphia Convention of 1787.

Assessing the quality of a constitution is a difficult task. If the degree of support for the final product is the measure, the convention succeeded admirably; the final vote in favor of the document was 31–1. In his inaugural address of 1777, George Clinton called it "our free and happy constitution," a judgment shared across the political spectrum, even by Anti-Federalists like Robert and Abraham Yates, who opposed the federal Constitution. Alan Nevins in his study of the states during the Revolution concluded: "At the time, and with reason, it was widely regarded as the best of the organic laws, and it exerted a considerable influence on the Federal Constitution."[10]

The constitution of 1777 remained in force unchanged until 1801. Two problems prompted the calling of a constitutional convention: the number and method of apportionment of members of the assembly and a bitter partisan dispute between Governor Jay, a Federalist, and the Republican members of the council of appointment over the question of who had the power to nominate appointees. Jay claimed that the governor nominated; the council claimed that the power was shared. The convention decided that the power to nominate was a concurrent right of both the governor and the council, putting effective control of nominations and appointments in the hand of the council and in effect the legislature, both weakening the executive and giving a great boost to the spoils system. The convention also adopted four other amendments stipulating the number of assemblymen and senators and their method of apportionment. None of these amendments was submitted to the voters for ratification.

THE CONSTITUTION OF 1821

A political bear-garden from beginning to end.

Ambrose Spencer,
convention delegate

The convention of 1821 owed its origins as much to the attempt by Tammany Hall to destroy its arch enemy, Governor De Witt Clinton, as it did to demands from new political forces for constitutional change. Its operation and product must be placed in the context of the chaotic factional conflicts that characterized New York politics between 1816 and 1828. Party lines at the convention were so fluid that one student of the convention found it more revealing to use a conservative-moderate-radical spectrum in analyzing voting patterns. The convention responded to the growing democratic forces by lowering the suffrage requirement, almost trebling the eligible voters. When dealing with parts of the constitution perceived to be defective, like the councils of appointment and revision and the creaking judiciary, the convention came up with reforms but in such a way as to reward the dominant political party.

When New York adopted its first constitution, the state's population stood at 190,000, with two-thirds of the people living on both sides of the Hudson River between Albany and New York. By 1820, that population had increased to 1.4

million, with two-thirds of the people living on lands farther west and north. New York City had grown at a similar rate, especially among the workingmen or "mechanics," as they were then called. The mechanics and the mortgaged farmers to the west were the groups least advantaged by the 1777 document. The first condition giving rise to calls for constitutional reform was the existence of groups demanding an expansion of the electorate and reapportionment. The second factor was the perceived defects in the constitution of 1777, particularly the councils of appointment and revision. The council of appointment had become a notorious center for the distribution of office, which numbered nearly 15,000 by 1820. A convention was proposed as early as 1819, but politicians were reluctant to respond. When popular discontent no longer could be safely ignored, party leaders embraced the cause of reform and then rather cautiously. In the absence of any constitutional provision for calling a convention, it fell to the legislature to make the decision and determine whether the results would be submitted to the people. A dispute over this question between the legislature and the council of revision resulted in a bill that placed the question of whether to convene a convention before the people and a provision that required the convention, if convened, to submit its results to the people. This decision of the legislature, made only reluctantly after the council of revision vetoed the bill without these provisions, established the tradition in New York of making con-stitutional conventions the creature of the people, not of the legislature. For the vote, the electorate was to include not only the freeholders but all taxpayers—men who worked on public roads and militiamen—making the vote the most democratic thus far in New York's history. The vote on the question of whether to hold the convention was overwhelming in favor, 109,396–34,901, with sup-port strongest in the western part of the state and New York City. The debates at the convention centered on four issues: suffrage, the appointing power, the council of revision, and the reorganization of the judiciary.

On the question of suffrage, the debate took place between the more radical and more conservative wings of the Bucktail party (a party formed by Martin Van Buren out of dissident Republicans and the Tammany Society). The result was compromise tilted slightly toward the radical side. Property qualifications for voting were removed, leaving only the requirements that the individual paid taxes or performed militia or highway service. The convention thus continued the earlier eighteenth-century Republican tradition that one prove some interest in the community as a qualification for voting. The arguments over a property qualification for voting have been called "one of the great suffrage debates in American history."[11] The change directly benefited citizens of New York City and the western farmers whose mortgaged farms did not give them a freehold status; however, the constitution required that men of color "be seized and possessed of a freehold estate of the value of two-hundred and fifty dollars over and above all debts and incumbrances charged thereon" (Art. II, sec. 1). The 1777 Constitution gave the vote to all male freeholders, allowing free African Americans the possibility of voting. The unwillingness to end African Americans' suffrage suggests a conflict between the racism of many of the delegates and their ideology of equal rights. The provision disenfranchised all but a handful of African Americans: in 1825, only 298 of the state's nearly 6,000 free adult black males could meet the requirement.[12]

When the delegates turned to a discussion of the council of appointments, the debate centered around its replacement. Even before the convention, a consensus had developed over the need to abolish it. The solution was a compromise, with some of the local offices made elective, some appointed by local bodies, and still others appointed by the governor and/or the legislature.[13]

The second institution that had come under attack, especially by the Democrats, was the council of revision. The union of judges and executive was attacked as a violation of the separation of powers, as antidemocratic, and for making the judiciary too partisan.[14] The question was not whether to abolish the council but whether any check on the legislative branch was necessary. The convention, responding to concerns about legislative abuses, modeled the executive on the presidency, giving the governor a veto that could be overridden only by a two-thirds vote of both houses. Thus in the midst of a rising tide of democratic expectations, the delegates maintained countermajoritarian elements in their constitutional tradition.

In addressing the question of executive power, the convention sought to balance each move to strengthen the governor's power with one to limit that power. He was given the sole power to veto laws but shorn of his power to adjourn the legislature. He was to receive a fixed compensation to protect his independence, but his term was reduced from three to two years. He was given the power to see that the laws were faithfully executed but was no longer allowed the customary privilege to address the legislature in person. The net result was a governor with a reduced role in party affairs but whose effectiveness was not significantly impaired.

The third institution to come under scrutiny was the judiciary. Overburdened and overcentralized, it was unable to keep pace with an expanding work load created by burgeoning population and economic growth. In New York City, for example, two-thirds of the cases in the supreme court could not be tried and had to be passed over.[15] This problem was addressed by the creation of a new system of circuit courts with four to eight circuit judges. Judges were also under personal attack by the Bucktails for their alleged partisanship. So strong was this sentiment that a movement gathered steam to abolish the judiciary, thus driving the judges from offices.[16] The moderate delegates, led by Van Buren, prevailed, however, and the most radical measure to pass was the dismissal of all members of the supreme court and the creation of a new one.

With thirty-two of the thirty-seven counties of the state located in the new growth areas in the west and north, redistricting was long overdue. The lines were drawn to make it likely that the Bucktails would win six of the eight districts.[17]

More significant, the convention added a provision that required a two-thirds vote of the legislature for passage of any bill appropriating money or property for local or private purposes (Art. VII, sec. 9). The provision had its origin in the scandals that had accompanied the chartering of banks in the state. Like the debate on the executive veto, traditional notions of checks and balances and distrust of power competed with democratic notions about the legislature as the embodiment of the will of the people. Delegates raised the question of whether the legislature would ever deliberately pass legislation contrary to the public good. The debates exposed the tension between a tradition of limited and balanced government and one of democracy and majority rule. The experience with the mistakes and machinations of legislators led even the advocates of popular sovereignty to support placing restrictions on the legislature in the constitution. Such restrictions were justified by making a distinction between the will of the people and that the legislature. As the public perceived a larger and larger gap between the two, the demand for further restrictions on legislative power grew and found expression in a variety of constitutional provisions adopted throughout the rest of the nineteenth century.

In the same vein were provisions pledging certain sums of money for payment of the canal debt. The delegates from the eastern part of the state, whose constituents had loaned the money, wanted constitutional assurances of payment. The delegates from the western regions resented the provision, and in response, the convention majority attempted to mollify these delegates by giving them a greater number of representatives in the legislature than their numbers warranted.

These provisions were attempts to deal with legislative abuse by limiting its power to act. Other similar restrictions were used by groups or regional interests to lock their policy goals into the basic document. They not only constitutionalized the canal policy already established by the legislature, making it more difficult to adjust that policy in the future, but also set a precedent for others seeking to insulate their policy objectives from legislative action.

Unlike its predecessor, the 1821 Constitution devoted a separate article (VII) to a bill of rights for its citizens, drawing it largely from the English Bill of Rights, the bill of rights adopted by the legislature in 1787, and the federal Bill of Rights. Provisions dealing with habeas corpus, double jeopardy, private property, and self-incrimination are identical to those found in the national Bill of Rights. However, some provisions exhibit the unique constitutional traditions of the state. Article VII provided an exemption from military service to any conscientious objector or any member of a religious denomination. The free speech clause (Art. VII, sec. 8) was written in a different form from its federal counterpart:

Every citizen has the right to speak, write, or publish freely anything he wishes, being responsible for the abuse of that right; and no law shall be passed to restrain or abridge the liberty of speech of the press.

The provision combines the absolute language of the First Amendment with responsibility for abuse of that right. It seems to provide a balancing test and suggests legislative specification of what constitutes abuse.

The convention also addressed the question of how to amend the constitution. Previously, there was no amendment procedure. The 1821 Constitution authorized amendment by a majority of the legislators in one of the sessions and two-thirds of the members elected to the legislature in the subsequent session. Amendments would become effective if ratified by a majority of the electorate. In New York, voters could do what no voter could do for the national Constitution: vote directly on whether to approve a constitutional amendment.

John Jay's name is most closely associated with the 1777 Constitution; Martin Van Buren, leader of the moderate Bucktails, deserves a similar association with the 1821 Constitution. He has been called the "most effective man at the convention."[18] After receiving the approval of all but nine of the delegates, the constitution was submitted as a single question to the electorate and was approved in 1822 by a vote of 75,422–41,497.

The 1821 Constitution: An Assessment

The convention restructured and rewrote the constitution in less than three months. What it accomplished was neither a democratic revolution nor a conservative triumph.[19] It is difficult to call a constitution that increased the electorate by 160,000 voters, abolished the councils of appointment and revision, adopted a bill of rights, reorganized the judiciary, made thousands of offices elective, and solidified the independence of each branch of government a conservative document. The convention was successful in mollifying the various regions of the state in connection with canal policy but less successful in terms of solving the policy problems connected with the canals. By freezing legislative policy in the constitution, the convention made it difficult to deal flexibly with changing economic and financial conditions, and it ensured that escalating resort to constitutional provisions would take place in the future. By reducing the governor's term and removing his control over patronage, the new constitution made it more difficult for the governor to challenge his party and paved the way for a reorganized Republican party led by Van Buren and a loosely knit council dubbed the Albany Regency, which would remain the model for party reorganization in the future. The convention was a political response to new forces and economic developments and a practical response to needed constitutional revision, both in turn shaped by the needs and goals of the party controlling the convention.

THE CONSTITUTION OF 1846

> [The] first constitution ever formed that rested, not nominally, but in fact, on a popular foundation.
>
> Churchill Cambreling,
> convention delegate

Between 1822 and 1845, eight amendments to the 1821 Constitution were adopted, continuing the democratizing trend begun in the convention of 1821. All justices of the peace were made elective, universal white male suffrage was achieved, and all property qualifications for holding office were eliminated. Despite this expansion of popular control, the 1821 document proved unsatisfactory in several respects. Many problems resulted from rapid social and economic developments in the state rather than deficiencies in the constitution. In the interim, New York had earned the title Empire State, enjoying unmatched prosperity. No other state had a more diversified industrial base in the first half of the nineteenth century. The building of a canal system and the rapid growth of the railroads were primarily responsible for this success. These developments brought changes in business organizations and the structure of financial institutions. The public works program of the state government, of which the canal system was the centerpiece, had sharply increased state indebtedness, yet the state imposed no direct taxes between 1826 and 1842. Instead it resorted to loans, and as these loans pyramided, state credit declined, and popular disapproval of grants and pledges mounted.

State indebtedness was a major factor in the drive for a convention but not the only one. The system of land tenure in the state prevented those who worked the land from ever owning it, a condition that sparked riots serious enough to require the militia to restore order. The antirent movement, a response to this land tenure system, was also an important factor in the agitation for the convention. A third factor was the feeling, no doubt part of the ethos of Jacksonian Democracy, that the 1821 Constitution did not put enough direct control of the government in the hands of the people. A final factor was the judiciary. The constitution of 1821 had established a rather rigid structure of courts, not allowing for the growth that took place in the next quarter century. Delays and the expense of litigation had become intolerable. The major courts were backlogged with the business of three to five years.

Reform movements of all stripes and colors proliferated, and the established parties increasingly splintered over single issues. Out of this cacophony of calls of reform, certain common refrains could be heard: more popular elections and more control by the people over their government. As early as 1837, a new constitution was drawn up at the Convention of Friends of Constitutional Reform at Utica. Each year from 1841 on, proposals were presented for a convention, but divisions within the Whig and Democratic parties prevented action. In 1844, twenty-four counties presented petitions to the legislature calling for a law authorizing the people to vote on the question of calling a constitutional convention. Although there was no provision for amending the constitution by convention, in 1845 the demand for reform overwhelmed the partisan divisions and conservative fears of a convention. A bill was enacted recommending a convention and providing for a referendum on the question. The vote to call the convention was overwhelmingly favorable: 213,257–33,860.

The convention responded in specific ways to the problems that had precipitated its convening. In response to the antirent agitation, it swept away the old feudal system of landownership, in part constitutionalizing reforms already accomplished by legislative action. On the issue of suffrage, universal white male suffrage having been achieved, the delegates focused on African American suffrage. The delegates cautiously avoided an unambiguous stand on this controversial issue, submitting to the voters a separate provision that provided equal suffrage for African Americans.

The gains in popular control came in other areas. Practically all state judicial and local offices were made elective. Senators' terms were reduced from four to two years, and both senators and assemblymen were to be elected from single-member districts to give better representation to smaller opinion clusters. The judiciary was made elective and completely reorganized, with a court of appeals established as the court of last resort in the state. Provisions making the secretary of state, treasurer, attorney general, comptroller, canal commissioners, state engineer, and state prison inspectors elective are vivid evidence of the desire to extend popular control as far as possible. These measures have earned the 1846 document the title "People's Constitution."

Having extended popular control well into both the judiciary and executive branches, the delegates proceeded to limit the power of the elected representatives in the legislative branch. The widely held view that the legislature had been fiscally irresponsible and overly generous with state aid to private enterprise prompted a provision depriving the legislature of the power to incur debts without the vote of the people. Reflecting the diminished confidence in state government, the 1846 Constitution added at least twenty-two new provisions that in one way or another restricted the power of the legislature to deal with taxation, appropriations of money, and some specific subject areas. The fear of a powerful executive expressed in 1777 had given way to fear of an irresponsible legislature. Jacksonian Democracy had swept over America, promoting frequent popular elections as the cure for defects in the political process. A corollary to that belief was that the solution to abuse of power was to limit or take that power away.

The executive branch did not fare much better. The convention transferred the appointive power to local governments, reducing the governor's patronage, and made major offices in the executive branch elective.

The constitution continued the devolution of powers to the people in the provision dealing with matters of local concern (Art. III, sec. 17), the first extension of constitutional protection to local government in New York. The convention devoted some attention to civil rights, adding provisions protecting against excessive bail or fines, cruel and unusual punishment, and unreasonable detention of witnesses. Specific policy issues were also addressed. Canal policy was constitutionalized and the bank monopoly was abolished by limiting the legislature's power to grant special charters or suspend specific payments. Some delegates attempted, unsuccessfully, to incorporate the right to free school and universal education. Apparently delegates thought the matter less important than specifying the debt structure for the canal system in the constitution. The document did repeat an 1821 provision guaranteeing a perpetual fund for the common schools.

The capstone of this convention's work was the addition of a second mode of initiating constitutional change. The delegates provided that in 1866 and in each twentieth year thereafter and also at such other times as the legislature may provide, the question, "Shall there be a Convention to revise the Constitution and amend the same?" be submitted to the voters (Art. XIII, sec. 2).

The constitution was approved overwhelmingly, 221,528–92,436. The special amendment allowing equal suffrage for African Americans was rejected by the same proportion.

The 1846 Constitution: An Assessment

The 1846 Constitution was essentially a new document; only eleven provisions remained unchanged. In the name of democracy, the convention made major executive offices elective. Combined with the two-year term mandated by the 1821 Constitution, the result was a diffusion of executive responsibility and a diminution of the governor's effectiveness. The convention's most significant change was the dramatic reduction in legislative power. In the name of grass-roots democracy, it required the election of numerous public officials in the executive and judicial branches and placed more authority in the hands of local governments; in the name of reform and efficiency, it required public approval for debt measures and either placed certain policies outside legislative control or restricted how these policies could be handled. The long list of restrictions adopted in 1846, typical of state constitutions in the second half of the nineteenth century, and the diffusion of governmental power made the effective positive exercise of political power almost impossible and marked a shift in the role of government in New York. From the opening of the century, the government had taken an active role in regulating and stimulating the economy. That role led to abuses by the legislature, which in turn prompted the movement to restrict its power. For example, special incorporation laws, whereby the legislature incorporated firms individually, had resulted in monopolistic practices and were replaced by general incorporation laws. Monopolistic concentrations were mitigated, but another step had been taken in effacing the idea of the corporation as a quasi-public instrument. While the economy was being transformed into a rational, integrated market system, with the corporation as its driving force, the political system was being decentralized. As L. Ray Gunn puts it: "The active, intimate, palpable connection between the political system and the social economic environment gave way to a passive, supervisory, formalized system. . . . The goal of such an arrangement was to give 'utmost latitude' to individual action and industry."[20] To be sure, a political culture deeply suspicious of power and authority would not have countenanced direct state control of the economy, but a tradition of active regulation and encouragement of the economy was in place. The great significance of the 1846 Convention was to move away from this tradition and redefine the role of the government in society, ensuring that the transformation of the socioeconomic order of New York would take place under the umbrella but not the active direction of the government.[21] Along with the long list of restrictions on legislative power, this constitution exhibited another tendency characteristic of state constitutions in the second half of the nineteenth century. The attempts to deal constitutionally with new problems created by economic expansion and the successful attempts of groups and regional interests to see their goals more permanently protected by ensconcing them in the constitution lengthened the document. The 1777 Constitution contained approximately 6,600 words, including the Declaration of Independence, which was adopted as its preamble. By 1846, that number had more than tribled to 20,400.

Between Constitutions, 1847–1867

There were few major alterations of the 1846 Constitution during this period, although a number of amendments dealing with the judiciary, gubernatorial succession, prohibition, and African American suffrage were introduced.

The one major change effected by constitutional amendment during this period concerned the canals. Previous provisions detailing proscriptions and prescriptions for the legislature on canal policy soon outlived their usefulness as the financial picture of the state changed. When the legislature tried to raise revenue by a direct loan, the court of appeals, pointing to the proscription in the constitution, declared the law unconstitutional. A constitutional amendment was necessitated and was adopted in 1854, but other provisions continued to pose obstacles to legislative action, and a variety of amendments were proposed. Falling revenues in 1858 prompted more calls for a convention.

THE CONSTITUTIONAL CONVENTION OF 1867

> To make proclamation . . . that every man . . . of whatever race or color, or however poor, helpless or lowly he may be, in virtue of his MANHOOD is entitled to the full enjoyment of every right appertaining to the most exalted citizenship.
>
> William A. Wheeler,
> Convention President

When the voters were given the option of calling a convention as mandated by the 1846 Constitution, they approved the call by a vote of 352,854–256,364. Republicans won a majority of delegates, with lawyers constituting the largest profession at the convention. Although most of its recommendations were rejected by the voters, it has generally received high marks for the quality of its work.

The judiciary article was the central issue with debate centered around the independence and effectiveness of the courts. By 1865, the docket of the court of appeals was four years in arrears. The convention recast the court of appeals.

It would consist of six associates and one chief judge to be elected statewide, with terms lengthened to fourteen years. A commission of appeals was also created to deal exclusively with cases backlogged on the docket of the court of appeals. For a brief time, New York had two courts of final jurisdiction and no way of resolving conflicting opinions. Lower courts were also revamped, providing stability and continuity by lengthening terms to fourteen years and extending the mandatory retirement age from sixty to seventy years. These changes, submitted to the electorate in 1869 separately from the rest of the recommendations, were ratified by a close vote. The adopted provisions directed the legislature to submit to the people in 1873 the question of whether the judiciary should be appointed or elected. By almost three to one, the voters chose to retain elective judgeships.

Another significant subject for debate was the suffrage. In many ways, the debates on this subject were remarkable. The convention declined to add a literacy test on the grounds that "men's relative capacity is not absolutely determined by their literacy acquirements." It was also the first convention to give serious attention to the question of women's suffrage. Although agitation for woman suffrage had been going on in New York since the Seneca Falls Convention of 1848, women's suffrage never received more than twenty-four votes on any resolution.

On the question of African American suffrage, there was reason to be more optimistic. Radical Republicans came to the convention strongly committed to that objective. However, as electoral returns from around the country indicated that strong identification with this cause was costly, Republicans began reassessing their commitment. The convention was adjourned until after the November elections, which proved disastrous for Republicans. The Democrats emerged as the state's dominant party, and many Republicans attributed these defeats to their close identification with the issue of African American suffrage. When the convention reconvened, the mood was sober and the Republicans subdued. They agreed to submit the suffrage amendment separately, ensuring its defeat. The rejection of much of their work by the voters was only a partial defeat for the convention. A number of their proposed reforms were accepted by the voters following the recommendations of the Constitutional Commission of 1872.

The defeat of the convention's work did not end the desire for reform. Indeed so many amendments were proposed that it did not seem likely that the legislature would be able to give the necessary time and energy to the task. For this reason, Governor John T. Hoffman in 1872 recommended a constitutional commission to be composed of twenty-two eminent citizens. The legislature accepted the proposal and charged the commission with the task of proposing amendments to the constitution. The commission, unique in New York history, was similar to that of a convention; the crucial difference was that its proposals required approval by the legislature before submission to the voters. Among the important measures adopted and subsequently approved were an extension of the governor's term to three years and an item veto. In 1876, two more amendments were added, giving the governor the power to appoint the superintendents of prisons and public works. The commission continued the practice of constitutionalizing canal policy (four amendments were adopted on this question), and amendments dealing with bribery, savings banks, and corporations were also approved. The commission added to the constitutional limits already placed on the legislative power. Six amendments were adopted, including prohibitions against special legislation and multiple subject laws.

The problems created by the growth of municipalities had been addressed in the abortive 1867 Convention, and the commission built on this work. It recommended that cities be given a measure of self-government or home rule and that mayors be granted adequate power to govern those cities. The legislature rejected these recommendations, allowing only an amendment mandating the legislature to authorize boards of supervisors for counties and accepting a provision limiting local indebtedness, a serious problem by the 1870s. Local government had accumulated debts amounting to more than 10 percent of the assessed valuation of real and personal property. Not until the Constitutional Convention of 1894 was municipal government incorporated into the constitutional structure of New York.

The constitutional commission was an innovation in the state's constitutional history, which seemed to fill a gap between a cumbersome convention and the ad hoc legislative amending process. This method allowed distinguished and informed individuals to recommend constitutional change to the legislature and then to the people.

Between 1875 and 1894, demands for constitutional reform continued unabated. Of the twelve amendments during this period, five related to the judiciary, four to canals, one to local indebtedness, and two to appointments of state officials. Agitation for women's suffrage continued, with amendments introduced in 1880, 1882, 1883, and 1885. The strength of the Prohibition party pressed the legislature into passing a prohibition amendment twice, although it was never submitted to the voters.

Governor Samuel Tilden made reform of the cities a major goal of his administration. In 1875, he established a commission to recommend legislation and constitutional amendments to bring about that reform. The commission made extensive recommendations, including reform of municipal governmental structures, home rule provisions, and classifications of cities according to population. The only proposal the legislature accepted placed further restrictions on local indebtedness. Nonetheless, the work of the 1867 Convention and the commissions of 1872 and 1875 provided the groundwork for many of the reforms adopted at the 1894 Convention.

Pursuant to the constitution of 1847, the question of holding a constitutional convention was submitted to the electorate in 1886 and approved by nearly 20–1. In spite of this lopsided vote, a convention was not convened until 1894 because the governor and the legislature could not agree on the method of selecting delegates. The problems with the judiciary, however, needed immediate attention, and the two branches did agree to authorize a judiciary commission in 1890. That commission made a series of recommendations; however, the election of 1891 put the Democrats in control of both the legislative and executive branches, rendering unnecessary action on the commission's proposals and allowing for agreement on delegate selection.

The bitter battle over the delegate selection process was protracted because those who controlled the convention controlled the apportionment under which the political parties would operate. It is not without irony that a delegate selection process controlled by the Democrats would produce a convention controlled by the Republicans. This convention produced a document that, as amended, is the current constitution of the state.

THE CONSTITUTION OF 1894

> This Constitution, we are not commissioned . . . to treat with any rude or sacrilegious hands.
>
> Joseph H. Choate,
> Presidential Address

With little hope they would control the convention, Republicans passed over party regulars to nominate a distinguished and less partisan slate of delegates at large, among them Joseph Choate and Elihu Root. The number of independent Republicans elected was also unusually large. A loose alliance of Independent Republicans and antimachine reformers would set the tone of the convention. Four-fifths of the delegates were members of the legal profession.

The convention made few alterations in the bill of rights (Art. I). A right of action to recover damages for injuries resulting in death was protected, which prevented the legislature from placing caps on monetary damages. Past legislatures had set such limits in response to railroad requests. Considering these caps an abuse of legislature power, the amendment made jurors not legislators the sole judge of damages. A proscription on various forms of gambling was added to the antilottery clause. None of the amendments proposed concerning labor rights was adopted.

The suffrage article (Art. II) was not given any extended consideration as far as general principles were concerned, and significant changes in the area of women's suffrage, compulsory voting, and a literacy requirement were rejected. Concern for the political role of immigrants prompted several measures. In response to the claim that Democrats were naturalizing large numbers of immigrants just before elections, a requirement was adopted that naturalization precede voting by ninety days. A requirement of personal registration only in cities and in villages over 5,000 in size was aimed at urban areas and, by implication, the political morality of the Democratic party and its voters. Provisions authorizing the use of voting machines, ensuring secrecy of the ballot, and disenfranchising anyone convicted of an infamous crime were also added.

In an attempt to reduce electoral fraud, a provision for bipartisan election boards was adopted. This was the first time New York gave a constitutional role to political parties—and de facto recognition to the two-party system. These measures have been viewed as partisan attempts by Republicans to destroy or limit the power of the urban Democratic machine. They can also be seen as reform measures aimed at machine abuse and were supported as such by reformers and antimachine Democrats. The coincidence of Republican party interest with the goals of independent reformers was in part responsible for the nonpartisan character of much of the convention's work and the limited impact of outside interest groups.

On the question of apportionment, however, partisan considerations were crucial. By 1894, the rapid growth of the counties that now make up New York City had made the issue even more politically sensitive. Republicans proposed an apportionment scheme that would ensure some representation for counties regardless of population and ensure that whatever the size of the population of the counties of New York City, they would not dominate the state legislative branch. Senate size was increased from thirty-two to fifty, restoring rural areas to the same numerical strength they enjoyed in the 1846 Constitution, and the assembly was enlarged from 132 to 150 members. Republican delegates were explicit in their arguments for the scheme. Numbers were not the only considerations in making a just apportionment; cities had too much impact on the legislature now and without this proposal would soon come to dominate the state. The rural upstate–urban downstate split was never so explicit as it was in the apportionment debate. The issue occasioned more bitter, lengthy debates than any other issue at the convention. The final vote was 96–60, with ninety-six Republicans voting for the plan.

To prevent legislation being rushed through unread and undigested, a provision was inserted requiring that all bills be presented to the legislators at least three days prior to final passage. A prohibition on riders to appropriation bills was also passed. Attempts to incorporate the initiative and referendum were not successful. Delegates argued they were incompatible with the principle of representative government, would allow legislators to shirk their responsibilities, and the ordinary citizen would not have the time to give careful consideration to legislative matters.

Only two changes of any importance were made in the executive article. The convention had separated municipal elections from state and national elections and thus had to change the governor's term from three years to either two or four years. In choosing a two-year term, the delegates took a step back from the movement, evident since the Civil War, to strengthen the powers of the executive. On the other hand, state officers were to be elected at the same time as the governor and serve for the same term. The most striking change in the executive branch was the introduction of a merit system of civil service appointment. Merit selection had already been embodied in statute but was now elevated to a constitutional principle.

One major problem facing the convention was the status of the judiciary. The court of appeals simply could not handle its work load, and an increasing number of conflicting opinions were being issued by the tribunals exercising intermediate appellate jurisdiction. The convention created an appellate division of the supreme court (the major trial court of the state) and limited the jurisdiction of the court of appeals to cases in which general principles could be enunciated and conflicting lower court decisions reconciled. The convention also consolidated by eliminating a number of courts and conferring their jurisdiction on the supreme court. No attempt was made to return to an appointive judiciary, but the convention did reject a move to reduce the term of judges from fourteen to eight years. The work of this convention created a judicial system that remains essentially intact.

The second major issue facing the convention was home rule. The extent to which municipalities would be free to decide their own affairs without legislative interference was the heart of the matter. A strong proposal emerged from committee but was considerably weakened by a combination of antimachine Democrats and Republicans concerned about relinquishing control over the cities.[22] Cities were divided into three classes according to population, and laws relating to these cities were designated general or special depending on whether they related to all cities in the class or otherwise. Local officials were given a veto power over special legislation, but that veto could be overridden by a majority of the legislature. Such was the extent of municipal reform. Though viewed by many as woefully inadequate, it was the first time New York gave home rule constitutional status.

The convention also dealt with various specific policy areas. Canals, a perennial topic since the 1821 Convention, no longer had the economic or constitutional significance they once possessed. Nevertheless, significant divisions still existed between those who wished to place specific directives as to canal development in the constitution and those who thought no constitutional action ought to be taken. The result was a provision stating that canals shall be improved in such a manner as the legislature shall deem appropriate and suggestions as to the methods of financing those improvements. Because the legislature unquestionably possessed such power, the amendment served to give symbolic assurance of the state's continuing commitment to canal development.

Conservation policy, on the other hand, was new to convention deliberations in New York. Like many other constitutional provisions, it had its origins in legislation. Concern for the destruction of the forests and the consequences for the health and well-being of the state resulted in a guarantee that the Adirondack Forest Preserve shall be forever kept as wild forestland. This provision, adopted without a single dissenting vote, was a laudable attempt to ensure that the state's great natural resources would not be sold off to commercial developers or otherwise dissipated. The very stringency of its wording, however, frequently interfered with legitimate and valuable uses of that land, and the provision has been amended fourteen times since its adoption.

The convention gave constitutional status to the University of the State of New York, placing all the educational work of the state under the direction of a board of regents and the commissioner of education. For the first time, the constitution mandated the state to maintain elementary, secondary, and higher education at public expense. A third provision concerning education was highly controversial: the convention adopted a provision forbidding any aid, direct or indirect, to institutions of learning under the direction of a religious denomination. Because it had been the policy of New York for all its history to combine religious and secular instruction in public schools without serious objection, the proposal marked a radical change of opinion concerning the legitimate function of public education. This change was precipitated by the growth of the Catholic population. Concentrated in the cities and Democratic in political affiliation, Catholics wished to create and maintain their own schools and social institutions. This alarmed many Protestants, extremist and nonextremist alike. Religious division seemed to reinforce the urban-rural conflict that was evident at the convention. Initially attempts were made to eliminate aid of any kind to all sectarian institutions. These proposals would have stopped the aid being provided to charitable institutions run by religious groups. A compromise was reached: aid to charitable institutions would continue, but aid to sectarian educational institutions would be prohibited. When this accommodation was threatened by those supporting the no-aid position, President Choate and Republican floor leader Elihu Root successfully invoked party discipline to maintain the compromise.

The force of the words used in the provision suggests a prohibition more stringent than that required by the establishment clause of the First Amendment, and in fact the immediate result of the amendment was to shut down a number of cooperative arrangements between public and parochial schools. The pressure for various forms of aid however did not disappear.

Released-time programs were upheld by the court of appeals and adopted statewide by the board of regents (People ex rel. Lewis v. Graves, 1927). When bus transportation aid for parochial school students was declared unconstitutional by the court of appeals in 1938, the constitutional convention then meeting promptly adopted an amendment overturning that decision and, in addition, authorized health services for parochial school children. In 1951, the board of regents approved a nondenominational prayer for all public schools. That requirement was upheld by the court of appeals, though it was reversed by the U.S. Supreme Court as a violation of the First Amendment.[23] A program providing textbooks for sectarian schools was upheld by both the court of appeals and the U.S. Supreme Court (Board of Education v. Allen, 1968). In spite of this stringent constitutional provision, the New York legislature and courts have supported measures that suggest a more accommodating approach to religion. The constitutional provision survives, but the consensus supporting it has been replaced by one with a more accommodationist character. This provision and its subsequent history show how a changing political consensus can affect the understanding and interpretation of constitutional provisions.

The 1894 Convention created a state board of prisons, a commission of lunacy, and a state board of charities, all charged with supervising and inspecting their respective clienteles. Constitutionalizing them did not add any functions beyond centralizing control not already being performed by the state, but it did reveal the convention's judgment about the permanency of these obligations.

The problem that had delayed the calling of the convention was settled by a provision specifying the date of the next convention and constitutionalized the procedure for selecting delegates. Upon completion of its work, the convention decided to submit the work as a whole, with the exceptions of the amendments on apportionment and the canals, which were submitted separately. The decision to submit the apportionment amendment separately was an acknowledgment of its partisan character and gave the voters an opportunity to reject it without jeopardizing the rest of the revisions. The constitution was approved, as were the separate amendments. The vote on the document itself was 410,697 for and 327,402 against.

The 1894 Convention: An Assessment

President Choate's judgment that "this was a conservative convention" is borne out in a number of ways.[24] Of the roughly four hundred proposals submitted, thirty-three were adopted. The number of new subjects was quite small, and changes were aimed at remedying problems requiring immediate attention. A number of reforms were enacted: civil service; bipartisan election boards; reorganization of the judiciary; significant commitments to education, conservation, and separation of church and state were made; and the problem of delegate selection was resolved. The convention continued the process of limiting legislative power. No fewer than thirteen changes removed subject matter from the discretionary control of the legislature. The 1894 Convention marks the high point of a period in New York's history in which the placing of restrictions on legislative power dominated the process of constitutional change.

The convention's failures were ones of omission. There was no attempt to deal with the problems of the haphazard growth of government boards and agencies; executive reorganization was not on the convention agenda. The proposed amendment granting women the franchise was defeated. Despite convening during a depression, the convention failed to address proposals for social and economic reforms, including stringent regulation of corporations, meals for school children, pensions for the elderly, the right of labor to organize, limitations on working hours, and banning of child labor, thus suggesting the narrow definition of reform most delegates held. As a result, the role of the government in the economy remained essentially unchanged by the work of the convention.

The 1894 Convention manifested, in a degree greater than any other in New

York's history, the tension between urban and rural New York. It is difficult to overestimate the impact of New York City, with its potential for dominating state government, on constitutional decision making. Apportionment, home rule, and limits on debt authorization were all affected by the existence of that city. It would be fair to characterize the work of the convention as pursuing a policy of placing constitutional restraints on the city. That policy has characterized New York's constitutional tradition well into the twentieth century. It was seen most clearly in the arguments over apportionment, but it was also obvious in the suffrage amendments, the dual registration systems for urban and rural areas, and the unwillingness to grant the cities a significant amount of home rule. The vision of a rural republic, Protestant and Republican, and that of an urban democracy, ethnic and Democratic, provided the ideological backdrop for many of the debates at this convention. The decisions of the convention succeeded in providing some protection for traditional New Yorkers against a new order emerging out of immigration, urbanization, and industrialization.

Between Conventions, 1894–1938

In the twenty years between the conventions of 1894 and 1915, twenty-two amendments were adopted. Seven dealt with limits on the payment of debt and six with the judiciary. A 1905 amendment gave the legislature the power to regulate wages, hours, and conditions of employment, and in the following year, such legislation was enacted. The amendment was aimed at preempting court intervention. Such concern was not unfounded. Federal courts had struck down similar legislation, and state judicial review in New York had been increasing since the Civil War, though it had not yet engendered major controversy.[25] In 1910, the legislature enacted a workmen's compensation program. The next year the court of appeals unanimously declared the law unconstitutional on both state and federal grounds (Ives v. South Buffalo Railway Co., 1911). The decision was attacked successfully by organized labor and groups associated with the progressive movement. The judge who wrote the decision was defeated for reelection, and the voters overwhelmingly approved an amendment in 1913 overruling the decision. In 1914 the legislation was repassed and subsequently upheld against a federal challenge. The relative ease with which the New York Constitution can be amended, coupled with the willingness of New Yorkers to invoke that process, prevented the state judiciary from becoming a significant obstacle in the path of social and economic legislation, though the judiciary has limited the development of home rule.[26] The willingness to resort to constitutional conventions and amendments to alter the constitution, as well as reverse court decisions, has meant that the high court in New York would not play the prominent role in the development of the state's constitution that the U.S. Supreme Court has played in the development of the national Constitution.

THE CONSTITUTIONAL CONVENTION OF 1915

This convention has risen above the plane of partisan politics.

Elihu Root,
president of the convention

The 1894 Constitution specified that 1916 would be the next year at which the question of holding a convention would be submitted to the voters. The Democratic governor, Martin Glynn, had argued that the question should be put to the voters in 1914, which, unlike 1916, was a nonpresidential election year, though the fact that the Democrats were in control of the legislature undoubtedly had something to do with the decision. An earlier convention would provide the Democrats with an opportunity to control the convention and rewrite the reapportionment provisions inserted by the Republican-controlled convention of 1894. The voters gave their approval by one of the lowest total votes on any other convention held in New York—305,291 and by the slim margin of 1,352. In spite of a large population increase, this was only half the total votes cast for the conventions of 1846 and 1867. Not all Republicans opposed the calling of the convention. The reform wing of the party—those who wanted to modernize and bring the party in line with the progressive movement—saw the convention as an opportunity to rejuvenate New York Republicanism and return state leadership to the party.[27] Republicans were successful in electing a majority of the delegates.

The convention took place in a decade in which "reformers played a major if not decisive role in New York's government and politics."[28] Not surprisingly, the issue that had exercised reformers for the last decade, executive reorganization, was the major focus of their efforts. The convention reduced the executive branch from nearly 180 agencies to 17, 10 of which would be under the direct control of the governor. An executive budget was approved, and the principle of the short ballot was adopted.

The convention's work was a complete victory for reorganization advocates. The New York Bureau of Municipal Research said that the convention had succeeded in making New York "the first state to frame the financial measures of its constitution around the budget ideal."[29] The voters were not as impressed: they rejected the proposed constitution by more than two to one. Organized labor, Tammany, progressive party leaders, upstate Republicans, and civil servants opposed the revisions.

The defeat of the convention's work did not end the push for reform, and attempts to accomplish piecemeal what had failed as a package continued unabated. In 1917, the women's suffrage amendment was approved two years before the Nineteenth Amendment to the federal Constitution provided the same for the nation. The proposals of the 1915 Convention concerning the judiciary reappeared in the form of recommendations of a judiciary convention (actually a commission consisting of thirty members) established in 1921 and approved by the voters in 1925. The proposals on the judiciary made by the 1915, 1938, and 1967 conventions were rejected by the voters, so the work of the 1921 Convention has provided the framework for all subsequent changes in the judicial article.

By 1927, through the work of Governor Al Smith and others, amendments were adopted that provided for the short ballot, executive consolidation, and an executive budget. It is fair to say that the work of the 1915 Convention prepared the way for these successes. Of the thirty-three changes recommended by that body, almost all were adopted between 1915 and 1935.

The focus of constitutional reform efforts had begun to shift. The period demarcated by the 1846 and 1894 conventions was characterized by a succession of provisions aimed at limited legislative power and diffusing governmental power and political responsibility. New York did not adopt the initiative or recall, but it did require direct popular approval of governmental decisions, especially those concerning state debt. It was a period in which groups resorted to the constitution to further their policy goals—what has been called "legislation through constitutional amendment."[30] By the end of the first decade of the twentieth century, a new focus for constitutional reform appeared, one concerned with governmental efficiency and reorganization. The emphasis was no longer on restricting governmental power but on making it more effective and responsible. Attempts in the state to meet new social problems had resulted in a multiplicity of governmental boards, agencies, and authorities. The focus inevitably shifted to the executive branch. An effective executive, one in control of his own house and budget, was identified with a responsible executive able to make government work to meet the needs of the people. It was an easy step to the conclusion that a more effective and responsive executive meant a more democratic government. One hundred and fifty years after the adoption of the first constitution, the branch of government most identified at the founding with tyranny came to be seen as the branch most likely to provide democratic responsiveness.[31]

For most of the period from 1867 to 1916, state leadership was primarily in the hands of Republicans and oriented toward the rural, upstate wing of that party. All that was to change with the election of Al Smith to the governor's office in 1918. New political forces such as labor unions and new social and economic problems would create the basis for the election of an almost unbroken succession of Democratic governors in the next two decades. These developments would provide the context for New York's last successful constitutional convention in 1938.

CONSTITUTIONAL REFORM: THE 1938 CONVENTION

> We are here to do one thing, if nothing else: To prove to the world that our form of government does work.
>
> Frederick E. Crane,
> convention president

The question of whether to hold a convention was placed on the ballot in 1936 as required by the "every twentieth year" provision of the constitution. With no groundswell of discontent and no single issue to focus interest, the vote on the convention question, not surprisingly, was less than half the vote cast in the governor's race. A convention, to be held in 1938, was approved by a margin of under 250,000 votes. For the third consecutive convention, Republicans gained control. It was the first convention in New York to seat women. Seventy percent of the delegates had legal training.

In 1937, voters approved a constitutional amendment extending to four years the terms of the governor, lieutenant governor, attorney general, and comptroller. This amendment, along with those passed in 1927 that provided for an executive budget and executive reorganization, created the constitutional basis for the governor's position as one of the strongest in the nation.

With no clear mandate, Republicans in the majority and Democrats divided between New Deal and anti–Deal factions, few expected any significant changes in the constitution. Yet there were factors that would make it difficult for delegates to ignore social and economic issues as they had in 1894 and 1915. The Great Depression had forced public officials to reevaluate their understanding of the role of government in society, labor was a more potent force than it had been in 1915, and the New Deal was in full swing both in the state and nation.

The convention produced nine amendments for consideration by the voters. The first of these was an omnibus amendment containing fifty separate proposals. They were lumped together on the grounds that they were "noncontroversial." The other eight were submitted separately because they were deemed controversial enough to jeopardize the bulk of the convention's work. The strategy paid off: voters approved the omnibus amendment and five of the separate amendments. The three rejected amendments were the most partisan: the addition of a new judicial district was expected to provide patronage for Republicans, the reapportionment provisions continued the Republican advantage in the legislature, and the ban on proportional representation, by discouraging the growth of third parties, would benefit both major parties.

The most striking features of the revised constitution were the additions of a statement of labor's rights of political and economic action and two new articles recognizing the state's responsibility for those who need support for the necessities of life, including provision for low-rent housing and slum clearance, and allowing for broad legislative discretion in the use of public monies for these social welfare programs. Labor's rights included a recognition that labor is not a commodity, the right to organize and bargain collectively, and the right to an eight-hour day, five-day week at prevailing wage rates in all public works projects. Constitutional recognition was also given to the state's role in protecting and providing for the mentally handicapped.

In addition to rights for labor, an unreasonable-search-and-seizure clause was added, though an amendment that would have excluded evidence from court that was gathered in violation of that provision (the exclusionary rule) was rejected. A provision was adopted that would not allow a defendant to waive jury trial in capital cases and would allow that waiver in noncapital cases only if it were made in open court in writing and with the approval of the judge. The convention added a provision prohibiting discrimination against one's civil rights on the basis of race, creed, or religion. This provision stands out because, unlike the national Constitution, which extends such protection only to state action, the New York provisions extend the protection to private action as well.

The issue of church and state arose in connection with a court of appeals decision declaring legislation providing transportation for parochial school students unconstitutional (Judd v. Board of Education, 1938). The decision was handed down during the convention and evoked an immediate response. An amendment drawn up specifically authorizing such transportation passed by an overwhelming majority. In addition to this amendment, welfare proposals approved by the convention ensured that children in all schools would have equal rights to health and welfare services.

The passage of a constitutional amendment did not end the matter. In almost all cases, provisions were written so as to require legislative implementation, and such implementation provided an opportunity for further opposition and modification. The 1939 legislature implemented the provisions requiring transportation aid to parochial students, the ban on discrimination in civil service and private businesses, and the new home rule provisions. Conflict over the housing provision, however, required legislative compromise, and the 1939 legislature took no action at all to put municipal pensions on a contractual basis as mandated by the revised constitution. The impact of constitutional change depends on the reaction of the courts, legislative implementation, and executive enforcement. None of these can be taken for granted.

Finally, the convention altered procedures concerning future constitutional change. Provision was made that any amendment passed by the legislature be submitted to the attorney general for opinion as to its impact on other parts of the constitution. It also required that the next question on a constitutional convention be submitted when no pending national or state election was being held, making 1957 the next year for submission.

The 1938 Convention: An Assessment

The constitutional convention, though ostensibly organized and operated on a nonpartisan basis, was in fact controlled by the Republicans, and party considerations were dominant on at least three issues: reapportionment, the new judicial district, and the ban on proportional representation. On other issues, upstate, downstate, and rural-urban cleavages cut across party lines. The fact that partisan considerations were felt throughout the convention while parties took no formal responsibility for its actions meant that there would be little accountability for the results. The absence of a party position on many of the issues and the resulting lack of direction allowed interest groups to play a major role at the convention. Their activity was open, pervasive, and intense. On all but one of the measures that were not party questions, the outcome was in line with the position of major groups that backed or opposed the measure.

The convention started with the goal of streamlining the 1894 document. While it eliminated several obsolete provisions, it nevertheless increased the length of the document by over 15,000 words. This reflected not attempts to place even more restrictions on governmental power but rather the expansion of governmental activities in fields heretofore thought to be in the private realm. The new articles represented successful attempts by interest groups and the new social forces they represented to gain constitutional recognition for their policies and goals.

The work of the 1938 Convention has been called "middle of the road conservatism."[32] Certainly this judgment is valid if it means that the delegates did not undertake a rewriting of the 1894 Constitution or that they did not inaugurate a new social democracy. But by committing the state to a new set of social responsibilities involving labor, welfare, housing, and health insurance, the revised constitution was more progressive than the national Constitution or the U.S. Supreme Court. Much of this constitutional material had already been embodied in statutory law. Nevertheless, its elevation to constitutional status had the effect of giving legitimacy and permanency to these responsibilities, removing doubts about their constitutionality, and giving the state high court an invitation to activism not otherwise available. From this perspective, labeling the work of the convention conservative is misleading. A more apt description would be "positive liberalism"—the belief that the state had the obligation to promote the welfare and protect the rights of as many people as possible.[33] What is remarkable is that a convention controlled by Republicans and a minority of anti–New Deal Democrats approved the liberal measures it did. A recognition of the power of party and pressure ought not to obscure the fact that the delegates recognized the real problems facing New York and reflected the spirit of the time in responding to them.

Between Conventions: 1939–1966

New Yorkers amended their constitutions ninety-three times during this period. Gubernatorial succession (1949), creation of the commerce department (1943), joint election of governor and lieutenant governor (1953), and the Department of Motor Vehicles (1959) were the major changes in the executive branch. Major court reorganization was accomplished in 1961, and additional home rule powers were extended to the cities and other local governments in 1963. Bingo games were permitted for certain organizations (1957), and state lotteries were approved to support education (1966).

In 1957, as mandated by the constitution, the question on whether to convene a convention was to be put to the voters. Unlike past conventions, where preparation of materials awaited the outcome of the vote, the state legislature in 1956 established the Temporary Commission on the Constitutional Convention, with Nelson Rockefeller as its chairman, to undertake extensive research and provide comprehensive background on the New York Constitution for the use of the delegates. In pursuit of that goal the commission held a series of public hearings around the state and published the varied proposals it had received.

After the voters defeated the proposal for a convention by 125,498 votes, the Temporary Commission was scheduled to go out of existence in February 1958. But the generally held view that some revision and simplification was in order led the legislature to set up the Special Committee on the Revision and Simplification of the Constitution, with Rockefeller as its chairman. This commission was charged with making specific recommendations for revision of the constitution. When Rockefeller resigned as chairman to assume the governorship in late 1958, he recommended formation of a Temporary Commission on the Revision and Simplification of the Constitution. This committee eventually produced thirty-five reports on all aspects of the constitution. The legislature allowed it to expire in 1961, in part at least because it took up the question of reapportionment. Up to that point, its work had been relatively noncontroversial. Its most notable accomplishment was the home rule amendment of 1963 whose origin can be traced to the work of these three commissions.

THE CONSTITUTIONAL CONVENTION OF 1967

Toward a Modern Constitution.

> Temporary Commission on the
> Revision and Simplification
> of the Constitution

Much had transpired in the ten years after the 1957 rejection. The landslide victory of President Lyndon Johnson helped deliver both state houses to the Democrats, who were anxious to call a convention they believed they would control. Organized pressure from a variety of groups, civic and otherwise, had also been growing. Prominent newspapers throughout the state published editorials in support of a convention. The greatest impetus, however, came from outside the state: a series of Supreme Court decisions declaring state reapportionment schemes unconstitutional.[34] These decisions were a catalyst for a number of civic groups to coordinate a statewide campaign for a convention. There were plenty of issues: welfare, reapportionment, simplification, reform of the judiciary, fragmentation of local government, and state and local finances. Although the next constitutionally mandated ballot proposal was not due until 1977, a convention was proposed and approved by the voters in 1965. When the voters gave their approval, Governor Rockefeller signed legislation setting up a Temporary Commission on the Constitutional Convention. From its inception, the commission was plagued by partisan divisions, which severely hampered its effectiveness. It managed to produce a series of short topical reports, but they were too little and too late to have any impact on the convention's decisions.

The delegation selection process gave Democrats control of the convention for the first time in over one hundred years. The alliance of Democrats, Liberal Party delegates, and civic reformers produced a substantially revised document, which made extensive constitutional changes. The length of the document was cut in half, and the number of articles was reduced from twenty to fifteen. The ban on aid to sectarian schools was removed. The state was to assume the cost of welfare programs over a ten-year period, as well as the costs of the statewide court system. The governor's item veto would be eliminated, but he would be given more flexibility in administering the executive branch. Apportionment would be taken out of legislative hands and placed with a special commission, and local governments would be apportioned on a population basis. A conservation bill of rights was adopted, and a provision was added permitting the legislature to lower the voting age to eighteen. The assumption of welfare costs and the elimination of the referendum on state bond issues were bold attempts to move in the direction of state responsibility for social problems rather than continuing the devolution of power to the cities.

Upon completion of their work, the delegates came to the crucial decision of the convention: whether to submit the revisions as a package or divide them as the 1938 Convention had, separating controversial issues like aid to sectarian schools and assumption of welfare costs from the main body of revisions. The delegates voted to submit their work as a whole, a fatal mistake: the proposed constitution was rejected by a three-to-one margin. The indifference of the parties, the highly charged issue of aid to religious schools, the failure to give more home rule to the cities (especially New York City), and the opposition of the League of Women Voters because the convention hardly touched the judiciary article were contributing reasons. On top of these, Governor Rockefeller's budget director released figures estimating that the cost of these reforms would be over $3 billion after ten years.

CONSTITUTIONAL DEVELOPMENT, 1967 TO THE PRESENT

It is not at all certain that the proposed constitution would have passed had the amendment been submitted separately, but future constitutional delegates are not likely to make any controversial changes in omnibus amendments. The combination of controversial issues and a factionalized and largely indifferent electorate have made major constitutional reform by the convention method increasingly difficult. The failure to pass significant constitutional revisions has not dampened the willingness to amend the constitution. The constitution has been amended thirty-five times between 1967 and 1990. Eight of the thirty-five amendments dealt with the judiciary. One approved in 1975 authorized the central administration of the courts, completing the step taken toward a unified court

system in 1961. In 1977, five constitutional amendments were approved, two
of which made major changes in the selection and removal of judges. Henceforth,
the governor would select members of the court of appeals from a list recommended by a judicial commission. A second amendment created a commission
on judicial conduct and provided procedures for admonition, censure, and retirement of judges or justices.

Eleven of the amendments concerned state and local finance, with the majority
of these loosening debt restrictions to allow state and local borrowing. The focus
on finance and the judiciary is not surprising in the light of the fact that nearly
half of the present constitution is taken up by the three articles on the judiciary
and state and local finance.

In 1977, the question of a convention was again submitted to the electorate
in accordance with the constitutional requirement. That proposal was rejected
by over a half-million votes. With the next proposal not scheduled until 1997
and the legislature unlikely to initiate a call for a constitutional convention, this
rejection means that New York will greet the twenty-first century with the constitution, as revised, it had adopted just prior to the opening of the twentieth
century.

The history of constitutional conventions since 1957 suggests that they will
not be the major vehicle for constitutional change they have proved to be in the
past. Interest groups committed to preserving advantages they have succeeded
in ensconcing in the constitution will likely oppose constitutional conventions,
and voters, fearful of the possibilities of drastic change and attendant large costs,
will be reluctant to approve the calling of a convention. Absent a major crisis,
constitutional change in the foreseeable future is likely to be incremental, initiated
by elected leadership, or, increasingly, will come from the decisions of the court
of appeals. That prospect is not likely to be greeted with much enthusiasm by
those for whom a model state constitution is the goal. For those who accept the
pluralistic and sometimes chaotic character of political decision making in a state
like New York, that prospect will not be so unsettling.

NOTES

1. Patricia Bonomi, *A Factious People* (New York: Columbia University Press,
1971), 286.

2. As quoted by Charles Z. Lincoln, in his five-volume *Constitutional History of
New York* (Rochester: Lawyers Co-Operative Corp., 1906), 1:428–29.

3. Robert C. Ritchie, *The Duke's Providence: A Study of New York Politics and
Society, 1664–1691* (Chapel Hill: University of North Carolina Press, 1977), 155.

4. "The Respectful Address of the Mechanics in Union for the City and County of
New York, represented in their General Committee," in Peter Force, comp., *American
Archives* (Washington, D.C.: M. St. Clair and Peter Force, 1837–53), 6:895–98.

5. Bernard Mason, "New York State's First Constitution," in *Essays on the Genesis
of the Empire State* (Albany: New York State Bicentennial Commission, 1979), 122–23.

6. Christopher Tappen and Gilbert Livingston to the Convention, August 24, 1776,

quoted in Willi Adams, *The First American Constitutions* (Chapel Hill: University of North Carolina Press, 1980), 85–86.

7. Mason, "New York State's First Constitution," 26.

8. As quoted in Milton Klein, "Shaping the American Tradition: The Microcosm of Colonial New York," *New York History* 59 (1978): 196.

9. Ibid., 197.

10. Alan Nevins, *The American States during and after the Revolution* (New York: Macmillan, 1924), 161.

11. Chilton Williamson, *American Suffrage from Property to Democracy, 1760–1860* (Princeton: Princeton University Press, 1960), 195.

12. Donald B. Cole, *Martin Van Buren and the American Political System* (Princeton: Princeton University Press, 1984), 70, and Phyllis Field, *The Politics Race in New York: The Struggle for Black Suffrage in the Civil War Era* (Ithaca: Cornell University Press, 1982), 35–37.

13. For example, the governor was authorized, with the consent of the senate, to appoint all judicial offices except justices of the peace, who were appointed locally. These justices were made elective by an amendment in 1846.

14. Nathanial Carter, William Stone, and Marcus Gould, *Reports of the Proceedings and Debates of the Convention of 1821* (Albany: E & E Hosford, 1821), 50–52.

15. Ibid., 501

16. Ibid., 502–7.

17. Cole, *Martin Van Buren*, 77.

18. Joseph O. Rayback, "Martin Van Buren: His Place in the History of New York and the United States," *New York History* 64 (1983): 128; Cole, *Martin Van Buren*, 81–82.

19. Merrill D. Peterson, *Democracy, Liberty, and Property: The State Constitutional Conventions of the 1820's* (Indianapolis: Bobbs-Merrill, 1966), 141.

20. L. Ray Gunn, *The Decline of Authority: Public Economic Policy and Political Development in New York State, 1800–1860* (Ithaca: Cornell University Press, 1988), 188.

21. Ibid., 184, 248. The foregoing is based on the work of Gunn and Marvin Meyers, *The Jacksonian Persuasion* (New York: Vintage Books ed., 1960), 261–75.

22. Samuel T. McSeveney, *The Politics of Depression: Political Behavior in the Northeast, 1893–1896* (New York: Oxford University Press, 1972), 68.

23. Engel v. Vitale (1961); rev'd Engel v. Vitale (1962).

24. *Rev. Rec.*, IV, 1277.

25. Edward S. Corwin, "The Extension of Judicial Review in New York, 1783–1905," *Michigan Law Review* 15 (February 1915): 285.

26. New York Central Railroad v. White, 243 U.S. 188 (1917), Franklin A. Smith, *Judicial Review of Legislation in New York, 1906–1938* (New York: Columbia University Press, 1952), 223–25.

27. Gerald McKnight, "The Perils of Reform Politics: The Abortive New York State Constitutional Reform Movement of 1915," *New-York Historical Society Quarterly* 63 (July 1979): 207.

28. David Ellis et al., *A History of New York*, rev. ed. (Ithaca: Cornell University Press, 1967), 376.

29. New York Bureau of Municipal Research, "The Budget Idea in the United States," *Municipal Research*, no. 69 (January 1916): 64.

30. Gerald Benjamin, "Constitutional Revision in New York: Retrospect and Prospect," in *Essays on the Genesis of the Empire State* (Albany: State Bicentennial Commission, 1979), 42.

31. Ibid., 43.

32. Vernon O'Rourke and Douglas W. Campbell, *Constitution-Making in a Democracy: Theory and Practice in New York State* (Baltimore: Johns Hopkins Press, 1943), 211.

33. Donald H. Roper, "The Governorship in History," in *Governing New York State: The Rockefeller Years*, ed. Robert H. Connery and Gerald Benjamin; *Proceedings of the Academy of Political Science* 31 (May 1974): 17.

34. Reynolds v. Sims (1964) and WMCA v. Lomenzo (1964). The latter specifically declared the New York apportionment scheme unconstitutional.

Part II

New York Constitution and Commentary

PREAMBLE

> WE, OF THE PEOPLE of the State of New York, grateful to Almighty God for our Freedom, in order to secure its blessings, DO ESTABLISH THIS CONSTITUTION. [1821; amend. 1846]

The 1777 Constitution had no preamble—at least not in the sense in which we think of that term today. Instead it was prefaced with the recommendations of the Continental Congress that governments be organized in various colonies, the action of the Third Provincial Congress of New York recommending the election of delegates with the power to act on that recommendation, and the text of the Declaration of Independence. In 1821 that prefatory material was dropped and a shorter preamble put in its place. As amended in 1846 that preamble has remained unchanged.

Unlike the preamble to the United States Constitution it does not set out in formal fashion the purposes of the instrument beyond that of securing the blessings of freedom. Unlike its national counterpart the source of that liberty was acknowledged to be God, but like the national preamble it asserts that a constitution is the best instrument to secure those blessings.

Article I

Bill of Rights

New York's tradition of liberty has its roots in the common law and documents like the Charter of Liberties and Privileges of 1683 and 1691. Though a formal Bill of Rights was not added to the New York Constitution until 1821, the 1777 Constitution contained a number of provisions concerning rights (Arts. 13, 34, 35, 38, and 41), and the legislature adopted a statutory bill of rights in 1787. The rights adopted in 1821 are an amalgam of the 1777 Constitution, the Statute of 1787, and the national Bill of Rights adopted in 1791. When the 1846 Constitutional Convention began its work, it recognized this tradition by making the bill of rights the first article of the new constitution.

The purpose of a bill of rights is to give fundamental legal status to individual liberties and place limits on the exercise of governmental power. For most of U.S. history, state bills of rights were the only protection available to citizens of the states (see Barron v. Baltimore, 1833) as the national Bill of Rights was not applicable to the states. With the gradual application of most of the provisions of the national Bill of Rights to the states, and the expansion of the meaning of those rights in the early 1960s by the Supreme Court under Chief Justice Earl Warren, state bills of rights were eclipsed. But state courts never fully relinquished their reliance on those provisions, and recently they have begun, with more regularity, to interpret those rights independently of their federal counterparts to grant greater protection to their citizens than is forthcoming from the federal Constitution.[1] Moreover, state bills of rights contain guarantees not found in the national document. New York's labor and welfare provisions are prime examples. All this is solid evidence of the continued viability of New York's constitutional tradition and the federal system.

SECTION 1

Rights, privileges and franchise secured; power of legislature to dispense with primary elections in certain cases. No member of this state shall be disfranchised, or deprived of any of the rights or privileges secured to any citizen thereof, unless by the law of the land, or the judgment of his peers, except that the legislature may provide that there shall be no primary election held to nominate candidates for public office or to elect persons to party positions for any political party or parties in any unit of representation of the state from which such candidates or persons are nominated or election whenever there is no contest or contests for such nominations or election as may be prescribed by general law. [Const. 1777, Art. XIII; amend. and renumbered Art. VII, sec. 1 Const. 1821; renumbered Art I, sec. 1, Const. 1846; amend. 1959][2]

This section, with its famous "law of the land" phrase, was meant to restrict the power of the legislature and forbid any act depriving a citizen of rights prior to a judicial determination. It does not so much delineate rights as provide a shield against unwarranted interference with existing rights. In this sense the phrase is synonymous with due process of law (Art. 1, sec. 6).

It is appropriate that the first substantive right mentioned in the constitution is the right of suffrage, the cornerstone of republican government. Suffrage in 1777 was restricted to males of "full age" who met property and residency qualifications. Today all persons eighteen years of age or older meeting minimal residency requirements can vote regardless of sex, race, or economic status (see Art. 2, sec. 1, 9 for other qualifications).

The clause has operated to strike down statutes denying the vote to those qualified and to monitor regulations dealing with the administration of elections and nominations not covered by Article II. A requirement that voters take a loyalty oath as a condition for voting was held to violate this section (Green v. Shumway, 1868). A regulation that excluded members of a political party from participating in an election because they did not attain the highest or next-highest representation on a common council was a disenfranchisement of a class of voters (Rathbone v. Wirth, 1896). The right of a candidate to have his or her name on more than one line on the ballot was affirmed (Matter of Button v. Donohue, 1966). Regulations are permitted when deemed fair and reasonable, for example, a statute requiring that no more than two civil service commissioners shall be of the same party (Rogers v. Buffalo, 1890).

The amendment concerning primaries added in 1959 was a cost-saving measure; holding uncontested primaries wasted time and money. Although there seemed to be no constitutional right to a primary system and the law in force protected full and fair participation in the nomination and election of candidates, the wording of certain court decisions raised doubts about the constitutionality of such legislation (People ex rel. Hotchkiss v. Smith, 1912). In such circumstances, an amendment was a safer way to proceed. Primaries would still be held when contests developed through the filing of independent petitions.

The amendment seems more appropriately placed in Article II, which deals with suffrage qualifications, elections, and registration.

SECTION 2

> **Trial by jury; how waived**. Trial by jury in all cases in which it has heretofore been guaranteed by constitutional provision shall remain inviolate forever; but a jury trial may be waived by the parties in all civil cases in the manner to be prescribed by law. The legislature may provide, however, by law, that a verdict may be rendered by not less than five-sixths of the jury in any civil case. A jury trial may be waived by the defendant in all criminal cases, except those in which the crime charged may be punishable by death, by a written instrument signed by the defendant in person in open court before and with the approval of a judge or justice of a court having jurisdiction to try the offense. The legislature may enact laws, not inconsistent herewith, governing the form, content, manner and time of presentation of the instrument effectuating such waiver. [Const. 1777, Art. XLI; amend. and renumbered, Art. VII, sec. 2, Const. 1821; renumbered Art. I, sec. 2, Const. 1846; amend. 1935, 1937, 1938]

This right had been guaranteed by the Charter of Liberties and Privileges of 1683. Trial by jury was considered by New Yorkers and the other colonists as a bedrock right: one's property and liberty could not be taken but by the unanimous consent of one's neighbors. The word *inviolate* suggests that this right cannot be amended (see Art. XIX), but, like other provisions of the document, it is probably not immune to constitutional modification. Its specifications were drawn largely from the common law: the general right to have questions of fact determined by the jurors composed in the higher courts of twelve and in the lower courts of six—a jury made up of one's peers or equals and held in the county where the offense was alleged to have occurred. The *heretofore been guaranteed* phrase now means that the right to jury applies to all causes of action to which the right attached at the time of the adoption of the 1894 Constitution (Motor Vehicles MFRS. v. State, 1990). The effect of this provision is to continue under the constitution all common law rights to a jury trial prior to 1777 and all statutory rights to such trial by jury enacted prior to 1894. These first two classes exist as constitutionally guaranteed rights. A third class, which grants jury trial by statute since 1894, does not have constitutional status.[3] Article I, section 18, constitutionalizing workmen's compensation, has removed this right with regard to an employee's right to have a jury assess the amount of liability, and Article VI, section 18 has abolished the right with regard to claims against the state (Graham v. Stillman, 1984). This does not mean that the legislature cannot add to the causes of action in which the right is guaranteed.

The section says nothing about a public trial, though that right is guaranteed by the Sixth Amendment to the U.S. Constitution (In re Oliver, 1948; Duncan v. Louisiana, 1968) and New York civil rights law. The right to a speedy trial is not mentioned, but again that right is protected by the Sixth Amendment and New York criminal procedure law.[4] Moreover, the court of appeals has held that lengthy and unjustifiable delay between crime and trial will, in certain circumstances, violate a defendant's due process rights (Art. I, sec. 6).[5]

When parties to a civil suit do not want a jury trial, mandating one simply added to the time and expense of litigation. With this is mind, the 1846 convention permitted mutually acceptable waivers for jury trials in civil cases. In 1935, the legislature was empowered to provide for less-than-unanimous verdicts in civil trials. This was expected to reduce the number of disagreements and make jury verdicts a fairer and sounder expression of jury will. Under the unanimity rule, the unyielding juror was given the power to extract compromises that otherwise would not occur. The amendment was necessary because of a strong judicial tradition supporting unanimous verdicts.[6] In 1937, waiver of jury trial in non-capital cases was permitted. The right to a jury trial had been considered so fundamental and essential to a defendant's rights that it could not be waived. Behind this amendment was the desire to reduce the expense of trials and to allow the defendant to avoid the adverse effects of publicity and prejudice on a jury in a sensational trial. Some of the philosophy of the earlier period remains in the denial of a waiver in capital cases. A desire to ensure that the waiver was made knowingly, intelligently, and voluntarily prompted a 1938 amendment requiring the waiver to be by written instrument in open court, thirty years before national recognition of the practice by the U.S. Supreme Court. The chief issue regarding the waiver is whether the right is absolute or whether the judge has any discretion in denying the waiver. The courts have held that the right to waive is not absolute but that a judge can refuse a waiver request only when that request is made in bad faith as a strategem to obtain an impermissible procedural advantage or when the defendant is not fully aware of the consequences of the choice he or she is making.[7]

Further aspects of the right to trial are specified in Article VI, section 18.

SECTION 3

Freedom of worship; religious liberty. The free exercise and enjoyment of religious profession and worship, without discrimination or preference, shall forever be allowed in this state to all mankind; and no person shall be rendered incompetent to be a witness on account of his opinions on matters of religious belief; but the liberty of conscience hereby secured shall not be so construed as to excuse acts of licentiousness, or justify practices inconsistent with the peace or safety of this state. [Const. 1777, Art. XXXVIII; amend. and renumbered Art. VII, sec. 3, Const. 1821; amend. and renumbered Art. I, sec. 3, Const. 1846]

There are three parts to this section. The first guarantees religious liberty, the second forbids any religious qualifications for competency as a witness, and the third, an abuse-of-liberty clause, preserves the state police power to prevent conduct inconsistent with the peace, welfare, and safety of the state. Unlike the First Amendment, the section makes no mention of an establishment of religion. Instead it allows for ''the exercise and enjoyment of religious profession without discrimination or preference.'' The provision contains no state action requirement but has been interpreted to apply only to governmental action (Zlotowitz v. Jewish Hospital, 1948). Finally, the section does not speak in the absolute terms of the First Amendment; instead it mandates balancing the free exercise of religious liberty against the interests of the state in preserving the peace and welfare of the community.

The Free Exercise Clause

The first clause, with only slight modification, was part of the first constitution of 1777. At the 1846 convention, the second clause of this section was added in the form it still retains. Even so, it was not until Brink v. Stratton (1903) that the clause was read to prohibit all discrimination against witnesses because of their religious views and to prevent their credibility from being attacked because they did not believe in a supreme being or an afterlife.[8] In line with more secular notions of legal proceedings, the court of appeals has interpreted the clause to allow individuals to affirm rather than swear to the truth of their testimony (People v. Wood, 1985).

The third clause of the section also dates from the 1777 Constitution. It is typical of early state constitutions in correlating a right with the responsibility for abuse of that right. Before the free exercise clause of the First Amendment was applied to the states (Cantwell v. Connecticut, 1940), New York courts had the opportunity to apply this clause on several occasions. In almost all cases, the free exercise claim was rejected.[9] In People v. Ruggles (1811), which sustained a conviction for blasphemy, Chancellor James Kent claimed the section was intended only to ''banish test oaths, disabilities and the burdens and oppressions of church establishment,''[10] and this narrow reading remained the basis for subsequent interpretations.[11]

Before 1940, this section was rarely applied to sustain religious liberty claims; after that date, it was rarely used as a separate basis for decision or to anticipate rulings of the Supreme Court that were to recognize more extensive free exercise claims.

In the 1980s, the court of appeals showed some signs of independent reliance on this section, at least where the Supreme Court had not provided guidance. In Matter of Rivera v. Smith (1984), the court relied exclusively on Article I, section 3 to sustain a Muslim prisoner's right to be free from frisk searches by women guards.

The No-Preference Clause and the Separation of Church and State

This provision merely required that no preference be given to one religious belief over another, especially in the form of a state-church establishment. The text itself has not been read to prohibit aid to religion or even require neutrality toward religious activities.[12] The practice throughout the nineteenth century was to provide financial and other support to religious institutions and activities.[13] Absent a state establishment clause and a Supreme Court decision applying the federal establishment clauses to the states, there were no constitutional limitations on state aid to religion. The principle of accommodation has been the policy of New York from the beginning to the present, and the clause has been interpreted in that spirit.[14]

Successful challenge to the various forms of aid to religion provided by New York had to wait passage of the so-called Blaine amendment (Art. XI, sec. 3) in 1894 and the Supreme Court decision to apply the establishment clause of the federal Constitution to the states. For further analysis of church-state issues, see Article XI, section 3.

SECTION 4

> **Habeas corpus**. The privilege of a writ or order of habeas corpus shall not be suspended, unless, in case of rebellion or invasion, the public safety requires it. [Const. 1821, Art. VII, sec. 6; renumbered Art. I, sec. 4, Const. 1846; amend. 1938]

The writ of habeas corpus can be traced to the Magna Carta (Arts. XXXIX–XXXX). Initially it was primarily a guarantee of the right to trial and protection against detention without trial. Today the writ is an important procedural right through which the legality of a detention can be challenged. It is a civil proceeding because its purpose is to inquire into the cause of the detention and is based on the civil right to be free from unlawful imprisonment. Habeas corpus is available when the jurisdiction of a court or agency is in question or when a denial of a constitutional or statutory right is alleged.[15] It requires for its issuance that a person actually be detained and be entitled to immediate release. Thus it would not be available if the only remedy were a new trial (People ex rel. Kaplan v. Commissioner of Corrections, 1983). It would be available to a pretrial detainee whose bail was so excessive as to constitute an abuse of discretion.[16]

Decisions of the court of appeals beginning in the 1940s considerably expanded the use of this writ, but the expansion was not sufficient to meet standards imposed by the Warren Court in the early 1960s. Although the New York judiciary quickly brought its procedures in line with the extension of federal habeas corpus,[17] this expansion eclipsed state habeas corpus as federal courts proved more receptive to granting such writs. State habeas corpus is still available and would be used where a state constitutional or statutory right not guaranteed by the national Constitution was in question. Even here, various other statutory and judicially fashioned remedies are available for direct as well as collateral review.

No attempt to suspend the writ has ever been made in New York, so no judicial interpretation of the clause exists on such questions as whether the governor or the legislature has the power of suspension. In 1915, an attempt was made to allow suspension only when civil courts were not operating. The 1938 Convention did tighten the wording by removing *may require* and substituting *requires*.[18]

The writ is known almost exclusively for its role in providing prisoners with a means to challenge their detention, but it functions in the areas of mental hygiene, domestic relations, and debtor and creditor law.[19]

SECTION 5

> **Bail; fines; punishments; detention of witnesses**. Excessive bail shall not be required nor excessive fines imposed, nor shall cruel and unusual punishments be inflicted, nor shall witnesses be unreasonably detained. [Const. 1846, Art. I, sec. 5]

The first three clauses of the section, found in the English Bill of Rights of 1689, were enacted into law by the legislature in 1787, and are contained in the Eighth Amendment to the U.S. Constitution. The 1846 convention added them to the constitution along with the clause relating to the detention of witnesses. With the exception of the last clause, the section is identical to the Eighth Amendment.

Bail functions as a complement to the presumption of innocence by permitting the accused freedom while at the same time ensuring his or her presence at trial. Traditionally New York courts have held that the only purpose of bail is to ensure the accused's presence at trial.[20] As the excessive-bail phrase of the Eighth Amendment has not been applied to the states, this provision is the only protection available to the citizens of New York. The clause prohibits only excessive bail; any right to bail in New York is statutory in nature.[21] The statute provides for release on one's own recognizance, release based on social ties to the community without money bond. The release is mandatory for misdemeanors and discretionary with the court in felony cases.[22] Courts have approached the question of excessive bail on an ad hoc basis with the general rule that the exercise of the discretion must have some underlying facts to support its exercise (People ex rel. Klein v. Krueger, 1969). On a number of occasions, bail has been declared excessive because the amount set was arbitrary (People ex rel. Fraser v. Britt, 1942).

New York has not adopted a full-fledged preventive detention law like the one embodied in the Comprehensive Crime Control Act of 1984,[23] but it has adopted a form of limited preventive detention. A defendant out on bail who is charged with a Class A felony or for whom there is reason to believe has intimidated a victim may have bail revoked.[24] This provision has not yet been tested in New York courts but given its limited nature and the fact that the provisions are triggered after bail has been granted, rather than denying bail in the first place, it is likely to withstand court scrutiny.

The situation is a bit different with regard to cruel and unusual punishment. Here the Supreme Court has applied the Eighth Amendment equivalent to the states (Robinson v. California, 1962), and courts in New York have given the same meaning to both clauses. The judiciary has given significant leeway to the legislature in determining the kind and range of punishments permissible. It is rare for the judiciary to strike down a legislative determination of punishment.[25] People v. Broadie (1975) laid down the criteria for determining whether punishments are cruel and unusual: comparison with punishment in the same jurisdiction for other offenses and with punishment for similar offenses prescribed in other jurisdictions. The clause would also prohibit punishment grossly disproportionate to the crime. In 1984, the New York Court of Appeals ruled the state's mandatory death penalty statute unconstitutional (People v. Smith, 1984). It did so, however, on Eighth Amendment grounds, explicitly refusing to reach the issue of whether the statute also contravened this section.[26] This is surprising since the court acknowledged that the Supreme Court had reserved decisions on the question of whether a mandatory death sentence for someone already serving life for murder is a violation of the federal constitution.

The little litigation dealing with excessive fines raises tantalizing questions about the relationship of wealth to the law and justice. In People v. Tennyson (1967), the court of appeals held that it was constitutionally permissible to allow an indigent defendant to work off a fine in prison. However, if the total time in prison exceeded the limit for the misdemeanors—one year—such imprisonment would violate the equal protection of the laws. More recently, a lower court judged a fine excessive by looking at the relative comparison between the fine and the wealth of the defendant. A fine of $350 was judged excessive for a defendant who had no economic resources (People v. Ingham, 1982).

The last clause concerning detention of witnesses has provoked little judicial activity. Courts have taken a case-by-case approach in handling these detentions and developed a list of factors to take into account when judging the reasonableness of a detention.[27]

SECTION 6

Grand jury; protection of certain enumerated rights; duty of public officers to sign waiver of immunity and give testimony; penalty for refusal. No person shall be held to answer for a capital or otherwise infamous crime (except in cases of impeachment, and in cases of militia when in actual service, and the land, air and naval forces in time of war, or which this state may keep with the consent of congress in time of peace, and in cases of petit larceny, under the regulation of the legislature), unless on indictment of a grand jury, except that a person held for the action of a grand jury upon a charge for such an offense, other than one punishable by death or life imprisonment, with the consent of the district attorney, may waive indictment by a grand jury and consent to be prosecuted on an information filed by the district attorney; such waiver shall be evidenced by written instrument signed by the defendant in open court in the presence of his counsel. In any trial in any court whatever the party accused shall be allowed to appear and defend in person and with counsel as in civil actions and shall be informed of the nature and cause of the accusation and be confronted with the witnesses against him. No person shall be subject to be twice put in jeopardy for the same offense; nor shall he be compelled in any criminal case to be a witness against himself, providing, that any public officer who, upon being called before a grand jury to testify concerning the conduct of his present office or of any public office held by him within five years prior to such grand jury call to testify, or the performance of his official duties in any such present or prior offices, refuses to sign a waiver of immunity against subsequent criminal prosecution, or to answer any relevant question concerning such matters before such grand jury, shall by virtue of such refusal, be disqualified from holding any other public office or public employment for a period of five years from the date of such refusal to sign a waiver of immunity against subsequent prosecution, or to answer any relevant question concerning such matters before such grand jury, and shall be removed from his present office by the appropriate authority or shall forfeit his present office at the suit of the attorney-general.

The power of grand juries to inquire into the wilful misconduct in office of the public officers, and to find indictments or to direct the filing of information in connection with such inquiries, shall never be suspended or impaired by law.

No person shall be deprived of life, liberty, or property without due process of law. [Const. 1821, Art. VII, sec. 7; renumbered Art. I, sec. 6, Const. 1846; amend. 1938, 1949, 1958, 1973]

This, the largest section in the article, contains the right to grand jury, counsel, notice of accusation, double jeopardy, self-incrimination, and due process of law.

Grand Jury

A grand jury protection was contained in the Charter of Liberties and Privileges, but no similar provision was included in the 1777 Constitution. The 1821 convention constitutionalized a 1787 statute providing for a grand jury.

The grand jury is designed to protect the individual against unjust prosecution. The right to a grand jury is solely a state constitutional right (the Supreme Court has not applied the federal counterpart to the states). Its primary function is accusatory, screening charges to determine whether there is sufficient evidence to proceed to trial. It also has a secondary function of investigating and reporting misconduct and neglect in public office.

The provision requires a grand jury for all felonies unless waived by the defendant, with four exceptions: impeachments; militia when in actual service; military forces in time of war and in peace, with the consent of Congress; and cases of petit larceny. The 1821 convention did not think the procedure necessary in petty crimes or misdemeanors. The crime of petit larceny was very common and contributed disproportionately to the backlogs in the city courts. At the time it was classified as a felony and had to be excepted explicitly from the protection.[28]

The waiver clause, adopted in 1973, was designed to speed disposition of cases and keep court calendars clear. The fact that a majority of defendants pleaded guilty to some charge, usually for consideration—plea bargaining—made the requirement, at least in these situations, an expensive and time-consuming charade. The waiver amendment was necessitated by People ex rel. Battista v. Christian (1928), which held that a waiver of the grand jury was not permitted. *Battista* represents a very different judicial attitude toward plea bargaining and the disposition of cases from the one now regnant. Remnants of the *Battista* approach were expressed in People v. Iannone (1978). There the court viewed the right to a grand jury proceeding not only as a protection for the defendant but also as serving important societal interests. Because the right is a fundamental public right and not only a personal privilege, the waiver is to be treated as a single exception and construed so as to maintain that fundamental principle.

An infamous crime today is synonymous with felonies; nonfelonies are not covered by the protection. When the state characterized as a misdemeanor a crime for which one could be punished for more than a year in the state prison, the court of appeals, eschewing form for substance, held that a grand jury proceeding was required (People v. Bellinger, 1935). Today statutory law defines a misdemeanor as a crime for which the punishment can be no more than one year of incarceration. Since the 1930s, there has been growing sentiment to abolish the grand jury for ordinary felonies. England and California have already done so. The device is cumbersome, duplicative of the preliminary hearing, secretive, and a tool of the prosecutor. On the other hand, its protective function remains valuable; it is one of the few remaining examples of self-government on the part of the citizenry.[29]

The Right to Counsel

The right to counsel is considered one of the fundamental principles of American law and indispensable to a fair trial; not surprisingly it appears in the first constitution (Art. XXIV). Until 1846, the constitution secured the right only in cases of impeachment and indictment. The 1846 Constitution expanded that right significantly by adding the phrase "in any trial in any court," and People ex rel. Garling v. Van Allen (1873) extended that right to court-martial proceedings.

As far back as 1883, the judiciary in New York has interpreted this right to include counsel at every stage of the proceedings (People ex rel. Burgess v. Riseley, 1883). The right-to-counsel tradition in New York has developed independently of the development of that right as embodied in the U.S. Constitution. Nowhere is this better illustrated than in the case of the indigent defendant. From the very beginning courts have claimed the power to assign counsel to indigent defendants (People ex rel. Saunders v. Board of Supervisors, 1875). A statute providing compensation for assigned counsel in capital cases was passed in 1877. In People v. Price (1933) the court ruled that regardless of the statutory distinction between capital and noncapital cases, when a defendant appears without counsel and desires counsel, the court must assign an attorney to defend him or her, capital charge or not. By 1875, a court concluded that the duty to assign counsel for the defense of the destitute has been ''by long and uniform practice as firmly established in the law of the state as if it were made imperative by express enactment.''[30] It was not until Gideon v. Wainwright (1963) that an equivalent right was established under the national Constitution. People v. Witenski (1965) mandated counsel for all misdemeanors, anticipating a similar Supreme Court ruling by seven years.[31] The primary responsibility for assigning counsel to indigent defendants was seen as a state responsibility and has been so recognized for most of New York's history.

A long line of cases has established that the right to counsel in New York and in certain circumstances includes the right to have counsel present before any waiver of rights can be made; that is, the right ''indelibly attaches.'' This rule has developed along two tracks. In the first, it has been held that a waiver of counsel after formal criminal proceedings have begun is ineffective unless counsel is present.[32] In the second, it has been held that the nonwaivability rule is applicable to a suspect in custody and represented by an attorney. It has been expanded to include persons in custody who do not have counsel but have requested assistance of counsel and to those who are not in custody but are represented by counsel.[33] New York has taken the position that without the nonwaiver rule, the right to counsel at trial would be empty. Once a matter is the subject of legal controversy, discussions of that controversy should be conducted by counsel because at that point defendants are in no position to safeguard their rights.

In addition, counsel is mandated in parole revocation hearings,[34] and, by statute, New York permits the presence of an attorney in the grand jury room to advise a client but not to take an active part in the proceedings.[35]

Although the right-to-counsel protection in New York is the most expansive in the nation, in July 1990 the court of appeals in People v. Bing overruled People v. Bartolomeo (1981). Under *Bartolomeo*, knowledge by police that one in costody is represented by counsel in an unrelated charge precluded interrogation in the absence of counsel and rendered invalid any purported waiver of counsel. Under *Bing* a suspect will be able to make a waiver of counsel in the absence of counsel and be questioned on the new charges.

Double Jeopardy

This provision originated in the 1821 Constitution. Its absence in the 1777 Constitution was not of great significance as the state had accepted the common law (Art. XXXV), which recognized the principle (People v. Goodwin, 1820). It was intended as a declaration of broad policy and an endorsement of the common law as it stood in 1821.[36] Its broad purpose is clear: to limit the awesome power of the government to prosecute or harass a defendant continuously. The wording is similar to that found in the Fifth Amendment, and it is likely that the inclusion followed the federal lead.

The clause prohibits not only a second punishment for the same offense but a second trial for the same offense. *Jeopardy* means "exposed to danger," and that point comes when a juror is sworn or a witness is sworn in a bench trial (People v. Jackson, 1967). The clause operates only in criminal settings and prevents second prosecution whether the outcome is acquittal or conviction.[37] A mistrial declared over the defendant's objections would also be barred under this protection unless the ends of justice would otherwise be defeated or on the grounds of manifest necessity (People v. Catten, 1987). A dismissal terminating the proceedings would not permit reprosecution if the dismissal was in the defendant's favor (e.g., a dismissal based on the evidence), but a dismissal requested by the defendant as a result of an error that does not relate to the question of guilt or innocence would not bar retrial (e.g., a good-faith procedural error by the prosecutor) (People v. Zagarino, 1980). The clause would not bar retrial when a defendant appeals a conviction because the appeal is tantamount to a waiver.

The double jeopardy clause of the Fifth Amendment was held applicable to the states in Benton v. Maryland (1969). The court of appeals has held the clause to provide similar protections, though it did rule that the right is so fundamental that failure to raise the issue before trial court does not automatically constitute a waiver preventing appellate review of the issue (People v. Michael, 1979). The state's high court has decided that neither the state nor the federal clause applies to sentencing proceedings under New York's second and "persistent felony" offender statutes (People v. Sailor, 1985).

A dispute of some complexity has arisen over the question of the meaning of *same offense*. The statute law of New York has expanded Fifth Amendment protection by providing additional grounds for prohibiting multiple prosecutions of offenses. The statute prohibits separate prosecution for two offenses based on the same act or transaction.[38] The U.S. Supreme Court has ruled that the provision does not prevent the state from trying someone for the same offense whom the federal courts have acquitted.[39] That decision rested on the doctrine of dual sovereignty. The New York clause does not prevent such prosecutions, but reprosecution is prohibited by the statute, which is regarded as constitutional in nature.

Self-Incrimination

The clause included in the 1821 Constitution is similar in wording to the self-incrimination clause of the Fifth Amendment. It prevents the state from requiring an individual to answer questions or otherwise give testimony that creates a substantial likelihood of criminal incrimination. The Fifth Amendment protection was applied to the states in Malloy v. Hogan (1964).

In most areas, the New York courts have interpreted the clause to provide the same protection provided by its Fifth Amendment counterpart. Among the areas of parallel interpretation are: conditions for requiring *Miranda* warnings (People v. Grant, 1978), public safety exception to *Miranda* requirements (People v. Krom, 1984), voluntariness test for confessions (People v. Huntley, 1965), admissibility of spontaneous statements (People v. Kaye, 1969), and the distinction between testimonial and physical evidence (People v. Damon, 1969). On the other hand, there are some areas where the section has been interpreted independently of the national clause to grant greater protection. The no-waiver-of-rights-absent-counsel rule provides significantly greater protection to one's right not to incriminate oneself. When a defendant has retained or is assigned counsel or has requested one, that person cannot be subjected to custodial interrogation or waive any rights without the presence of counsel (People v. Cunningham, 1980; People v. Rogers, 1979).

In another departure from the Supreme Court, the court of appeals has ruled that when a defendant makes statements under interrogation without *Miranda* warnings and later repeats those statements after having received *Miranda* warnings, the latter statements will be held inadmissible when there is a close sequence between the warned and unwarned statements.[40]

The Supreme Court has held that a grant of immunity to testify can be limited to use immunity, which leaves open the possibility of subsequent prosecution on the basis of evidence obtained independently of the immunized testimony (Kastigar v. United States, 1972). The other type of immunity, transactional immunity, is immunity from prosecution for offenses to which the testimony relates and provides complete immunity from prosecution. New York's self-incrimination clause has not required transactional immunity, but such immunity is required by statutory provision.[41]

A significant qualification to the privilege added in 1938 provided a powerful weapon in the hands of prosecutors for obtaining evidence of official misconduct. The prosecutor may seek to compel any public officer to testify before a grand jury about conduct in public office under pain of loss of employment. The officer may also be required to sign a waiver of immunity, again under penalty of loss of job for refusal. The testimony could then be used in subsequent criminal prosecutions. The prosecutor could do to public officials what would not be permitted with private citizens. The provision was occasioned by the Seabury investigation of public officials, many of whom refused to answer questions concerning their office on the basis of the self-incrimination clause.[42] The amendment was aimed at preventing this from happening again.

In 1944, a city official refused to waive immunity and testify concerning conduct in office. He was removed, and a new position was created for him in the same department. The court of appeals ruled that there was no provision disqualifying the official from holding any other office (People v. Harris, 1945). The section was amended in 1949 to prevent an official removed under the section from holding any public office for five years. One more amendment was added to alter the effect of another court decision. A public official refused to testify under waiver of immunity as to his conduct in an office he had held prior to the one he was holding when called before the grand jury. When an attempt to remove him from office was made, an appellate court determined that without "explicit constitutional direction," it could not hold one removable from office because of refusal under waiver to testify about conduct as to a prior office (People v. Doyle, 1955). A 1959 amendment made removable possible from office if one refused to testify about conduct in any office held within five years of the grand jury call.

All this changed when the Supreme Court called into question the validity of the waiver provision. In a series of cases, the Court reasoned that the imposition of any sanction that makes assertion of the Fifth Amendment privilege "costly" is not permissible. If the officer waived immunity and testified, such testimony was coerced and could not be used in criminal prosecution (Garrity v. New Jersey, 1967). If he or she refused to waive immunity, he or she could not be dismissed from office for exercise of a constitutional right (Gardner v. Broderick, 1968). The 1967 convention rewrote the provision to conform to the *Garrity* decision, but that constitution was rejected. The Court did suggest that the state would be permitted to dismiss one who, not required to waive immunity, refused to answer questions specifically, directly, and narrowly related to the performance of his or her official duties.[43] The provision remains in the constitution but is unenforceable as long as the Supreme Court adheres to its interpretation of the Fifth Amendment.[44]

The power of the grand jury never to be suspended was adopted in 1938 in response to actions by the legislature and governor of Pennsylvania to suspend the operation of a grand jury investigating official misconduct.[45] The "by-law" phrase was added so that the amendment would not be interpreted to prevent a court from granting stays of grand jury actions while litigation was taking place.[46] The paragraph as amended does not apply to court action.

Due Process

The clause was added by the 1821 Constitutional Convention. Its wording is almost exactly the same as that of the federal due process clause in the Fifth Amendment. It has generally been equated with the law-of-the-land clause found in Article I, section 1 and has superseded that clause (People v. Priest, 1912).

Due process has two components: procedural and substantive. Procedural due process refers to the manner in which a law or administrative practice is carried out. It requires that the government follow fair and nonarbitrary steps before depriving a person of life, liberty, or property. At its core is the notion of fundamental fairness, some part of which is expressed in the requirements of notice, reasonable definiteness in the law, and a hearing appropriate to the nature of the case. When the court of appeals, in People v. Isaacson (1978), found police conduct "egregious and deprivative" and a violation of the state due process clause, though not reaching entrapment levels, it was shaping the contours of police behavior in terms of notions of fairness and reasonableness.

Substantive due process refers to the substance of the law or practice that deprives a person of life, liberty, or property. Under this review, courts attempt to ensure that the law is not unreasonable, arbitrary, or capricious. If a fundamental right is involved, the state interest must be compelling, and the law must have a real and substantial relationship to the goal sought. If no fundamental right is at stake, the law must have a rational relationship to a legitimate governmental purpose. Generally New York courts have followed the federal approach, adopting a strict scrutiny test when fundamental rights are involved and a minimal scrutiny or rational relationship when they are not.[47] The minimum scrutiny test permits the state wide latitude in exercising regulatory powers. Nonetheless, state due process has provided protection for property rights against arbitrary actions of the state.[48] Where a fundamental right is involved, the more demanding test is applied. In Cooper v. Morin (1979), the court voided a regulation restricting contact visits with inmates because it infringed on the fundamental right to "marriage and family life."[49] In Rivers v. Katz (1986), the court held there was no compelling state interest established to override a person's fundamental liberty interest to control his or her own care and treatment. Both cases were based squarely on the state due process clause, extending protection beyond that provided by federal due process.

Due process also functions in areas where no specific rights are mentioned. The right to counsel does not apply to lineups conducted before an accustory instrument has been filed, and the privilege against self-incrimination is not grounds for refusal to participate.[50] Nevertheless, due process requires that such lineups be conducted in a fair and nonsuggestive manner.[51] The right to a speedy trial is not mentioned in the state constitution. It is protected by the Sixth Amendment and statutory provisions, but the court of appeals has ruled that the state due process requirement of a speedy trial is broader than the protection found in the statute or the Sixth Amendment. A lengthy and unjustifiable delay may require dismissal though no actual prejudice to the defendant is shown and though the defendant was not formally accused or incarcerated (People v. Singer, 1978).

When a town zoning ordinance restricted occupancy of single-family housing based generally on biological or legal relationships, the court found that the restrictions bore no rational relationship to the goals put forth by the village in justification for the ordinance (McMinn v. Town of Oyster Bay, 1985). A village ordinance prohibiting possession in a public place of an alcoholic beverage without requiring proof of intent to consume did not meet the minimal scrutiny test in that it bore no reasonable relationship to the public good (People v. Lee, 1983).

Statutes frequently provide significant due process protections. The Family Court Act of 1962 had already embodied most of the due process requirement laid down by the Supreme Court for juvenile proceedings in the *Gault* decision.[52]

Unlike the federal due process clause, the state provision contains no state action requirement. In Sharrock v. Dell-Buick Cadillac, Inc. (1978), the court focused on this absence and applied the protection of the clause to a situation held to be private action by federal courts. In the conclusion, with potentially far-reaching implications, the court wrote that the state and federal clauses were "adopted to combat entirely different evils." Aware of these implications, the court continued: "This is not to say that . . . the clause . . . eliminated the necessity of any state involvement in the objected to activity."[53] Nonetheless, the absence of a state action requirement enables New York to apply a more flexible state government involvement standard than the one required by the U.S. Constitution.

The state due process clause has provided the judiciary with a flexible tool it has used to fashion a variety of protections.[54] In a number of cases, these protections are broader than those afforded by the due process clause of the U.S. Constitution.

SECTION 7

Compensation for taking private property; private roads; drainage of agricultural lands. (a) Private property shall not be taken for public use without just compensation.

[(b) repealed by vote of the people November 3, 1964.]

(c) Private roads may be opened in the manner to be prescribed by law; but in every case the necessity of the road and the amount of all damage to be sustained by the opening thereof shall be first determined by a jury of freeholders, and such amount, together with the expenses of the proceedings, shall be paid by the person to be benefited.

(d) The use of property for the drainage of swamp or agricultural lands is declared to be a public use, and general laws may be passed permitting the owners or occupants of swamp or agricultural lands to construct and maintain for the drainage thereof, necessary drains, ditches and dykes upon the lands of others, under proper restrictions, on making just compensation, and such compensation together with the cost of such drainage may be assessed, wholly or partly, against any property benefited thereby; but no special laws shall be enacted for such purposes. [Const. 1821, Art. VII, sec. 7; amend. and renumbered Art. I, sec. 7, Const. 1846; amend. Const. 1894, 1919]

Although the taking of private property for public use—the power of eminent domain—is an attribute of sovereignty, the clause requires that it be done for a public purpose and with just compensation. The relationship of this clause to due process in section 6 has been the occasion for some confusion. When regulations passed under the police power constitute a taking, due process of law has been violated, and absent any damages irreversibly inflicted, the remedy is a declaration of unconstitutionality (Lutheran Church in America v. City of New York, 1974). In this role the due process clause has been an important protection for property rights. It has, for example, placed some limit on the zoning power of local governments (Fred F. French Investing Co. v. New York, 1976). The exercise of eminent domain for opening private roads, does not include a jury trial.[55] When property is acquired under eminent domain, due process is satisfied by reasonable notice, public hearings, publication of findings, and opportunity for court review on the questions of public purpose and just compensation.[56] In the absence of a statutory requirement, due process does not include a right to a hearing to determine the right and necessity of the exercise of the power of eminent domain (Charles v. Diamond, 1977).

The phrase *public purpose* has been interpreted as a limitation on the government. When an easement will suffice for the public purpose, acquisition by complete ownership will not be permitted. The issue is justiciable, but the courts have demanded a "clear showing of bad faith" or government actions that are "irrational" or baseless.[57] Since the clause was meant to protect the individual and not the government, the government can acquire land in excess of public need with the consent of the property owners (Embury v. Connor, 1850). Most of the litigation concerning this clause has centered on the question of compensation. The standards for state due process and eminent domain have paralleled the interpretations of the federal due process and taking clauses.[58]

Paragraph (c) has remained unaltered since its adoption in 1846. It was included to ensure the constitutionality of eminent domain proceedings for private roads, a power put in doubt by Taylor v. Porter (1843), which declared a statute providing for the laying of private roads unconstitutional. The law constituted a deprivation of property without due process of law and was a taking of property for a private, not a public, purpose. No doubt this section was also included to further the public policy of the state "that facilities should be furnished for private ways so that property of citizens might be made accessible." (In Re Tuthill, 1900).

Legislative attempts to permit farmers to improve their lands by draining them across the land of others were curtailed by court decisions that limited such takings to maintaining the public health.[59] Undrained land was considered valueless as far as production was concerned, as well as a health hazard. Farmers pressed for constitutional relief, and the 1894 convention responded with this section enabling them to "properly improve their land."[60] The use of eminent domain to improve some property when that improvement was seen as a means to economic prosperity was not unusual in the nineteenth century, as its use by the railroads attests, and this argument was made explicitly at the convention.[61]

The court narrowed the meaning of this section by ruling that assessments for improvements could be made only on the landowner whose land was being drained (In re Tuthill, 1900). A 1919 amendment allowed assessments to be levied on any property benefited. Because swampland could be profitably drained, it was included in the section. The third clause (d), declaring drainage of both a public purpose, was ostensibly to ensure the constitutionality of legislation implementing this section.[62]

SECTION 8

Freedom of speech and press; criminal prosecutions for libel. Every citizen may freely speak, write and publish his sentiments on all subjects, being responsible for the abuse of that right; and no law shall be passed to restrain or abridge the liberty of speech or of the press. In all criminal prosecutions or indictments for libels, the truth may be given in evidence to the jury; and if it shall appear to the jury that the matter charged as libelous is true, and was published with good motives and for justifiable ends, the party shall be acquitted; and the jury shall have the right to determine the law and the fact. [Const. 1821, Art. VII, sec. 8; amend. and renumbered Art. I, sec. 8, Const. 1846]

The great importance delegates attached to freedom of speech and the press led to securing those rights in the 1821 constitution. The explicit reason was to prevent the legislature from restricting these freedoms by statute.[63] The section differs from its federal counterpart in a number of ways: the freedoms are stated in the affirmative, the initial sentence makes no mention of state action, the provision is set off by a responsibility-for-abuse clause, and there is a lengthy statement of the conditions governing prosecutions from criminal libel.

The entire debate was taken up with the question of libel.[64] What was finally adopted was substantially similar to the provisions of an 1805 statute governing libel prosecutions. That statute in turn was based on Chancellor Kent's arguments in People v. Croswell (1804).[65] The provision does not apply to civil libel cases (Hunt v. Bennett, 1859).

The requirement that only truth told for good motives or justifiable ends was acceptable as a defense in libel suits strikes us today as quaint and perhaps dangerous. But the conditions placed in the section were meant to ensure that the jury, and not the judges would decide all crucial aspects of the libel suit. Criminal libel was meant to cover blasphemous publications and guard public morality, as well as protect private individuals. The provisions are remnants of a tradition of free speech that saw speech limited to forms necessary for self-government. Other types of speech could be considered abuses of the right, which added nothing of value to the community. The abuse constraint was added to make this understanding clear. What constituted abuse was not defined, but Justice Joseph Story summed up a widespread understanding when he wrote: "[E]very man shall have the right to speak, write, and print his opinions upon any subject whatsoever without any prior restraints, so always, that he does not injure any other person in his rights, person, property, or reputation; and so always that he does not hereby disturb the public peace or attempt to subvert the government."[66] In a short compass, Story anticipated the areas that would precipitate the great battles over free speech in the twentieth century.

New York's commitment to protect the press from censorship was demonstrated early in Brandreth v. Lance (1839). There a chancery court concluded that it had no power to restrain publication of a pamphlet alledged to be libelous. Such prior restraint "would endanger the freedom of the press."[67] For most of its history, New York permitted prosecutions for criminal libel, but there is no tradition of seditious libel in New York, and the criminal libel statute now omitted from the penal law was interpreted to exclude group libel prosecutions (People v. Edmondson, 1938). Civil libel has been shaped by the transforming decisions of the Supreme Court between 1964 and 1975. Under those decisions truth is no longer the only or even the primary defense in libel suits. Falsehoods about public officials are protected unless made with malice (knowing falsehoods or reckless disregard of truth) and about private figures unless made negligently.[68] The New York courts have required the higher standard of gross irresponsibility when private figures are in question.[69]

Claims involving free speech under the New York Constitution involve the same principles and tests that apply under the First Amendment (Pico v. Board of Education Island Trees Union Free School, 1979; reversed on other grounds). In recent years, the court of appeals has extended press protection significantly, especially in the area of journalist privilege. In Matter of Beach v. Shanley (1984), a subpoena issued to a reporter to appear before a grand jury investigating public misconduct was held to violate section 79-h of New York's civil rights law, which grants an absolute privilege to a journalist's sources gained in confidence—this in spite of Article I, section 6 forbidding the legislature to suspend or impair the power of the grand jury to inquire into the wilful misconduct of public officials. A subsequent case held that a similar privilege did not apply to nonconfidential sources (Knight-Ridder v. Greenberg, 1987). However, in O'Neill v. Oakgrove Construction Co. (1988), the court of appeals held that journalists possess a qualified right to withhold sources under this section even though those sources are not gained in confidence. The right is founded on the statute's explicit language and the strong tradition of freedom of the press in the state. New York's protection of the press in the areas of confidentiality of sources and libel is among the strongest in the nation.

Freedom of speech has not received the same solicitude as the freedom of the press, however. Prior to the application of the free speech clause of the First Amendment to the states in 1925 (Gitlow v. New York, 1925), the New York judiciary had not done much in the way of protecting free speech; the emphasis was more on the abuse than the right. Obscene, indecent, and immoral publications were considered an "abuse of right" and made criminal.[70] It was not until after World War I that successful constitutional challenges were made, and then on the basis of the First Amendment.[71] The Poletti report in 1938 concluded that the "clear and present danger [test] imposed appreciably greater restrictions on the government and achieves a broader guarantee of individual freedom than that employed by the Court of Appeals."[72]

The New York judiciary readily adapted to the expansive readings of the First Amendment rendered by the Warren Court between 1955 and 1970 (Larking v. G. P. Putnam's Sons, 1964). Starting in the 1980s, the court of appeals, in a series of decisions, began to develop an independent jurisprudence based on this section. People v. Calbud (1980) made the standard for determining obscenity a statewide rather than a local community standard. In Bellanca v. New York Liquor Authority (1981), on remand from the Supreme Court, which had held that a ban on topless dancing was not a violation of the First Amendment, the court of appeals held that Article I, section 8 protects topless dancing as a form of expression. Two 1986 cases also were decided on state constitutional grounds after Supreme Court rulings that no federal constitutional rights had been violated. People ex rel. Arcara v. Cloud Books (1986) held that the use of a public health law to close an adult bookstore was a violation of this section. It justified its departure from federal standards by referring to New York's long history and tradition of fostering freedom of expression.[73] The court suggested that if there was a nuisance, the government, under constitutional standards, was required to explore less restrictive remedies before resorting to the more drastic closure measure. People v. P. J. Video (1986), though a Fourth Amendment case, required a higher probable cause standard for warrants issued to search and seize allegedly obscene materials because such materials "presumptively enjoy First Amendment protections."[74]

The fullest discussion of this section occurred in Shad Alliance v. Smith Haven Mall (1985). The case concerned the question of whether free speech rights are protected in private shopping malls. The Supreme Court had ruled they were not (Pruneyard Shopping Center v. Robins, 1980). Shad required the court to face the questions of whether the state clause required state action and whether to expand the protective reach of the clause beyond federal limits. Finding little evidence that the 1821 Constitutional Convention meant to apply the protection to private actions, the court concluded that for it to take that step would be an act of "judicial arrogance" in that the court "would displace the legislature in settling conflicting interests among citizens."[75] The court found no significant state action in the operation of the shopping mall.

SECTION 9

Right to assemble and petition; divorce; lotteries; pool-selling and gambling; laws to prevent; parimutuel betting on horse races permitted;

games of chance, bingo, or lotto authorized under certain restrictions.
1. No law shall be passed abridging the rights of the people peaceably to assemble and to petition the government, or any department thereof; nor shall any divorce be granted otherwise than by due judicial proceedings; except as hereinafter provided, no lottery or sale of lottery tickets, pool-selling, book-making, or any other kind of gambling, except lotteries operated by the state and the sale of lottery tickets in connection therewith as may be authorized and prescribed by the legislature, the net proceeds of which shall be applied exclusively to or in aid or support of education in this state as the legislature may prescribe, and except pari-mutuel betting on horse races as may be prescribed by the legislature and from which the state shall derive a reasonable revenue for the support of government, shall hereafter be authorized or allowed within the state; and the legislature shall pass appropriate laws to prevent offenses against any of the provisions in this section.

2. Notwithstanding the foregoing provisions of this section, any city, town or village within the state may by an approving vote of the majority of the qualified electors in such municipality voting on a proposition therefor submitted at a general or a special election authorize, subject to state legislative supervision and control, the conduct of one or both of the following categories of games of chance commonly known as: (a) bingo or lotto, in which prizes are awarded on the basis of designated numbers or symbols on a card conforming to numbers or symbols selected at random; (b) games in which prizes are awarded on the basis of a winning number or numbers, color or colors, or symbol or symbols determined by chance from among those previously selected or played, whether determined as the result of the spinning of a wheel, a drawing or otherwise by chance. If authorized, such games shall be subject to the following restrictions, among others which may be prescribed by the legislature: (1) only bona fide religious, charitable or non-profit organizations of veterans, volunteer firemen and similar non-profit organizations shall be permitted to conduct such games; (2) the entire net proceeds of any game shall be exclusively devoted to the lawful purposes of such organizations; (3) no person except a bona fide member of any such organization shall participate in the management or operation of such game; and (4) no person shall receive any remuneration for participating in the management or operation of any such game. Unless otherwise provided by law, no single prize shall exceed two hundred fifty dollars, nor shall any series of prizes on one occasion aggregate more than one thousand dollars. The legislature shall pass appropriate laws to effectuate the purposes of this subdivision, ensure that such games are rigidly regulated to prevent commercialized gambling, prevent participation by criminal and other undesirable elements and the diversion of funds from the purposes authorized hereunder and establish a method by which a municipality which has authorized such games may rescind or revoke such authorization. Unless permitted by the legislature, no municipality shall have the power to pass local laws or ordinances relating to such games. Nothing in this section shall prevent the legislature from passing laws more restrictive

than any of the provisions of this section. [Const. 1846, Art. I, sec. 10; amend. and renumbered Art. I, sec. 9, Const. 1894; amend. 1939, 1957, 1966, 1975, 1984]

The right to assemble peaceably and petition the government are closely related to the protection of freedom of speech and press found in section 8. In many instances, they give occasion and force to freedom of expression. Picketing and demonstrations are obvious examples of activities that combine freedom of speech, assembly, and right to petition government. It is not surprising that the court of appeals has almost always combined the sections when deciding issues implicating assembly of right (People v. Nahman, 1948). As a result, no law has developed interpreting this section independently of section 8. Earlier decisions upheld a variety of regulations in the face of challenges based on this clause. In People v. Kopezak (1935), picketing (actually demonstrating) to protest firetrap conditions was held disorderly on the grounds that a more orderly procedure was available to the demonstrator by appealing to the proper official.

The court of appeals has not interpreted this clause to provide protection beyond that available on the basis of the First Amendment.[76]

In 1787, the legislature gave jurisdiction to the court of chancery to grant divorces in cases of adultery. With no statement of intent, the 1846 Constitutional Convention adopted this provision concerning divorce, probably to prevent the legislature or any other agency from granting divorces. No legislative divorces have been attempted, so there is no case law on this particular issue, but the clause has had the effect of invalidating divorces granted by religious authorities.[77] The legislature has made the granting of a divorce without proper judicial proceedings (defined as a proceeding in a court of justice recognized by the constitution and with statutory jurisdiction to grant decrees of divorce) a misdemeanor.[78]

Generally all kinds of gambling not expressly authorized are prohibited in New York by this constitutional provision. Prior to 1821, lotteries had been used to raise revenues. However, the 1821 convention eliminated lotteries altogether, and subsequent legislatures banned lotteries and gambling in general. When the Ives Pool Hall Law exempted gambling at race tracks in 1877, it was challenged on the grounds that it constituted a lottery, but the court of appeals held that pool betting was not a lottery (Reilly v. Gray, 1894). The decision was handed down two months before the 1894 Constitutional Convention convened. Concern over the corruption of public life and the moral character of the citizenry were dominant themes during the debates,[79] and the amendment banning gambling passed overwhelmingly 109–4.

Eighteen hundred ninety-four was the high-water mark for antigambling sentiment in New York. From that point on, the state constitution has been amended to permit various forms of state or private gambling. The first step was taken in 1939 when parimutuel betting on horse races was permitted. It was permissive only and did not create a right to parimutuel betting (Application of Stewart, 1940).

The fact that many religious and charitable organizations play bingo to raise funds for worthy purposes and were risking criminal penalties in doing so prompted a 1957 amendment authorizing bingo and lotto on a local option basis but only to bona-fide religious, charitable, and nonprofit organizations of veterans, volunteer firemen, and similar groups.

In 1966, a third amendment to this section allowed New York, for the first time in the twentieth century, to operate a lottery system, with the proceeds earmarked exclusively for the support of education. The main justification for the amendment was to open a heretofore untapped source of revenue for the state. The provisions were not self-executing. The legislature had to "authorize and prescribe" the game by statute. That statute is known as the New York State Lottery for Education Law (1967). The debate in the state senate suggests that there was no intention to do more than carve out an exception to the general prohibition against lotteries and gambling.[80]

The 1957 amendment broadened the category of games of chance that eligible groups could conduct, and a 1984 amendment allowed the legislature to increase the amount of prizes specified in this section as it deemed necessary in the light of inflation and other factors.[81] In two formal opinions, the attorney-general has defined the lottery exception to the antigambling clause narrowly, concluding that the exception does not permit computer programmed games ("computerized slot machines") or allow a sports card betting game for wagering on professional football games.[82]

SECTION 10

[Dealt with ownership of lands, allodial tenures, and escheats; was repealed by amendment approved by vote of the people November 6, 1962.]

SECTION 11

Equal protection of laws; discrimination in civil rights prohibited. No person shall be denied the equal protection of the laws of this state or any subdivision thereof. No person shall, because of race, color, creed or religion, be subjected to any discrimination in his civil rights by any other person or by any firm, corporation, or institution, or by the state or any agency or subdivision of the state. [1938]

This section marks the first appearance of a provision against discrimination in the New York Constitution. At the time it was adopted there were a number of antidiscrimination statutes. The section was meant to announce a broad state-

The first sentence prohibits discriminatory action by the state and functions as the state equivalent to the Fourteenth Amendment's equal protection clause. The New York courts have held that the protection provided by the state clause is no broader than the federal provision.[83]

The second sentence relates to private parties and prohibits the state, its subdivisions, private individuals, corporations, and institutions from subjecting any person to discrimination in his or her civil rights on account of race, color, creed, or religion. The first major test of the scope of this clause came in Dorsey v. Stuyvesant Town Corporation (1949). A town corporation refused to accept African American applicants for housing. In answering the question of whether the civil rights of appellant were violated, the court of appeals reasoned that the civil rights as defined in this section refer to those elsewhere declared. The court pointed to the 1938 convention debates in which the phrase *civil rights* was added to limit its scope to "rights found in the constitution in the civil rights law and in the statutes."[84] Since there was no statute recognizing the opportunity to acquire interests in real property as a civil right, the court concluded that the section could not apply to individuals in appellant's situation.[85] In effect, the court said the clause is not self-executing; for its prohibitions to be effective, legislation is necessary. The remaining claim was that there was, in fact, state action in violation of the first sentence of the section. In response, the court said that tax exemptions and use of eminent domain for private developers and the town corporation did not amount to state action. To hold otherwise would come close to saying that any state assistance to an organization constitutes state action.[86] Within a year of the decision, legislation was adopted implementing this civil right.[87]

While state action provision has undergone some expansion since *Dorsey*, the court of appeals has not expanded its scope beyond that required by the Fourteenth Amendment.[88]

The court has adopted the three-tiered scrutiny test used by the Supreme Court when applying the equal protection clause, although its decisions have not always made this clear.[89]

People v. Liberta (1984) held that a statute exempting females from criminal liability for forcible rape and providing a marital exemption for rape, violates both state and federal equal protection.[90] The level of scrutiny was not mentioned. *Liberta* initiated habeas corpus proceedings in federal court, and a federal appeals court subsequently overruled that part of the decision based on federal equal protection (Liberta v. Kelly, 1988).

In general, the court of appeals has not stepped beyond the standards set by the Supreme Court under the three levels of scrutiny. In Levittown Union Free School District v. Nyquist (1982),[91] the court refused to put wealth in a suspect category and declare spending disparities among school districts no violation of equal protection. It has upheld the bail system against challenges based on equal protection, followed federal precedent in allowing a landownership requirement for voting in water district elections,[92] and has not placed age or the handicapped in the suspect category.[93]

In the area of criminal procedure, the court has used the equal protection clause to ensure that guaranteed rights are available to all regardless of economic status. When the state constitutionally or statutorily affords a defendant a right, that right cannot be conditioned on the defendant's ability to pay (People v. Montgomery, 1966). In New York, every defendant has an absolute right to appeal a conviction, and when denial or obstruction of the right occurs because of indigency, equal protection is violated.[94] In People v. Kerns (1990), the court of appeals held that use of pre-emptory challenges by defense counsel to exclude jurors solely on the basis of race was prohibited by both the civil rights and equal protection clauses of section 11. In doing so that court extended the United States Supreme Court ruling of Batson v. Kentucky (1986) wherein racially based exclusions by the prosecutor were held to violate the equal protection clause of the Fourteenth Amendment.

On the other hand, even under the minimal scrutiny, rational relationships test, the court has declared a variety of law or regulations violations of equal protection. In Berenson v. New Castle (1975), for example, the court declared zoning regulations that were exclusionary in intent and impact a violation of the equal protection clause. Subsequent decisions have made it clear, however, that the court will be reluctant to impose "drastic essentially legislative intervention by the judiciary."[95] In Allen v. Town of Hempstead (1984), a rule requiring senior citizens to live in the town for at least one year before qualifying for a golden age residence district was exclusionary. Geographically based disparities in judges' salaries were voided (Kendall v. Evans, 1988), and Sunday blue laws, selectively enforced only at the initiation of interest groups, also failed an equal protection challenge (People v. Acme Markets, Inc., 1975). Even in the area of taxation, which courts generally consider an area of nearly unconstrained power, the court has found violations of equal protection. In Foss v. City of Rochester (1985), assessment policy creating a disparity in tax rate between homestead property in the city of Rochester and similar property in the county were voided. Tax and assessment policies that created differences in exemptions between similarly situated veterans also failed to meet the rational relationship standard (Burrows v. Town of Chatham, 1984). In each of these cases, minimal scrutiny was applied, and in each case the actions in question were struck down.

The range of issues illustrated by these cases suggests that minimal scrutiny equal protection analysis is not synonymous with judicial abdication. The U.S. Supreme Court is physically incapable of and not inclined to give much attention to the kinds of cases that state courts handle regularly. In this respect, even when the state judiciary is not expanding the suspect category, it is playing a significant role in ensuring equal protection under the laws.[96]

SECTION 12

Security against unreasonable searches, seizures, and interceptions. The right of the people to be secure in their persons, houses, papers, and effects, against unreasonable searches and seizures, shall not be violated, and no warrants shall issue, but upon probable cause, supported by oath or affirmation, and particularly describing the place to be searched, and the persons or things to be seized.

The right of the people to be secure against unreasonable interception or telephone and telegraph communications shall not be violated, and ex parte orders or warrants shall issue only upon oath or affirmation that there is reasonable ground to believe that evidence of crime may be thus obtained, and identifying the particular means of communication, and particularly describing the person or persons whose communications are to be intercepted and the purpose thereof. [1938]

Prior to 1938, the New York State Constitution contained no guarantees against unreasonable searches and seizures. A proposal at the 1867 Constitutional Convention to make this protection part of the constitution was rejected. There was, however, a statutory provision embodying the protection, which goes back to 1828.[97] The U.S. Supreme Court did not apply the Fourth Amendment to the states until Wolf v. Colorado in 1949, so New Yorkers had no constitutional protection against unreasonable searches and seizures until 1938. The wording of the section is almost identical to that of the Fourth Amendment, with the addition of the paragraph on the use of wiretapping.

The purpose of the section is to protect personal privacy and security against arbitrary intrusions of official power. Blanket or general warrants are prohibited, and searches must meet the test of reasonableness. The debate over the section in the 1938 convention focused on two areas: the use of wiretapping and whether a clause ought to be added that would exclude from court any evidence seized in violation of the section (the exclusionary rule).[98] Until Mapp v. Ohio in 1961, the chief difference between the state and federal clauses was with respect to the application of the exclusionary rule: the federal rule excluded illegally seized evidence (Weeks v. United States, 1914); the state law did not mandate an exclusionary rule (People v. Defore, 1926). In People v. Richter's Jeweler's, Inc. (1943), the court of appeals held that the refusal of the 1938 convention to adopt an exclusionary rule left the common law rule of admissibility unchanged.

In the past, the general policy of the court of appeals has been to promote a uniformity of interpretation between federal and state courts in this area of law. The identity of the language supported this policy of consistency of interpretation. The wiretapping statute adopted under the constitutional provision was upheld, as were stop-and-frisk laws (People v. Sibron, 1966), warrantless arrests in the home (People v. Payton, 1978), and warrantless investigative arrests (People v. Dunaway, 1975). The latter two decisions were overruled by the Supreme Court in Payton v. New York (1980) and Dunaway v. New York (1979).

In the early 1980s, the court began to diverge from federal law, adopting independent standards under the state constitution when doing so would best promote "predictability and precision in judicial review of search and seizure cases and in the protection of the individual rights of our citizens."[99]

The development of a position independent of national Fourth Amendment law appeared first in the area of automobile searches. Prior to United States v. Robinson (1973), allowing police to conduct full searches incident to traffic arrests, New York courts did not permit such searches (People v. Marsh, 1967; People v. Adams, 1973). Decisions subsequent to *Robinson* allowed for some exceptions to this rule (e.g., People v. Troiano, 1974), but the broad doctrine of *Marsh* has survived *Robinson*. In People v. Class (1986), on remand from a Supreme Court decision finding no violation of federal law in police action in entering a vehicle to read the vehicle identification number after stopping a suspect for a traffic offense, the court of appeals ruled that the search violated this section of the state constitution.

The court of appeals has invalidated routine traffic checks of single vehicles absent reasonable suspicion that a violation has taken place but has sustained use of permanent or movable sobriety checkpoints carried out under clear guidelines.[100]

The state's commitment to the exclusionary rule was explicitly based on this section of the constitution after the U.S. Supreme Court adopted a "good faith" exception to that rule,[101] and in People v. Stith (1987), the court of appeals refused to rule admissible evidence seized illegally from the cab of a truck under the inevitable discovery exception to the exclusionary rule. The decision was apparently in line with federal law; nevertheless, the court of appeals, anticipating any possible changes in federal law, relied on this section, apparently insulating the decision from federal court review.

People v. Elwell (1980) laid down a per se rule that warrantless searches and seizures will require the police to confirm conduct suggestive of or directly involving criminal activity when the informer did not indicate the basis for knowledge about that activity, a rule more demanding than the test then required by the Supreme Court. When the Supreme Court in Illinois v. Gates (1983) adopted the less stringent totality-of-circumstances test for judging the worth of an informant's tip, the New York high court refused to follow the relaxed standard and reaffirmed *Elwell*.[102]

People v. P. J. Video (1986) involved a warranted search of an adult bookstore. After the Supreme Court ruled that the search was not a violation of the Fourth Amendment, the court of appeals reaffirmed its initial ruling on state constitutional grounds. In overturning the search, the court said that because the material in question "presumptively enjoyed First Amendment protection, the magistrate was required to perform his duties with scrupulous exactitude."[103]

The New York judiciary has been particularly active on the question of the scope of a search incident to a lawful arrest. People v. Belton (1980) held that a warrantless search of a zippered pocket jacket within the passenger compartment of a vehicle is permissible only when there is a possibility of the arrestee's gaining access to the article. The Supreme Court reversed in New York v. Belton (1981), allowing warrantless searches of closed articles. On remand in People v. Belton (1982) (Belton II) the court sustained the search but on state constitutional grounds: the search fell within the automobile exception to the warrant requirement. The court further specified that for the exception to be applied validly, there must be reason to believe that the vehicle contains evidence related to the crime for which the occupant was arrested. If that condition is met, the whole automobile may be searched.[104] With regard to searches incident to lawful arrest not involving vehicles, court decisions have established the position that searches of closed containers possessed by the subject are not automatically "searchable" unless exigent circumstances involving safety of officers or possibility of destruction or concealment of evidence exists.[105] The extension of state-based protection continued in People v. Torres (1989). In Torres, police had ordered two men out of their automobile and conducted a limited protective frisk of the suspects (permitted under Terry v. Ohio, 1968). They then conducted a more intrusive search of the automobile's interior. This latter search, justified under Michigan v. Long (1983), was declared a violation of section 12 of the state constitution. In one of the few cases involving obligations of citizens to respond to police questions in street encounters, People v. Howard (1980) the court held that a suspect's refusal to answer police questions and flight from the officer, absent any other evidence of criminal activity, were not sufficient grounds for search or seizure or pursuit of suspect.

The question of drug testing reached the court of appeals in Patchogue-Medford Congress of Teachers v. Board of Education (1987). In *Patchogue-Medford* a school district's policy of random drug testing requiring all probationary teachers to submit to urinalysis prior to decision on tenure, was held to violate both federal and state guarantees against unreasonable searches and seizures. The court was not clear as to whether the case rested on state grounds independent of federal law, suggesting that a decision ought to involve both state and federal law when the results would be similar under both clauses and when the Supreme Court has not yet ruled on the particular issue in question. In Matter of Caruso v. Ward (1988) the court ruled that periodic random urinalysis drug testing for members of the Organized Crime Division of the New York City Police Department did not facially violate the search-and-seizure clauses of the state and federal constitutions.

In the 1980s, the most significant developments in the creation of a body of independent state constitutional law were in the area of search and seizure.[106] The court of appeals has not yet worked out a consistent basis for determining when protection ought to be extended beyond that guaranteed by federal law, and it has not yet determined when state constitutional grounds ought to be relied on exclusively, when the ground ought to be exclusively federal, and when both should be cited, but cases like People v. Johnson, *Patchogue-Medford*, and *P. J. Video* indicate that the court is working toward a resolution of these issues.

The second paragraph of the section is an application of the principles of the first section to the specific area of wiretapping, but instead of probable cause "reasonable cause" is required, and only two types of electronic surveillance are mentioned. Under earlier statutes adopted pursuant to this provision, any supreme court or county court judge could issue such a warrant, and police officers down to the rank of sergeant could apply for one. The constitutional provision did little more than authorize eavesdropping. The statute passed under this provision was declared unconstitutional in Berger v. New York (1967).[107] Subsequently New York revised its eavesdropping legislation to conform to the requirements of *Berger* and the Federal Omnibus Crime Control and Safe Streets Act of 1968. As a result of the federal activity in this area, the state constitutional provision has not been a significant factor in determining the wiretapping policy of the state. The revised statute specifies five conditions that must be met for the issuance of a warrant. The fourth condition, that there must be no reasonable alternative means for acquisition of the evidence, is not required by the *Berger* decision and is an example of a state statutory requirement more demanding than either federal or state constitutional law.[108] The impact of this provision was blunted by People v. Gallina (1983) wherein it was held that electronic surveillance need not be sought only as a last resort after all possible investigative techniques have been exhausted. In general, the courts have interpreted the statute strictly, holding that some crimes included in the New York law, for which such warrants could be issued, were not included under the "danger to life, limb or property" phrase of the federal law, and requiring that tapes presented to the judge must be done immediately upon expiration of the eavesdropping warrant and not, as federal law allows, at the termination of the final order.[109]

SECTION 13

[Dealt with purchase of lands of Indians, repealed by amendment approved by vote of the people November 6, 1962.]

SECTION 14

Common law and acts of the colonial and state legislatures. Such parts of the common law, and of the acts of the legislature of the colony of New York, as together did form the law of the said colony, on the nineteenth day of April, one thousand seven hundred seventy-five, and the resolutions of the congress of the said colony, and of the convention of the State of New York, in force on the twentieth day of April, one thousand seven hundred seventy-seven, which have not since expired, or been repealed or altered; and such acts of the legislature of this state as are now in force, shall be and continue the law of this state, subject to such alterations as the legislature shall make concerning the same. But all parts of the common law, and such of the said acts, or parts thereof, as are repugnant to this constitution, are hereby abrogated. [Const. 1777, Art. XXXV; amend. and renumbered Art. VII, sec. 13, Const. 1821; renumbered Art. I, sec. 17, Const. 1846; renumbered Art. I, sec. 16, Const. 1894; amend. and renumbered Art. I, sec. 14, 1938]

There was no formal bill of rights in the 1777 Constitution, but the common law was seen by the colonists as their natural heritage and shield. The principles and rules found in the common law were a vast source of substantive liberties and procedural rights. This section, continuing the English statutory and common law colonial legislation in force on April 20, 1775, was aimed at preserving the rights and principles embodied therein.

There are two qualifications in the section. The first allows the legislature to modify this statutory and common law as it sees fit. Pursuant to this authorization, the legislature declared both English and colonial statutes to have no force and effect in the state.[110] The second qualification is that parts of the common law inconsistent with the constitution are abolished. The 1777 Constitution specifically abrogated all parts of the common law of England that required the maintenance or establishment of any denomination of Christianity (Art. XXXV). The 1821 convention eliminated this specific exception, leaving the general statement as it now appears. The clause operates to ensure that common law principles that have not been abolished by legislature or the courts are applied. In Chandler v. Avery (1888),[111] it was held that, at common law, a party in a civil suit had an absolute right personally to appear and defend his or her interests and could not be excluded at any stage of the trial. The rule continues by virtue of this section, and its violation is reversable error.

What of the role of the judiciary in altering or abolishing the common law?[112] The common law developed over a long period of time by virtue of decisions of the judges. Did the provision mean to freeze the common law at a certain point save for the exceptions made by the legislature? Was the judiciary limited to refusing to apply the common law when it was inconsistent with the constitution? Or was the judiciary also empowered to deviate from the common law? In the nineteenth century, courts asserted the right to alter or abolish the common law where it is judged to be inapplicable to contemporary circumstances or situations.

It has been suggested that the courts should modify the common law only when there is a substantial body of agreement that such change is necessary and when it is manifest that change can be better effected by the judiciary (Duhan v. Milanowski, 1973). Whatever constraints exist with regard to Article I, section 14, the judiciary of New York has played a major role in altering the common law in a variety of areas, abolishing what it perceived to be anachronistic rules and establishing new ones.[113]

SECTION 15

[Dealt with certain grants of lands and of charters made by the king of Great Britain and the state and obligations and contracts not to be impaired; repealed by amendment approved by vote of the people November 6, 1962.]

SECTION 16

Damages for injuries causing death. The right of action now existing to recover damages for injuries resulting in death, shall never be abrogated; and the amount recoverable shall not be subject to any statutory limitation. [Const. 1894, Art. I, sec. 18; renumbered Art. I, sec. 16, 1938]

This section was occasioned by attempts on the part of various groups, especially the railroads, to limit recoverable damages for wrongful deaths. The legislature in 1847 had altered the common law prohibition on such suits.[114] In response to these pressures, a limit of $5,000 was placed on damages.[115] The 1894 Constitutional Convention added this section to ensure that the right of action for wrongful death, which until then was purely statutory in nature, could not be abolished solely by legislative action and to eliminate what was perceived as an arbitrary limit on damages. Since the legislature undoubtedly had the power to abolish the limit, the provision's assumption is that it could not be trusted to do so and its power must be restricted by constitutional provision. There was unquestionably an undercurrent of sentiment at the convention that the railroad corporations had too much influence with the legislature. As one delegate put it: "The legislators of this state cannot be trusted."[116]

The "now existing" phrase means a right of action that existed prior to January 1, 1895, the effective date of the new constitution (In re Meng, 1919). It does not prevent the state from enacting statutes of limitations on the filing of actions to recover damages.[117] In addition, the legislature can and has limited the kinds of damages one can collect to "pecuniary injuries resulting from the decedent's death to the person to whose benefits the action is brought."[118] Because the provision allows judges and jurors to be the sole judges of damages awarded, courts have the power to reduce damages as "excessive."[119]

The existence of this right-to-access provision creates a property right that may not be arbitrarily altered or restricted. Short of a constitutional amendment, the legislature could not remove jurisdiction from civil courts unless it provides alternative remedies as it has in the no-fault provisions of the insurance law.[120] In fact, section 8 of Article I restricts the scope of this section by barring initiation of wrongful death suits where fatal injury is caused by the negligence of the decedent's employer or a coemployee.

The strong commitment to this policy represented by its inclusion in the constitution has meant that New York courts will not apply laws from other jurisdiction limiting recoverable damages even when conflict-of-law principles support such an application.[121]

SECTION 17

Labor not a commodity; hours and wages in public work; right to organize and bargain collectively. Labor of human beings is not a commodity nor an article of commerce and shall never be so considered or construed.

No laborer, workman or mechanic, in the employ of a contractor or subcontractor engaged in the performance of any public work, shall be permitted to work more than eight hours in any day or more than five days in any week, except in cases of extraordinary emergency; nor shall he be paid less than the rate of wages prevailing in the same trade or occupation in the locality within the state where such public work is to be situated, erected or used.

Employees shall have the right to organize, and to bargain collectively through representatives of their own choosing. [1938]

This section, sometimes referred to as a bill of rights for labor, contains three parts: a declaration that labor is not a commodity or an article of commerce, a limitation of hours of labor and payment of prevailing wage rates in public works, and a guarantee to labor of the right to organize and bargain collectively. These should be read in conjunction with other constitutional provisions concerning labor (Art. I, sect. 18; Art. VII, sec. 8; Art. IX, sec 2(c)(9)).

Like many other parts of the constitution, the provisions of this section were preceded by statutory enactments. The provision declaring labor not a commodity is found in the Clayton Anti-Trust Act (1914) and in the state equivalent, the Donnelly Act.[122] The first paragraph exempted labor unions from the effect of the state's antitrust law, which had been used to restrict organized union activity. It was also felt that if the rights in question were fundamental, they ought to have a status commensurate with that fact.

The second paragraph also constitutionalizes a policy with a long history in the state. By 1894, both the regulation of wages and hours as well as the prevailing wage rate requirement had become state law. An attempt to apply the law to municipalities was declared unconstitutional by the court of appeals (People ex rel. Rodgers v. Coler, 1900). The effects of that decision were overcome by an amendment in 1905 authorizing appropriate legislative action, and the statute was reenacted in 1906. The desire to make this public policy the constitutional policy of the state, giving it more permanency and status and to immunize legislative action from adverse court review, were the major reasons offered to justify its inclusion.

The third paragraph follows the pattern of the first two, placing in the document a policy already recognized by the legislature and the judiciary. New York was a leader in recognizing the right to picket and to have collective bargaining agreements recognized. It has not been read as preventing the state from outlawing strikes by public employees (New York v. DeLury, 1968) or as permitting supervisory personnel the right to organize and be recognized for purposes of collective bargaining (District 2 Marine Engineers Beneficial Association (AFL-CIO) v. New York Shipping Association, 1968).

Much of the protection provided by this section is now provided by federal labor law. The occupancy of the field by federal law has had the effect of preempting this section, as well as much other state labor law, giving it primarily a standby character.[123] The value of these provisions, aside from their symbolic importance, lies in their potential use should federal policy change radically.

SECTION 18

Workers' compensation. Nothing contained in this constitution shall be construed to limit the power of the legislature to enact laws for the protection of the lives, health, or safety of employees; or for the payment, either by employers, or by employers and employees or otherwise, either directly or through a state or other system of insurance or otherwise, of compensation for injuries to employees or for death of employees resulting from such injuries without regard to fault as a cause thereof, except where injury is occasioned by the wilful intention of the injured employee to bring about the injury or death of himself or of another, or where the injury results solely from the intoxication of the injured employee while on duty; or for the adjustment, determination and settlement, with or without trial by jury, of issues which may arise under such legislation; or to provide that the right of such compensation, and the remedy therefor shall be exclusive of all other rights and remedies for injuries to employees or for death resulting from such injuries; or to provide that the amount of such compensation for death shall not exceed a fixed or determinable sum; provided that all moneys paid by an employer to his employees or their legal representatives, by reason of the enactment of any of the laws herein authorized, shall be held to be a proper charge in the cost of operating the business of the employer. [Const. 1894, Art. I, sec. 19 as added in 1913; renumbered Art. I, sec. 18, 1938]

In 1910, New York State became the first state in the nation to adopt a comprehensive workers' compensation law.[124] It was designed to overcome the inability of employees to recover damages for loss of income and needed expenses relating to industrial accidents. Under the common law, employers were not liable unless negligent, and employees could not collect if they contributed in any way to the accident. In 1911, the court of appeals struck this law down on both state and federal due process grounds (Ives v. South Buffalo Railroad Co., 1911). The decision aroused such opposition that within two years an amendment overruling it was approved, and legislation pursuant to the amendment was passed.[125] Within four years of the *Ives* decision, the state had amended its constitution and reinstated workers' compensation legislation. The swiftness of the action suggests the extent to which a consensus had formed supporting the program.[126] The section serves as an enabling authorization; it does not enact any program, so it cannot be construed to prohibit the adoption of a provision that allows injured workers to file separate first-party benefit claims under no-fault law (Ryder Truck Lines, Inc. v. Maiorano, 1978).

The extensive power granted to the legislature by the amendment was meant to override other provisions in the constitution that otherwise might be seen as inconsistent with it (e.g., Art. I, sec. 16). Challenges to the legislation on the grounds that it did not allow for trial by jury (Art. I, sec. 8) in determining settlement and that it was an unconstitutional delegation of judicial power in violation of Article III, section 1 were rebuffed on the grounds that the extensive power granted to the legislature both to compensate and set up procedures to arbitrate and settle claims immunized legislation adopted pursuant to its provisions.[127]

The program ensures a swift and sure source of benefits to insured or dependents of deceased employees by eliminating the delays and expenses of pursuing claims in the courts. It also affords protection to employers against excessive claims. The provision contains exceptions: compensation will not be paid to an employee who intentionally causes his or her own injury or death or is injured while intoxicated.

In the light of its purpose to protect working women and men and their dependents from want in case of injury or death, its provisions have been interpreted liberally by the courts.[128]

The conditions that necessitated this amendment have seemingly passed into history, but its presence continues to allow for a bypassing of traditional common law remedies, as well as the limitation of other provisions in the constitution. The use of administrative and regulatory boards with quasi-judicial and quasi-executive powers has moved the courts out of this arena and gave impetus to the growth of administrative law. Of course, the activities of the Workers' Compensation Board must comport with the terms of the legislation, and the legislation must conform to due process constraints, however broadly defined they may be (W. H. H. Chamberlin Inc. v. Andrews, 1936), but the impact of this section has been to reduce constitutional review to a bare minimum in the name of an efficient and effective solution to a serious social problem.

Article II

Suffrage

The right of suffrage is at the heart of republican government. This article attempts to ensure each qualified voter the fullest and freest exercise of that right and to protect that right from dilution by electoral fraud or irregularities. It provides the qualifications, disqualifications, and procedures governing the exercise of the right to vote in New York. It should be read in conjunction with Article I, Section 1, which contains a general guarantee of the right to vote.

SECTION 1

Qualifications of voters. Every citizen shall be entitled to vote at every election for all officers elected by the people and upon all questions submitted to the vote of the people provided that such citizen is twenty-one years of age or over and shall have been a resident of this state, and of the county, city, or village for three months next preceding an election.

Notwithstanding the foregoing provisions, after January first, one thousand nine hundred twenty-two, no persons shall become entitled to vote by attaining majority, by naturalization or otherwise, unless such person is also able, except for physical disability, to read and write English. [Const. 1894, Art. II, sec. 1 as amend. in 1921; amend. 1966]

Section 1 sets forth the qualifications for voting: an age of twenty-one, an English literacy requirement, and a residency requirement of three months in the state, county, city, or village.

The section removes all disqualifications that had attached to persons in earlier times and ensures that citizens qualified by age, residency, and literacy are guaranteed the right to vote. Inspectors at elections can do no more than make use of the machinery provided by law to test the voters' qualifications; they cannot decide the truth or falsity of answers given. The legislature cannot add to the qualifications authorized by the constitution. Hence, a provision requiring voters to take a loyalty oath was voted as imposing a qualification not specified in the constitution (Green v. Shumway, 1868).

These requirements apply only to general elections relating to government affairs of the whole state (Turco v. Union Free School District No. 4 Town of North Hemstead, 1964). A statutory requirement that one own property to vote in a water district election was held not to violate this section or Article I, section 1. The court gave as its justification that it has always been the established policy of the state "to limit the right of suffrage in such elections" (Elser v. Walters, 1982).

In response to the increasingly mobile character of Americans, a 1966 amendment substantially reduced residency requirements. The earlier requirement of one year was estimated to disenfranchise upwards of 20 percent of the voters. The three-months' standard, however, was not short enough to meet federal standards, and the court of appeals, following Dunn v. Blumstein (1972), held the requirement a violation of the equal protection clause of the Fourteenth Amendment. The current standard set by the Supreme Court is thirty days.

The adoption of the Twenty-sixth Amendment to the U.S. Constitution, establishing eighteen as the age for voting in all elections, eclipsed the state requirement of twenty-one. Amendments to the Voting Rights Act of 1965 suspended all literacy tests until 1975, and in that year the suspensions were made permanent. The New York literacy requirements were held to be in violation of the 1965 act insofar as they disenfranchised Puerto Ricans whose native tongue was Spanish (Katzenbach v. Morgan, 1966). In 1977, the legislation implementing the literacy requirement was dropped from the recompiled election law. As a result, section 1 bears no relation to the actual requirements for voting in New York.

SECTION 2

Absentee voting. The legislature may, by general law, provide a manner in which, and the time and place at which, qualified voters who, on the occurrence of any election, may be absent from the county of their residence or, if residents of the city of New York, from the city, and qualified voters who, on occurrence of any election, may be unable to appear personally at the polling place because of illness or physical disability, may vote and for the return and canvass of their votes. [Const. 1894, Art. II, sec. 1-a as added in 1919; renumbered Art. II, sec. 2, 1938; amend. 1955, 1963]

This section gives the legislature broad authority to establish procedures for absentee voting. The legislature is permitted but not required to provide absentee voting procedures for voters absent from the state, county, or city and those suffering physical disabilities. It was first adopted in 1919 when studies revealed that over 300,000 voters were disenfranchised by virtue of unavoidable absence.[1] Since that time, the classes eligible have been expanded. In 1963, the legislature was authorized to grant absentee voting privileges to any persons who, for any reason, may be absent from their place of residence, in effect turning over to the legislature the power to decide who can exercise the privilege and under what conditions. This amendment eliminated the cumbersome process of having to amend the constitution each time a new class is made eligible. The section does not grant a constitutional right to an absentee ballot, and the courts have been deferential with regard to legislation passed pursuant to this section (Colaneri v. McNabb, 1975). The state's failure to provide absentee ballots for a person on vacation during a special election was sustained.[2] Absentee ballot procedures are governed by the state election law, and, with regard to presidential and vice-presidential elections, by amendments to the Federal Voting Rights Act of 1970 (see section 9 of this article).

SECTION 3

Persons excluded from the right of suffrage. No person who shall receive, accept, or offer to receive, or pay, offer or promise to pay, contribute, offer or promise to contribute to another, to be paid or used, any money or other valuable thing as a compensation or reward for the giving or withholding a vote at an election, or who shall make any promise to influence the giving or withholding any such vote, or who shall make or become directly or indirectly interested in any bet or wager depending upon the result of any election, shall vote at such election; and upon challenge for such cause, the person so challenged, before the officers authorized for that purpose shall receive his vote, shall swear or affirm before such officers that he has not received or offered, does not expect to receive, has not paid, offered or promised to pay, contributed, offered or promised to contribute to another, to be paid or used, any money or other valuable thing as a compensation or reward for the giving or withholding a vote at such election, and has not made any promise to influence the giving or withholding of any such vote, nor made or become directly or indirectly interested in any bet or wager depending upon the result of such election. The legislature shall enact laws excluding from the right of suffrage all persons convicted of bribery or of any infamous crime. [Const. 1846, Art. II, sec. 2 as amend. in 1874; renumbered Art. II, sec. 3, 1938]

Election chicanery and fraud, along with the American penchant for betting, have been part of the American republic at least since the beginning of the nineteenth century. Various legislative attempts to deal with this problem were made, culminating in this section, which combines material from 1821, 1846, and 1874.

The 1821 Constitution allowed the legislature to exclude those convicted of an infamous crime, which today is synonymous with a felony. No debate occurred on the amendment, but the assumption, widely shared, that only those who contributed to the public service or supported the government in some way were entitled to vote, thus excluding the rootless and impoverished, would apply more strongly to a convicted felon. The right is not lost if no sentence of death or imprisonment occurs, and felons once discharged from parole, pardoned, or who have their civil rights restored by the governor are again allowed to vote.[3] The legislature has added a further restriction by excluding all those who have been judged incompetent or committed to an institution for the mentally ill.[4]

In 1874, the section was amended to nearly its present form. It is no longer left to legislative discretion to pass laws excluding those convicted of bribery; they were directly barred from voting. Every conceivable form of bribery was detailed. Such elaborate detail is testimony to the gross and open electoral fraud characteristic of New York politics after the Civil War, when open payment to voters at the polls and other blatant corrupt practices were common.[5] Putting into the constitution a provision that reads like an election code no doubt reflected the frustration created by the failure of other attempts to correct the problem.

The line between a candidate's promises to voters and an offer of inducement constituting a bribe is a fine one, as the case of People ex rel. Bush v. Thorton (1881) indicates. A candidate's promise that if elected he would only take half his salary was held to be a bribe of the electors!

A voter challenged on grounds specified in this section is required to swear under oath that he or she is not guilty of any of these practices before being allowed to vote. This provision, currently implemented in the election law, would seem to raise problems involving the privilege against self-incrimination as interpreted by Garrity v. New Jersey (1967) (see Art. I, sec. 6).

SECTION 4

Certain occupations and conditions not to affect residence. For the purpose of voting, no person shall be deemed to have gained or lost a residence, by reason of his presence or absence, while employed in the service of the United States; nor while engaged in the navigation of the waters of this state, or of the United States, or of the high seas; nor while a student of any seminary of learning; nor while kept at any almshouse, or other asylum, or institution wholly or partly supported at public expense or by charity; nor while confined in any public prison. [Const. 1846, Art. II, sec. 3; amend. and renumbered Art. II, sec. 4, 1938]

This section qualifies the residency requirements of section 1. It means that presence at a new location for one of the enumerated reasons does not create a residence, nor does absence from the original domicile for any of the reasons create the loss of a residence. The amendment was in part a response to the possibility that voters in the military or in school who were ignorant of local affairs would create political imbalances, especially in small towns and villages. The courts have interpreted the clause as creating a rebuttable presumption—one that can be overcome by clear and convincing evidence.[6] The establishment of a new residence must be demonstrated by evidence other than the mere presence at the new location. The conditions for establishing a residence for those in the categories in question are spelled out in the state's election law.[7] Most cases interpreting this section have involved the military and students.

SECTION 5

Registration and election laws to be passed. Laws shall be made for ascertaining, by proper proofs, the citizens who shall be entitled to the right of suffrage hereby established, and for the registration of voters; which registration shall be completed at least ten days before each election. Such registration shall not be required for town and village elections except by express provision of law. In cities and villages having five thousand inhabitants or more, voters shall be registered upon personal application only; but voters not residing in such cities or villages shall not be required to apply in person for registration at the first meeting of the officers having charge of the registry of voters; however, voters who are in the actual military service of the state or of the United States, in the army, navy, air force or any branch thereof, or in the coast guard, or inmates of a veterans' bureau hospital and voters who are unable to appear personally for registration because of illness or physical disability or because their duties, occupation or business require them to be outside the counties of their residence or, in the case of residents of the city of New York, their duties, occupation or business require them to be in a county outside such city; and a spouse, parent or child of such a voter in the actual military service or of such an inmate or of such a voter unable to appear personally for registration, accompanying or being with him or her, if a qualified voter and a resident of the same election district, shall not be required to register personally. The number of such inhabitants shall be determined according to the latest census or enumeration, federal or state, showing the population of the city or village, except that the federal census shall be controlling unless such state enumeration, if any, shall have been taken and returned two or more years after the return of the preceding federal census. [Const. 1821, Art. II, sec. 3, amend. and renumbered Art. II, sec. 4, Const. 1846; amend. Const. 1894, 1931; amend. and renumbered Art. II, sec. 5, 1938; amend. 1951, 1955, 1966]

SECTION 6

Permanent registration. The legislature may provide by law for a system or systems of registration whereby upon personal application a voter may be registered and his registration continued so long as he shall remain qualified to vote from the same address, or for such shorter period as the legislature may prescribe. [1938]

Both sections deal with registration. Section 5 directs the legislature to enact laws for registering voters and requires that such registration be completed ten days before each election. No registration is required in towns or villages, but it may be required by express provision of the law. In cities with more than five thousand inhabitants, registration must be personal—a classification that was added in 1894 in order to establish two uniform systems for registration throughout the state (one for rural and one for urban areas). Various justifications were offered, but city delegates considered it a measure aimed at the political morality of the cities, and no doubt the Tammany machine was in the minds of delegates when they proposed the division. The article prescribes three possible types of registration: permanent personal, annual personal, and nonpersonal registration. Section 6 authorizes the legislature to establish a permanent personal registration system. The legislature did so in 1965. Citizens register in person in the first instance and retain that registration as long as they do not change address and vote in at least one general election every four years. The effect of the legislation was to ban annual personal registration and nonpersonal registration in the state.

New York had taken a census of its inhabitants every seven years pursuant to Article V of the 1777 Constitution. With the existence of a federal census, the taking of a state census for reapportionment purposes seemed duplicative and wasteful. A 1932 amendment made the federal census the basis for computing the number of inhabitants in a community unless the state census is more recent by a period of two years or more. Similar reliance on the federal census is found in Article III, section 4 and Article VII, sections 4, 10, 11(b).

SECTION 7

Manner of voting; identification of voters. All elections by the citizens, except for such town officers as may by law be directed to be otherwise chosen, shall be by ballot, or by such other method as may be prescribed by law, provided that secrecy in voting be preserved. The legislature shall provide for identification of voters through their signatures in all cases where personal registration is required and shall also provide for the signatures, at the time of voting, of all persons voting in person by ballot or voting machine, whether or not they have registered in person, save only in cases of illiteracy or physical disability. [Const. 1821, Art. II, sec. 4; renumbered Art. II, sec. 5, Const. 1846; amend. Const. 1894; amend. and renumbered Art. II, sec. 7, 1938]

The 1777 Constitution authorized the legislature to determine whether voting would be viva voce (by voice) or ballot. The 1821 Constitution mandated voting by ballot for all but town officials. In the 1894 convention, explicit provision was made requiring secrecy of the ballot and allowing the use of the newly invented voting machines because there was doubt as to whether the use of voting machines would be deemed voting by ballot.

In 1938, a signature verification requirement was added to this section in all cases where personal registration was in effect in order to combat fraud. Now that the legislature has mandated permanent registration, the signature can be compared with the one given at registration. The requirement was declared self-executing in the absence of legislative action.[8]

SECTION 8

Bi-partisan registration and election boards. All laws creating, regulating or affecting boards or officers charged with the duty of registering voters, or of distributing ballots to voters, or of receiving, recording or counting votes at elections, shall secure equal representation of the two political parties which, at the general election next preceding that for which such boards or officers are to serve, cast the highest and the next highest number of votes. All such boards and officers shall be appointed or elected in such manner, and upon the nomination of such representatives of said parties respectively, as the legislature may direct. Existing laws on this subject shall continue until the legislature shall otherwise provide. This section shall not apply to town, or village elections. [Const. 1894, Art. II, sec. 6; amend. and renumbered Art. II, sec. 8, 1938]

Shortly before the 1894 Constitutional Convention met, the state legislature adopted a statute providing for equal representation of the two major parties on election boards. To secure the protection intended, the convention decided to make the policy part of the constitution. The stated purpose was to "secure purity" and "absolute impartiality in the conduct of elections."[9] The convention exempted town meetings and village elections from the requirement. The exemptions occasioned bitter debate, as they were seen by city delegates as an anticity measure. A variety of explanations were offered for the distinction, some of them embarrassingly weak, including "antiquity." It was argued that such boards were unnecessary in village elections and would inject partisanship where none existed.[10] The 1938 additions involved changing "distributing ballots at the polls" to "distributing ballots to voters." The changed language was necessitated by a court of appeals decision, Matter of Adams v. Flanagan (1922), permitting county clerks to distribute absentee ballots, thus frustrating the requirement that all elections shall be conducted by bipartisan boards.

The amendment provides no details as to the basis for determining the highest vote. The election law relies on the statewide vote for governor. The adoption of this section marks the first time political parties were given constitutional status and function and constitutes a de jure recognition of the two-party system as the basis for New York's electoral system.

SECTION 9

Presidential elections; special voting procedures authorized. Notwithstanding the residence requirements imposed by section one of this article, the legislature may, by general law, provide special procedures whereby every person who shall have moved from another state to this state or from one county, city or village within this state to another county, city or village within this state and who shall have been an inhabitant of this state in any event for ninety days next preceding an election at which electors are to be chosen for the office of president and vice president of the United States shall be entitled to vote in this state solely for such electors, provided such person is otherwise qualified to vote in this state and is not able to qualify to vote for such electors in any other state. The legislature may also, by general law, prescribe special procedures whereby every person who is registered and would be qualified to vote in this state but for his removal from this state to another state within one year next preceding such election shall be entitled to vote in this state solely for such electors, provided such person is not able to qualify to vote for such electors in any other state. [1963]

This section allows the legislature to prescribe reduced residency requirements and special voting procedures in presidential and vice-presidential elections for those who have moved into New York State from another state, or who have moved from one governmental unit to another, if they have resided in the state at least ninety days and are not eligible to vote in any other state. It also allows those who have moved from the state within one year next preceding the election to vote in the presidential election provided they have not qualified to vote in that state.

Article III

The Legislature

For a large part of the state's history, the legislature was constitutionally and politically the dominant branch of the government. The 1777 Constitution ignored the separation of powers and created a constitutional order that revolved around the legislative branch. That dominance faded as the nineteenth century wore on, however. A series of restraints were placed on the legislative branch in response to legislative abuses. In the twentieth century, the demand for governmental reorganization and leadership in government gave the executive branch the dominant position. For the last half-century or so, the center of energy and power has been located in the governor's office. In the 1960s, the legislature took steps to make it a more effective and efficient partner, with some success; it was rated the second most effective state legislative body in the country in the early 1970s.[1]

This article sets the size of the two bodies and determines such basic matters as qualifications for membership, time of elections, votes needed for passage of various types of legislation, and a series of restrictions on the power of the legislature. Other powers and responsibilities of the legislature exist elsewhere in the constitution: concerning its role in the budget process, Article VII, sections 3–5; with respect to the judiciary, Article VI, sections 4, 6, 16–20, 22; with respect to local finance, Article VII, section 7; and with respect to local government, Article IX, sections 2a, 9b, 3a–b.

Unlike the national government, one of delegated powers, state governments are governments of plenary power, possessing all inherent powers necessary to govern. The state legislature possesses the police power and all powers inherent in government except where specifically limited by the national or the state constitution. For this reason, a list of enumerated powers comparable to that found in Article I of the U.S. Constitution does not appear in Article III. In practice the addition of a variety of restrictions on the exercise of legislative power and the application by the courts of the doctrine that the mention of one power implies the exclusion of another power has attenuated the distinction between the two types of government. As part of the separation-of-powers doctrine, the judiciary presumes the constitutionality of legislation that comes before it and refrains from judging the wisdom or propriety of laws (Trump v. Chu, 1985).

SECTION 1

Legislative power. The legislative power of this state shall be vested in the senate and assembly. [Const. 1777, Art. II; amend. and renumbered Art. I, sec. 1, Const. 1821; amend. Const. 1894]

This section announces that the legislature shall establish the policies and standards of the state and embraces the bicameral principle that the legislative branch should be divided into two houses. The commitment to a representative form of government means that attempts to pass legislation by more direct or democratic methods like referenda are constitutionally suspect. In Barto v. Himrod (1853), an act sustaining free schools throughout the state was declared void because its becoming law depended on the results of a popular vote. Courts have allowed referenda approving local actions by resorting to a distinction between "administrative" and legislative actions (Stanton v. Board of Supervisors, 1908). Nonetheless, the referendum is used frequently in New York as a result of constitutional provision mandating it in certain circumstances, including those found in this article (sec. 20), the requirements for amendments (Art. XIX), and those found in the local government article (IX). The statement that the legislature possesses the power to legislate reflects the notion of the separation of powers whereby each branch of the government is confined primarily to its particular function. This doctrine is also the basis for the view that legislative power cannot be delegated—not to the people, not to administrative agencies, and not to committees of the legislature itself.

The legislature cannot delegate power to enact or repeal laws or establish policies and standards (People v. Blanchard, 1942). On the other hand, the realities of the twentieth-century administrative state have required that some responsibilities be turned over to executive or other specialized agencies. Such delegation has been permitted as long as reasonable guidelines are set forth in the legislation. These guidelines need be only as specific as is reasonably practicable in the light of the area being regulated. This test grants the legislature wide discretion (Barney's Inc. v. Department of Finance of City of New York, 1983). For example, the legislature may enact a number of statutes dealing with the same subject, leaving to the executive the responsibility of selecting the statute that will eventually become law (Teeval v. Stern, 1950).

The legislative function belongs to the legislature as a whole and cannot be delegated even to its own committees (New York Public Interest Research Group v. Carey, 1977).

SECTION 2

Number and terms of senators and assemblymen. The senate shall consist of fifty members, except as hereinafter provided. The senators elected in the year one thousand eight hundred and ninety-five shall hold their offices for three years, and their successors shall be chosen for two years. The assembly shall consist of one hundred and fifty members. The assemblymen elected in the year one thousand nine hundred and thirty-eight, and their successors, shall be chosen for two years. [Const. 1821, Art. I, sec. 2; amend. Const. 1894, 1937]

The section sets the absolute limit on assembly seats at 150 but allows for the expansion of senate seats. Nowhere does the constitution specify single-member districts, but they have generally been assumed.[2] The one-year assembly term was raised to two in 1937, with the change justified on the grounds that assemblymen "never get away from the polls" or from the influence of active private interest groups detrimental to the public interest.[3]

SECTION 3

Senate districts. The senate districts described in section three of article three of this constitution as adopted by the people on November sixth, eighteen hundred ninety-four are hereby continued for all of the purposes of future reapportionments of senate districts pursuant to section four of this article. [1962]

SECTION 4

Readjustments and reapportionments; when federal census to control. Except as herein otherwise provided, the federal census taken in the year nineteen hundred thirty and each federal census taken decennially thereafter shall be controlling as to the number of inhabitants in the state or any part thereof for the purposes of the apportionment of members of assembly and readjustment or alteration of senate and assembly districts next occurring, in so far as such census and the tabulation thereof purport to give the information necessary therefor. The legislature, by law, shall provide for the making and tabulation by state authorities of an enumeration of the inhabitants for the entire state to be used for such purposes, instead of a federal census, if the taking of a federal census in any tenth year from the year nineteen hundred thirty be omitted or if the federal census fails to show the number of aliens or Indians not taxed. If a federal census, though giving the requisite information as to the state at large, fails to give the information as to any civil or territorial divisions which is required to be known for such purposes, the legislature, by law, shall provide for such an enumeration of the inhabitants of such parts of the state only as may be necessary, which shall supersede in part the federal census and be used in connection therewith for such purposes. The legislature, by law, may provide in its discretion for an enumeration by state authorities of the inhabitants of the state, to be used for such purposes, in place of a federal census, when the return of a decennial federal census is delayed so that it is not available at the beginning of the regular session of the legislature in the second year after the year nineteen hundred thirty or after any tenth year therefrom, or if an apportionment of members of assembly and readjustment or alteration of senate districts is not made at or before such a session. At the regular session in the year nineteen hundred thirty-two, and at the first regular session after the year nineteen hundred forty and after each tenth year therefrom the senate districts shall be readjusted or altered, but if, in any decade, counting from and including that which begins with the year nineteen hundred thirty-one, such a readjustment or alteration is not made at the time above prescribed, it shall be made at a subsequent session occurring not later than the sixth year of such decade, meaning not later than nineteen hundred thirty-six, nineteen hundred forty-six, nineteen hundred fifty-six, and so on; provided, however, that if such districts shall have been readjusted or altered by law in either of the years nineteen hundred thirty or nineteen hundred thirty-one, they shall remain unaltered until the first regular session after the year nineteen hundred forty. Such districts shall be so readjusted or altered that each senate district shall contain as nearly as may be an equal number of inhabitants, excluding aliens, and be in as compact form as practicable, and shall remain unaltered until the first year of the next decade as above defined, and shall at all times consist of contiguous territory, and no country shall be divided in the formation of a senate district except to make two or more senate districts wholly in such county. No town, except a town having more than a full ratio of apportionment, and no block in a city inclosed by streets or public ways, shall be divided in the formation of senate districts; nor shall any district contain a greater excess in population of the town or block therein adjoining such district. Counties, towns or blocks which, from their location, may be included in either of two districts, shall be so placed as to make said districts most nearly equal in number of inhabitants, excluding aliens.

No county shall have four or more senators unless it shall have a full ratio for each senator. No county shall have more than one-third of all the senators; and no two counties or the territory thereof as now organized, which are adjoining counties, or which are separated only by public waters, shall have more than one-half of all the senators.

The ratio for apportioning senators shall always be obtained by dividing the number of inhabitants, excluding aliens, by fifty, and the senate shall always be composed of fifty members, except that if any county having three or more senators at the time of any apportionment shall be entitled on such ratio to an additional senator or senators, such additional senator or senators shall be given to such county in addition to the fifty senators, and the whole number of senators shall be increased to that extent.

The senate districts, including the present ones, as existing immediately before the enactment of a law readjusting or altering the senate districts, shall continue to be the senate districts of the state until the expirations of the terms of the senators then in office, except for the purpose of an election of senators for full terms beginning at such expirations, and for the formation of assembly districts. [Const. 1894, Art. II, sec. 3, 4 as amend. 1931; renumbered Art. III, sec. 4, 1938; amend. 1945]

SECTION 5

Apportionment of assemblymen; creation of assembly districts. The members of the assembly shall be chosen by single districts and shall be apportioned by the legislature at each regular session at which the senate districts are readjusted or altered, and by the same law, among the several counties of the state, as nearly as may be according to the number of their respective inhabitants, excluding aliens. Every county heretofore established and separately organized, except the county of Hamilton, shall always be entitled to one member of assembly, and no county shall hereafter be erected unless its population shall entitle it to a member. The county of Hamilton shall elect with the county of Fulton, until the population of the county of Hamilton shall, according to the ratio, entitle it to a member. But the legislature may abolish the said county of Hamilton and annex the territory thereof to some other county or counties.

The quotient obtained by dividing the whole number of inhabitants of the state, excluding aliens, by the number of members of assembly, shall be the ratio for apportionment, which shall be made as follows: One member of assembly shall be apportioned to every county, including Fulton and Hamilton as one county, containing less than the ratio and one-half over. Two members shall be apportioned to every other county. The remaining members of assembly shall be apportioned to the counties having more than two ratios according to the number of inhabitants, excluding aliens. Members apportioned on remainders shall be apportioned to the counties having the highest remainders in the order thereof respectively. No county shall have more members of assembly than a county having a greater number of inhabitants, excluding aliens.

The assembly districts, including the present ones, as existing immediately before the enactment of a law making an apportionment of members of assembly among the counties, shall continue to be the assembly districts of the state until the expiration of the terms of members then in office, except for the purpose of an election of members of assembly for full terms beginning at such expirations.

In any county entitled to more than one member, the board of supervisors, and in any city embracing an entire county and having no board of supervisors, the common council, or if there be none, the body exercising the powers of a common council, shall assemble at such times as the legislature making an apportionment shall prescribe, and divide such counties into assembly districts as nearly equal in number of inhabitants, excluding aliens, as may be, of convenient and contiguous territory in as compact form as practicable, each of which shall be wholly within a senate district formed under the same apportionment, equal to the number of members of assembly to which such county shall be entitled, and shall cause to be filed in the office of the secretary of state and of the clerk of such county, a description of such districts, specifying the number of each district and of the inhabitants thereof, excluding aliens, according to the census or enumeration used as the population basis for the formation of such districts; and such apportionment and districts shall remain unaltered until after the next reapportionment of members of assembly, except that the board of supervisors of any county containing a town having more than a ratio of apportionment and one-half over may alter the assembly districts in a senate district containing such town at any time on or before March first, nineteen hundred forty-six. In counties having more than one senate district, the same number of assembly districts shall be put in each senate district, unless the assembly districts cannot be evenly divided among the senate districts of any county, in which case one more assembly district shall be put in the senate district in such county having the largest, or one less assembly district shall be put in the senate district in such county having the smallest number of inhabitants, excluding aliens, as the case may require. No town, except a town having more than a ratio of apportionment and one-half over, and no block in a city inclosed by streets or public ways, shall be divided in the formation of assembly districts, nor shall any districts contain a greater excess in population over an adjoining district in the same senate district, than the population of a town or block therein adjoining such assembly district. Towns or blocks which, from their location may be included in either of two districts, shall be so placed as to make said districts most nearly equal in number of inhabitants, excluding aliens. Nothing in this section shall prevent the division, at any time, of counties and towns and the erection of new towns by the legislature.

An apportionment by the legislature, or other body, shall be subject to review by the supreme court, at the suit of any citizen, under such reasonable regulations as the legislature may prescribe; and any court before which a cause may be pending involving an apportionment, shall give precedence thereto over all other causes and proceedings and if said court be not in session it shall convene promptly for the disposition of the same. [Const. 1821, Art. I, sec. 7; amend. and renumbered Art. III, sec. 5, Const. 1846; amend. Const. 1894, 1931, 1945]

SECTION 5–a

Definition of inhabitants. For the purpose of apportioning senate and assembly districts pursuant to the foregoing provisions of this article, the term "inhabitants, excluding aliens" shall mean the whole number of persons. [1969]

For political parties and candidates, reapportionment is a matter of political life and death, so it is not surprising that these sections have been the most bitterly contested in the constitution.

They provide for the method of apportioning senate and assembly seats. Largely the work of the 1894 convention, they are structured in such a way as to favor rural and upstate interests at the expense of the downstate New York City area. Section 3 provides for the use of the federal census unless that census proves inadequate for the state's purposes. New York has not undertaken a full census since 1925 and has relied on the federal census since that time. The first paragraph speaks of equality of district population as the basis for representation and requires that districts be compact and contiguous, a clause meant to protect against gerrymandering.

The provision not allowing any county to be divided except to form two senate districts creates the first imbalance. In addition, no single county was permitted to have more than one-third the senators regardless of its population (New York City counties were in mind), and no two counties divided by a public waterway could have half the senate seats within their borders (Manhattan and Brooklyn were in mind). Finally, no county could have four or more senators unless it had a full ratio for each senator.

The method of apportioning senate seats is complicated. The formula used was expressly designed to perpetuate rural control.[4] The citizen population, now called inhabitants (see sec. 5–a), is divided by fifty, the number of senators at the time of the 1894 convention. The number obtained from this division is called the first ratio. The inhabitant population is then compared with this ratio. Counties having a population between three and four times greater than the ratio are eligible for three senate seats; counties having four or five times the ratio are entitled to four seats; and so forth. When these computations have been made, a list is compiled of all the counties entitled to three or more senate seats or all counties with three-fiftieths (6 percent of the state's population). A comparison is then made between the seats these counties were entitled to and those they had in 1894. If any of these counties is found to be entitled to more seats than it had in 1894, the total number of senate seats is increased by that amount. Each time a larger county was entitled to a new seat, the senate size was increased by the same number, so increases in some counties were not accompanied by decreases in areas that would otherwise lose seats. After this process was completed, the remaining seats were divided among the remaining counties by an apportionment method known as the second ratio. Though not mandated by the constitution, it was necessary to complete the reapportionment. This ratio was obtained by dividing the number of senate seats left over after the earlier steps were completed. This system was declared a violation of the equal protection clause of the Fourteenth Amendment in WMCA Inc. v. Lomenzo (1964). To the extent that equal population in all senate districts can be achieved only by breaking county lines, the requirement that no county shall be divided in the formation of senate district lines is void (In re Orans, 1965). The one-third senate seat limit for any county and the one-half limit for counties separated by waterways are not operative because no counties have ever been entitled to that number of senators. The court of appeals in Matter of Schneider v. Rockefeller (1973) upheld a reapportionment plan that segmented nine lesser populated counties. The court sustained the segmentations on the grounds that state constitutional requirements must conform to the federal standard. The court decided that the one-person, one-vote principle required overriding county lines. While it was so deciding, the U.S. Supreme Court was backing away from the mathematical equality standard for state legislatures and allowing states to deviate from population standards to preserve the jurisdictional lines of cities and towns (Abate v. Mundt, 1971; Mahan v. Howell, 1973). Overriding local subdivisions in the name of population equality made manipulation of district lines for purposes of political gerrymandering much easier.

The method for apportioning the assembly differs in a number of ways. Every county except Hamilton, which shares one assembly seat with Fulton, was entitled to one assembly seat. That accounted for sixty-one seats. The remaining eighty-nine were apportioned as follows. The inhabitants of the state were divided by the total number of assemblymen, and the quotient becomes the "ratio." Every county whose inhabitant population equals one and one-half times the ratio was entitled to a second assembly seat, with the rest of the seats apportioned to counties having more than twice the ratio. The remainders were distributed on the basis of highest remainders, a system that divided the state's counties into three categories. The provision allowing one assembly seat for each county was voided, as was the clause in section 5 giving local legislative bodies power to draw assembly lines in counties having more than one assembly seat, since at least in some instances assembly districts will have to be partly in one county and partly in another (WMCA Inc. v. Lomenzo, 1964).

The state has complied with the federal court rulings, and substantial equality has been achieved. This compliance has not prevented the legislature from engaging in partisan or bipartisan gerrymandering, and a bipartisan gerrymander characterized legislative apportionment plans in the 1970s and 1980s.

The provisions requiring districts to be compact and contiguous are potential safeguards against such gerrymandering, but the court of appeals has not applied these requirements with much rigor. In Bay Ridge Community Council Inc. v. Carey (1985), the court reaffirmed its unwillingness to review issues involving challenges based on partisan gerrymanders. In *Bay Ridge*, the court said that districts need be only as compact as "practicable" and would be contiguous as long as all parts of the district are connected geographically. The court's position seems to be that it is not the judiciary's duty to police the political effects of legislatively proposed reapportionment plans (Prentice v. Cahill, 1973).

Section 5–a makes the general population—"persons"—the basis for apportioning legislative districts rather than the citizen population base specified in sections 4 and 5. New York relies on the federal decennial census, which does not make a distinction between aliens and citizens for purposes of congressional apportionment. As a result, New York was forced to wait four years until special census figures concerning aliens were made available to comply with the citizen base mandate in the state constitution. This amendment cut that time in half and saved the state money as well. At the turn of the century, when the alien population in New York was concentrated in New York City, this distinction would have had significance. Today that heavy concentration no longer exists.

SECTION 6

Compensation, allowances, and traveling expenses of members. Each member of the legislature shall receive for his services a like annual salary, to be fixed by law. He shall also be reimbursed for his actual traveling expenses in going to and returning from the place in which the legislature is in session. Senators, when the senate alone is convened in extraordinary session, or when serving as members of the court for the trial of impeachments, and such members of the assembly, not exceeding nine in number, as shall be appointed managers of an impeachment, shall receive an additional per diem allowance, to be fixed by law. Any member, while serving as an officer of his house or in any other special capacity therein or directly connected therewith not hereinbefore in this section specified, may also be paid and receive, in addition, any allowance which may be fixed by law for the particular and additional services appertaining to or entailed by such office or special capacity. Neither the salary of any member nor any other allowance so fixed may be increased or diminished during, and with respect to, the term for which he shall have been elected, nor shall he be paid or receive any other extra compensation. The provisions of this section and laws enacted in compliance therewith shall govern and be exclusively controlling, according to their terms. Members shall continue to receive such salary and additional allowance as heretofore fixed and provided in this section, until changed by law pursuant to this section. [Const. 1894, Art. III, sec. 6; amend. 1938, 1947, 1964]

Until 1947, legislators' salaries were specified in the constitution; every time a salary change was warranted, a constitutional amendment was required. A 1947 amendment to this section put that decision in the hands of the legislature, which also determines expenses and extra allowances for added responsibilities, such as speaker of the assembly. An election must intervene between a vote to increase salaries or allowances and receipt of those increases by legislators (New York Public Research Interest Group v. Steingut, 1976). In 1946, the Joint Legislative Committee on Legislative Methods, Practices, Procedures and Expenditures recommended this change, arguing that the legislature would be responsible and that public opinion would control any urge to abuse that power.

SECTION 7

Qualification of members; certain civil appointments prohibited. No person shall serve as a member of the legislature unless he or she is a citizen of the United States and has been a resident of the state of New York for five years, and, except as hereinafter otherwise prescribed, of the assembly or senate district for the twelve months immediately preceding his or her election; if elected a senator or member of assembly at the first election next ensuing after a readjustment or alteration of the senate or assembly districts becomes effective, a person, to be eligible to serve as such, must have been a resident of the county in which the senate or assembly district is contained for the twelve months immediately preceding his or her election. No member of the legislature shall, during the time for which he or she was elected, receive any civil appointment from the governor, the governor and the senate, the legislature or from any city government, to an office which shall have been created, or the emoluments whereof shall have been increased during such time. If a member of the legislature be elected to congress, or appointed to any office, civil or military, under the government of the United States, the state of New York, or under any city government except as a member of the national guard or naval militia of the state, or of the reserve forces of the United States, his or her acceptance thereof shall vacate his or her seat in the legislature, providing, however, that a member of the legislature may be appointed commissioner of deeds or to any office in which he or she shall receive no compensation. [Const. 1821, Art. I, secs. 10–11; amend. and renumbered Art. III, sec. 7, Const. 1846; amend. 1874, 1938, 1943]

This section establishes residency requirements for New York's legislators. Residency requirements are meant to ensure some knowledge of the state and district from which one is elected. *Residence* with reference to this section means domicile—that is, bodily presence as well as intent to make it one's domicile (Isaacson v. Heffernan, 1946).

"Civil appointments" is broadly defined to include any civil office of public trust relating to the exercise of power and authority of government of the state that is not reasonably incidental to duties of a member of the legislature (People v. Tremaine, 1929). Such restrictions serve to prevent subservience of the legislative branch to the executive. The prohibition against municipal appointment was added for similar reasons. The sight of Boss Tweed holding both a state senate seat and the powerful commissioner of public works office in New York City precipitated this restriction. The restriction on holding national office was meant to prevent any control by the federal government of state government policy or personnel. It should be noted that this section does not prevent legislators from accepting executive posts. Only those created or the salaries of which have been increased during the term of office are off-limits. It does not prevent a justice of the peace or mayor from serving as a legislator, but persistent failure to attend duties of either office would be grounds for charge of misconduct in office.[5] The section does allow service in the military reserves without the individual's having to relinquish office.

SECTION 8

Time of elections of members. The elections of senators and members of assembly, pursuant to the provisions of this constitution, shall be held on the Tuesday succeeding the first Monday of November, unless otherwise directed by the legislature. [Const. 1846, Art. III, sec. 9; renumbered Art. III, sec. 8, 1938]

This section specifies the day but not the time or place for elections. These are spelled out in the state's election law.[6]

SECTION 9

Powers of each house. A majority of each house shall constitute a quorum to do business. Each house shall determine the rules of its own proceedings, and be the judge of the elections, returns and qualifications of its own members; shall choose its own officers; and the senate shall choose a temporary president and the assembly shall choose a speaker. [Const. 1821, Art. I, sec. 3; amend. and renumbered Art. III, sec. 10, Const. 1846; renumbered Art. III, sec. 9, 1938; amend. 1963]

A majority of the members of each house is necessary to conduct business. Each house is given the power to determine its own rules and to judge the election returns and the qualifications of its own members. These latter two powers have been called judicial powers. By statute, the legislature has delegated part of this power to the judiciary, allowing suits to be brought pursuant to the state's election law. Outside that proceeding, the courts have no power to review decisions of the legislature on these questions (Scaringe v. Ackerman, 1986). With the scandalous exception of the expulsion of five socialists in 1920, the legislature has exercised these powers only for cause as specified in statute.[7]

The only two officers of the legislature specified in the constitution are the temporary president of the senate and the speaker of the assembly. All other officers are provided for by statute. These two officers are the most powerful members of the legislative branch. The temporary president is third in line as a successor to the governor (Art. IV, sec. 6).

SECTION 10

Journals; open sessions; adjournments. Each house of the legislature shall keep a journal of its proceedings, and publish the same, except such parts

as may require secrecy. The doors of each house shall be kept open, except
when the public welfare shall require secrecy. Neither house shall, without
the consent of the other, adjourn for more than two days. [Const. 1777,
Art. XV; amend. and renumbered Art. I, sec. 4, Const. 1821; renumbered
Art. III, sec. 11, Const. 1846; amend. and renumbered Art. III, sec. 10,
1938]

All state constitutions require their legislature to keep a journal of proceedings.
The provision allowing secrecy when state welfare requires it is modeled on the
national Constitution (Art. I, sec. 5). The journals are considered competent
evidence in courts of law. In a suit collaterally attacking a legislative enactment,
the journals were deemed binding on the courts, and judicial review of the
accuracy of these records was not warranted (City of Rye v. Ronan, 1971).

SECTION 11

Members not to be questioned for speeches. For any speech or debate in
either house of the legislature, the members shall not be questioned in any
other place. [Const. 1846, Art. III, sec. 12; renumbered Art. III, sec. 11,
1938]

Freedom to debate openly any issue or question without reservation is indispensable to effective representative government. The protection guaranteed here
is similar to that found in the national Constitution (Art. I, sec. 6). It first appeared
in New York in the Duke of York's Laws of 1683 and was readopted in the
statutory bill of rights in 1787 before it found its way into the constitution in
1846. The privilege includes immunity from arrest in civil action, with a few
exceptions, during the legislative session and two weeks before and after that
session.[8] Speeches to constituents and similar actions outside the legislative halls
do not enjoy this absolute immunity, and legislators are vulnerable to libel and
slander suits.

SECTION 12

Bills may originate in either house; may be amended by the other. Any
bill may originate in either house of the legislature, and all bills passed by
one house may be amended by the other. [Const. 1821, Art. I, sec. 8;
renumbered Art. III, sec. 13; renumbered Art. III, sec. 12, 1938]

This section was added to remove any doubts as to whether money bills could
originate in or be amended in the senate. The federal rule (Art. I, sec. 7) was
not considered inapplicable to the state since both houses were based on the
immediate representation of the people and both equally represented the taxable
property of the state.

SECTION 13

Enacting clause of bills; no law to be enacted except by bill. The enacting clause of all bills shall be "The People of the State of New York, represented in Senate and Assembly, do enact as follows," and no law shall be enacted except by bill. [Const. 1846, Art. III, sec. 14; renumbered Art. III, sec. 13, 1938]

An enacting clause contains a statement of the authority by which the law is made. At a minimum, this clause declares the republican form of government and, more strongly, that the will of the people should be reflected by the legislature. Without this enacting clause, legislation is null and void (Noonan v. O'Leary, 1954).

SECTION 14

Manner of passing bills; message of necessity for immediate vote. No bill shall be passed or become a law unless it shall have been printed and upon the desks of the members, in its final form, at least three calendar legislative days prior to its final passage, unless the governor, or the acting governor, shall have certified, under his hand and the seal of the state, the facts which in his opinion necessitate an immediate vote thereon, in which case it must nevertheless be upon the desks of the members in final form, not necessarily printed, before its final passage; nor shall any bill be passed or become a law, except by the assent of a majority of the members elected to each branch of the legislature; and upon the last reading of a bill, no amendment thereof shall be allowed, and the question upon its final passage shall be taken immediately thereafter, and the ayes and nays entered on the journal. [Const. 1846, Art. III, sec. 15; amend., Const. 1894; amend. and renumbered Art. III, sec. 14, 1938]

This section requires a three-day delay after a bill has been perfected before it can be put to a final vote. The delay was to prevent hasty and careless legislation, to enable constituents to contact their representatives about the bill, and to help make sure legislators know what they are voting for. The requirement that a vote be taken immediately after the final reading was to prevent logrolling, whereby three or four bills are laid on the table until sufficient support is generated in the assembly to logroll them through.[9] Failure to provide a printed copy of a bill in final form three days before final passage renders the bill void even if signed by the governor (People v. Reardon, 1906). Judicial rulings support the view that the requirement that the ayes and nays be entered and that a vote be taken immediately after final reading are merely directions to the legislature and not provisions meant to be enforceable in the courts.

Passage of legislation requires a majority of the members elected, not just a majority of those present and voting. This requirement of a majority of elected members was designed to ensure full attendance of both houses when legislation is adopted and to make individuals take responsibility for the results (Barto v. Himrod, 1853). This would seem to make passage of legislation more difficult, but the legislature has devised ingenious ways to count as affirmative votes those who are not physically present in the chambers.[10] The three-day rule can be waived if the governor sends a message of necessity to the legislature. In practice, the governor does not do so unless so requested by the legislature. The message of necessity is used most frequently at the end of the session when a mass of legislation has accumulated and there is a need to expedite action. Frequent use for this purpose has led many to conclude that it has been subject to abuse. It has the effect of enabling the governor and the legislative leadership to control bills introduced once the legislature is within three days of adjournment.[11] Challenges to the sufficiency of a governor's message of necessity have been rebuffed by the courts. According to Norwick v. Rockefeller (1972), courts may not consider the sufficiency of the facts underlying such messages.

SECTION 15

Private or local bills to embrace only one subject. No private or local bill, which may be passed by the legislature, shall embrace more than one subject, and that shall be expressed in the title. [Const. 1846, Art. III, sec. 16; renumbered Art. III, sec. 15, 1938]

This section imposes a procedural limitation on the legislature. Private or local bills are to be limited to one subject, which must be expressed in the bill's title. It has two purposes: to limit logrolling by preventing the accumulation of unrelated subjects in one bill and to give adequate notice to the legislature and the public as to what is contained in the bill, thus preventing fraudulent insertion of material not related to the title of the bill. A local bill has been defined, rather loosely, as one that operates within a limited territory or specified locality and whose benefits relate directly to those within that specified locality or their property. Special or private laws relate only to a particular person or things of their class.[12] It is unusual for any law to be voided on the basis of this provision. One reason is that the courts give a strong presumption of constitutionality regarding an issue of this sort (Knapp v. Fashender, 1956). Another is that the courts have not given a strict interpretation of any of the crucial terms employed in this section. If the title of a local law expresses a general object or purpose, all matters reasonably related to that purpose are considered one subject (Economic Power and Construction Co. v. Buffalo, 1909). Courts have allowed state legislation to deal with specific entities or persons and yet remain general as opposed to local laws (Hotel Dorset v. Trust for Cultural Resources of the City of New York, 1978).

SECTION 16

Existing law not to be made applicable by reference. No act shall be passed which shall provide that any existing law, or any part thereof, shall be made or deemed a part of said act, or which shall enact that any existing law, or part thereof, shall be applicable, except by inserting it in such act. [Const. 1846, Art. III, sec. 17 as added in 1874; renumbered Art. III, sec. 16, 1938]

This section prevents inadvertent enactment of a law relating to one subject from being made applicable to a law passed on another subject. Such a bill as submitted fails to disclose its scope and contents. By prohibiting legislation by reference, legislators would know what they are accepting or rejecting. Prior to this section, legislation could by mere reference revive a repealed statute (Blauvelt v. Village of Nyack, 1876). An attempt to incorporate by reference the provisions of a private association's rules and standards pertaining to flammable and combustible liquids was held to violate this section (People v. Mobil Oil Co., 1979; Opin. St. Compt. 68–625).

A literal construction of this section would make all referential legislation impossible, so the judiciary has construed this section in line with the evil it was intended to remove, not in terms of the letter of the law (People v. Lorillard, 1892). For example, under this construction, the section would prevent only affirmative legislation—the nature of which is explained only by reference instead of actually being set forth (Brandt v. City of New York, 1962).

SECTION 17

Cases in which private or local bills shall not be passed. The legislature shall not pass a private or local bill in any of the following cases:

Changing the names of persons.

Laying out, opening, altering, working or discontinuing roads, highways or alleys, or for draining swamps or other low lands.

Loading or changing county seats.

Providing for changes of venue in civil or criminal cases.

Incorporating villages.

Providing for election of members of boards of supervisors.

Selecting, drawing, summoning or empaneling grand or petit jurors.

Regulating the rate of interest on money.

The opening and conducting of elections or designating places of voting.

Creating, increasing or decreasing fees, percentages or allowances of public officers, during the term for which said officers are elected or appointed.

Granting to any corporation, association or individual the right to lay down railroad tracks.

Granting to any private corporation, association or individual any exclusive privilege, immunity or franchise whatever.

Granting to any person, association, firm or corporation, an exemption from taxation on real or personal property.

Providing for the building of bridges, except over the waters forming a part of the boundaries of the state, by other than a municipal or other public corporation or a public agency of the state. [Const. 1846, Art. III, sec. 18 as added in 1874; amend. and renumbered Art. III, sec. 17, 1938]

This section prohibits the legislature from passing local or private bills concerning the subjects specified. This prohibition attempted to reduce the pressure on legislators from interested parties to pass bills that provided private benefits, and prevent legislators from passing local legislation in an area in which they were neither well informed nor competent. By establishing a policy, wherever possible, of legislating by general laws, it was hoped that the sheer amount of legislation would also be reduced. This section does not limit the power of the legislature to legislate by general laws in any of the areas specified.[13] If there was a need to act, it could be done by general legislation. Such general legislation would receive more careful attention from the legislature as a whole than would special or local bills.

This section has not limited the legislature as much as its framers intended because the courts have allowed the term *general law* to apply to less than all places or persons in the state. A statute may be limited in its application according to specified conditions common to a class reasonably related to the subject matter (Cutler v. Herman, 1957). An act applying to cities of over 1 million was not a local law even though only one city, New York City, fell into that category (Matter of McAneny v. Board of Estimates and Apportionment, 1972).

The exception for the waters forming the boundaries of the state, mainly the Niagara and St. Lawrence rivers, was meant to protect the property interests of private owners of bridges on these waterways who were operating under charters issued by authority of the state.

This section also prevents the state from granting any individual or corporation exclusive privileges or franchises. Incorporation must be done by general laws (see the similar prohibition in Art. X, sec. 1). This prohibition contains aspects of equal protection of the laws because it prevents the state from arbitrarily conferring on one class benefits from which others similarly situated are denied.

SECTION 18

Extraordinary sessions of the legislature; power to convene on legislative initiative. The members of the legislature shall be empowered, upon the

presentation to the temporary president of the senate and the speaker of the
assembly of a petition signed by two-thirds of the members elected to each
house of the legislature, to convene the legislature on extraordinary occasions
to act upon the subjects enumerated in such petition. [1975]

This section is designed to give the legislature more power over its own affairs
and lessen what many legislators perceived was undue control over the legislative
branch by the executive. Prior to this amendment, only the governor could call
an extraordinary session (Art. IV, sec. 3). Its chief sponsor, Perry Durea, then
speaker of the assembly, expected it would give the legislature some recourse
when the governor vetoed a bill after the session had adjourned. It would also
allow the legislature to take up issues it proposed in the petition and not just
those the governor specified. No extraordinary session has been called by the
legislature. It has preferred to recess and reconvene, avoiding the need for a
two-thirds vote and the restriction of acting on only those items listed in the
petition.

SECTION 19

**Private claims not to be audited by legislature; claims barred by lapse
of time.** The legislature shall neither audit nor allow any private claim or
account against the state, but may appropriate money to pay such claims as
shall have been audited and allowed according to law.

No claim against the state shall be audited, allowed or paid which, as
between citizens of the state, would be barred by lapse of time. But if the
claimant shall be under legal disability, the claim may be presented within
two years after such disability is removed. [Const. 1846, Art. III, sec. 19,
as added in 1874; amend. Const. 1894, 1938]

Before 1874, the legislature would pass special legislation aimed at private
claimants in which the legislature would fix the amount of the claim without
prior determination that the claims were meritorious—a procedure that was open
to abuse and soon depleted the public treasury. By the terms of this section, the
legislature is prohibited from auditing the claims itself but can provide by law
for an audit and appropriate moneys to pay those audited claims, which the state
did in 1876. In 1897, a court of claims was established to adjudicate these claims,
and that court was later constitutionalized (see Art. VI, sec. 9). The section
extends only to private claims against the state and does not embrace public
claims, such as a county's claim for reimbursement of moneys expended prosecuting certain criminals (Cayuga County v. State, 1897).

No claim against the state is to be paid or allowed if it would be barred by a
lapse of time if brought by a citizen against another citizen. This ensures that
the state is not in a less advantageous situation than private citizens would be
in suits of this kind. The legislature may impose even shorter time limitations

for claims against the state if it so desires (Kilbourne v. State, 1980). If the claimant was under legal disability, preventing him or her from bringing the claim, this section allows that claimant to present that claim within two years after the disability has been removed.

SECTION 20

> **Two-thirds bills.** The assent of two-thirds of the members elected to each branch of the legislature shall be requisite to every bill appropriating the public moneys or property for local or private purposes. [Const. 1821, Art. VII, sec. 9; renumbered Art. I, sec. 9, Const. 1846; renumbered Art. III, sec. 20, 1894]

If the moneys of the state belonging to the whole state are going to be used for the benefit of a part, that appropriation measure ought to be meritorious enough to gain the assent of two-thirds rather than a majority of the legislature. Again, the target of this requirement was the mass of special legislation that was the chief product of the legislature in the nineteenth century. When the appropriation is for a state purpose, the two-thirds requirement is not triggered. The major issues concerning this section are what constitutes appropriation of the money or property of the state and what are local or private purposes. This section is not operative when the state receives equivalent consideration for its money or property; it concerns transfers as a gift or gratuity. It applied only to the public moneys of the state as opposed to public revenues levied for local purposes by towns and cities under state authority (People ex rel. Einsfeld v. Murray, 1896). When the city of Syracuse was given permission by the state to use excess water from the waters making up the barge canal, the courts held that such public waters were not appropriations of state property (Sweet v. City of Syracuse, 1891). Appropriation and transfer of property to railroads was also determined to be a state and not a private purpose (People v. Kerr, 1863). An appropriation for an exhibit at the World's Fair in 1964, which was run by a private corporation, and the placing of "World's Fair" on state license plates were not private purposes in violation of this section. In each of these cases, the courts found some state purpose. In the last case, it was to promote intra- and interstate tourism.

A local purpose has been defined as an expenditure that is exclusively and purely local and directly benefits a particular locality (Matter of Froslid v. Hults, 1964). If the purpose is public but the bill is local, the provision is applicable. These interpretations, along with the judicial requirement that the party challenging the enactment demonstrate its invalidity beyond a reasonable doubt, have attenuated the power of this section (People v. Pagnotta, 1969).

SECTION 21

Certain sections not to apply to bills recommended by certain commissioners or public agencies. Sections 15, 16 and 17 of this article shall not apply to any bill, or the amendments to any bill, which shall be recommended to the legislature by commissioners or any public agency appointed or directed pursuant to law to prepare revisions, consolidations or compilations of statutes. But a bill amending an existing law shall not be excepted from the provisions of sections 15, 16 and 17 of this article unless such amending bill shall itself be recommended to the legislature by such commissioners or public agency. [Const. 1846, Art. III, sec. 23 as added in 1874; amend, Const. 1894; amend. and renumbered Art. III, sec. 21, 1938]

Commissions created by law to revise and consolidate statutes are not limited by the restrictions found in sections 15–17. For example, section 17 provides that the legislature shall not pass a local law concerning the selection of jurors, but because such a law was recommended by a judicial council, a public agency, that limitation does not apply. These exemptions are allowed for public agencies to enable them to be effective in carrying out their responsibilities of integrating and revising the laws and because the danger of narrow private interest legislation emanating from such agencies was deemed minimal. The last sentence was added because the section had been interpreted to allow the legislature to call a local law an amendment to a statute adopted on the recommendations of an agency responsible for consolidating the laws.[14]

SECTION 22

Tax laws to state tax and object distinctly; references to federal tax laws authorized. Every law which imposes, continues or revives a tax shall distinctly state the tax and the object to which it is to be applied, and it shall not be sufficient to refer to any other law to fix such tax or object.

Notwithstanding the foregoing or any other provision of this constitution, the legislature, in any law imposing a tax or taxes on, in respect to or measured by income, may define the income or, in respect to or by which such tax or taxes are imposed or measured, by reference to any provision of the laws of the United States as the same may be or become effective at any time or from time to time, and may prescribe exceptions or modifications to any such provision. [Const. 1846, Art. VII, sec. 13; renumbered Art. III, sec. 20, 1874; renumbered Art. III, sec. 24, Const. 1894; renumbered Art. III, sec. 22, 1938; amend. 1959]

Three requirements with regard to tax laws are set forth in this section: the tax must be distinctly stated, the object to which the tax applies must also be distinctly stated, and no reference can be made to any other law to fix the tax or object. This provision, like most of the other restrictions on legislative power, was added in the nineteenth century to protect against the problem of extended debt and permanent taxation, both connected with canal expenditures and the panic of 1837. By specifying these three conditions, the public as well as the legislators would know for what purposes the taxes were imposed without consulting other statutes. The courts have given the section a practical construction that accomplishes its purpose of informing the public and legislators without applying it to every tax the legislature imposes (In re McPherson, 1887). The courts have held that this section applies only to general taxes levied for general purposes. License fees, transfer taxes, and local taxes, for example, are not covered by the prohibition (Sweeny v. Cannon, 1965; Berkshire Fine Spinning Associates Inc. v. New York City, 1959).

The second paragraph, added in 1959, allows the legislature to adopt the federal definition of income for purposes of the state income tax. The object was to simplify the preparation of state income returns. It does not affect tax rates.

SECTION 23

When yeas and nays necessary; three-fifths to constitute quorum. On the final passage, in either house of the legislature, of any act which imposes, continues or revives a tax, or creates a debt or charge, or makes, continues or revives any appropriation of public or trust money or property, or releases, discharges or commutes any claim or demand of the state, the question shall be taken by yeas and nays, which shall be duly entered upon the journals, and three-fifths of all the members elected to either house shall, in all such cases, be necessary to constitute a quorum therein. [Const. 1846, Art. VII, sec. 14 as renumbered Art. III, sec. 21, 1874; renumbered Art. III, sec. 25, Const. 1894; renumbered Art. III, sec. 23, 1938]

This section requires three-fifths of all members elected to either house to be present any time an act is passed that imposes or revives a tax or makes an appropriation of moneys of the state. It is an additional guarantee for safe legislation in matters affecting taxes and appropriations of public moneys. It applies only to taxes that are general in their operation and coextensive with the state (People ex rel. Scott v. Chenango, 1853). A variety of taxes, including militia commutation taxes, license fees, and transfer taxes, have been held to be special taxes not within the compass of this section (People ex rel. Scott v. Chenango, 1853; Matter of Weeks, 1905; Exempt Firemen's Benevolent Fund v. Roome, 1897).

SECTION 24

Prison labor; contract system abolished. The legislature shall, by law, provide for the occupation and employment of prisoners sentenced to the several state prisons, penitentiaries, jails and reformatories in the state; and no person in any such prison, penitentiary, jail or reformatory, shall be required or allowed to work, while under sentence thereto, at any trade, industry or occupation, wherein or whereby his work, or the product or profit of his work, shall be farmed out, contracted, given or sold to any person, firm, association or corporation. This section shall not be construed to prevent the legislature from providing that convicts may work for, and that the products of their labor may be disposed of to, the state or any political division thereof, or for or to any public institution owned or managed and controlled by the state, or any political division thereof. [Const. 1894, Art. III, sec. 29; amend. and renumbered Art. III, sec. 24, 1938]

This section constitutionalized previous state policy. It embodies three mandates to the legislature: not to allow convict labor to be sold on the open market, to employ inmates in useful work, and to use the state to provide the market for the goods produced by the inmates. The last would be accomplished by having the state (its political subdivision and public institutions) purchase the products of inmates. The section attempts to combine punishment and reformation of the offender with reimbursement of the taxpayer for expenses of prosecuting and incarcerating the criminal and, at the same time, remove what they saw as a legitimate grievance on the part of free labor.

SECTION 25

Continuity of state and local governmental operations in periods of emergency. Notwithstanding any other provision of this constitution, the legislature, in order to insure continuity of state and local governmental operations in periods of emergency caused by enemy attack or by disasters (natural or otherwise), shall have the power and the immediate duty (1) to provide for prompt and temporary succession to the powers and duties of public offices, of whatever nature and whether filled by election or appointment, the incumbents of which may become unavailable for carrying on the powers and duties of such offices, and (2) to adopt such other measures as may be necessary and proper for insuring the continuity of governmental operations.

Nothing in this article shall be construed to limit in any way the power of the state to deal with emergencies arising from any cause. [1963]

This section is an enabling measure designed to empower the legislature to ensure, as far as possible, the continuity of governmental operations in time of grave emergency brought on by nuclear attack or natural disaster. It requires legislation for its implementation. Various attempts have been made to use this section to circumvent constitutional restrictions. When the federal courts declared New York's apportionment plans unconstitutional, this provision was invoked as a basis for suspending section 2 of this article. The court in Matter of Orans

(1965) rejected this argument. Similar attempts to invoke this section were made in connection with the various fiscal crises that faced local governments in the 1970s. In all cases, the courts rejected these arguments on the grounds that this section was meant to cover disasters of the kind associated with nuclear attacks and natural disasters that disrupt the operations of the state (Flushing National Bank v. Municipal Assistance Corporation, 1976; Waldert v. City of Rochester, 1977). Without such a narrow interpretation of emergency, section 25 is an open invitation to trump the constitution any time a crisis develops.

Article IV

The Executive

The governor is unquestionably the most important decision maker in New York government and one of the strongest governors in the nation. The strength of the office is derived from both constitutional and extraconstitutional roles and powers. The significant major developments in the constitutional powers of the office took place in the twentieth century. These include the four-year term, an executive budget, executive reorganization, and increases in appointment powers. The state's tradition of strong governors going back to 1777 and including George Clinton, the two Roosevelts, Herbert Lehman, Al Smith, and Nelson Rockefeller, Jr., has also contributed to strong and effective state leadership. The union of active political leadership and broad constitutional prerogatives placed the governor in a position of exceptional strength in relation to the legislature.

The governor's powers are not confined to those found in this article. Other powers and responsibilities are found in Articles V; VI, sections 2, 4, 9, 21, 22; VII, sections 1–6; and XIII, section 13.

SECTION 1

Executive power; election and terms of governor and lieutenant-governor. The executive power shall be vested in the governor, who shall hold his office for four years; the lieutenant-governor shall be chosen at the same time, and for the same term. The governor and lieutenant-governor shall be chosen at the general election held in the year nineteen hundred thirty-eight, and each fourth year thereafter. They shall be chosen jointly, by the casting by each voter of a single vote applicable to both offices, and the legislature by law shall provide for making such choice in such manner.

The respective persons having the highest number of votes cast jointly for
them for governor and lieutenant-governor respectively shall be elected.
[Const. 1821, Art. IV, secs. 1, 3; amend. Const. 1846; 1937; amend. and
renumbered Art. IV, sec. 1, 1938; amend. 1953]

The question of whether the phrase *executive power* confers on the governor
powers or simply the title has not occasioned the same controversy in New York
as it has at the national level (Cf. U.S. Constitution, Art. II, sec. 1). The phrase
was added in 1821 and likely was patterned after the federal equivalent. While
the courts have accorded great flexibility to the governor in carrying out the
duties of the office, they have also held that the governor has only those powers
delegated by the constitution and statutes (Rapp v. Carey, 1978). There is no
executive power independent of enumerated powers granted the governor in the
constitution. For this reason, the court struck down an executive claim to impound
funds (Oneida County v. Berle, 1980). The court had occasion to elaborate on
this position in a challenge to an executive order requiring financial disclosure,
prohibiting service at party office, and regulating outside employment of state
employees. The court held that such an order involved a broad question of policy
resolvable only by the lawmaking branch of the government (Rapp v. Carey, at
165). The court surveyed the history of executive actions before 1950, concluding
that those orders did not involve rule-making components and that while orders
after 1950 were more ambiguous, they were emergency measures later ratified
by the legislature. In any case, none went as far as this order. The court narrowed
the range of executive orders, claiming that the executive may not "go beyond
state legislative policy and prescribe a remedial device not embraced by the
policy" (at 163). Going even further, the court held that an executive order is
wholly contingent on whether there exists a statute specifically authorizing the
gubernatorial act (at 166). On the other hand, in Clark v. Cuomo (1984), seven
years later, the same court held that an executive order establishing a program
to encourage voter registration using existing state agencies was constitutional.
The order had been challenged as a violation of the separation of powers and
an infringement on the legislative power to "provide for a system of registration"
(Art. II, sec. 6). In sustaining the order, the court recognized some overlap was
inevitable and that the doctrine of separation of powers does not require "airtight
compartments." The court pulled back from the restrictive limits imposed in the
Rapp decision: "It is only when the executive acts inconsistently with the legislature, or usurps its prerogatives, that the doctrine of separation is violated"
(at 189). Since this program merely facilitates the process of registration and
does not actually register voters, it is consistent with and not invasive of the
legislative power and purpose. Clark v. Cuomo stands for the proposition that
an executive order is valid as long as it implements state legislative policy and
does not reach the level of policy or formulate a remedy not explicitly provided
for by the legislature.

The courts have given the executive wide berth in carrying out the duties of supervising the executive branch and implementing legislative policy (Gaynor v. Rockefeller, 1965). They have refused to adjudicate issues concerning the administration of programs. The court rejected a claim of correctional workers that an executive decision to close the correctional facility would place workers in danger of bodily injury or death. By seeking to vindicate their legally protected interests in a safe workplace, petitioner "calls for a remedy which would embroil the judiciary in the management and operation of the state correction system" (New York State Inspection, Security and Enforcement Employees v. Cuomo, 1984). That would violate the principle that "each department of government should be free from interference in carrying out their lawful responsibilities." When a policy matter has "demonstrably and textually been committed to a coordinate, political branch of government, any consideration of such matters by a branch or body other than that which the power expressly reposed would, absent extraordinary or emergency circumstances . . . constitute an *ultra vires* act" (239–40).

The political question doctrine, however, has its limits, and the judiciary has made it clear that it will declare the vested rights of specifically protected class of individuals in a fashion recognized by statute (Klosterman v. Cuomo, 1984).

The tenure of office has changed a number of times, reaching the present term of four years in 1937. Until 1953, the governor and the lieutenant governor were not elected jointly, and candidates from different parties could and were elected to office. The 1953 amendment prevented that possibility by bracketing the two offices on the voting machine so that a vote for one gubernatorial candidate is automatically a vote for the running mate. Since the governor does not necessarily select the running mate, the provision guarantees only that the two will be of the same party. It does not guarantee that they will be personally or politically compatible.

SECTION 2

Qualifications of governor and lieutenant-governor. No person shall be eligible to the office of governor or lieutenant-governor, except a citizen of the United States, of the age of not less than thirty years, and who shall have been five years next preceding his election a resident of this state. [Const. 1846, Art. IV, sec. 2 as amend. in 1874; renumbered Art. IV, sec. 2, 1894]

There has been little activity with regard to this section. It follows the form, if not the specifics, of the comparable federal provision (Art. II, sec. 2) and was likely based on it. The residency, age, and citizenship requirements were added in 1821. No record of legislative intent exists at the convention, but the 1846 convention debates indicate that the age requirement was set to prevent inexperienced men or, as one delegate put it, "raw boys" from gaining office.[1]

The five-year residency requirement was added to ensure that those elected would have some familiarity with the state. The next-preceding-election condition was added to ensure that the five-year residency would be the five years preceding the election in question and not any five years in the candidate's life. The residency requirement has not been interpreted strictly. Residency has been equated with domicile or the permanent home and principal establishment to which, whenever absent, the individual has the intention of returning. This allows a presumption of intent to remain a citizen of a state in spite of residing outside the state for a period of time. A candidate for attorney general who had lived in Virginia for five years but maintained a residence in New York was declared eligible for that office (Matter of Mechan v. Lomenzo, 1970).

SECTION 3

Powers and duties of governor; compensation. The governor shall be commander-in-chief of the military and naval forces of the state. He shall have power to convene the legislature, or the senate only, on extraordinary occasions. At extraordinary sessions convened pursuant to the provisions of this section no subject shall be acted upon, except as the governor may recommend for consideration. He shall communicate by message to the legislature at every session the condition of the state, and recommend such matters to it as he shall judge expedient. He shall expedite all such measures as may be resolved upon by the legislature, and shall take care that the laws are faithfully executed. He shall receive for his services an annual salary to be fixed by joint resolution of the senate and assembly, and there shall be provided for his use a suitable and furnished executive residence. [Const. 1777, Art. XXVIII; amend. and renumbered Art. III, sec. 4, Const. 1821; amend. and renumbered Art. IV, sec. 4, Const. 1846; amend. 1874; amend. Const. 1894, 1927; renumbered Art. IV, sec. 3, Const. 1938, amend. 1953, 1975]

Section 3 makes the governor commander in chief, gives the power to convene extraordinary sessions of the legislature, communicate by message to the legislature on the condition of the state, and see that the laws are faithfully executed. It also provides that compensation be fixed by joint act of the senate and assembly.

Regulations issued by the governor consistent with federal military law on the training and organization of the militia have the force of law. The governor has full and exclusive power to make rules governing the military forces of the state. Judicial review of the military decisions of the governor is limited. Acts of the governor concerning the organization of the militia and the discharging of the enlistees are not reviewable by the courts (Nistal v. Hausauer, 1954).

The governor's power to convene extraordinary sessions enables him or her to call the legislature into session when pressing matters arise. When in extraordinary session, the constitution requires that no subject be acted upon except those recommended by the governor. This clause put the session very much in the hands of the governor in every matter but the final vote. The prohibition does not extend to amendments of senate or assembly rules[2] or to impeachments. The case deciding the impeachment question was occasioned by one of the most unusual, not to say shameful, events in New York's political history. Governor William Sulzer (1912–1913) had called an extraordinary session of the legislature in 1913 and in that session was impeached. In upholding the impeachment, the court concluded that for purposes of impeachment, the assembly is the assembly, whatever type of session it might be in. The impeachment power was judicial in nature and therefore did not constitute a ''legislative subject'' (People ex rel. Robin v. Hayes, 1913). The governor is not obliged to submit interim appointments for confirmation at such a session.

During the colonial period, the governor customarily addressed the legislature in person, making such recommendations as he deemed proper. This practice was changed, and the word *speech* was removed and replaced by *message*. It was claimed that that personal address was a relic of monarchy, and, furthermore, the legislature consumed much time and expense responding to the speech.[3] The governor's message is an important tool in setting the policy agenda of the state. In it, the governor lays out his or her understanding of the problems the state faces, the progress made in solving them, and what remains to be done.

In words imitated by the national Constitution, the governor is directed to take care that the laws are faithfully executed. This clause and the ''executive power'' phrase of section 1 provide the governor with power to supervise and control the executive branch. This power and provisions of the executive law of the state allow the governor to direct the attorney general to supersede elected district attorneys. This power is at the governor's discretion, and judicial review of decisions in this respect is severely circumscribed (Mulroy v. Carey, 1977). In 1972, Governor Rockefeller, acting on recommendations of the Knapp Commission investigating police corruption in New York City, named a special prosecutor to take over from New York City's five district attorneys in all cases of corruption.

The faithfully-execute-the-laws clause, however, acted as a limit on executive power when the governor attempted to impound funds. The court in *Berle* held that this clause put the governor under the obligation to spend the funds in question.

SECTION 4

Reprieves, commutations, and pardons; powers and duties of governor relating to grants of. The governor shall have the power to grant reprieves, commutations and pardons after conviction, for all offenses except treason and cases of impeachment, upon such conditions and with such restrictions and limitations, as he may think proper, subject to such regulations as may be provided by law relative to the manner of applying for pardons. Upon conviction for treason, he shall have power to suspend the execution of the sentence, until the case shall be reported to the legislature at its next meeting, when the legislature shall either pardon, or commute the sentence, direct the execution of the sentence, or grant a further reprieve. He shall annually communicate to the legislature each case of reprieve, commutation or pardon granted, stating the name of the convict, the crime of which he was convicted, the sentence and its date, and the date of the commutation, pardon or reprieve. [Const. 1777, Art. XVIII; amend. and renumbered Art. III, sec. 5, Const. 1821; amend. and renumbered Art. IV, sec. 5, Const. 1846; and renumbered sec. 4, Const. 1938]

The cases interpreting this section support the view that the governor has unlimited power to grant reprieves, commutation, and pardons on such conditions and with such restrictions as he or she shall see fit. That discretion cannot be limited by the judiciary or the legislature. A reprieve postpones execution of sentence; a commutation shortens the sentence. A commutation of sentence allows an inmate to come before the parole board for consideration of release at an earlier time than permitted by sentence of the court, but it is not a guarantee of automatic release. Because the governor cannot be expected to become familiar with all the petitions for pardons and commutations, an agency has been set up to screen these petitions and make recommendations to the governor.

SECTION 5

When lieutenant-governor to act as governor. In case of the removal of the governor from office or of his death or resignation, the lieutenant-governor shall become governor for the remainder of the term.

In case the governor-elect shall decline to serve or shall die, the lieutenant-governor-elect shall become governor for the full term.

In case the governor is impeached, is absent from the state or is otherwise unable to discharge the powers and duties of his office, the lieutenant-governor shall act as governor until the inability shall cease or until the term of the governor shall expire.

In case of the failure of the governor-elect to take the oath of office at the commencement of his term, the lieutenant-governor-elect shall act as governor until the governor shall take the oath. [1949; amend. 1963]

SECTION 6

Duties and compensation of lieutenant-governor; succession to the governorship. The lieutenant-governor shall possess the same qualifications of eligibility for office as the governor. He shall be the president of the senate but shall have only a casting vote therein. The lieutenant-governor shall receive for his services an annual salary to be fixed by joint resolution of the senate and assembly.

In case of vacancy in the offices of both governor and lieutenant-governor, a governor and lieutenant-governor shall be elected for the remainder of the term at the next general election happening not less than three months after both offices shall have become vacant. No election of a lieutenant-governor shall be had in any event except at the time of electing a governor.

In case of vacancy in the offices of both governor and lieutenant-governor or if both of them shall be impeached, absent from the state or otherwise unable to discharge the powers and duties of the office of governor, the temporary president of the senate shall act as governor until the inability shall cease or until a governor shall be elected.

In case of vacancy in the office of lieutenant-governor alone, or if the lieutenant-governor shall be impeached, absent from the state or otherwise unable to discharge the duties of his office, the temporary president of the senate shall perform all the duties of lieutenant-governor during such vacancy or inability.

If, when the duty of acting as governor devolves upon the temporary president of the senate, there be a vacancy in such office or the temporary president of the senate shall be absent from the state or otherwise unable to discharge the duties of governor, the speaker of the assembly shall act as governor during such vacancy or inability.

The legislature may provide for the devolution of the duty of acting as governor in any case not provided for in this article. [Const. 1821, Art. III, sec. 7; amend. and renumbered Art. IV, secs. 7, 8, Const. 1846; amend. 1874, Const. 1894; amend. and renumbered Art. IV, sec. 6, 1938; amend. 1945, 1953, 1963]

These two sections deal with gubernatorial succession. Their importance is underscored by the frequency with which governors of New York have resigned. Governor Daniel Tompkins resigned to become vice-president of the United States; Martin Van Buren left office to become president Andrew Jackson's secretary of state; Grover Cleveland was elected president of the United States and resigned his office a few weeks before inauguration; Governor Herbert Lehman resigned in 1943, as did Nelson Rockefeller in 1973.

The tradition of succession by lieutenant governor goes back to colonial times. In the earliest cases when governors died or resigned, there was some confusion as to whether the lieutenant governor became governor or acting governor. This section makes it clear that in such situations, the lieutenant governor becomes governor. The phrase *or die* was added in 1949 to cover the possibility of the death of the governor-elect following the death of the governor-elect of Georgia. The article was substantially revised in 1963. As a result, the conditions under which the lieutenant governor would be acting governor and when governor were made clear. Provision is also made for the case where the governor-elect declines to serve or fails to take the oath of office. When the governor leaves the state, he or she remains the governor. If he or she plans to be absent for extended periods of time, the practice has been to inform the lieutenant governor of that fact.

Section 6 spells out the actual, as opposed to potential, powers of the office

of lieutenant governor. The requirement that he or she possess the same qualifications as the governor is undoubtedly connected with the status as potential
successor. As president of the senate, he or she presides over sessions and casts
a vote in case of a tie only on votes concerning legislative procedure. This latter
restriction stems from the fact that he or she is not a member of the senate and
no legislative power is vested in the office. The lieutenant governor votes in
procedural matters so that the business of lawmaking does not come to a halt.

For some time, this section specified the salary of the lieutenant governor,
necessitating a constitutional amendment every time the salary was raised. The
current provision allows the legislature to keep the salary in line with changing
financial realities.

The line of succession runs from the lieutenant governor to the temporary
president of the senate and from there to the speaker of the assembly. The last
paragraph of this section, enabling the legislature to provide for further devolution
by statute, was added with the possibility of nuclear catastrophe in mind. A
ruling of the court of appeals held that upon the death of the lieutenant governor,
an election for a successor had to be held at the next general election (Ward v.
Curran, 1943). This provision overrules the court of appeals decision by mandating that no election for lieutenant governor shall take place except at the time
of electing the governor.

SECTION 7

Action by governor on legislative bills; reconsideration after veto. Every
bill which shall have passed the senate and assembly shall, before it becomes
a law, be presented to the governor; if he approve, he shall sign it; but if
not, he shall return it with his objections to the house in which it shall have
originated, which shall enter the objections at large on the journal, and
proceed to reconsider it. If after such reconsideration, two-thirds of the
members elected to that house shall agree to pass the bill, it shall be sent
together with the objections, to the other house, by which it shall likewise
be reconsidered; and if approved by two-thirds of the members elected to
that house, it shall become a law notwithstanding the objections of the
governor. In all such cases the votes in both houses shall be determined by
yeas and nays, and the names of the members voting shall be entered on
the journal of each house respectively. If any bill shall not be returned by
the governor within ten days (Sundays excepted) after it shall have been
presented to him, the same shall be a law in like manner as if he had signed
it, unless the legislature shall, by their adjournment, prevent its return, in
which case it shall not become law without the approval of the governor.
No bill shall become a law after the final adjournment of the legislature,
unless approved by the governor within thirty days after such adjournment.
If any bill presented to the governor contain several items of appropriation
of money, he may object to one or more of such items while approving of
the other portion of the bill. In such case he shall append to the bill, at the

time of signing it, a statement of items to which he objects; and the
appropriation so objected to shall not take effect. If the legislature be in
session, he shall transmit to the house in which the bill originated a copy
of such statement, and the items objected to shall be separately reconsidered.
If on reconsideration one or more of such items be approved by two-thirds
of the members elected to each house, the same shall be part of the law,
notwithstanding the objections of the governor. All the provisions of this
section, in relation to bills not approved by the governor, shall apply in
cases in which he shall withhold his approval from any item or items
contained in a bill appropriating money. [Const. 1821, Art. I, sec. 12; amend.
and renumbered Art. IV, sec. 9, Const. 1846 as amend. in 1874; renumbered
Art. IV, sec. 7, 1938]

Every bill that passes both houses in the same form must be presented to the
governor for action before it becomes law. An attempt to redraw the state's
congressional district lines by concurrent resolution without submission to the
governor was held unconstitutional (Matter of Koenig v. Flynn, 1932). The court
argued that while not all actions of the legislature require submission to the
governor (e.g., proposed amendments), when the legislature prescribes or enacts
rules that must be followed and obeyed by the people of the state, it is engaged
in lawmaking, and such acts are subject to the governor's action. Congressional
districting has always been considered in that category (at 301).

On the meaning of "presented to the governor," the court held the phrase to
mean physically presented to him or her and not merely in the hands of those
responsible for delivery (City of Rye v. Ronan, 1971). The mere fact that the
governor was aware that the bill had passed the legislature is not sufficient. In
the same case, the court held that the return of a vetoed bill on the day of
adjournment did not deprive the legislature of adequate opportunity to override
the veto.

The section provides the governor with an item veto of appropriations. The
practice of placing in appropriation bills a great number of objects in order to
get a favorable vote on projects that might have trouble standing on their own
was the evil the item veto meant to eradicate. The governor may approve portions
of the bill and return those portions he or she objects to. The item veto has
declined in importance with the adoption of the executive budget since the
legislature is usually reluctant to add items to the governor's budget.[4] Items in
the governor's budget submitted to the legislature and not changed require no
further action by the governor except that appropriations for the legislature or
the judiciary and separate additional items added to the governor's budget are
subject to his or her approval (see Art. IV, sec. 4). Ostensibly restricted to
appropriations, the item veto has been stretched on occasion. Governor Hugh
Carey approved a deficiency line item appropriation but disallowed the item's
language prohibiting the use of the name or photo of any state or local official.
An attorney general's opinion sustained this "veto."[5]

The governor has ten days, excluding Sundays, to veto a bill. It becomes law if he or she does not sign it within that period unless the legislature adjourns before the ten days are up. Following the adjournment of the legislature, the governor has thirty days to sign or veto the bill. If he or she does not issue a memorandum of approval or veto, the bill is pocket vetoed.

The veto power of the governor in New York is formidable. Since 1873, only one full veto has been overridden.[6] There are a number of reasons for this unprecedented record: the requirement that two-thirds of the whole membership of each house must override; the fact that the bulk of bills passed are transmitted to the governor at the end of the session, leaving the governor the opportunity to veto them during the thirty-day adjournment period; and the strength and popular support of many of the governors who have wielded the veto with regularity. Since 1976, the legislature has had the power to call itself into special session at which time it could consider the vetoed bills, but so far, it has not availed itself of this power (Art. III, sec. 18).

In the twentieth century, governors have adopted the practice of providing reasons for their vetos when the bills are acceptable and when they need corrective action. This practice has undoubtedly helped smooth legislative-executive relations in the policymaking process. Frequently the governor will request or allow bills to be recalled from his desk, especially when he needs more time to consider the legislation or when there are correctable problems and the legislature wishes to amend the objectionable provision(s).[7] Governors and the legislature cooperate in this area by using the message of necessity, which allows the legislature to waive the constitutional requirement that all bills be in their final form on the desks of members at least three days before final passage. For the use of this provision in connection with the veto, see Art. III, sec. XIV.

SECTION 8

> **Departmental rules and regulations; filing; publication.** No rule or regulation made by any state department, board, bureau, authority or commission, except such as relates to the organization or internal management of a state department, board, bureau, authority or commission shall be effective until it is filed in the office of the department of state. The legislature shall provide for the speedy publication of such rules and regulations, by appropriate laws. [1938]

The purpose of this section is to provide proper notice to citizens concerned with the activities of the state and to provide one common place, the Department of State, where all regulations and rules of the various government agencies shall be on file. Prior to this provision, with few exceptions, there were no public rules or regulations of which the public had any notice. Its adoption was a reflection of the growing size and importance of the bureaucracy and administrative law in the daily lives of the citizens.

The judiciary is not covered by this provision nor are local government bodies and housing authorities (People v. Granatelli, 1981; Smalls v. White Plains Housing Authority, 1962). The major judicial question that has been the basis for litigation is the kind of rules and regulations that must be filed. The courts have held that matters of internal management or organization are not covered by the filing requirement. On the other hand, a correction institution's rules that affect a prisoner's liberty interests are matters of public interest and must be filed, though police rules governing the taking of blood tests were held to be purely matters of internal management.[8]

The failure to file such rules generally renders action taken during the no-filing period invalid (Connell v. Regan, 1986). The enforcement of this provision has created notice and due process protection for citizens by requiring agencies to file rules and then abide by them (Johnson v. Smith, 1981). The strict enforcement of this provision has helped to create regularity in bureaucratic procedures and eliminate some of the arbitrariness frequently associated with bureaucratic behavior.

Article V

Officers and Civil Departments

Article V provides the constitutional ground rules for the organization of the executive departments, the "fourth branch of government." Coordinating, controlling, and making New York's large and complex bureaucracy responsive is a major responsibility of the governor. This article provides for executive appointment of all but three of the regular departments. It creates an executive office, which is composed of the Division of Budget and over thirty other subdivisions, some so large that their budgets and personnel exceed those of the regular departments. It provides for a merit system of selection of public employees, gives veterans preferences on the competitive examinations, and makes the retirement system contractual, preventing any impairments of benefits by the state legislature.

Many of the agencies of the executive branch exercise rule-making, enforcement, licensing, and investigatory powers and have a substantial influence on the lives of citizens. A body of administrative law has developed, and while this regulation is subject to statutory and constitutional law, such restraint has not always been effective. Three limits on bureaucratic decision making exist in New York: the statute establishing the agency sets limits on its powers and responsibilities, allowing challenge to agency decisions on the basis that the agency acted *ultra vires* (beyond its authority); the internal rule-making process of each agency, which has been defined by the state's Administrative Procedure Act (SAPA); and the broad concept of reasonableness. Judges generally defer to the findings of experts, but they require that such decisions be reasonable and not arbitrary or capricious. In addition, section 8 of Article IV has been interpreted to require public notice and regularity in the administrative process.

SECTION 1

Comptroller and attorney-general; payment of state moneys without audit void. The comptroller and attorney-general shall be chosen at the same general election as the governor and hold for the same term, and shall possess the qualifications provided in section 2 of article IV. The legislature shall provide for filling vacancies in the office of comptroller and of attorney-general. The comptroller shall be required: (1) to audit all vouchers before payment and all official accounts; (2) to audit the accrual and collection of all revenues and receipts; and (3) to prescribe such methods of accounting as are necessary for the performance of the foregoing duties. The payment of any money of the state, or of any money under its control, or the refund of any money paid to the state, except upon audit by the comptroller, shall be void, and may be restrained upon the suit of any taxpayer with the consent of the supreme court in appellate division on notice to the attorney-general. In such respect the legislature shall define his powers and duties and may also assign to him: (1) supervision of the accounts of any political subdivision of the state; and (2) powers and duties pertaining to or connected with the assessment and taxation of real estate, including determination of ratios which the assessed valuation of taxable property bears to the full valuation thereof, but not including any of those powers and duties reserved to officers of a county, city, town or village by virtue of sections seven and eight of article nine of this constitution. The legislature shall assign to him no administrative duties, excepting such as may be incidental to the performance of these functions, any other provision of this constitution to the contrary notwithstanding. [Const. 1894, Art. V, sec. 1 as amend. in 1925, 1938, 1953, 1955]

The attorney general and the comptroller are the only two department heads elected directly by the people. This provides them with an independence deemed necessary by virtue of their functions as watchdogs of the law and treasury, respectively. The comptroller, for example, acts in a quasi-judicial capacity when exercising the power to audit (City of New York v. State of New York, 1976). The importance of these two offices is underscored by the fact that the qualifications for the positions are made similar to those for the governor. When a vacancy occurs in either office, no special election is held; rather an interim appointment is made until the next regularly scheduled statewide election is held (see Art. IV, sec. 1).

The attorney general heads the Department of Law and is in charge of the legal affairs of all state departments and agencies. The office has had numerous powers assigned to it by the legislature.[1] These include the power to investigate, at the governor's request or on the initiative of the office, all matters concerned with public peace, safety, or justice, enforcement of consumer fraud, and environmental and human rights legislation. In carrying out investigations, the attorney general possesses subpoena power. The office issues formal and informal opinions on points of law to all governmental agencies or officials when requested. These formal opinions are deemed to be controlling unless and until they have been set aside by judicial determination. Finally, the attorney general is permitted to appear in any legal proceeding in which the constitutionality of a statute is brought into question.

The comptroller is the chief fiscal officer of the state and heads the Department of Audit and Control. That office is charged with maintaining the accounts of the state, paying state bills and payrolls, and auditing the financial practices of all state departments and divisions and public authorities, as well as the fiscal affairs of all units of local government. The comptroller invests the funds of the state, as well as the moneys of others held by the state. Like the attorney general, the comptroller issues advisory opinions of fiscal legal matters to state agencies and local governments. Not all public entities are under the pre-audit authority of the comptroller. The courts have held that the Urban Development Corporation (UDC) and other public corporations are not state agencies and thus not subject to pre-audit under this provision. UDC bonds are not ''money of the state'' or ''money under its control'' as those terms are used in this section (Smith v. Levitt, 1972).

This section spells out the powers of the comptroller and authorizes the legislature to pass implementing legislation and to assign to the office the additional powers specified. The legislature is forbidden, however, to assign to the office any administrative duties except those incidental to the performance of the specified functions. Article X, section 5 gives the comptroller the additional power to supervise the accounts of any public benefit corporation but not the power of pre-audit. The power is discretionary with the comptroller. Any attempt by the legislature to mandate that obligation impermissibly infringes on the comptroller's discretionary power to supervise the accounts of public authorities, thus compromising the independence of an elected official (Patterson v. Carey, 1977). Concern for the independence of the offices was also in evidence when the court held that reports of the comptroller or subordinates had absolute privilege with regard to libel actions (Ward Telecommunication v. State, 1977).

SECTION 2

Civil departments in the state government. There shall be not more than twenty civil departments in the state government, including those referred to in this constitution. The legislature may by law change the names of the departments referred to in this constitution. [Const. 1894, Art. V, sec. 2 as amend. in 1925, 1961]

SECTION 3

Assignment of functions. Subject to the limitations contained in this constitution, the legislature may from time to time assign by law new powers and functions to departments, officers, boards, commissions or executive offices of the governor, and increase, modify or diminish their powers and functions. Nothing contained in this article shall prevent the legislature from creating temporary commissions for special purposes or executive offices of the governor and from reducing the number of departments as provided for in this article, by consolidation or otherwise. [Const. 1894, Art. V, sec. 3, as added in 1925; amend. 1961]

By specifying the number at twenty, this section sought to halt the proliferation of agencies and departments that had plagued the state in the past. Although the number of office remains at twenty, hundreds of agencies have been created by the legislature and by executive order.

These sections provide for an executive office that functions as a kind of umbrella, or *omnium gatherum*, for over thirty subdivisions. The executive office, originally added to provide the governor with more flexibility in reorganizing the executive branch, has been one way in which the limitation on the number of departments has been circumvented. The courts have also given a rather broad interpretation to the clause, allowing for the creation of temporary commissions for special purposes. When the legislature transferred powers vested in the superintendent of insurance to a mortgage commission on the grounds that an emergency (the Great Depression) called for prompt action and no agency was equipped for prompt action, the court gave its blessing. The "special purpose" can be the "need for prompt and effective action" (Matter of People [Westchester Title and Trust Insurance Co.], 1935).

SECTION 4

Department heads. The head of the department of audit and control shall be the comptroller and of the department of law, the attorney-general. The head of the department of education shall be The Regents of the University of the State of New York, who shall appoint and at pleasure remove a commissioner of education to be the chief administrative officer of the department. The head of the department of agriculture and markets shall be appointed in a manner to be prescribed by law. Except as otherwise provided in this constitution, the heads of all other departments and the members of all boards and commissions, excepting temporary commissions for special purposes, shall be appointed by the governor by and with the advice and consent of the senate and may be removed by the governor, in a manner to be prescribed by law. [Const. 1894, Art. V, sec. 4, as added in 1925]

This section confirms the governor's power to appoint and remove heads of the executive departments, which—with the executive budget—is the basis for the governor's power to supervise and control the executive branch. It also creates exceptions to this power. The head of the Department of Education is the board of regents, who are appointed by the legislature and, in turn, appoint the commissioner of education, who serves at the pleasure of the board. This places both control and management of educational affairs with the board of regents and the commissioner of education and gives them a degree of independence from the governor. Since the department was set up to remove ''as far as practicable and as possible all matters pertaining to the general school system from controversies in the courts,'' it is subject to limited judicial review (Donohue v. Copiague Union Free School District, 1979).

The fourth exception to the governor's appointment and removal power is the commissioner of agriculture and markets. The section allows the legislature to determine how the post shall be filled. It has elected to allow the governor to appoint the commissioner with the advice and consent of the senate and be removed by the governor for cause as prescribed by law.[2]

SECTION 5

[Repealed, 1962].

SECTION 6

Civil service appointments and promotions; veterans' credits.
Appointments and promotions in the civil service of the state and all of the civil divisions thereof, including cities and villages, shall be made according to merit and fitness to be ascertained, as far as practicable, by examination which, as far as practicable, shall be competitive; provided, however, that any member of the armed forces of the United States who served therein in time of war, who is a citizen or an alien lawfully admitted for permanent residence in the United States and a resident of this state and was honorably discharged or released under honorable circumstances from such service, shall be entitled to receive five points additional credit in a competitive examination for original appointment and two and one-half points additional credit in an examination for promotion or, if such member was disabled in the actual performance of duty in any war, is receiving his disability payments therefor from the United States veterans administration, and his disability is certified by such administration to be in existence at the time of his application for appointment or promotion, he shall be entitled to receive ten points additional credit in a competitive examination for original appointment and five points additional credit in an examination for promotion. Such additional credit shall be added to the final earned rating of such member after he has qualified in an examination and shall be granted only at the time of establishment of an eligible list. No such member shall receive the additional credit granted by this section after he has received one appointment, either original entrance or promotion, from an eligible list on which he was allowed the additional credit granted by this section. [Const. 1894, Art. V, sec. 9; renumbered sec. 5, 1925; amend. 1929, 1945; renumbered Art. V, sec. 6, 1938; amend. 1949, 1987]

New York was the first state to constitutionalize a merit system of civil service appointment. The section contains two exceptions to the competitive examination requirement: competitive examinations are required only where practicable, and bonus points are awarded to veterans who served during time of war.

The provision replaces the spoils system with a system of merit selection protecting both the public and individual employees. The legislature has adopted a statutory scheme for its implementation. That law created the Civil Service Commission, a system of classification and compensation, and embodies the holdings of various court decisions concerning the constitutional provision.[3] The vast majority of state positions are now part of the civil service system. Employees are placed in two broad classifications: unclassified and classified positions. The former includes elected officials, legislative officers and employees, gubernatorial appointees, officers, members and employees of the board of elections, teachers and professors in public schools, certain community colleges, and the state university and supervisory personnel. These positions are exempt from the requirements of this section. The classified services are divided into four subgroupings: competitive class, for which competitive examinations are required (about 80 percent of the classified positions fall into this category); noncompetitive, where examinations are required but competitive examinations are not practicable; the labor class, where a qualifying examination may be required but is not mandated; and an exempt class, which includes, inter alia, one secretary for each department. Court decisions have helped shape the contours of these classifications by deciding such questions as who are and who are not state employees and what exemptions are legitimate under the ''as far as practicable'' clause. For example, the court has held that positions requiring qualities such as fairness, patience, common sense, and judgment do not require competitive examination (Powers v. Taylor, 1955). The courts have not permitted block certification in which all candidates within a block of scores would be considered on an equal basis, but a rule of three is generally followed whereby departments and agencies can select from the top three candidates on the eligibility list. This allows some flexibility for managers, but supporters of affirmative action argue that it limits recruitment of minorities and women.

Recent attempts to develop affirmative action plans by executive order have created some tension between this clause and the goal of equal employment opportunities. An attempt to appoint the highest-ranking female without regard to placement on the eligibility list was held violative of this provision. If the examination is fair and related to the position in question, any such skipping is not consistent with this section (Ruddy v. Connelie, 1978). On the other hand, experience with racial, religious, or ethnic problems may be considered if shown to be reasonably related to job performance and ability (Jackson v. Poston, 1972).

Decisions of the Civil Service Commission are subject to limited judicial review. Only if the classification ''lacks any harmony with the institutionally mandated merit selection system . . . may the determination be overturned by the courts'' (Dillon v. Nassau Civil Service, 1978). State policies with regard to civil service must conform to the national Constitution. In Elrod v. Burns (1976), the Supreme Court held that patronage dismissals of nonpolicymaking public employees violate the First Amendment. A New York appellate court following *Burns* declared the dismissal of a housing counselor by a newly elected mayor void because the position was in the ''nonpolicymaking'' category (Corbeil v. Canestrari, 1977). The veterans' preference provision has been upheld against a Fourteenth Amendment equal protection challenge alleging gender discrimination (Personnel Administrator of Massachusetts v. Feeney, 1979).

SECTION 7

Membership in retirement systems; benefits not to be diminished or impaired. After July first, nineteen hundred forty, membership in any pension or retirement system of the state or of a civil division thereof shall be a contractual relationship, the benefits of which shall not be diminished or impaired. [1938]

This section was added to the constitution by the 1938 Constitutional Convention in response to pressure from civil service organizations. The court of appeals in Roddy v. Valentine (1934) noted that the public moneys set aside for pensions could not be deemed contractual and such statutory schemes were ''subject to change or even to revocation at the will of the legislature'' (at 231). Concern that the system was susceptible to political manipulation and possible collapse led to this section, which makes pension obligations contractual guarantees. The effective date of the section was postponed until July 1, 1940, presumably to allow state and civil divisions of the state to make any adjustments or modifications of their pension systems then in force before the amendment took effect. The courts have enforced this section rigorously. In Birnbaum v. NYS Teachers Retirement System (1958), the court voided an attempt by the state to apply newly adopted mortality tables to all members who had not previously retired. The new tables had the effect of reducing the annuities of all members by about 5 percent. The court held that the mortality tables in effect at the time of the contract must be enforced. The court has refused to extend the reach of the provision. In Lippman v. Board of Education (1985), health insurance benefits were declared not within the coverage of this provision. The section protects only benefits of membership in the retirement system; more than an incidental relationship to the retirement system must be found before employee benefits will be held to be within the protection of this section.

Article VI

The Judiciary

New York's judiciary is of the largest, busiest, and most expensive in the world. Because it has jurisdiction over the financial district in New York City, the First Department of the Appellate Division is the country's most important appellate court in the commercial field, and New York's Criminal Court is the busiest criminal court in the world.

The 1894 Constitution shaped the structure that remains intact to the present. Amendments in 1962 and 1977 created a unified court system with a centralized administration, a single state-financed court budget, and streamlined procedures for disciplining judges.

The courts comprising the judicial system can be divided as follows: (1) appellate courts, including the court of appeals, the state's highest court, and the appellate division of the supreme court, the state's intermediate appellate courts; (2) trial courts of superior jurisdiction including the supreme court, a trial court of general jurisdiction, a court of claims, surrogate's court, family court, and county courts; and (3) trial courts of inferior jurisdiction, including New York City's civil and criminal courts and various district, city, town, and village courts outside New York City.

With the exception of full court consolidation, New York's Constitution embodies most of the reforms connected with effective court administration: centralized management and rule making, a unitary budget, and state financing.

SECTION 1

Establishment and organization of unified court system; courts of record; service and execution of process. (a) There shall be a unified court system for the state. The state-wide courts shall consist of the court of appeals, the supreme court including the appellate divisions thereof, the court of claims, the county court, the surrogate's court and the family court, as hereinafter provided. The legislature shall establish in and for the city of New York, as part of the unified court system for the state, a single, city-wide court of civil jurisdiction and a single, city-wide court of criminal jurisdiction, as hereinafter provided, and may upon the request of the mayor and the local legislative body of the city of New York, merge the two courts into one city-wide court of both civil and criminal jurisdiction. The unified court system for the state shall also include the district, town, city and village courts outside the city of New York, as hereinafter provided.

(b) The court of appeals, the supreme court including the appellate divisions thereof, the court of claims, the county court, the surrogate's court, the family court, the courts or court of civil and criminal jurisdiction of the city of New York, and such other courts as the legislature may determine shall be courts of record.

(c) All processes, warrants and other mandates of the court of appeals, the supreme court including the appellate divisions thereof, the court of claims, the county court, the surrogate's court and the family court may be served and executed in any part of the state. All processes, warrants and other mandates of the courts or court of civil and criminal jurisdiction of the city of New York may, subject to such limitation as may be prescribed by the legislature, be served and executed in any part of the state. The legislature may provide that processes, warrants and other mandates of the district court may be served and executed in any part of the state and that processes, warrants and other mandates of town, village and city courts outside the city of New York may be served and executed in any part of the county in which such courts are located or in any part of any adjoining county. [1961]

Prior to the adoption of this section, New York had no statewide system of courts. Courts were organized on the basis of cities, towns, and counties, as well as the state. For the most part, they were independent of one another as far as administrative and financial matters were concerned. This section establishes a unified statewide court system encompassing all the courts of the state. In spite of a move toward a unified court system, eleven different courts of original jurisdiction are continued.

Recommendations to merge the family court, the court of claims, and the surrogate's courts into the jurisdiction of the supreme court were rejected. The decision to maintain these courts strikes a balance between a system of courts of broad powers and jurisdiction and specialized courts handling special types of litigation.

The legislature was left the task of integrating the New York City and the town, village, and city courts outside New York City into the system. The unified system simplified procedures, made for a more efficient use of court personnel, eliminated restrictive jurisdictional lines among courts, and brought some administrative coordination to the operation of the courts (c).[1] In addition, a number of independent courts with overlapping and conflicting court jurisdiction were abolished (sec. 35).

The courts of record mentioned in 1(b) are simply those courts defined as such by constitutional or legislative enactment. Some statutory and constitutional provisions apply only to courts of record.

SECTION 2

Court of appeals; organization; designation; vacancies, how filled; commission on judicial nomination. (a) The court of appeals is continued. It shall consist of the chief judge and the six elected associate judges now in office, who shall hold their offices until the expiration of their respective terms, and their successors, and such justices of the supreme court as may be designated for service in said court as hereinafter provided. The official terms of the chief judge and the six associate judges shall be fourteen years.

Five members of the court shall constitute a quorum, and the concurrence of four shall be necessary to a decision; but not more than seven judges shall sit in any case. In case of the temporary absence or inability to act of any judge of the court of appeals, the court may designate any justice of the supreme court to serve as associate judge of the court during such absence or inability to act. The court shall have power to appoint and to remove its clerk. The powers and jurisdiction of the court shall not be suspended for want of appointment when the number of judges is sufficient to constitute a quorum.

(b) Whenever and as often as the court of appeals shall certify to the governor that the court is unable, by reason of the accumulation of causes pending therein, to hear and dispose of the same with reasonable speed, the governor shall designate such number of justices of the supreme court as may be so certified to be necessary, but not more than four, to serve as associate judges of the court of appeals. The justices so designated shall be relieved, while so serving, from their duties as justices of the supreme court, and shall serve as associate judges of the court of appeals until the court shall certify that the need for the services of any such justices no longer exists, whereupon they shall return to the supreme court. The governor may fill vacancies among such designated judges. No such justices shall serve as associate judge of the court of appeals except while holding the office of justice of the supreme court. The designation of a justice of the supreme court as an associate judge of the court of appeals shall not be deemed to affect his existing office any longer than until the expiration of his designation as such associate judge, nor to create a vacancy.

(c) There shall be a commission on judicial nomination to evaluate the qualifications of candidates for appointment to the court of appeals and to prepare a written report and recommend to the governor those persons who by their character, temperament, professional aptitude and experience are well qualified to hold such judicial office. The legislature shall provide by law for the organization and procedure of the judicial nominating commission.

(d) (1) The commission on judicial nomination shall consist of twelve members of whom four shall be appointed by the governor, four by the chief judge of the court of appeals, and one each by the speaker of the assembly, the temporary president of the senate, the minority leader of the senate, and the minority leader of the assembly. Of the four members appointed by the governor, no more than two shall be enrolled in the same political party, two shall be members of the bar of the state, and two shall not be members of the bar of the state. Of the four members appointed by the chief judge of the court of appeals, no more than two shall be enrolled in the same political party, two shall be members of the bar of the state, and two shall not be members of the bar of the state. No member of the commission shall hold or have held any judicial office or hold any elected public office for which he receives compensation during his period of service, except that the governor and the chief judge may each appoint no more than one former judge or justice of the unified court system to such commission. No member of the commission shall hold any office in any political party. No member of the judicial nominating commission shall be eligible for appointment to judicial office in any court of the state during the member's period of service or within one year thereafter.

(2) The members first appointed by the governor shall have respectively one, two, three and four year terms as he shall designate. The member first appointed by the temporary president of the senate shall have a one year term. The member first appointed by the minority leader of the senate shall have a two year term. The member first appointed by the speaker of the assembly shall have a four year term. The member first appointed by the minority leader of the assembly shall have a three year term. Each subsequent appointment shall be for a term of four years.

(3) The commission shall designate one of their number to serve as chairman.

(4) The commission shall consider the qualifications of candidates for appointment to the offices of judge and chief judge of the court of appeals and, whenever a vacancy in those offices occurs, shall prepare a written report and recommend to the governor persons who are well qualified for those judicial offices.

(e) The governor shall appoint, with the advice and consent of the senate, from among those recommended by the judicial nominating commission, a person to fill the office of chief judge or associate judge, as the case may be, whenever a vacancy occurs in the court of appeals; provided, however, that no person may be appointed a judge of the court of appeals unless such person is a resident of the state and has been admitted to the practice of law in this state for at least ten years. The governor shall transmit to the senate the written report of the commission on judicial nomination relating to the nominee.

(f) When a vacancy occurs in the office of chief judge or associate judge of the court of appeals and the senate is not in session to give its advice and consent to an appointment to fill the vacancy, the governor shall fill the vacancy by interim appointment upon the recommendation of a commission on judicial nomination as provided in this section. An interim appointment shall continue until the senate shall pass upon the governor's selection. If the senate confirms an appointment, the judge shall serve a term as provided in subdivision a of this section commencing from the date of his interim appointment. If the senate rejects an appointment, a vacancy in the office shall occur sixty days after such rejection. If an interim appointment to the court of appeals be made from among the justices of the supreme court or the appellate divisions thereof, that appointment shall not affect the justice's existing office, nor create a vacancy in the supreme court, or the appellate division thereof, unless such appointment is confirmed by the senate and the appointee shall assume such office. If an interim appointment of chief judge of the court of appeals be made from among the associate judges, an interim appointment of associate judge shall be made in like manner; in such case, the appointment as chief judge shall not affect the existing office of associate judge, unless such appointment as chief judge is confirmed by the senate and the appointee shall assume such office.

(g) The provisions of subdivisions c, d, e, and f of this section shall not apply to temporary designations or assignments of judges or justices. [Const. 1846, Art. VI, sec. 2, 13 as amend. in 1869; amend. and renumbered Art. VI, sec. 7, 8, Const. 1894; amend. 1899; amend. and renumbered Art. VI, sec. 5, 1925; amend. (sec. revised) and renumbered Art. VI, sec. 2, 1961; amend. 1977]

Established in 1846, the court of appeals has become a great common law court, sitting at the apex of the judicial system. It consists of a chief judge and six associate judges. This section changed the mode of selection of these judges from election, which was deemed inappropriate and demeaning for judges, to selection by the governor from candidates recommended by a commission of judicial nominations. All appointments must be approved by the state senate. To be eligible for appointment, candidates must have been admitted to the state bar for at least ten years. This provision was added to ensure experience and familiarity with New York and its law. Successful candidates serve for a term of fourteen years.

The commission itself consists of twelve members serving four-year staggered terms. Four are appointed by the governor, four by the chief judge of the court of appeals, and one each by the temporary president of the senate, the speaker of the assembly, and the two legislative minority leaders. The section ensures bipartisan membership. All members must be residents of the state. This elaborate distribution of appointment power was meant to prevent any one branch of the government from dominating the commission, to prevent it from becoming partisan, and to ensure public confidence in its independence and impartiality.

In order to avoid the necessity of adjournment when temporary absences prevent a quorum (five members), subdivision (a) allows the court to designate a supreme court justice to serve as an associate judge during the absence. Subdivision (b) permits the governor, upon certification from the court of appeals that it is unable to accommodate its work load, to appoint up to four additional justices of the supreme court to sit on the court of appeals. The procedures for operation of the commission are spelled out in (c) and the state judiciary law.

SECTION 3

Jurisdiction of court of appeals. (a) The jurisdiction of the court of appeals shall be limited to the review of questions of law except where the judgment is of death, or where the appellate division, on reversing or modifying a final or interlocutory judgment in an action or a final or interlocutory order in a special proceeding, finds new facts and a final judgment or a final order pursuant thereto is entered; but the right to appeal shall not depend upon the amount involved.

(b) Appeals to the court of appeals may be taken in the classes of cases hereafter enumerated in this section:

In criminal cases, directly from a court of original jurisdiction where the judgment is of death, and in other criminal cases from an appellate division or otherwise as the legislature may from time to time provide.

In civil cases and proceedings as follows:

(1) As of right, from a judgment or order entered upon the decision of an appellate division of the supreme court which finally determines an action or special proceeding wherein is directly involved the construction of the constitution of the state or of the United States, or where one or more of the justices of the appellate division dissents from the decision of the court, or where the judgment or order is one of reversal or modification.

(2) As of right, from a judgment or order of a court of record of original jurisdiction which finally determines an action or special proceeding where the only question involved on the appeal is the validity of a statutory provision of the state or of the United States under the constitution of the state or of the United States; and on any such appeal only the constitutional question shall be considered and determined by the court.

(3) As of right, from an order of the appellate division granting a new trial in an action or a new hearing in a special proceeding where the appellant stipulates that, upon affirmance, judgment absolute or final order shall be rendered against him.

(4) From a determination of the appellate division of the supreme court in any department, other than a judgment or order which finally determines an action or special proceeding, where the appellate division allows the same and certifies that one or more questions of law have arisen which, in its opinion, ought to be reviewed by the court of appeals, but in such case the appeal shall bring up for review only the question or questions so certified;

and the court of appeals shall certify to the appellate division its determination upon such question or questions.

(5) From an order of the appellate division of the supreme court in any department, in a proceeding instituted by or against one or more public officers or a board, commission or other body of public officers or a court or tribunal, other than an order which finally determines such proceeding, where the court of appeals shall allow the same upon the ground that, in its opinion, a question of law is involved which ought to be reviewed by it, and without regard to the availability of appeal by stipulation for final order absolute.

(6) From a judgment or order entered upon the decision of an appellate division of the supreme court which finally determines an action or special proceeding but which is not appealable under paragraph (1) of this subdivision where the appellate division or the court of appeals shall certify that in its opinion a question of law is involved which ought to be reviewed by the court of appeals. Such an appeal may be allowed upon application (a) to the appellate division, and in case of refusal, to the court of appeals, or (b) directly to the court of appeals. Such an appeal shall be allowed when required in the interest of substantial justice.

(7) No appeal shall be taken to the court of appeals from a judgment or order entered upon the decision of an appellate division of the supreme court in any civil case or proceeding where the appeal to the appellate division was from a judgment or order entered in an appeal from another court, including an appellate or special term of the supreme court, unless the construction of the constitution of the state or of the Untied States is directly involved therein, or unless the appellate division of the supreme court shall certify that in its opinion a question of law is involved which ought to be reviewed by the court of appeals.

(8) The legislature may abolish an appeal to the court of appeals as of right in any or all of the cases or classes of cases specified in paragraph (1) of this subdivision wherein no question involving the construction of the constitution of the state or of the United States is directly involved, provided, however, that appeals in any such case or class of cases shall thereupon be governed by paragraph (6) of this subdivision.

(9) The court of appeals shall adopt and from time to time may amend a rule to permit the court to answer questions of New York law certified to it by the Supreme Court of the United States, a court of appeals of the United States or an appellate court of last resort of another state, which may be determinative of the cause then pending in the certifying court and which in the opinion of the certifying court are not controlled by precedent in the decisions of the courts of New York.

[Const. 1894, Art. VI, sec. 9; amend. and renumbered Art. VI, sec. 7, 1925; amend. 1943, 1951; amend. (sec. revised) and renumbered Art. VI, sec. 3, 1961; amend. 1985)

This section delineates the appellate jurisdiction of the court of appeals. That court has no original jurisdiction except to hear matters coming from the commission on judicial conduct (sec. 22) and reviews only questions of law with two exceptions: on appeal from a criminal judgment imposing the death penalty and on an appeal from the appellate division, which has reversed or modified a judgment finding new fact or directing that a final judgment be entered on those facts. The reason for this first exception is that death penalty cases bypass the appellate division and go directly to the court of appeals. New York's policy of providing at least one review of the facts explains both situations. A finding of new facts means that appellate review of those facts has not taken place.[2] The distinction between law and fact is not always clear. The court will review a finding of fact when those facts as a matter of law are unsupportable or incredible (People v. Gruttola, 1977). The legislature has allowed review of the law or "upon the law and such facts which *but for* the determination of law would not have led to reversal or modification."[3] The *but for* phrase keeps the statute within the constitutional requirement that the court review only issues of law. Generally disposition must be final before an appeal to the court can be taken. With the exception of a criminal case involving the death penalty, criminal appeals require the permission of an appellate division justice or a judge of the court of appeals. All other criminal appeals are granted as a result of statutory provision.

In contrast, appeal as a matter of right in civil cases exists in a number of instances, though the legislature has limited those appeals to matters involving a substantial right. In the recent past, more than 70 percent of the cases decided by the court were appeals as a matter of right.[4] Appeals exist as a matter of right from the appellate division if a substantial constitutional question is involved ((b)(1)), from a court of original jurisdiction when the only question is the validity of a statutory provision of the state or the United States is challenged under the state or national constitution ((b)(2)), or on the basis of a dissent on a question of law in favor of the party taking the appeal ((b)(1)). There is no appeal from a unanimous appellate division unless a constitutional question is involved (Pendleton v. New York State Department of Correctional Services, 1987). Appeal as a right lies when the appellate division reverses or modifies an order from one of the other superior courts in the state ((a), (b)(1)). The legislature, under the authority granted in (b)(8), no longer permits review as a matter of right unless two dissents exist at the appellate level, and it has eliminated appeal as a matter of right when the appellate division reverses or modifies a decision of a superior court of original jurisdiction.[5] Finally, appeal as a right exists when the appellate division grants a new trial or hearing where the appellant stipulates that upon affirmance, judgment absolute shall be entered against him or her ((b)(3)). If plaintiff appeals the appellate division's grant of a new trial to defendant and the court of appeals finds the judgment of a new trial was correct, there will be no new trial; instead a final judgment dismisses the plaintiff's action. This procedure, rarely used, has been called a vindictive provision that tells the appellant that he or she "imposes on the court of appeals at his peril."[6]

Appeals as a matter of permission from the appellate division lie with regard to certain nonfinal actions ((b)(4)) and by permission of the court of appeals with regard to certain nonfinal determinations, without stipulation for final order, in proceedings instituted by or against a public body or officer ((b)(5)).

An appellant shall be allowed by permission of either the court of appeals or the appellate division in an action arising from a court of original jurisdiction, administrative agency, or appellate division "when required in the interests of substantial justice" ((b)(6)). This subdivision allows the court discretion to review cases where review might otherwise not be available and when the court believes it necessary to achieve justice. For example, the court will review technically unpreserved law questions involving fundamental constitutional error or the right to counsel (People v. Jones, 1981).

Subdivision (b)(7) denies review powers to the court of appeals of any civil case that has been reviewed by the appellate division unless a constitutional question is involved or the appellate division grants permission. This general denial of review power beyond those stipulated aimed at preventing an overload of cases at the court of appeals.

When reviewing issues involving state and federal constitutional questions, the court of appeals is not bound by the interpretation of the U.S. Supreme Court if adequate and independent state grounds exists for its decision. For example, if the U.S. Supreme Court decides that the First Amendment to the national Constitution does not give protesters the right to free speech in privately owned shopping malls, the court of appeals is free to interpret its free speech clause (Art. I, sec. 8) to guarantee that right as a matter of state constitutional law. Conversely if the Supreme Court were to decide that the First Amendment does guarantee protesters the right to exercise free speech in these shopping malls, the court of appeals, though bound to follow that decision and allow those protests, can nevertheless interpret its free speech clause as not providing that protection. In the first situation, the result would be an expansion of right's protection in New York State; in the latter situation, the reading of the state clause would have only potential impact depending on what the Supreme Court did in the future with the particular case in question (People ex rel. Arcara v. Cloud Books, 1986).

Subdivision (b)(8) allows the legislature to limit appeals as a matter of right in the cases specified in (b)(1) where no question of constitutionality is involved, and the legislature has done that, providing the court with the opportunity to take fewer appeals as a matter of right, enabling it to exercise more discretionary power in deciding what cases to hear. These appeals as a matter of right can be abolished only if appeal by permission is substituted in their place ((b)(6)).

Subdivision (b)(9) allows the court of appeals to answer questions of New York law certified to it from federal courts or courts of last resort from other states when the outcome turns on the meaning of state law and when no controlling precedent exists. It was adopted to eliminate the need for other courts to guess what New York law is and to save time and resources. The certification procedure is an example of cooperative federalism. Federal courts are not forced to choose between giving their interpretation of state law or remitting the case to a state tribunal, requiring litigants to start another lawsuit.

SECTION 4

Judicial departments; appellate divisions of supreme court and justices thereof; temporary designation of additional justices; transfer of appeals; jurisdiction. (a) The state shall be divided into four judicial departments. The first department shall consist of the counties within the first judicial district of the state. The second department shall consist of the counties within the second, ninth, tenth and eleventh judicial districts of the state. The third department shall consist of the counties within the third, fourth, and sixth judicial districts of the state. The fourth department shall consist of the counties within the fifth, seventh, and eighth judicial districts of the state. Each department shall be bounded by the lines of judicial districts. Once every ten years the legislature may alter the boundaries of the judicial departments, but without changing the number thereof.

(b) The appellate divisions of the supreme court are continued, and shall consist of seven justices of the supreme court in each of the first and second departments, and five justices in each of the other departments. In each appellate division, four justices shall constitute a quorum, and the concurrence of three shall be necessary to a decision. No more than five justices shall sit in any case.

(c) The governor shall designate the presiding justice of each appellate division, who shall act as such during his terms of office and shall be a resident of the department. The other justices of the appellate divisions shall be designated by the governor, from all the justices elected to the supreme court, for terms of five years or the unexpired portions of their respective terms of office, if less than five years.

(d) The justices heretofore designated shall continue to sit in the appellate divisions until the terms of their respective designations shall expire. From time to time as the terms of the designations expire, or vacancies occur, the governor shall make new designations. He may also, on request of any appellate division, make temporary designations in case of the absence or inability to act of any justice in such appellate division, for service only during such absence or inability to act.

(e) In case any appellate division shall certify to the governor that one or more additional justices are needed for the speedy disposition of the business before it, the governor may designate an additional justice or additional justices; but when the need for such additional justice or justices shall no longer exist, the appellate division shall so certify to the governor, and thereupon service under such designation or designations shall cease.

(f) A majority of the justices designated to sit in any appellate division shall at all times be residents of the department.

(g) Whenever the appellate division in any department shall be unable to dispose of its business within a reasonable time, a majority of the presiding justices of the several departments, at a meeting called by the presiding justice of the department in arrears, may transfer any pending appeals from such department to any other department from hearing and determination.

(h) A justice of the appellate division of the supreme court in any department may be temporarily designated by the presiding justice of his department to the appellate division in another judicial department upon agreement by the presiding justices of the appellate division of the departments concerned.

(i) In the event that the disqualification, absence or inability to act of justices in any appellate division prevents there being a quorum of justices qualified to hear an appeal, the justices qualified to hear the appeal may transfer it to the appellate division in another department for hearing and determination. In the event that the justices in any appellate division qualified to hear an appeal are equally divided, said justices may transfer the appeal to the appellate division in another department for hearing and determination. Each appellate division shall have power to appoint and remove its clerk.

(j) No justice of the appellate division shall, within the department to which he may be designated to perform the duties of an appellate justice, exercise any of the powers of a justice of the supreme court, other than those of a justice out of court, and those pertaining to the appellate division, except that he may decide causes or proceedings theretofore submitted, or hear and decide motions submitted by consent of counsel, but any such justice, when not actually engaged in performing the duties of such appellate justice in the department to which he is designated, may hold any term of the supreme court and exercise any of the powers of a justice of the supreme court in any judicial district in any other department of the state.

(k) The appellate divisions of the supreme court shall have all the jurisdiction possessed by them on the effective date of this article and such additional jurisdiction as may be prescribed by law, provided, however, that the right to appeal to the appellate division from a judgment or order which does not finally determine an action or special proceeding may be limited or conditioned by law. [Const. 1846, Art. VI, sec. 6 as amend. in 1869; amend. and renumbered Art. VI, sec. 2, 1894; 1925; amend. and renumbered Art. VI, sec. 4, 1961 (sec. revised); amend. 1977]

The principal intermediate appellate court in New York is the appellate division of the supreme court. There are four departments, which correspond to four geographic regions of the state. Their primary purpose is to sift appeals to the court of appeals, supervise local courts, and promote substantial justice. They possess all of the powers and general jurisdiction of the supreme court except where limited by law. They have the power to review both the law and the facts in civil and criminal matters. They are the final arbiters of the fact except where they make new findings of fact, in which case such findings are subject to court of appeals review. For all practical purposes, they are the court of last resort; 90 percent of the cases they hear are not reviewed.

The appellate division is a division of the supreme court, the trial courts of general and original jurisdiction. Members are chosen by the governor from among supreme court justices for terms of five years. The governor is also given power to fill vacancies and, on request, make temporary assignments and designate additional justices when work loads become too onerous. Four departments are fixed by the constitution, but every ten years, the legislature is permitted to adjust the boundaries to meet changing demographic patterns and judicial loads. From five to seven justices are assigned in each department, though only five can sit on a case, with four necessary to a quorum and three concurrences for a decision.

Sections (g–i) provide flexibility to meet needs in whatever divisions or departments they may arise. A majority of the justices must be residents of their respective departments, but nonresident justices can be assigned. Doing so adds a further element of impartiality, especially in cases involving strong local prejudice.[7]

Subdivision (j) reserves justices' time for appellate work by preventing them from holding any court other than that which they were specially assigned. They are permitted to exercise powers that any unassigned justice of the supreme court can exercise out of court, such as appointments of special juror commissioners.

The section allows the legislature to prescribe additional jurisdiction to the appellate division beyond that granted them at the time this provision was adopted, but it cannot impose limitations or conditions on that jurisdiction except as noted in subdivision (k). An attempt by the state to disallow an appeal to the appellate division when the sole issue was the excessiveness of a negotiated sentence imposed by the court on acceptance of a guilty plea was such a limitation in violation of this section (People v. Pollenz, 1986).

SECTION 5

Power of appellate courts upon appeal from judgment or order; transfer of appeals taken to improper appellate court. (a) Upon an appeal from a judgment or an order, any appellate court to which the appeal is taken which is authorized to review such judgment or order may reverse or affirm, wholly or in part, or may modify the judgment or order appealed from, and each interlocutory judgment or intermediate or any other order which it is authorized to review, and as to any or all of the parties. It shall thereupon render judgment of affirmance, judgment of reversal and final judgment upon the right of any or all of the parties, or judgment of modification thereon according to law, except where it may be necessary or proper to grant a new trial or hearing, when it may grant a new trial or hearing.

(b) If any appeal is taken to an appellate court which is not authorized to review such judgment or order, the court shall transfer the appeal to an appellate court which is authorized to review such judgment or order. [Const. 1894, Art. VI, sec. 8 as added in 1925; amend. (sec. revised) and renumbered Art. VI, sec. 5, 1961]

This section spells out the actions an appellate court may take with regard to the disposition of an appeal on the merits of the case. The authority of the appellate division is that of a trial court; that is, it can review both the law and the facts. This reviewing power is not limited to cases where the trial judgment is clearly erroneous. In cases that cannot be tried by a jury as a matter of right, the appellate division may make new findings and render judgment on those findings (Jacques v. Sears & Roebuck, 1972; Bernadine v. City of New York, 1945).

SECTION 6

Judicial districts, number and composition; supreme court, continuation and composition; election and terms of justices. a. The state shall be divided into eleven judicial districts. The first judicial district shall consist of the counties of Bronx and New York. The second judicial district shall consist of the counties of Kings and Richmond. The third judicial district shall consist of the counties of Albany, Columbia, Greene, Rensselaer, Schoharie, Sullivan, and Ulster. The fourth judicial district shall consist of the counties of Clinton, Essex, Franklin, Hamilton, Montgomery, St. Lawrence, Saratoga, Schenectady, Warren and Washington. The fifth judicial district shall consist of the counties of Herkimer, Jefferson, Lewis, Oneida, Onondaga, and Oswego. The sixth judicial district shall consist of the counties of Broome, Chemung, Chenango, Corland, Delaware, Madison, Otsego, Schuyler, Tioga and Tompkins. The seventh judicial district shall consist of the counties of Cayuga, Livingston, Monroe, Ontario, Seneca, Steuben, Wayne and Yates. The eighth judicial district shall consist of the counties of Allegany, Cattaraugus, Chautauqua, Erie, Genesee, Niagara, Orleans, and Wyoming. The ninth judicial district shall consist of the counties of Dutchess, Orange, Putnam, Rockland, and Westchester. The tenth judicial district shall consist of the counties of Nassau and Suffolk. The eleventh judicial district shall consist of the county of Queens.

b. Once every ten years the legislature may increase or decrease the number of judicial districts or alter the composition of judicial districts and thereupon re-apportion the justices to be thereafter elected in the judicial districts so altered. Each judicial district shall be bounded by county lines.

c. The justices of the supreme court shall be chosen by the electors of the judicial district in which they are to serve. The terms of the justices of the supreme court shall be fourteen years from and including the first day of January next after their election.

d. The supreme court is continued. It shall consist of the number of justices of the supreme court including the justices designated to the appellate divisions of the supreme court, judges of the county court of the counties of Bronx, Kings, Queens and Richmond and judges of the court of general sessions of the county of New York authorized by law on the thirty-first day of August next after the approval and ratification of this amendment by the people, all of whom shall be justices of the supreme court for the remainder of their terms. The legislature may increase the number of justices of the supreme court in any judicial district, except that the number in any district shall not be increased to exceed one justice for fifty thousand, or fraction over thirty thousand, of the population thereof as shown by the last federal census or state enumeration. The legislature may decrease the number of justices of the supreme court in any judicial district, except that the number in any district shall not be less than the number of justices of the supreme court authorized by law on the effective date of this article.

e. The clerks of the several counties shall be clerks of the supreme court, with such powers and duties as shall be prescribed by law. [Const. 1846, Art. VI, sec. 3; amend. and renumbered Art. VI, sec. 1, 4, Const. 1894; amend. 1905; amend. (sec. revised) and renumbered Art. VI, sec. 6, 1961]

The supreme court, as now understood, was established in 1846. The heart of the judicial system, it is a court of statewide jurisdiction with a branch in each county and the power to serve process anywhere in the state. The name *supreme court* is misleading—the court of appeals is the highest court in the state—but it is the only court of general jurisdiction, meaning that it has just about all the jurisdiction the state can confer. The only limitations are those actions for which exclusive jurisdiction has been conferred by the U.S. Congress on federal courts and actions against the state for which exclusive jurisdiction has been conferred on the court of claims. The pivotal position of these courts is underscored by the fact that the intermediate appellate courts in New York are appellate divisions of the supreme court, whose members are drawn from supreme court justices.

There are, at present, twelve judicial districts even though this section speaks of eleven because the legislature has exercised its authority under subdivision (b) to increase the number of districts. Supreme court justices are elected by the voters in the judicial districts in which they serve. Candidates are nominated by judicial district conventions held by each political party. Supreme court members must have been members of the bar for at least ten years, and they serve for terms of fourteen years. The legislature is empowered to increase or decrease the number of justices in any judicial district using the formula set forth in subdivision (d).

SECTION 7

Jurisdiction of supreme court; new classes of action. (a) The supreme court shall have general original jurisdiction in law and equity and the appellate jurisdiction herein provided. In the city of New York, it shall have exclusive jurisdiction over crimes prosecuted by indictment, provided, however, that the legislature may grant to the city-wide court of criminal jurisdiction of the city of New York jurisdiction over misdemeanors prosecuted by indictment and to the family court in the city of New York jurisdiction over crimes and offenses by or against minors or between spouses or between parent and child or between members of the same family or household.

(b) If the legislature shall create new classes of actions and proceedings, the supreme court shall have jurisdiction over such classes of actions and proceedings, but the legislature may provide that another court or other courts shall also have jurisdiction and that actions and proceedings of such classes may be originated in such other court or courts. [1961; amend. 1977]

Section 7 gives the supreme court jurisdiction in law and equity, and that jurisdiction cannot be limited by the legislature (Matter of Realty Corp. v. Weinberger, 1963). The court is presumed to have jurisdiction unless the contrary plainly appears (Jones v. McNeill, 1966).

Its power has been described as "original, unlimited and unqualified" (Kagen v. Kagen, 1968). Subdivision (b) explicitly provided for the exercise of concurrent jurisdiction in cases where the legislature establishes a new class of action and specifies the court in which the action may originate. That action does not have the effect of depriving the supreme court of jurisdiction. In the face of a legislative grant of "exclusive original jurisdiction over support proceedings to family court," the court held that sections 13(d) and 7(b) grant the supreme court concurrent jurisdiction in such matters. Legislation which affects the jurisdiction of the Supreme Court is not necessarily void. Under section 30 of this article the legislature is given the power to alter and regulate the jurisdiction and proceedings in law and equity of that court. Under such authority the legislature may grant jurisdiction to other tribunals to abolish or change common law causes of action or substitute new remedies (Loretto v. Teleprompter Manhattan CATV Corp., 1983; Montgomery v. Daniels, 1975). In Motor Vehicle MFRS. v. State (1990) the court of appeals upheld provisions of the so-called "lemon law" which limits Supreme Court's jurisdiction to reviewing when a consumer elected compulsory arbitration in the first place. Since the statute allows a consumer to litigate the claim in court and allows either party to seek review of arbitration proceedings, the Supreme Court's jurisdiction is not unconstitutionally diminished.

SECTION 8

Appellate terms of supreme court; composition and jurisdiction. a. The appellate division of the supreme court in each judicial department may establish an appellate term in and for such department or in and for a judicial district or districts or in and for a county or counties within such department.

Such an appellate term shall be composed of not less than three nor more than five justices of the supreme court who shall be designated from time to time by the chief administrator of the courts with the approval of the presiding justice of the appropriate appellate division, and who shall be residents of the department or of the judicial district or districts as the case may be and the chief administrator of the courts shall designate the place or places where such appellate terms shall be held.

b. Any such appellate term may be discontinued and re-established as the appellate division of the supreme court in each department shall determine from time to time and any designation to service therein may be revoked by the chief administrator of the courts with the approval of the presiding justice of the appropriate appellate division.

c. In each appellate term no more than three justices assigned thereto shall sit in any action or proceeding. Two of such justices shall constitute a quorum and the concurrence of two shall be necessary to a decision.

d. If so directed by the appellate division of the supreme court establishing an appellate term, an appellate term shall have jurisdiction to hear and determine appeals now or hereafter authorized by law to be taken to the supreme court or to the appellate division other than appeals from the supreme court, a surrogate's court, the family court or appeals in criminal cases prosecuted by indictment or by information as provided by section six of article one.

e. As may be provided by law, an appellate term shall have jurisdiction to hear and determine appeals from the district court or a town, village or city court outside the city of New York. [Const. 1894, Art. VI, sec. 3 as added, in 1925; amend. and renumbered Art. VI, sec. 8, 1961; amend. (sec. revised) 1977]

The constitution authorizes the appellate division in each judicial department to establish an appellate term for that department or part of that department. An appellate term consists of three to five justices of the supreme court. Two justices constitute a quorum, and two concurrences are necessary for a decision. The chief administrator of the courts, in consultation with the presiding judge of the appellate division, can discontinue or reestablish these terms as the circumstances warrant. The appellate term exercises jurisdiction over civil and criminal appeals from local courts and certain appeals from county courts. Appeals from the appellate term go to the appellate division.

The appellate term was created to ease the volume of cases coming directly to the appellate division and to provide a less expensive forum closer to the people than the appellate division. With only four departments throughout the entire state, taking an appeal to the division could be more costly than the case is worth. Now only the First and Second departments have established an appellate term. These departments are located in the downstate area, which includes New York City and Long Island, the most heavily populated areas of the state.

SECTION 9

Court of claims; composition; appointment of judges; jurisdiction. The court of claims is continued. It shall consist of the eight judges now authorized by law, but the legislature may increase such number and may reduce such number to six or seven. The judges shall be appointed by the governor by and with the advice and consent of the senate and their terms of office shall be nine years. The court shall have jurisdiction to hear and determine claims against the state or by the state against the claimant or between conflicting claimants as the legislature may provide. [1949; amend. (sec. revised) and renumbered Art. VI, sec. 9, 1961]

The court of claims has exclusive jurisdiction to adjudicate private claims against the state and claims against certain agencies of the state. It came into existence because a state as a sovereign entity cannot be sued without its permission. From 1777 to 1897, New York State did not permit claims for damages in any court. Redress for such grievances during that period had to be taken to the legislature. From 1897, a court of claims existed by statutory authority. This section constitutionalized that court. The governor appoints its members with the consent of the senate. Appointees must have been members of the state bar for at least ten years, and they serve for terms of nine years. The court is made up of a minimum of six judges, but the legislature may increase that number. At present, seventeen judges sit on the court. Its jurisdiction is determined by statute.

Various commissions have recommended that this court be abolished and its functions merged with the supreme court,[8] arguing that its separate existence created jurisdictional difficulties and since the state has almost completely waived sovereign immunity, such a court was no longer necessary. Nevertheless, when the 1961 reorganization took place, the court was retained. Appeals from this court go to the appellate division in which the claim arose.

SECTION 10

County court; judges; terms of office. The county court is continued in each county outside the city of New York. There shall be at least one judge of the county court in each county and such number of additional judges in each county as may be provided by law. The judges shall be residents of the county and shall be chosen by the electors of the county.

The terms of the judges of the county court shall be ten years from and including the first day of January next after their election. [Const. 1846, Art. VI, sec. 14, as amend. in 1869; and renumbered Art. VI, sec. 11, 1925; amend. (sec. revised) and renumbered Art. VI, sec. 10, 1961]

SECTION 11

County court; jurisdiction. a. The county court shall have jurisdiction over the following classes of actions and proceedings which shall be originated in such county court in the manner provided by law, except that actions and proceedings within the jurisdiction of the district court or a town, village or city court outside the city of New York may, as provided by law, be originated therein: actions and proceedings for the recovery of money, actions and proceedings for the recovery of chattels and actions and proceedings for the foreclosure of mechanics liens and liens on personal property where the amount sought to be recovered or the value of the property does not exceed twenty-five thousand dollars exclusive of interest and costs; over all crimes and other violations of law; over summary proceedings to recover possession of real property and to remove tenants therefrom; and over such other actions and proceedings, not within the exclusive jurisdiction of the supreme court, as may be provided by law.

b. The county court shall exercise such equity jurisdiction as may be provided by law and its jurisdiction to enter judgment upon a counterclaim for the recovery of money only shall be unlimited.

c. The county court shall have jurisdiction to hear and determine all appeals arising in the county in the following actions and proceedings: as of right, from a judgment or order of the district court or a town, village or city court which finally determines an action or proceeding and, as may be provided by law, from a judgment or order of any such court which does not finally determine an action or proceeding. The legislature may provide, in accordance with the provisions of section eight of this article, that any and all of such appeals be taken to an appellate term of the supreme court instead of the county court.

d. The provisions of this section shall in no way limit or impair the jurisdiction of the supreme court as set forth in section seven of this article. [1961; amend. 1983]

Although part of the statewide court system, county courts, unlike supreme courts, are treated as distinct to each county. Every county outside New York City has a county court, with each county designated a district of the state court system. Justices of these courts are elected on a county-wide basis and must be residents of the county in which they serve. These requirements ensure a strong local orientation.

Section 11 gives the county courts unlimited criminal jurisdiction, but their civil jurisdiction is limited to claims of no more than $25,000. Subdivision (b) allows these courts to entertain counterclaims without limit as to the amount and authorizes the legislature to confer additional equity jurisdiction on the court. County courts in the Third and Fourth departments have limited appellate jurisdiction to hear cases from justice and city courts. In general, county courts handle cases over which the supreme court does not exercise its jurisdiction, so the actual cases handled by these courts may vary from county to county. Subdivision (d) makes clear that the jurisdiction granted to county courts in no way derogates from that of the supreme court.

SECTION 12

Surrogate's court; composition; term of office; jurisdiction. a. The surrogate's court is continued in each county in the state. There shall be at least one judge of the surrogate's court in each county and such number of additional judges of the surrogate's court as may be provided by law.

b. The judges of the surrogate's court shall be residents of the county and shall be chosen by the electors of the county.

c. The terms of the judges of the surrogate's court in the city of New York shall be fourteen years, and in other counties ten years, from and including the first day of January next after their election.

d. The surrogate's court shall have jurisdiction over all actions and proceedings relating to the affairs of decedents, probate of wills, administration of estates and actions and proceedings arising thereunder or pertaining thereto, guardianship of the property of minors, and such other actions and proceedings, not within the exclusive jurisdiction of the supreme court, as may be provided by law.

e. The surrogate's court shall exercise such equity jurisdiction as may be provided by law.

f. The provisions of this section shall in no way limit or impair the jurisdiction of the supreme court as set forth in section seven of this article. [Const. 1894, Art. VI, sec. 15; renumbered Art. VI, sec. 13, 1925; amend. (sec. revised) and renumbered Art. IV, sec. 12, 1961]

Surrogate's court can be traced back to colonial times. During the colonial period, the governor took on the responsibility of granting letters to probate wills. In carrying out this responsibility, he was authorized to appoint a delegate to act in his place—as one of these delegates called himself, a surrogate.

The court exists in every county and has jurisdiction over all actions relating to the affairs of decedents, probate of wills, administration of estates, guardianship of minors, and other actions and proceedings not within the exclusive jurisdiction of the supreme court. The supreme court exercises concurrent jurisdiction with the surrogate's court in matters involving decedents' estates (Dunham v. Dunham, 1972). In sustaining a surrogate court's opinion in an eviction proceeding affecting an estate before it, the court of appeals gave an expansive reading of this court's powers under subdivision (d) (Matter of Piccione, 1982).

Unlike the supreme court, it is a court of limited original jurisdiction. There is some authority for the view that the legislature can enlarge but not restrict the court's jurisdiction (In re Estate of Fornason, 1976).

Surrogate judges must be residents of the county in which they serve and are elected by the voters of the county to serve for terms of fourteen years within the five county areas of New York City and for ten years in the counties outside of the city.

In spite of recommendations to abolish this court and make it a division of the supreme court, the reorganization amendment in 1961 continued its existence, chiefly because of the special skills and knowledge possessed by surrogates and their courts.[9]

SECTION 13

Family court established; composition; election and appointment of judges; jurisdiction. a. The family court of the state of New York is hereby established. It shall consist of at least one judge in each county outside the city of New York and such number of additional judges for such counties as may be provided by law. Within the city of New York it shall consist of such number of judges as may be provided by law. The judges of the family court within the city of New York shall be residents of such city and shall be appointed by the mayor of the city of New York for terms of ten years. The judges of the family court outside the city of New York, shall be chosen by the electors of the counties wherein they reside for terms of ten years.

b. The family court shall have jurisdiction over the following classes of actions and proceedings which shall be originated in such family court in the manner provided by law: (1) the protection, treatment, correction and commitment of those minors who are in need of the exercise of the authority of the court because of circumstances of neglect, delinquency or dependency, as the legislature may determine; (2) the custody of minors except for custody incidental to actions and proceedings for marital separation, divorce, annulment of marriage and dissolution of marriage; (3) the adoption of persons; (4) the support of dependents except for support incidental to actions and proceedings in this state for marital separation, divorce, annulment of marriage or dissolution of marriage; (5) the establishment of paternity; (6) proceedings for conciliation of spouses; and (7) as may be provided by law: the guardianship of the person of minors and, in conformity with the provisions of section seven of this article, crimes and offenses by or against minors or between spouses or between parent and child or between members of the same family or household. Nothing in this section shall be construed to abridge the authority or jurisdiction of courts to appoint guardians in cases originating in those courts.

c. The family court shall also have jurisdiction to determine, with the same powers possessed by the supreme court, the following matters when referred to the family court from the supreme court: habeas corpus proceedings for the determination of the custody of minors; and in actions and proceedings for marital separation, divorce, annulment of marriage and dissolution of marriage, applications to fix temporary or permanent support and custody, or applications to enforce judgments and orders of support and of custody which may be granted only upon the showing to the family court that there has been a subsequent change of circumstances and that modification is required.

d. The provisions of this section shall in no way limit or impair the jurisdiction of the supreme court as set forth in section seven of this article. [1961]

The establishment of a statewide family court to replace the domestic relations and children's courts was considered at the time one of the major achievements of the 1961 amendment reorganizing the judiciary. It was maintained as a separate court in spite of recommendations for its merger with the supreme court because of the special character of family problems and the strong support of legal and social agencies.[10] The court's jurisdiction is limited to certain well-defined classes of action and proceedings to be brought pursuant to Article 6 of the Family Court Act. Seven areas of jurisdiction or responsibility are specified in subdivision (b). The jurisdiction is divided between matters that originate in that court and those that are transferred to it from the supreme court. In spite of its name, the supreme court, and not the family court, has jurisdiction over matrimonial actions such as divorce, annulment, and separation, though the family court can entertain actions referred to it by the supreme court, such as habeas corpus proceedings for determining the custody of minors and actions connected with custody and support of minors (subdivision c).

In New York City, the judges are appointed by the mayor for ten-year terms; in all other counties, they are elected on a county-wide basis for ten-year terms.

The court was intended to remove from criminal court a limited class of offenses arising from family conflicts. The assumption was that complex problems of family life would be better handled, at least initially, in a noncriminal context. For this reason, it is generally regarded as a civil court. In recent years, concern over abuse of spouses and children has resulted in a change in the relationship of family to criminal courts. Previously matters would go to family court for decision as to whether the matter might be better handled in criminal court. Recent amendments to the Family Court Act allow the victim of that abuse to choose whether the action will be initiated in family or criminal court.[11]

SECTION 14

Discharge of duties of county judge, surrogate or judge of family court by single person outside New York City. The legislature may at any time provide that outside the city of New York the same person may act and discharge the duties of county judge and surrogate or of judge of the family court and surrogate, or of county judge and judge of the family court, or of all three positions in any county. [Const. 1894, Art. IV, sec. 14 as added in 1925; amend. and renumbered Art. VI, sec. 14, 1938; amend. (sec. revised) 1961]

This provision authorizes the legislature to provide that the same individual may hold two or all three positions of county, surrogate, and family court judge at the same time. It was adopted so that the more sparsely populated counties with small caseloads would not have to support two or three judges when one or two would suffice. There are many ''two-hat'' or ''three-hat'' judges in upstate counties.

SECTION 15

Civil and criminal courts in New York City; merger into single court; judges, election and term of office, jurisdiction. a. The legislature shall by law establish a single court of city-wide civil jurisdiction and a single court of city-wide criminal jurisdiction in and for the city of New York and the legislature may, upon the request of the mayor and the local legislative body of the city of New York, merge the two courts into one city-wide court of both civil and criminal jurisdiction. The said city-wide courts shall consist of such number of judges as may be provided by law. The judges of the court of city-wide jurisdiction shall be residents of such city and shall be chosen for terms of ten years by the electors of the counties included within the city of New York from districts within such counties established by law. The judges of the court of city-wide criminal jurisdiction shall be residents of such city and shall be appointed for terms of ten years by the mayor of the city of New York.

b. The court of city-wide civil jurisdiction of the city of New York shall have jurisdiction over the following classes of actions and proceedings which shall be originated in such court in the manner provided by law: actions and proceedings for the recovery of money, actions and proceedings for the recovery of chattels and actions and proceedings for the foreclosure of mechanics liens and liens on personal property where the amount sought to be recovered or the value of the property does not exceed twenty-five thousand dollars exclusive of interest and costs, or such smaller amount as may be fixed by law; over summary proceedings to recover possession of real property and to remove tenants therefrom and over such other actions and proceedings, not within the exclusive jurisdiction of the supreme court, as may be provided by law. The court of city-wide civil jurisdiction shall further exercise such equity jurisdiction as may be provided by law and its jurisdiction to enter judgment upon a counterclaim for the recovery of money only shall be unlimited.

c. The court of city-wide criminal jurisdiction of the city of New York shall have jurisdiction over crimes and other violations of law, other than those prosecuted by indictment, provided, however, that the legislature may grant to said court jurisdiction over misdemeanors prosecuted by indictment; and over such other actions and proceedings, not within the exclusive jurisdiction of the supreme court, as may be provided by law.

d. The provisions of this section shall in no way limit or impair the jurisdiction of the supreme court as set forth in section seven of this article.

[Const. 1894, Art. VI, sec. 14 as added in 1925; amend. and renumbered Art. VI, sec. 15, 1938; amend. (sec. revised) 1961]

This section consolidated a number of courts in New York City into two city-wide courts of civil and criminal jurisdiction. The legislature was given the power to merge these two courts into a single city-wide court at the request of the mayor and the city's legislative body. This provision allows the merger without resort to another constitutional amendment. The provision of special courts in New York City reflects the unique character and problems of that city.

The criminal court has jurisdiction to try misdemeanors and offenses less than misdemeanors, as well as hold preindictment felony hearings. Most of this court's business consists of traffic violations and violations of New York City's administrative code or multiple dwelling law. The judges must be residents of the city and are appointed by the mayor for a term of ten years. The legislature is given power to add additional judges. Appeals from this court go to appellate term.

The civil court has jurisdiction over such actions as contracts, real property actions, actions for personal injury, and actions in equity. Its jurisdiction is limited in monetary actions to a maximum of $25,000. This limitation does not apply to counterclaims. It has a special housing section and a small claims section that handles claims up to $2,000.[12] Judges, unlike those of the civil courts, are elected for terms of ten years from districts established by the legislature. Appeals go the county courts unless an appellate term has been established for such appeals. A challenge to the system on the ground that judges had to be appointed on the basis of the one-man, one-vote principle was rejected on both state and federal constitutional grounds (Cox v. Katz, 1968).

SECTION 16

District courts; establishment; jurisdiction; judges. a. The district court of Nassau county may be continued under existing law and the legislature may, at the request of the board of supervisors or other elective governing body of any county outside the city of New York, establish the district court for the entire area of such county or for a portion of such county consisting of one or more cities, or one or more towns which are contiguous, or of a combination of such cities and such towns provided at least one of such cities is contiguous to one of such towns.

b. No law establishing the district court for an entire county shall become effective unless approved at a general election on the question of the approval of such law by a majority of the votes cast thereon by the electors within the area of any cities in the county considered as one unit and by a majority of the votes cast thereon by the electors within the area outside the cities in the county considered as one unit.

c. No law establishing the district court for a portion of a county shall become effective unless approved at a general election on the question of the approval of such law by a majority of the votes cast thereon by the electors within the area of any cities included in such portion of the county considered as one unit and by a majority of the votes cast thereon by the electors within the area outside of cities included in such portion of the county considered as one unit.

d. The district court shall have such jurisdiction as may be provided by law, but not in any respect greater than the jurisdiction of the courts for the city of New York as provided in section fifteen of this article, provided, however, that in actions and proceedings for the recovery of money, actions and proceedings for the recovery of chattels and actions and proceedings for the foreclosure of mechanics liens and liens on personal property, the amount sought to be recovered or the value of the property shall not exceed fifteen thousand dollars inclusive of interest and costs.

e. The legislature may create districts of the district court which shall consist of an entire county or of an area less than a county.

f. There shall be at least one judge of the district court for each district and such number of additional judges in each district as may be provided by law.

g. The judges of the district court shall be apportioned among the districts as may be provided by law, and to the extent practicable, in accordance with the population and the volume of judicial business.

h. The judges shall be residents of the district and shall be chosen by the electors of the district. Their terms shall be six years from and including the first day of January next after their election.

i. The legislature may regulate and discontinue the district court in any county or portion thereof. [1961; amend. 1983]

Provision for adoption of district courts was made because full-time lawyers and judges were needed in counties with large populations. Counties wishing such courts can request action from the state legislature, but that request, if approved, does not become effective until approved by a concurrent majority in any cities in the county considered as one unit and of the voters in areas outside the cities in the county. A similar procedure is required for district courts established for a portion of the county. Jurisdiction is to be established by the legislature, but in no case can it exceed that for city courts, and monetary damages in civil suits cannot exceed $15,000.

District courts are distinguished from justice courts in that the jurisdiction of the former is substantially greater, terms of office are different (cf. sec. 17), and judges of district courts must be members of the bar. As of 1990, only Nassau and Suffolk counties have established district courts. When adopted, they supersede local justice courts. Judges are elected from the district for terms of six years and must be residents of the districts in which they serve.

SECTION 17

Town, village and city courts; jurisdiction; regulation; judges. a. Courts
for towns, villages and cities outside the city of New York are continued
and shall have the jurisdiction prescribed by the legislature but not in any
respect greater than the jurisdiction of the district court as provided in section
sixteen of this article.

b. The legislature may regulate such courts, establish uniform jurisdiction,
practice and procedure for city courts outside the city of New York and may
discontinue any village or city court outside the city of New York existing
on the effective date of this article. The legislature may discontinue any
town court existing on the effective date of this article only with the approval
of a majority of the total votes cast at a general election on the question of
a proposed discontinuance of the court in each such town affected thereby.

c. The legislature may abolish the legislative functions of town boards of
justices of the peace and provide that town councilmen be elected in their
stead.

d. The number of the judges of each of such town, village and city courts
and the classification and duties of the judges shall be prescribed by the
legislature. The terms, methods of selection and method of filling vacancies
for the judges of such courts shall be prescribed by the legislature, provided,
however, that the justices of town courts shall be chosen by the electors of
the town for terms of four years from and including the first day of January
next after their election. [1961]

Town, village, and city courts outside New York City are provided for in this
section, but almost all matters concerning jurisdiction, number of judges, procedure, terms of office (with the exception of town courts who are elected to
four year terms), and method of election are left to legislative discretion.[13]
Collectively they are called justice courts. They possess nonfelony, criminal
jurisdiction, handling preliminary criminal functions such as setting bail, warrant
issuance, and preliminary hearings to determine probable cause for detention
until grand jury action. Generally these justices are elected and serve four-year
terms. The legislature may discontinue any of these courts, but a discontinuance
of a town court requires approval of the voters of the town at a referendum.
Justices of these courts are not required to be lawyers, but they must take training
courses (sec. 20c).

Recommendations were made by a Judicial Conference and the Temporary
Commission on Court Reform to abolish these courts, but strong opposition from
the approximately 2,500 justices threatened to jeopardize the reorganization
amendment, and they were included in the 1961 amendment submitted to the
people. Towns are prohibited from discontinuing town courts because that authority is vested in the legislature.[14]

The use of nonlawyers on these courts was challenged as a violation of the

Sixth and Fourteenth amendments to the U.S. Constitution. In People v. Skrynski (1977), the court of appeals rejected those challenges, arguing that as long as the defendant in a criminal case has the alternative of a criminal trial before a law-trained judge, no violation takes place.

SECTION 18

Trial by jury; number of jurors; trial of certain criminal cases without jury; claims against state; manner of trial. a. Trial by jury is guaranteed as provided in article one of this constitution. The legislature may provide that in any court of original jurisdiction a jury shall be composed of six or of twelve persons and may authorize any court which shall have jurisdiction over crimes and other violations of law, other than crimes prosecuted by indictment, to try such matters without a jury, provided, however, that crimes prosecuted by indictment shall be tried by a jury composed of twelve persons, unless a jury trial has been waived as provided in section two of article one of this constitution.

b. The legislature may provide for the manner of trial actions and proceedings involving claims against the state. [1961]

This section should be read in conjunction with Article I, section 2 guaranteeing the right to trial by jury. The force of its terms suggests it is primarily concerned with trial by jury in criminal cases. It allows for six-person juries in all prosecutions not undertaken by indictment but requires twelve-person juries for all crimes prosecuted by indictment. This twelve-person jury requirement is more demanding than the six-person minimum allowed under the Sixth Amendment as interpreted in Williams v. Florida (1970). On the other hand, the provision allows for nonjury trials for crimes that could result in imprisonment of more than six months in violation of the Sixth Amendment requirement that jury trials must be granted all defendants who could be imprisoned for six months or more. In Baldwin v. New York (1970), the U.S. Supreme Court struck down a New York provision that denied jury trials to defendants in New York City who, as misdemeanants, were liable for a year's imprisonment. New York had complied with *Baldwin*, but it has not required more. A statute providing for bench trials in New York City but not in other parts of the state for crimes punishable for six months or less was upheld by the court of appeals in Morgenthau v. Erlbaum (1983) and was sustained against an equal protection challenge in People v. Carroll (1987).

SECTION 19

Transfer of actions and proceedings. a. The supreme court may transfer any action or proceeding, except one over which it shall have exclusive jurisdiction which does not depend upon the monetary amount sought, to any other court having jurisdiction of the subject matter within the judicial department provided that such other court has jurisdiction over the classes of persons named as parties. As may be provided by law, the supreme court may transfer to itself any action or proceeding originating or pending in another court within the judicial department other than the court of claims upon a finding that such a transfer will promote the administration of justice.

b. The county court shall transfer to the supreme court or surrogate's court or family court any action or proceeding which has not been transferred to it from the supreme court or surrogate's court or family court and over which the county court has no jurisdiction. The county court may transfer any action or proceeding, except a criminal action or proceeding involving a felony prosecuted by indictment or an action or proceeding required by this article to be dealt with in the surrogate's court or family court, to any court, other than the supreme court, having jurisdiction of the subject matter within the county provided that such other court has jurisdiction over the classes of persons named as parties.

c. As may be provided by law, the supreme court or the county court may transfer to the county court any action or proceeding originated or pending in the district court or a town, village or city court outside the city of New York upon finding that such a transfer will promote the administration of justice.

d. The surrogate's court shall transfer to the supreme court or the county court or the family court or the courts for the city of New York established pursuant to section fifteen of this article any action or proceeding which has not been transferred to it from any of said courts and over which the surrogate's court has no jurisdiction.

e. The family court shall transfer to the supreme court or the surrogate's court or the county court or the courts for the city of New York established pursuant to section fifteen of this article any action or proceeding which has not been transferred to it from any of said courts and over which the family court has no jurisdiction.

f. The courts for the city of New York established pursuant to section fifteen of this article shall transfer to the supreme court or the surrogate's court or the family court any action or proceeding which has not been transferred to them from any of said courts and over which the said courts for the city of New York have no jurisdiction.

g. As may be provided by law, the supreme court shall transfer any action or proceeding to any other court having jurisdiction of the subject matter in any other judicial district or county provided that such other court has jurisdiction over the classes of persons named as parties.

h. As may be provided by law, the county court, the surrogate's court, the family court and the courts for the city of New York established pursuant to section fifteen of this article may transfer any action or proceeding, other than one which has previously been transferred to it, to any other court, except the supreme court, having jurisdiction of the subject matter in any other judicial district or county provided that such other court has jurisdiction over the classes of persons named as parties.

i. As may be provided by law, the district court or a town, village or city court outside the city of New York may transfer any action or proceeding, other than one which has previously been transferred to it, to any court, other than the county court or the surrogate's court of the family court or the supreme court, having jurisdiction of the subject matter in the same or any adjoining county provided that such other court has jurisdiction over the classes of persons named as parties.

j. Each court shall exercise jurisdiction over any action or proceeding transferred to it pursuant to this section.

k. The legislature may provide that the verdict or judgment in actions and proceedings so transferred shall not be subject to the limitation or monetary jurisdiction of the court to which the actions and proceedings are transferred if that limitation be lower than that of the court in which the actions and proceedings were originated. [1961].

This section is a broad constitutional provision allowing for the transfer of cases among the various courts from superior to inferior courts, and vice versa, when such transfer "will promote the interest of justice" or when the court does not have the jurisdiction to hear the case before it. Transfers to courts of lesser jurisdiction cannot be made if the monetary jurisdiction of the lower court limits the claim in question unless the legislature authorizes suspension of the limitation for purposes of the transfer (subdivision k). Such liberal transfer powers enable the courts to equalize caseloads and to shift the many cases initiated at a higher court that should have been brought at a lower court. It was also hoped that strict enforcement of this provision would reduce the number of misfiled cases.

SECTION 20

Judicial office, qualifications and restrictions. a. No person, other than one who holds such office at the effective date of this article, may assume the office of judge of the court of appeals, justice of the supreme court, or judge of the court of claims unless he has been admitted to practice law in this state at least ten years. No person, other than one who holds such office at the effective date of this article, may assume the office of judge of the county court, surrogate's court, family court, a court for the city of New York established pursuant to section fifteen of this article, district court or city court outside the city of New York unless he has been admitted to practice law in this state at least five years or such greater number of years as the legislature may determine.

b. A judge of the court of appeals, justice of the supreme court, judge of the court of claims, judge of a county court, judge of the surrogate's court, judge of the family court or judge of a court for the city of New York established pursuant to section fifteen of this article who is elected or appointed after the effective date of this article may not: (1) hold any other public office or trust except an office in relation to the administration of the courts, member of a constitutional convention or member of the armed forces of the United States or of the state of New York in which latter event the legislature may enact such legislature as it deems appropriate to provide for a temporary judge or justice to serve during the period of the absence of such judge or justice in the armed forces; (2) be eligible to be a candidate for any public office other than judicial office or member of a constitutional convention, unless he resigns his judicial office; in the event a judge or justice does not so resign his judicial office within ten days after his acceptance of the nomination of such other office, his judicial office shall become vacant and the vacancy shall be filled in the manner provided in this article; (3) hold any office or assume the duties or exercise the powers of any office of any political organization or be a member of any governing or executive agency thereof; (4) engage in the practice of law, act as an arbitrator, referee or compensated mediator in any other profession of business which interferes with the performance of his judicial duties. Judges and justices of the courts specified in this subdivision shall also be subject to such rules of conduct as may be promulgated by the chief administrator of the courts with the approval of the court of appeals.

c. Qualifications for and restrictions upon the judges of district, town, village or city courts outside the city of New York, other than such qualifications and restrictions specifically set forth in subdivision a of this section, shall be prescribed by the legislature, provided, however, that the legislature shall require a course of training and education to be completed by justices of town and village courts selected after the effective date of this article who have not been admitted to practice law in this state. Judges of such courts shall also be subject to such rules of conduct not inconsistent with law as may be promulgated by the chief administrator of the courts with the approval of the court of appeals. [1961]

This section safeguards the independence, integrity, and impartiality of the judiciary. A separation of powers philosophy undergirds its specific provisions. Subdivision (a) requires that judges of the court of appeals, justices of the supreme court, and judges of the court of claims be members of the bar for at least ten years prior to assuming their position. For surrogate, family, and county court judges, the period is set at five years. Acquaintance with the laws of the state as well as a measure of experience and knowledge of state affairs seemed to the proponents of this requirement to be "sound as a general principle for ascendency to the bench."[15] Judges outside the inferior courts of New York City were not required to be lawyers but were required to take training courses.

To ensure that judges would be impartial and devote full time to their tasks, they were prohibited by subdivision (b)(1–4) from holding any elected or appointed public office not connected with the administration of the courts and any party position. Two exceptions were granted: judges were permitted to be members of constitutional conventions, presumably because of their expertise and experience, and members of the armed forces. It was felt that judges should have the privilege of entering military service without having to pay the penalty of forfeiture of office. This exception put judges on the same footing as other officials and employees of the state. When a judge enters the military service, the governor is authorized to appoint a temporary judge until such service is completed. Requiring judges to resign congressional office was sustained on the grounds that such a prohibition was necessary to protect the integrity and independence of the judicial branch (Signorelli v. Evans, 1980). Judges are not prohibited from engaging in other business activities unless those activities interfere with the performance of their judicial duties. Such interference could come in the form of time constraints or the need to recuse oneself constantly.

Judges and justices of the courts specified in this section are subject to rules of conduct as promulgated by the chief administrator of the courts with the approval of the court of appeals. Rules implementing (b)(4) have been promulgated;[16] they are both more detailed and more demanding than the requirements of this subdivision, in effect superseding them as far as the behavior of judges and justices is concerned. Although the section places no restriction on justices of the inferior courts outside New York City as far as office-holding is concerned, these justices are governed by the rules of conduct promulgated by the chief administrator of the courts with the approval of the court of appeals (Dworsky v. Farano, 1977).

SECTION 21

Filling of vacancies occurring otherwise than by expiration of term of judge or justice. a. When a vacancy shall occur, otherwise than by expiration of term, in the office of justice of the supreme court, of judge of the county court, of judge of the surrogate's court or judge of the family court outside the city of New York, it shall be filled for a full term at the next general election held not less than three months after such vacancy occurs and, until the vacancy shall be so filled, the governor by and with the advice and consent of the senate, if the senate shall be in session, or, if the senate not be in session, the governor may fill such vacancy by an appointment which shall continue until and including the last day of December next after the election at which the vacancy shall be filled.

b. When a vacancy shall occur, otherwise than by expiration of term, in the office of judge of the court of claims, it shall be filled for the unexpired term in the same manner as an original appointment.

c. When a vacancy shall occur, otherwise than by expiration of term, in the office of judge elected to the city-wide court of civil jurisdiction of the city of New York, it shall be filled for a full term at the next general election held not less than three months after such vacancy occurs and, until the vacancy shall be so filled, the mayor of the city of New York may fill such vacancy by an appointment which shall continue until and including the last day of December next after the election at which the vacancy shall be filled. When a vacancy shall occur, otherwise than by expiration of term on the last day of December of any year, in the office of judge appointed to the family court within the city of New York or the city-wide court of criminal jurisdiction of the city of New York, the mayor of the city of New York shall fill such vacancy by an appointment for the unexpired term.

d. When a vacancy shall occur, otherwise than by expiration of term, in the office of judge of the district court, it shall be filled for a full term at the next general election held not less than three months after such vacancy occurs and, until the vacancy shall be so filled, the board of supervisors or the supervisor or supervisors of the affected district if such district consists of a portion of a county or, in counties with an elected county executive officer, such county executive officer may, subject to confirmation by the board of supervisors or the supervisor or supervisors of such district, fill such vacancy by an appointment which shall continue until and including the last day of December next after the election at which the vacancy shall be filled. [Const. 1894, Art. VI, sec. 16 as added in 1925; amend. and renumbered Art. VI, sec. 18, 1938; amend. (sec. revised) and renumbered Art. VI, sec. 21, 1961]

When vacancies occur in elective courts, the positions are filled in an election held not less than three months after the vacancy has occurred, giving citizens time to receive notice of the election and to acquaint themselves with the candidates. Between the vacancy and the election, the governor, with the consent of the senate, can fill vacancies on the supreme, surrogate, county, and family courts outside New York City. In New York City, interim appointments to the civil court are made by the mayor. Vacancies in the city-wide criminal and family courts are filled by the mayor, and those appointees serve the rest of the unexpired term. Temporary vacancies in district court are filled by boards of supervisors or county executives.

SECTION 22

Commission on judicial conduct; membership; organization and procedure; review by court of appeals; discipline of judges. a. There shall be a commission on judicial conduct. The commission on judicial conduct shall receive, initiate, investigate, and hear complaints with respect to the conduct, qualifications, fitness to perform or performance of official duties of any judge or justice of the unified court system, in a manner provided by law; and, in accordance with subdivision d of this section, may determine that a judge or justice be admonished, censured or removed from office for cause, including, but not limited to, misconduct in office, persistent failure to perform his duties, habitual intemperance, and conduct, on or off the bench, prejudicial to the administration of justice, or that a judge or justice be retired for mental or physical disability preventing the proper performance of his judicial duties. The commission shall transmit any such determination to the chief judge of the court of appeals who shall cause written notice of such determination to be given to the judge or justice involved. Such judge or justice may either accept the commission's determination or make written request to the chief judge, within thirty days after receipt of such notice, for a review of such determination by the court of appeals.

b. (1) The commission on judicial conduct shall consist of eleven members, of whom four shall be appointed by the governor, one by the temporary president of the senate, one by the minority leader of the senate, one by the speaker of the assembly, one by the minority leader of the assembly and three by the chief judge of the court of appeals. Of the members appointed by the governor one person shall be a member of the bar of the state but not a judge or justice, two shall not be members of the bar, justices or judges or retired justices or judges of the unified court system, and one shall be a judge or justice of the unified court system. Of the members appointed by the chief judge one person shall be a justice of the appellate division of the supreme court and two shall be judges or justices of a court or courts other than the court of appeals or appellate divisions. None of the persons to be appointed by the legislative leaders shall be justices or judges or retired justices or judges.

(2) The persons first appointed by the governor shall have respectively, one, two, three, and four year terms as he shall designate. The persons first appointed by the chief judge of the court of appeals shall have respectively two, three, and four year terms as he shall designate. The person first appointed by a temporary president of the senate shall have a one year term. The person first appointed by the minority leader of the senate shall have a two year term. The person first appointed by the speaker of the assembly shall have a four year term. The person first appointed by the minority leader of the assembly shall have a three year term. Each member of the commission shall be appointed thereafter for a term of four years. Commission membership of a judge or justice appointed by the governor or the chief judge shall terminate if such member ceases to hold the judicial position which qualified him for such appointment. Membership shall also terminate if a member attains a position which would have rendered him ineligible for appointment at the time of his appointment. A vacancy shall be filled by the appointing officer for the remainder of the term.

c. The organization and procedure of the commission on judicial conduct shall be as provided by law. The commission on judicial conduct may establish its own rules and procedures not inconsistent with law. Unless the legislature shall provide otherwise, the commission shall be empowered to designate one of its members or any other person as a referee to hear and report concerning any matter before the commission.

d. In reviewing a determination of the commission on judicial conduct, the court of appeals may admonish, censure, remove or retire, for the reasons set forth in subdivision (a) of this section, any judge of the unified court system. In reviewing a determination of the commission on judicial conduct, the court of appeals shall review the commission's findings of fact and conclusions of law on the record of the proceedings upon which the commission's determination was based. The court of appeals may impose a less or more severe sanction prescribed by this section than the one determined by the commission, or impose no sanction.

e. The court of appeals may suspend a judge or justice from exercising the powers of his office while there is pending a determination by the commission on judicial conduct for his removal or retirement, or while he is charged in this state with a felony by an indictment or an information filed pursuant to section six of article one. The suspension shall continue upon conviction and, if the conviction becomes final, he shall be removed from office. The suspension shall be terminated upon reversal of the conviction and dismissal of the accusatory instrument. Nothing in this subdivision shall prevent the commission on judicial conduct from determining that a judge or justice be admonished, censured, removed, or retired pursuant to subdivision a of this section.

f. Upon the recommendation of the commission on judicial conduct or on its own motion, the court of appeals may suspend a judge or justice from office when he is charged with a crime punishable as a felony under the laws of this state, or any other crime which involves moral turpitude. The suspension shall continue upon conviction and, if the conviction becomes final, he shall be removed from office. The suspension shall be determined upon reversal of the conviction and dismissal of the accusatory instrument. Nothing in this subdivision shall prevent the commission on judicial conduct from determining that a judge or justice by admonished, censured, removed, or retired pursuant to subdivision (a) of this section.

g. A judge or justice who is suspended from office by the court of appeals shall receive his judicial salary during such period of suspension, unless the court directs otherwise. If the court has so directed and such suspension is thereafter terminated, the court may direct that he shall be paid his salary for such period of suspension.

h. A judge or justice retired by the court of appeals shall be considered to have retired voluntarily. A judge or justice removed by the court of appeals shall be ineligible to hold other judicial office.

i. Notwithstanding any other provision of this section, the legislature may provide by law for review of determinations of the commission on judicial conduct with respect to justices of town and village courts by an appellate division of the supreme court. In such event, all references in this section to the court of appeals and the chief judge thereof shall be deemed references to an appellate division and the presiding justice thereof, respectively.

j. If a court on the judiciary shall have been convened before the effective date of this section and the proceeding shall not be concluded by that date, the court on the judiciary shall have continuing jurisdiction beyond the effective date of this section to conclude the proceeding. All matters pending before the former commission on judicial conduct on the effective date of this section shall be disposed of in such manner as shall be provided by law. [1977]

This section contains the first of three methods provided in this article by which a judge or justice can be removed from office. The other two, concurrent resolutions of the legislature (sec. 23) and impeachment (sec. 24), have been rarely used and are thought to be appropriate only in cases involving flagrant abuse of judicial power. What was needed was a method that would provide a range of sanctions short of but including removal so that abuses not reaching impeachable offenses could be dealt with effectively. The adoption of the section was prompted by a rise in the number of incidents reported in the press in the late 1960s and early 1970s concerning judicial misconduct. Despite dispute as to how effective the system then in place was in responding to these charges, the perception on the part of the public that the judiciary had not responded decisively led to the procedures embodied in this section.[17]

A commission on judicial conduct was established to receive, investigate, and make a determination with regard to the conduct of judges. It can recommend sanctions ranging from admonishment to removal. Members of the commission are selected in such a way as to ensure its independence from legislative or executive dominance and from any direct or overt partisanship. The requirement that only two judges sit on the commission and that at least two members be nonlawyers protects against the charge that the judiciary had structured the tribunal to serve its own interests. Most of subdivision (b)(2) is obsolete because all members are now four-year appointees. Review of the decisions of the commission is by the court of appeals, except that the legislature may provide for appellate division review of cases involving town and village justices (2)(i).

The "for cause" phrase in subdivision (a) appeared in earlier constitutional provisions and has been upheld against claims that it was void for vagueness (Friedman v. State, 1969). In addition, the court of appeals has ruled that the "but not limited to" phrase includes "general moral and ethical standards expected of judicial officers" (In re Steinberg, 1980). The standard of proof in all determinations is that used in civil suits, the preponderance of evidence, a less demanding standard than clear and convincing evidence (In re Seiffert, 1985). The commission's investigative power includes the subpoena power, but the information sought in the subpoena must bear a reasonable relationship to the matter under investigation (New York State Commission on Judicial Conduct v. Doe, 1984). Organization and procedures for the commission are established by the legislature, but the commission can establish its own rules consistent with the statute.

Subdivision (j) is a transitional provision, now obsolete. The court of the judiciary was the mechanism for removing judges prior to the adoption of this section. It was permitted to continue in existence until cases commenced but not decided at the time this section was adopted were completed.

SECTION 23

Removal of judges or justices by legislature for cause. a. Judges of the court of appeals and justices of the supreme court may be removed by concurrent resolution of both houses of the legislature, if two-thirds of all the members elected to each house concur therein.

b. Judges of the court of claims, the county court, the surrogate's court, the family court, the courts for the city of New York established pursuant to section fifteen of this article, the district court and such other courts as the legislature may determine may be removed by the senate, on the recommendation of the governor, if two-thirds of all the members elected to the senate concur therein.

c. No judge or justice shall be removed by virtue of this section except for cause, which shall be entered on the journals, nor unless he shall have been served with a statement of the cause alleged, and shall have had an opportunity to be heard. On the question of removal, the yeas and nays shall be entered on the journal. [Const. 1846, Art. VI, sec. 11 as amend. in 1869; renumbered Art. VI, sec. 9, 1925; amend. 1945; amend. (sec. revised) and renumbered Art. VI, sec. 23, 1961]

SECTION 24

Court for trial of impeachments; procedure; judgment. The assembly shall have the power of impeachment by a vote of a majority of all the members elected thereto. The court for the trial of impeachments shall be composed of the president of the senate, the senators, or the major part of them, and the judges of the court of appeals, or the major part of them. On the trial of an impeachment against the governor or lieutenant-governor, neither the lieutenant-governor nor the temporary president of the senate shall act as a member of the court. No judicial officer shall exercise his office after articles of impeachment against him shall have been preferred to the senate, until he shall have been acquitted. Before the trial of an impeachment, the members of the court shall take an oath or affirmation truly and impartially to try the impeachment according to the evidence, and no person shall be convicted without the concurrence of two-thirds of the members present. Judgment in cases of impeachment shall not extend further than to removal from office, or removal from office and disqualification to hold and enjoy any public office on honor, trust, or profit under this state; but the party impeached shall be liable to indictment and punishment according to law. [Const. 1777, Art. XXXIII; amend. and renumbered Art. V, sec. 2, Const. 1821; amend. and renumbered Art. VI, sec. 1, Const. 1846 as amend. in 1869; amend. and renumbered Art. VI, sec. 13, Const. 1894; amend. and renumbered Art. VI, sec. 10, 1925; amend. (sec. revised) 1961]

Section 23 is aimed at removing judges who through no fault of their own are unable to discharge their judicial duties—for example, because of senility or physical debilitation.[18] It has never been applied to any judge.

Section 24 is the general impeachment clause by which civil offices of the state, as well as judges, can be removed from office. Unlike the national impeachment clause (Art. I, sec. 2, 3; Art. II, sec. 4), the trial on the impeachment includes members of the court of appeals as well as senators. Little of substance is provided in this section. Nowhere, for example, are the grounds for impeachment spelled out. Earlier constitutions had specified "mal and corrupt conduct" as well as "high crimes and misdemeanors" (Const. 1821, Art. V). Nor does the article tell exactly who is eligible to be impeached. The Judiciary Law addresses the issue by stating that "impeachment shall lie against" all civil officers of the state except justices of the peace, justices of justice courts, police court justices and their clerks." The Public Officer law defines "state officer," but nowhere is there a definition of "civil officer" though the Public Officer's law contains the qualifications necessary to hold civil office.[19] A report of the State Senate Judiciary Committee concluded that at present a "state officer is one who holds civil office and therefore is a civil officer as referred to in sec. 240 [of the Judiciary Law]."[20] Failure to include such a definition in the constitution allows the legislature, if it wishes, to exempt its members from impeachment proceedings.

There is evidence that impeachment was intended to be invoked for other than criminal offenses. The language of the 1821 Constitution, as well as the debates at the 1821 convention, suggest that criminal acts were not prerequisites for impeachment proceedings.[21] Impeachment proceedings have been initiated against officials for conduct that took place while in office during a prior term of office and conduct that took place while a candidate for public office.[22]

Impeachment has served more as a shadowy threat than a ready sanction or remedy for misconduct in office. Only one judge has ever been removed by impeachment proceedings, and one governor, William Sulzer, was also successfully impeached and convicted in 1913 for filing false statements regarding use of campaign funds and use of campaign funds for speculation in the stock market (see Art. IV, sec. 3). Article XIII, section 5 provides for the removal of a public officer for misconduct. Questions about who can be impeached for what grounds remain unsettled under the New York Constitution.

SECTION 25

Compensation and retirement of judges and justices; continuation of services after retirement. a. The compensation of a judge of the court of appeals, a justice of the supreme court, a judge of the court of claims, a judge of the county court, a judge of the surrogate's court, a judge of the family court, a judge of a court for the city of New York established pursuant to section fifteen of this article, a judge of the district court or of a retired judge or justice shall be established by law and shall not be diminished during the term of office for which he was elected or appointed. Any judge or justice of a court abolished by section thirty-five of this article, who pursuant to that section becomes a judge or justice of a court established or continued by this article, shall receive without interruption or diminution for the remainder of the term for which he was elected or appointed to the abolished court the compensation he had been receiving upon the effective date of this article together with any additional compensation that may be prescribed by law.

b. Each judge of the court of appeals, justice of the supreme court, judge of the court of claims, judge of the county court, judge of the surrogate's court, judge of the family court, judge of a court for the city of New York established pursuant to section fifteen of this article and judge of the district court shall retire on the last day of December in the year in which he reaches the age of seventy. Each such former judge of the court of appeals and justice of the supreme court may thereafter perform the duties of a justice of the supreme court, with power to hear and determine actions and proceedings, provided, however, that it shall be certificated in the manner provided by law that the services of such judge or justice are necessary to expedite the business of the court and that he is mentally and physically able and competent to perform the full duties of such office. Any such certification shall be valid for a term of two years and may be extended as provided by law for additional terms of two years. A retired judge or justice shall serve no longer than until the last day of December in the year in which he reaches the age of seventy-six. A retired judge or justice shall be subject to assignment by the appellate division of the supreme court of the judicial department of his residence. Any retired justice of the supreme court who had been designated to and served as a justice of any appellate division immediately preceding his reaching the age of seventy shall be eligible for designation by the governor as a temporary or additional justice of the appellate division. A retired judge or justice shall not be counted in determining the number of justices in a judicial district for purposes of section six subdivision d of this article.

c. The provisions of this section shall also be applicable to any judge or justice who has not reached the age of seventy-six and to whom it would otherwise have been applicable but for the fact that he reached the age of seventy and retired before the effective date of this article. [Const. 1894, Art. VI, sec. 19 as amend. in 1925; amend. (sec. revised) and renumbered Art. VI, sec. 25, 1961; amend. 1966]

Compensation for the judges specified is set by the legislature but shall not be diminished during the term of office to which the judge was elected or appointed. This clause protects the independence of judges by insulating their salaries from punitive legislative actions. Subdivision (a) is a transitional clause, allowing judges whose courts have been abolished under the new article and who have been assigned to new courts to receive the same compensation for the new position as prescribed by law. Subdivision (b) provides for mandatory retirement at age seventy for all judges listed but provides exceptions that dilute the force of the mandatory retirement clause. When it is determined that court of appeals or supreme court judges are needed to "expedite the business of the court," and those judges are deemed mentally and physically competent by the administrative board of the courts (sec. 28), these judges may be certified, for two-year periods, to perform the duties of a supreme court justice. This certification can be renewed for additional two-year periods until the individual judge reaches the age of seventy-six. Retired justices or judges are to be assigned by the appellate division in the judicial department of his or her residence. In addition, supreme court justices who had served prior to retirement on the appellate division are eligible to serve at the appellate division under the same requirements noted above. The intent of these exceptions to the mandatory retirement rule is to give the courts the benefit of well-qualified, experienced judges or justices who, except for their age, are otherwise qualified to serve.

An amendment to the Federal Age Discrimination in Employment Act outlawed discrimination in employment against those who had reached seventy years or older.[23] The New York State Administrative Board of Courts has construed that act as preventing the mandatory retirement of appointed but not elective judges.[24] That distinction was upheld in Diamond v. Cuomo (1987). In EEOC v. State of New York (1990), a federal district court ruled that the New York practice of classifying judges as elected officials and thus not eligible to serve after the age of seventy-six violated the federal Age Discrimination in Employment Act. The effect of this federal law, as interpreted, is to supersede and place in abeyance the constitutional policy of New York with regard to the mandatory retirement of appointive judges.

Subdivision (c) permits judges under seventy-six at the transition date but who retired because of age before the adoption of this section to be used as retired judges if certified as provided. This section allowing justices of the supreme court and judges of the court of appeals to continue to serve, but requiring other judges to retire at seventy, was challenged on equal protection grounds. The court of appeals in Maresca v. Cuomo (1984) rejected the challenge, finding a rational basis for the distinction in the greater experience and manpower needs in these particular courts.

SECTION 26

Temporary assignments of justices or judges to other courts. a. A justice of the supreme court may perform the duties of his office or hold court in any county and may be temporarily assigned to the supreme court in any judicial district or to the court of claims. A justice of the supreme court in the city of New York may be temporarily assigned to the family court in the city of New York or to the surrogate's court in any county within the city of New York when required to dispose of the business of such court.

b. A judge of the court of claims may perform the duties of his office or hold court in any county and may be temporarily assigned to the supreme court in any judicial district.

c. A judge of the county court may perform the duties of his office or hold court in any county and may be temporarily assigned to the supreme court in the judicial department of his residence or to the county court or the family court in any county or to the surrogate's court in any county outside the city of New York or to a court for the city of New York established pursuant to section fifteen of this article.

d. A judge of the surrogate's court in any county within the city of New York may perform the duties of his office or hold court in any county and may be temporarily assigned to the supreme court in the judicial department of his residence.

e. A judge of the surrogate's court in any county outside the city of New York may perform the duties of his office or hold court in any county and may be temporarily assigned to the supreme court in the judicial department of his residence or to the county court or the family court in any county or to a court for the city of New York established pursuant to section fifteen of this article.

f. A judge of the family court may perform the duties of his office or hold court in any county and may be temporarily assigned to the supreme court in the judicial department of his residence or to the county court or the family court in any county or to the surrogate's court in any county outside of the city of New York or to a court for the city of New York established pursuant to section fifteen of this article.

g. A judge of a court for the city of New York established pursuant to section fifteen of this article may perform the duties of his office or hold court in any county and may be temporarily assigned to the supreme court in the judicial department of his residence or to the county court of the family court in any county or to the other court for the city of New York established pursuant to section fifteen of this article.

h. A judge of the district court in any county may perform the duties of his office or hold court in any county and may be temporarily assigned to the county court in the judicial department of his residence or to a court for the city of New York established pursuant to section fifteen of this article or to the district court in any county.

i. Temporary assignments of all the foregoing judges and justices listed in this section shall be made by the chief administrator of the courts in accordance with standards and administrative policies established pursuant to section twenty-eight of this article.

j. The legislature may provide for temporary assignments within the county of residence or any adjoining county, of judges of town, village or city courts outside the city of New York,

k. While temporarily assigned pursuant to the provisions of this section, any judge or justice shall have the powers, duties and jurisdiction of a judge or justice of the court to which assigned. After the expiration of any temporary assignment, as provided in this section, the judge or justice assigned shall have all the power, duties and jurisdiction of a judge or justice of the court to which he was assigned with respect to matters pending before him during the term of such temporary assignment. [1961; amend. 1977, 1983]

This section enables the chief administrator of the courts, in accordance with the standards laid down in section 28 of this article, to transfer judges from court to court. Absent unconstitutional or illegal use, the discretion of the court administrator in reassigning judges is not subject to judicial review (Schwartz v. Williams, 1986). This centralized administration is one of the major advantages of a unified court system.

SECTION 27

Extraordinary terms of the supreme court. The governor may, when in his opinion the public interest requires, appoint extraordinary terms of the supreme court. He shall designate the time and place of holding the terms and the justice who shall hold the term. The governor may terminate the assignment of the justice and may name another justice in his place to hold the term. [1961]

This section constitutionalized a former section of the judiciary law allowing the governor to convene a special term of the supreme court. The governor may do so for whatever reason, and the judiciary is not empowered to review those reasons. The power is that of creating a judicial forum for pressing or special needs. Governor Rockefeller appointed an extraordinary term of supreme court in 1972 in the face of strong evidence of corruption in New York City among police, prosecutors, and judges. It has not been interpreted as an attempt by the executive branch to direct the outcome. When a governor terminated the assignment of a justice of the supreme court's extraordinary term, that action was attacked as a denigration of the independence of the judiciary in violation of the separation of powers. The court rejected the challenge but left open the question of whether a challenge alleging corrupt use of the extraordinary term would be reviewable and grounds for reversal (Steinman v. Nadjari, 1976).

SECTION 28

Administrative supervision of the courts. a. The chief judge of the court of appeals shall be the chief judge of the state of New York and shall be the chief judicial officer of the unified court system. There shall be an administrative board of the courts which shall consist of the chief judge of the court of appeals as chairman and the presiding justice of the appellate division of the supreme court of each judicial department. The chief judge shall, with the advice and consent of the administrative board of the courts, appoint a chief administrator of the courts who shall serve at his pleasure.

b. The chief administrator, on behalf of the chief judge, shall supervise the administration and operation of the unified court system. In the exercise of such responsibility, the chief administrator of the courts shall have such powers and duties as may be delegated to him by the chief judge and such additional powers and duties as may be provided by law.

c. The chief judge, after consultation with the administrative board, shall establish standards and administrative policies for general application throughout the state, which shall be submitted by the chief judge to the court of appeals, together with the recommendations, if any, of the administrative board. Such standards and administrative policies shall be promulgated after approval by the court of appeals. [1977]

This section provides the state's judicial system with sound administrative authority and leadership in the form of a chief administrator who has broad powers delegated by the chief judge to supervise and manage the flow of cases through the courts. It replaces a cumbersome and fragmented system that had diffused administrative authority. Although policies must be approved by the administrative board, no limitations are placed by the constitution on the duties the chief judge may delegate to the chief administrator. Neither consultation with the administrative board nor approval of the court of appeals is necessary for the exercise of his or her administrative powers (Corkum v. Bartlett, 1979).

SECTION 29

Allocation of cost of maintenance and operation of courts; determination of annual financial needs of the courts. a. The legislature shall provide for the allocation of the cost of operating and maintaining the court of appeals, the appellate division of the supreme court in each judicial department, the supreme court, the court of claims, the county court, the surrogate's court, the family court, the courts for the city of New York established pursuant to section fifteen of this article and the district court, among the state, the counties, the city of New York and other political subdivisions.

b. The legislature shall provide for the submission of the itemized estimates of the annual financial needs of the courts referred to in subdivision a of this section to the chief administrator of the courts to be forwarded to the appropriating bodies with recommendations and comment.

c. Insofar as the expense of the courts is borne by the state or paid by the state in the first instance, the final determination of the itemized estimates of the annual financial needs of the courts shall be made by the legislature and the governor in accordance with articles four and seven of this constitution.

d. Insofar as the expense of the courts is not paid by the state in the first instance and is borne by the counties, the city of New York or other political subdivisions, the final determination of the itemized estimates of the annual financial needs of the courts shall be made by the appropriating governing bodies of such counties, the city of New York or other political subdivisions. [1961; amend. 1977]

This section centralized responsibility for budgeting for the unified court system. The state assumed the entire noncapital costs of operating all courts and court-related agencies with the exception of town and village courts. A single budget is submitted to the executive and the legislature (see Art. VII, sec. 1). Insofar as local bodies bear the costs of their courts, they are the appropriate forums to make the final decision on itemized budget estimates. For the state to appropriate funds and then charge local governments their allocable shares would violate the principle of home rule. By 1980, the state had taken over the entire costs of the court system without any reimbursements from the localities.

SECTION 30

Regulations of jurisdiction, practice and procedure of the courts. The legislature shall have the same power to alter and regulate the jurisdiction and proceedings in law and in equity that it has heretofore exercised. The legislature may, on such terms as it shall provide and subject to subsequent modification, delegate, in whole or in part, to a court, including the appellate division of the supreme court, or to the chief administrator of the courts, any power possessed by the legislature to regulate practice and procedure in the courts. The chief administrator of the courts shall exercise any such power delegated to him with the advice and consent of the administrative board of the courts. Nothing herein contained shall prevent the adoption of regulations by individual courts consistent with the general practice and procedure as provided by statute or general rules. [1961, amend. 1977]

Section 30 declares that this article does not change the power the legislature has exercised in the past with regard to the judiciary. The court of appeals, the appellate division, and the administrative board are the only bodies capable of exercising rule-making authority delegated by the legislature. The section allows the legislature to choose how it wishes to delegate that rule-making power. Individual courts are permitted to adopt regulations not inconsistent with the general rules or statutes (see comments under section 7 of this article).

SECTION 31

Indian courts excepted from application of article. This article does not apply to the peacemakers courts or other Indian courts, the existence and operation of which shall continue as may be provided by law. [1961]

This section left unchanged the status of peacemaker courts on Indian reservations. Peacemaker courts, a creation of treaties and Indian law, have jurisdiction with respect to all controversies between Indians on the reservations.[25] These courts are not part of the unified court system and are specifically exempted from the provisions of Article VI.

SECTION 32

Children committed by courts to be placed in custody of persons of same religious persuasion. When any court having jurisdiction over a child shall commit it or remand it to an institution or agency or place it in the custody of any person by parole, placing out, adoption or guardianship, the child shall be committed or remanded or placed, when practicable, in an institution or agency governed by persons, or in the custody of a person, of the same religious persuasion as the child. [1961]

This section, which constitutionalizes previous statutory law, represents an attempt to accommodate the free exercise and the establishment clauses of the First Amendment. Matching the child's religion to the religious affiliation of the person or facility is a reasonable accommodation between the demands of the two clauses (Wilder v. Sugarman, 1974). The directive is not written in absolute language but is more than a matter of the exercise of mere discretion on the part of the court (Starr v. De Rocco, 1968).

SECTION 33

Continuation of existing laws consistent with article; enactment of new laws to promote purposes of article. Existing provisions of law not inconsistent with this article shall continue in force until repealed, amended, modified or superseded in accordance with the provisions of this article. The legislature shall enact appropriate laws to carry into effect the purposes and provisions of this article, and may, for the purpose of implementing, supplementing or clarifying any of its provisions, enact any laws, not inconsistent with the provisions of this article, necessary or desirable in promoting the objectives of this article. [1961]

SECTION 34

Hearing and determination of appeals, actions or proceedings pending in certain courts; continuation in office of certain judges until expiration of terms. a. The court of appeals, the appellate division of the supreme court, the supreme court, the court of claims, the county court in counties outside the city of New York, the surrogate's court and the district court of Nassau county shall hear and determine all appeals, actions and proceedings pending therein on the effective date of this article except that the appellate division of the supreme court in the first and second judicial departments or the appellate term in such departments, if so directed by the appropriate appellate division of the supreme court, shall hear and determine all appeals pending in the appellate term of the supreme court in the first and second judicial departments and in the court of special sessions of the city of New York and except that the county court or an appellate term shall, as may be provided by law, hear and determine all appeals pending in the county court or the supreme court other than an appellate term. Further appeal from a decision of the county court, the appellate term or the appellate division of the supreme court, rendered on or after the effective date of this article, shall be governed by the provisions of this article.

b. The justices of the supreme court in office on the effective date of this article shall hold their offices as justices of the supreme court until the expiration of their respective terms.

c. The judges of the court of claims in office on the effective date of this article shall hold their offices as judges of the court of claims until the expiration of their respective terms.

d. The surrogates, and county judges outside the city of New York, including the special county judges of the counties of Erie and Suffolk, in office on the effective date of this article shall hold office as judges of the surrogate's court or county judge, respectively, of such counties until the expiration of their respective terms.

e. The judges of the district court of Nassau county in office on the effective date of this article shall hold their offices until the expiration of their respective terms.

f. Judges of courts for towns, villages and cities outside the city of New York in office on the effective date of this article shall hold their offices until the expiration of their respective terms. [1961]

Section 33 is a transitional provision clarifying the status of legislation adopted prior to the approval of this article. It is now largely obsolete. Section 34 is also a transitional provision accommodating pending actions and proceedings and previously existing terms of judges until expiration of their respective terms.

SECTION 35

Abolition of certain courts; transfer of judges and pending actions and proceedings to other courts; abolition of official referee's office; continuation of non-judicial personnel; appeals taken after effective date of article. a. The children's court, the court of general sessions of the county of New York, the county courts of the counties of Bronx, Kings, Queens and Richmond, the city court of the city of New York, the domestic relations court of the city of New York, the municipal court of the city of New York, the court of special sessions of the city of New York and the city magistrates' courts of the city of New York are abolished from and after the effective date of this article and thereupon the seals, records, papers and documents of or belonging to such courts shall, unless otherwise provided by law, be deposited in the offices of the clerks of the several counties in which these courts now exist.

b. The judges of the county court of the counties of Bronx, Kings, Queens and Richmond and the judges of the court of general sessions of the county of New York in office on the effective date of this article shall for the remainder of the terms for which they were elected or appointed, be justices of the supreme court in and for the judicial district which includes the county in which they resided on that date. The salaries of such justices shall be the same as the salaries of the other justices of the supreme court residing in the same judicial district and shall be paid in the same manner. All actions and proceedings pending in the county court of the counties of Bronx, Kings, Queens and Richmond and in the court of general sessions of the county of New York on the effective date of this article shall be transferred to the supreme court in the county in which the action or proceedings was pending, or otherwise as may be provided by law.

c. The legislature shall provide by law that the justices of the city court of the city of New York and the justices of the municipal court of the city of New York in office on the date such courts are abolished shall, for the remainder of the term for which each was elected or appointed, be judges of the city-wide court of civil jurisdiction of the city of New York established pursuant to section fifteen of this article and for such district as the legislature may determine.

d. The legislature shall provide by law that the justices of the court of special sessions and the magistrates of the city magistrates' courts of the city of New York in office on the date such courts are abolished shall, for the remainder of the term for which each was appointed, be judges of the city-wide court of criminal jurisdiction of the city of New York established pursuant to section 15 provided, however, that each term shall expire on the last day of the year in which it would have expired except for the provisions of this article.

e. All actions and proceedings pending in the city court of the city of New York and the municipal court in the city of New York on the date such courts are abolished shall be transferred to the city-wide court of civil jurisdiction of the city of New York established pursuant to section fifteen of this article or as otherwise provided by law.

f. All actions and proceedings pending in the court of special sessions in the city of New York and the city magistrates' court of the city of New York on the date such courts are abolished shall be transferred to the city-wide court of criminal jurisdiction of the city of New York established pursuant to section fifteen of this article or as otherwise provided by law.

g. The special county judges of the counties of Broome, Chautauqua, Jefferson, Oneida and Rockland and the judges of the children's courts in all counties outside the city of New York in office on the effective date of this article shall, for the remainder of the terms for which they were elected or appointed, be judges of the family court in and for the county in which they hold office. Except as otherwise provided in this section, the office of special county judge and the office of special surrogate is abolished from and after the effective date of this article and the terms of the persons holding such offices shall terminate on that date.

h. All actions and proceedings pending in the children's courts in the counties outside the city of New York on the effective date of this article shall be transferred to the family court in the respective counties.

i. The justices of the domestic relations court of the city of New York in office on the effective date of this article shall, for the remainder of their terms for which they were appointed, be judges of the family court within the city of New York.

j. All actions and proceedings pending in the domestic relations court of the city of New York on the effective date of this article shall be transferred to the family court in the city of New York.

k. The office of official referee is abolished, provided, however, that official referees in the office on the effective date of this article shall, for the remainder of the terms for which they were appointed or certified, be official referees of the court in which appointed or certified or the successor court, as the case may be. At the expiration of the term of any official referee, his office shall be abolished and thereupon such former official referee shall be subject to the relevant provision of section twenty-five of this article.

l. As may be provided by law, the non-judicial personnel of the courts affected by this article in office on the effective date of this article shall, to the extent practicable, be continued without diminution of salaries and with the same status and rights in the courts established or continued by this article; and especially skilled, experienced and trained personnel shall, to the extent practicable, be assigned to like functions in the courts which exercise the jurisdiction formerly exercised by the courts in which they were employed. In the event that the adoption of this article shall require or make possible a reduction in the number of non-judicial personnel, or in the number of certain categories of such personnel, such reduction shall be made, to the extent practicable, by provision that the death, resignation, removal or retirement of an employee shall not create a vacancy until the reduced number of personnel has been reached.

m. In the event that a judgment or order was entered before the effective date of this article and a right to appeal existed and notice of appeal therefrom is filed after the effective date of this article, such appeal shall be taken from the supreme court, the county courts, the surrogate's court, the children's courts, the court of general sessions of the county of New York and the domestic relations court of the city of New York to the appellate division of the supreme court in the judicial department in which such court was located; from the court of claims to the appellate division of the supreme court in the third judicial department, except for those claims which arose in the fourth judicial department, in which case the appeal shall be to the appellate division of the supreme court in the fourth judicial department; from the city court of the city of New York, the municipal court of the city of New York, the court of special sessions of the city of New York and the city magistrates' courts of the city of New York to the appellate division of the supreme court in the judicial department in which such court was located, provided, however, that such appellate division of the supreme court may transfer any such appeal to an appellate term, if such appellate term be established; and for the district court, town, village and city courts outside the city of New York to the county court in the county in which such court was located, provided, however, that the legislature may require the transfer of any such appeal to an appellate term, if such appellate term be established. Further appeal from a decision of a county court or an appellate term or the appellate division of the supreme court shall be governed by the provisions of this article. However, if in any action or proceeding decided prior to the effective date of this article, a party had a right to direct appeal from a court of original jurisdiction to the court of appeals, such appeal may be taken directly to the court of appeals.

n. In the event that an appeal was decided before the effective date of this article and a further appeal could be taken as of right and notice of appeal therefrom is filed after the effective date of this article, such appeal may be taken from the appellate division of the supreme court to the court of appeals and from any other court to the appellate division of the supreme court. Further appeal from a decision of the appellate division of the supreme court shall be governed by the provisions of this article. If a further appeal could not be taken as of right, such appeal shall be governed by the provisions of this article. [1961]

In line with the unified court system's goal of consolidation and coordination, certain courts listed in (a) were abolished and justices of those courts assigned to other courts (b)(c)(d)(g). Attempts were made to continue the positions and salaries of nonjudicial court personnel. Because the transition to the new courts has long since been completed, much of the section is now obsolete.

SECTION 36

Continuation and transfer of pending appeals, actions, or proceedings; jurisdiction of court on appeal; law governing proceedings on appeal. No civil or criminal appeal, action or proceeding pending before any court or any judge or justice on the effective date of this article shall abate but such appeal, action or proceeding so pending shall be continued in the courts as provided in this article and, for the purposes of disposition of such actions or proceedings only, the jurisdiction of any court to which any such action or proceeding is transferred by this article shall be coextensive with the jurisdiction of the former court from which the action or proceeding was transferred. Except to the extent inconsistent with the provisions of this article, subsequent proceedings in such appeal, action or proceeding shall be conducted in accordance with the laws in force on the effective date of this article until superseded in the manner authorized by law. [1975; amend. 1977]

SECTION 36–a

Effective date of certain amendments to Articles VI and VII. The amendments to the provisions of section two, four, seven, eight, eleven, twenty, twenty-two, twenty-six, twenty-eight, twenty-nine and thirty of article six and to the provisions of section one of article seven, as first proposed by a concurrent resolution passed the legislature in the year nineteen hundred seventy-six and entitled "Concurrent Resolution of the Senate and Assembly proposing amendments to article six and seven of the constitution, in relation to the manner of selecting judges of the court of appeals, creation of a commission on judicial conduct and administration of the unified court system, providing for the effectiveness of such amendments and the repeal of subdivision c of section two, subdivision b of section seven, subdivision b of section eleven, section twenty-two and section twenty-eight of article six thereof relating thereto", shall become a part of the constitution on the first day of January next after the approval and ratification of the amendments proposed by such concurrent resolution by the people but the provisions thereof shall not become operative and the repeal of subdivision c of section two, section twenty-two and section twenty-eight shall not become effective until the first day of April next thereafter which date shall be deemed the effective date of such amendments and the chief judge and the associate judges of the court of appeals in office on such effective date shall hold their offices until the expiration of their respective terms. Upon a vacancy in the office of any such judge, such vacancy shall be filled in the manner provided in section two of article six. [1975; amend. 1977]

SECTION 36–b

[No section 36–b has been adopted.]

SECTION 36–c

Effective date of certain amendments to Article VI, section 22. The amendments to the provisions of section twenty-two of article six as first proposed by a concurrent resolution passed by the legislature in the year nineteen hundred seventy-four and entitled "Concurrent Resolution of the Senate and Assembly proposing an amendment to section twenty-two of article six and adding section thirty-six-c to such article of the constitution, in relation to the powers of and reconstituting the court on the judiciary and creating a commission on judicial conduct", shall become a part of the constitution on the first day of January next after the approval and ratification of the amendments proposed by such concurrent resolutions by the people but the provisions thereof shall not become operative until the first day of September next thereafter which date shall be deemed the effective date of such amendments. [1976; amend. 1977]

SECTION 37

Effective date of article. This article shall become a part of the constitution on the first day of January next after the approval and ratification of this amendment by the people but its provisions shall not become operative until the first day of September next thereafter which date shall be deemed the effective date of this article. [1961]

Section 36–a set the effective date for the amendment passed in 1977. It allowed four additional months before the amendment would take effect to give the judiciary time to adjust to the requirements of the amendment. For similar reasons, section 36–c set the operative date as September 1976, giving the courts and legislature eight additional months to phase out the old court of the judiciary and create the new commission of judicial conduct. Section 37 allowed a transition time of an additional eight months for reasons similar to those noted in section 36.

Article VII

State Finances

Article VII contains the executive budget and the debt system of the state. Sections 1–7 describe the procedures for creation of a budget. The roles and powers of the governor, as well as of the legislature, are specified. The seven sections present a sequence of stages for budgeting and appropriating funds. The governor is assigned the principal responsibility for preparing the budget, an integrated plan of revenues and expenditures, and the legislature is assigned the primary responsibility for authorizing expenditures. The executive budget system is a major source of the governor's power, promoting integration of and control over the executive branch. The administrative linchpin of this system is the Division of the Budget, which makes recommendations to the governor as to what each agency ought to receive and how state agencies will be allowed to spend appropriated moneys.

The debt system remains, in broad outline, similar to that adopted in 1846. The legislature may authorize short-term debt in anticipation of taxes and revenues to be repaid in one year or in anticipation of authorized bond issues to be repaid within two years. Unlimited debt may be incurred to repel invasions or suppress forest fires. To incur full faith and credit debt beyond these, the legislature must propose debt for a single purpose and present that proposal to the people for approval in a referendum at which no other issues are being decided. The article provides three exceptions to this requirement: $300 million for the elimination of grade crossings, $400 million for veterans' bonuses, and $250 million for the State University of New York.

Debt limitation by constitutional provision is controversial, and scholars disagree as to its effect. There is some evidence that borrowing is higher in states without the referendum requirements. New York, however, has one of the highest debts in the country, standing at just over $24 billion in 1989. Only $4.5 billion of this is constitutionally authorized debt under the provisions of this article.[1] To be sure, most of the indirect nonconstitutional debt is serviced by nontax revenues, such as highway tolls, student fees, or local revenues; nonetheless, the state is ultimately responsible for that debt should those revenue sources prove inadequate for any reason. The efficacy of these debt restrictions is difficult to measure because the state has resorted to a variety of devices, such as public authorities, lease-purchasing agreements, and moral obligation bonds, to circumvent the constitutional limitations. The New York courts have approved these devices by adopting a posture of judicial restraint with regard to these provisions and redefining the authorities so as to exclude them from constitutional coverage.

SECTION 1

Estimates by departments, the legislature and the judiciary of needed appropriations; hearings. For the preparation of the budget, the head of each department of state government, except the legislature and judiciary, shall furnish the governor such estimates and information in such form and at such times as he may require, copies of which shall forthwith be furnished to the appropriate committees of the legislature. The governor shall hold hearings thereon at which he may require the attendance of heads of departments and their subordinates. Designated representatives of such committees shall be entitled to attend the hearings thereon and to make inquiry concerning any part thereof.

Itemized estimates of the financial needs of the legislature, certified by the presiding officer of each house, and of the judiciary, approved by the court of appeals and certified by the chief judge of the court of appeals, shall be transmitted to the governor not later than the first day of December in each year for inclusion in the budget without revision but with such recommendations as he may deem proper. Copies of the itemized estimates of the financial needs of the judiciary also shall forthwith be transmitted to the appropriate committees of the legislature. [Const. 1894, Art. IV-A, sec. 1 as added in 1927; amend. and renumbered Art. VII, sec. 1, 1938; amend. 1977]

This provision centralizes budgetary procedures and enables the governor to impose a degree of responsibility on the various departments. Department heads are required to prepare financial estimates as instructed by the governor and to appear for the governor's budget hearings. Copies of estimates are provided to the appropriations committees of the legislature, and representatives of those committees are entitled to attend the budget hearings. The second paragraph provides for the preparation of the budgets for the legislature and judiciary. As separate and coequal branches of government, these budgets are given separate treatment from those involving departments of the executive branch. The provision of a unified budget for the courts eliminates dependence on local funding and provides an overview of the cost of dispensing justice. This 1977 addition was part of a series of amendments to Article VI concerning the administration of a unified court system.

SECTION 2

Executive budget. Annually, on or before the first day of February in each year following the year fixed by the constitution for the election of governor and lieutenant governor, and on or before the second Tuesday following the first day of the annual meeting of the legislature, in all other years, the governor shall submit to the legislature a budget containing a complete plan of expenditures proposed to be made before the close of the ensuing fiscal year and all moneys and revenues estimated to be available therefor, together with an explanation of the basis of such estimates and recommendations as to proposed legislation, if any, which he may deem necessary to provide moneys and revenues sufficient to meet such proposed expenditures. It shall also contain such other recommendations and information as he may deem proper and such additional information as may be required by law. [Const. 1894, Art. IV-A, sec. 2 as added in 1927; amend. and renumbered Art. VII, sec. 2, 1938; amend. 1965]

This section provides a timetable for the submission of the budget. The governor usually presents the annual message at the end of the first week in January and the proposed budget two weeks later. The mandate that revenues "which he may deem necessary to meet such proposed expenditures" be factored into the budget has been interpreted to require a balanced budget. A balanced budget requirement does not mean a balanced budget will in fact take place. In Wein v. Carey (1977), the court of appeals ruled that "Proof of improper budget manipulation must be found in the estimates of revenue and expenditures." Two successive deficits are not sufficient to shift the burden of proof to the state. Such a shift would "convert the court into a super-auditing office." In reviewing state budget plans, judicial intervention "may be invoked only in the narrowest of instances" (at 504–505). While the court and the legislature were authorizing taxpayer suits challenging appropriation and/or disbursements of moneys—for example, Boryszewski v. Brydges (1975)—the court of appeals in a series of decisions adopted a distinctly deferential stance to budget decisions reached by the political branches of the government.

It had traditionally been assumed that the governor was in charge of budget execution once the legislature had approved the appropriation bills, but in Oneida County v. Berle (1980), the court of appeals held that the governor's duty to present a balanced budget does not entail the power to impound funds to avert a deficit.

SECTION 3

Budget bills; appearance before legislature. At the time of submitting the budget to the legislature the governor shall submit a bill or bills containing all the proposed appropriations and reappropriations included in the budget and the proposed legislation, if any, recommended therein.

The governor may at any time within thirty days thereafter and, with the consent of the legislature, at any time before the adjournment thereof, amend or supplement the budget and submit amendments to any bills submitted by him or submit supplemental bills.

The governor and the heads of departments shall have the right, and it shall be the duty of the heads of departments when requested by either house of the legislature or an appropriate committee thereof, to appear and be heard in respect to the budget during the consideration thereof, and to answer inquiries relevant thereto. The procedure for such appearances and inquiries shall be provided by law. [Const. 1894, Art. IV-A, secs. 2 and 3 as added in 1927; amend. and renumbered Art. VII, sec. 3, 1938]

The governor is required to submit bills appropriating the money to cover the expenditures proposed in the submitted budget and is also authorized to amend or supplement his original proposals. The legislature can compel department heads to appear as witnesses before budget hearings, and conversely, the governor and those department heads have the right to appear at those hearings if they so desire. In addition to ensuring cooperation and sharing of information, this requirement ensures that the governor's budget will receive publicity and criticism throughout the state.

The constitution does not explicitly mandate a line-item budget, but the court of appeals has held that there is a constitutional mandate to itemize (People v. Tremaine, 1939; Saxton v. Carey, 1978). Partial support for this view is found in Section 4 in which the word *item* is used throughout. The court of appeals in People v. Tremaine required that itemization must take place with "reasonable particularity," with the particularity required determined by the circumstances. In Saxton v. Carey, the court of appeals held that itemization is required only insofar as it is necessary to facilitate proper legislative review of the budget, and that decision is best left to the legislature and the political process. Should the legislature fail in its responsibility to require a sufficiently itemized budget, "the remedy lies not in the courtroom but in the voting booth" (at 551).

SECTION 4

Action on budget bills by legislature; effect thereof. The legislature may not alter an appropriation bill submitted by the governor except to strike out or reduce items therein, but it may add thereto items of appropriation provided that such additions are stated separately and distinctly from the original items of the bill and refer each to a single object or purpose. None of the restrictions of this section, however, shall apply to appropriations for the legislature or judiciary.

Such an appropriation bill shall when passed by both houses be a law immediately without further action by the governor, except that appropriations for the legislature and judiciary and separate items added to the governor's bills by the legislature shall be subject to his approval as provided in section 7 of article IV. [Const. 1894, Art. IV-A, sec. 3 as added in 1927; amend. and renumbered Art. VII, sec. 4, 1938]

This section ensures political accountability on the part of the governor and the legislature for their spending decisions by adopting the itemization principle. The governor submits a single integrated plan with items, and the legislature must address this budget as a single plan in terms of the specific items. The legislature can reduce or eliminate items: these actions are not subject to gubernatorial veto. If the legislature wishes to increase funding for an item, it can only do so by adding a separate item for the same purpose. New programs added must also be submitted as separate items, each with a single object or purpose. These increases or additions, however, are subject to the governor's item veto (Art. IV, sec. 7). These restrictions are not applicable to the appropriations for the judicial or legislative branches. The section is an attempt to ensure discipline and responsibility in the budgetary process while enabling the legislature to correct any misuse of power or obvious inequities revealed in legislative committee hearings.

When the legislature enacted a law amending the budget submitted by the governor by striking out all the itemizations contained in the bill and substituting a lump sum appropriation for each department, bureau, and division, the court of appeals struck the revision down as a violation of this section (People v. Tremaine). For the legislature to substitute lump sum appropriations was a violation of the itemization principle, the purpose of which was to ensure accountability for appropriations. The legislature can strike lump sum appropriations and substitute items; it cannot do the reverse.

The judiciary will continue to adjudicate disputes between the legislature and the executive over the budget process, but approval by the legislature of the governor's budget precludes review of the degree of itemization.

SECTION 5

Restrictions on consideration of other appropriations. Neither house of the legislature shall consider any other bill making an appropriation until all the appropriation bills submitted by the governor shall have been finally acted on by both houses, except on message from the governor certifying to the necessity of the immediate passage of such a bill. [Const. 1894, Art. IV-A, sec. 4 as added in 1927; amend. and renumbered Art. VII, sec. 5, 1938]

This section assumes action on an integrated plan in order to provide a coherent budgetary process. Only upon receipt of a "message of necessity" from the governor or after adoption of the budget can the legislature add appropriations. This restriction, along with the provision in section 4 that additions by the legislature must refer to a single object or purpose, are attempts to protect the budget process from riders and logrolling while safeguarding it against executive abuse.

SECTION 6

Restrictions on content of appropriation bills. Except for appropriation contained in the bills submitted by the governor and in a supplemental appropriation bill for the support of government, no appropriations shall be made except by separate bills each for a single object or purpose. All such bills and such supplemental appropriation bill shall be subject to the governor's approval as provided in section 7 of article IV.

No provision shall be embraced in any appropriation bill submitted by the governor or in such supplemental appropriation bill unless it relates specifically to some particular appropriation in the bill, and any such provision shall be limited in its operation to such appropriation. [Const. 1894, Art. III, sec. 22, and Art. IV-A, sec. 4 as added, in 1927; amend. (sec. revised) and renumbered Art. VII, sec. 6, 1938]

In addition to the appropriations originally submitted in the governor's budget, this section contains one exemption from the separate bills: single-object or -purpose limitation. At the close of each legislative session, there is a need for some changes in the budget—some political—and a need for a deficiency budget for various departments, the courts, and the legislature. Since these changes are numerous and frequently involve small amounts, they can not be conveniently embodied in separate bills for single objects. The exemption balances constitutional control with the realities of the appropriations process. All the changes are subject to the governor's veto.

The second paragraph was added to prevent the inclusion of general legislation sometimes called riders in appropriation bills. Prior to this addition, it was a common legislative practice to tack onto annual appropriations various provisions that probably could not stand on their own merit. The single-object or -purpose clause has not occasioned much litigation, though its meaning is far from clear.

SECTION 7

Appropriation bills. No money shall ever be paid out of the state treasury or any of its funds, or any of the funds under its management, except in pursuance of an appropriation by law; nor unless such payment be made within two years next after the passage of such appropriation act; and every such law making a new appropriation or continuing or reviving an appropriation, shall distinctly specify the sum appropriated, and the object or purpose to which it is to be applied; and it shall not be sufficient for such law to refer to any other law to fix such sum. [Const. 1846, Art. VII, sec. 8; amend. and renumbered Art. III, sec. 21, Const. 1894; amend. and renumbered Art. VII, sec. 7, 1938]

The object of this section is to ensure responsibility in the appropriations process by requiring that appropriations be made by law, that they be made for no more than two year periods, and that the law distinctly specify the amount appropriated and the object or purpose for which it is intended. The hope was that every administration would "collect and pay as it went."[2] Prior to this provision, the legislature could appropriate far in excess of anticipated revenues, and these appropriations could remain on the books for extended periods. The effect of this practice was to delegate to the executive the discretion as to when, how, and on what the funds were used. By eliminating this practice, this section preserves the roles and responsibilities of the two branches.

Although the language of the section seems clear and emphatic, its reach is complicated by the fact that not all state moneys are deposited in the state treasury or are funds under its management. Funds administered by a legislatively created benefit corporation are not covered by this section. Moreover, the practice of off-budgeting (that is, placing certain revenues such as federal aid and lottery funds outside the treasury or otherwise deeming them not funds of the state for purposes of this section) also has limited its impact.

In the first constitutional challenge to this practice, the court of appeals in Anderson v. Regan (1981) held that this section applied to federal funds deposited in the state treasury, which was considered to comprise accounts in the custody of the commissioner of finance and the comptroller. Such funds required legislative appropriation even though the funds had already been appropriated for general purposes at the federal level and the state legislature had passed program legislation governing their use at the state level. In dicta, the court took notice of the practice of off-budgeting, saying that it raised "serious questions" but left for future decision the question of whether and under what conditions the legislature can avoid the requirements of this section by simply directing revenues to a public benefit corporation or to other funds rather than to the state treasury itself.

State finance law provides for the expenditure of fund in emergencies when the legislature is not in session. The governor is authorized to draw money for governmental emergencies as specified by that law.[3]

SECTION 8

Gift or loan of state credit or money prohibited; exceptions for enumerated purposes. 1. The money of the state shall not be given or loaned to or in aid of any private corporation or association, or private undertaking; nor shall the credit or the state be given or loaned to or in aid of any individual, or public or private corporation or association, or private undertaking, but the foregoing provisions shall not apply to any fund or property now held or which may hereafter be held by the state for educational, mental health or mental retardation purposes.

2. Subject to the limitations on indebtedness and taxation, nothing in this constitution contained shall prevent the legislature from providing for the aid, care, and support of the needy directly or through subdivisions of the state; or for the protection by insurance or otherwise, against the hazards of unemployment, sickness and old age; or for the education and support of the blind, the deaf, the dumb, the physically handicapped, the mentally ill, the emotionally disturbed, the mentally retarded or juvenile delinquents as it may deem proper; or for health and welfare services for all children, either directly or through subdivisions of the state, including school districts; or for the aid, care and support of neglected and dependent children and of the needy sick, through agencies and institutions authorized by the state board of social welfare or other state department having the power of inspection thereof, by payments made on a per capita basis directly or through the subdivisions of the state; or for the increase in the amount of pensions of any member of a retirement system of the state, or of a subdivision of the state; or for an increase in the amount of pension benefits of any widow or widower of a retired member of a retirement system of the state or of a subdivision of the state to whom payable as beneficiary under an optional settlement in connection with the pension of such member. The enumeration of legislative powers in this paragraph shall not be taken to diminish any power of the legislature hitherto existing.

3. Nothing in this constitution shall prevent the legislature from authorizing the loan of the money of the state to a public corporation to be organized for the purpose of making loans to non-profit corporations or for the purpose of guaranteeing loans made by banking organizations, as that term shall be defined by the legislature, to finance the construction of new industrial or manufacturing plants, the construction of new buildings to be used for research and development, the construction of other eligible business facilities, and for the purchase of machinery and equipment related to such new industrial or manufacturing plants, research and development buildings, and other eligible business facilities in this state or the acquisition, rehabilitation or improvement of former or existing industrial or manufacturing plants, buildings to be used for research and development, other eligible business facilities, and machinery and equipment in this state, including the acquisition of real property therefor, and the use of such money by such public corporation for such purposes, to improve employment opportunities in any area of the state, provided, however, that any such plants, buildings or facilities or machinery or equipment therefor shall not be (i) primarily used in making retail sales of goods or services to customers who personally visit such facilities to obtain such goods or services or (ii) used primarily as a hotel, apartment house or other place of business which

furnishes dwelling space or accommodations to either residents or transients, and provided further that any loan by such public corporation shall not exceed sixty per centum of the cost of any such project and the repayment of which shall be secured by a mortgage thereon which shall not be a junior incumbrance thereon by more than fifty per centum of such cost or by a security interest if personalty, and that the amount of any guarantee of a loan made by a banking organization shall not exceed eighty per centum of the cost of any such project. [Const. 1846, Art. VII, sec. 9, as amend. in 1874; amend. and renumbered Arts. VII, sec. 8 and Art. VIII, sec. 9; Const. 1894; amend. and renumbered Art. VII, sec. 8, 1938; amended 1951, 1961, 1966, 1973, 1977, 1985]

Subdivision (1) of this section was adopted to restrain certain financial practices that forced the state to make good on its loans of credit to private corporations such as the railroads and to limit increases in public funds appropriated to charities, many of which were sectarian in character and, in any case, received the money free of any governmental control. Public corporations were added to this restriction in 1938. The target is primarily cities or authorities, which, finding themselves in trouble or unable to sell their securities, could run to the state for assistance. It was felt that state credit should be reserved for the state with only those exceptions as set forth in the constitution. The state may give or lend its money, as distinguished from its credit, to assist municipal or other public corporations.

The constitution clearly distinguishes between lending money and lending credit. The distinction is based on the fact that the granting of the state's moneys does not create dangers of collapse, insolvency, and crisis associated with the abuse of credit. Wein v. State (1976) did allow the state to use its short-term credit (tax and revenue anticipation notes) to fund an emergency appropriation for New York City.

Subdivision (2) contains eight explicit exemptions from the restrictions. These exemptions allow the state to provide aid and/or credit to public or private agencies, provided that other constitutional and statutory requirements are met. The list of exemptions has grown over the last hundred years, reflecting an expanded conception as to the proper role of the government (see Arts. XVII and XVIII for other exemptions). The provision has effectively rendered the federal public purpose doctrine academic in New York. That doctrine holds that under the due process clause of the Fourteenth Amendment, public funds can be expended only for public purposes. Federal courts have given the legislature wide latitude in determining what a public purpose is, and the federal public purpose doctrine has played little or no role in restricting state legislation (see Art. I, sec. 7).

A series of court decisions in the 1970s occasioned by the fiscal crisis in New York has rendered the efficacy of this provision problematic. In response to a desperate fiscal crisis in New York City in 1975, the legislature appropriated for New York City an advance grant of $250 million and $500 million to the

Municipal Assistance Corporation, a public authority financed by short-term borrowing in the form of revenue or tax anticipation notes. It was claimed that these moneys constituted a gift or loan of the credit of the state in violation of section 8 of this article and section 5 of Article X. In Wein v. State, the court of appeals sustained the law, reasoning that section 9 allowed for the contracting of short-term debt in anticipation of taxes and revenues and that since the state could appropriate money for assistance to the city, that borrowing was for a state purpose. Since the purpose of section 8 was to prevent the state from shifting the tax burden to future generations and this program involved only short-term debt, there was no danger of that happening. The decision minimized the significance of this section with regard to the short-term debt on the financial practices of the state. The majority recognized this fact when it described the state scheme as poised on "the brink of valid practice" and acknowledged that "the device under scrutiny, even if it is not identifiable at this stage as a violation of constitutional limitations in control of the state's temporary debt, may in the course of time prove violative" (at 142, 151). Here the court had reference to planned rollovers of the short-term debt. A narrow reading of these provisions and a deferential stance toward state financial measures have combined to make these sections less effective as restrictions on the use of the state's credit.

Subdivision (3) established the Job Development Authority in 1961 with the purpose of stimulating the expansion of business, thus securing jobs and creating new ones, encouraging new plants to locate in the state, and encouraging existing plants to stay in the state rather than relocating. The scope of responsibilities and borrowing power of the agency have been expanded periodically since its inception. The authority may loan up to 60 percent of project costs in connection with acquisitions, rehabilitations, or improvement to enterprises. Such loans must be secured by real property mortgages that may not be junior to other mortgages by more than 50 percent of the project costs. The agency guarantees loans made by banking institutions for either realty or machinery and equipment projects as long as the agency's guarantee does not exceed 80 percent of the project costs. This subdivision was made necessary by the restrictions contained in subdivision (1). The full faith and credit support of the Job Development Authority obligation now stands at $600 million as a result of an amendment approved in 1985. The new limit is specified in Article X, section 8.

SECTION 9

Short-term state debts in anticipation of taxes, revenues and proceeds of sale of authorized bonds. The state may contract debts in anticipation of the receipt of taxes and revenues, direct or indirect, for the purposes and within the amounts of appropriations theretofore made. Notes or other obligations for the moneys so borrowed shall be issued as may be provided by law, and shall with the interest thereon be paid from such taxes and revenues within one year from the date of issue.

The state may also contract debts in anticipation of the receipt of the proceeds of the sale of bonds theretofore authorized, for the purpose and within the amounts of the bonds so authorized. Notes or obligations for the money so borrowed shall be issued as may be provided by law, and shall with the interest thereon be paid from the proceeds of the sale of such bonds within two years from the date of issue, except as to bonds issued or to be issued for any of the purposes authorized by article eighteen of this constitution, in which event the notes or obligations shall with the interest thereon be paid from the proceeds of the sale of such bonds within five years from the date of issue. [Const. 1894, Art. VII, sec. 2 as amend. in 1920; amend. and renumbered Art. VII, sec. 9, 1938; amend. 1958]

This section allows the legislature to incur short-term debt to be repaid in one year in anticipation of tax receipts and other revenues or short-term debt to be paid in two years in anticipation of revenues from bonds. Debt contracted under this section is not subject to the referendum requirement of section 11 or other provisions of this article. Housing projects financed under section 18 are given a five-year limitation because short-term financing provides funds quickly at low interest rates while the life of housing projects under construction frequently extends beyond the two-year limit on temporary funding.

Anticipation notes issued by the state in the wake of a failure to balance the budget were challenged in Wein v. Carey (1977). The court held that only when "estimates of revenues and expenditures are dishonest" may budget plans be questioned and the use of anticipation notes to balance the imbalanced budget plan be declared unconstitutional. The decision allows successive budget deficits and reliance on anticipation notes as long as the deficits are not planned. Only in the latter case would there be an "ill-disguised roll-over" or unconstitutional refinancing of a planned deficit (at 503). Wein v. Carey illustrates the leeway courts have given the political branches of the government in their attempts to solve the financial problems of the state.

SECTION 10

State debts on account of invasion, insurrection, war, and forest fires. In addition to the above limited power to contract debts, the state may contract debts to repel invasion, suppress insurrection, or defend the state in war, or to suppress forest fires; but the money arising from the contracting of such debts shall be applied to the purpose for which it was raised, or to repay such debts, and to no other purpose whatever. [Const. 1846, Art. VII, sec. 11; renumbered Art. VII, sec. 3, Const. 1894; as amend. in 1929; amend. and renumbered Art. VII, sec. 10, 1938]

Section 10 is an emergency provision allowing the state to contract debt for the reasons specified. Concern over the constitutionality of a revision of the

conservation law allowing the state to obtain temporary loans to suppress forest
fires led to a 1929 amendment allowing debt to "suppress forest fires."[4]

SECTION 11

State debts generally; manner of contracting; referendum. Except the
debts specified in sections 9 and 10 of this article, no debt shall be hereafter
contracted by or in behalf of the state, unless such debt shall be authorized
by law, for some single work or purpose, to be distinctly specified therein.
No such law shall take effect until it shall, at a general election, have been
submitted to the people, and have received a majority of all the votes cast
for and against it at such election nor shall it be submitted to be voted on
within three months after its passage nor at any general election when any
other law or any bill shall be submitted to be voted for or against. The
legislature may, at any time after the approval of such law by the people,
if no debt shall have been contracted in pursuance thereof, repeal the same;
and may at any time, by law, forbid the contracting of any further debt or
liability under such law. [Const. 1846, Art. VII, sec. 12; renumbered Art.
VII, sec. 4, Const. 1894 as amend. in 1905 and 1920; amend. and
renumbered Art. VII, sec. 11, 1938]

No single section of the state constitution has had more effect on the state's
financial practices than this one. It was originally a response to the accumulation
of excessive state debt by the legislature. With the exception noted in sections
8 and 9, the faith and credit debt of the state cannot be created by the legislature
unless the proposal for such debt relates to a single purpose or object distinctly
stated and is submitted to the voters for their approval or disapproval at the next
general election. The three months interim was to give the public enough time
to ponder the issue presented to them. The clause disallowing any other law to
be on the ballot at the same time was meant to ensure that the voters would not
be distracted and would focus on the issue of state debt. This section exemplified
American distrust of governmental power and the belief that all governments,
even free ones, are disposed to the "besetting sin" of contracting debt. The
single-purpose or -object phrase of this section has been the subject of much
litigation. Its purpose is to prevent multipurpose debt, but its meaning is anything
but clear. Courts have given the legislature a fair amount of leeway in interpreting
the phrase but have set outer limits to that discretion. When the state sought a
bond authorization under the title "Comprehensive Community Development,"
which included industrial development, conservation and environment, tourism
and recreation, and local transportation access, the court said use of semantics
cannot obscure the fact that this bonded indebtedness lumped three or four
different purposes together into one bond issue in order to gain support from
adherents of each to approve the authorization (New York Public Interest Research Group, Inc. v. Carey, 1977). Resort to public authorities to which this
section does not apply has undermined the efficacy of this section (see Art. X).

SECTION 12

State debts generally; how paid; restrictions on use of bond proceeds. Except the debts specified in sections 9 and 10 of this article, all debts contracted by the state and each portion of any such debt from time to time so contracted shall be paid in equal annual installments, the first of which shall be payable not more than one year, and the last of which shall be payable not more than forty years, after such debt or portion thereof shall have been contracted, provided, however, that in contracting any such debt the privilege of paying all or any part of such debt prior to the date on which the same shall be due may be reserved to the state in such manner as may be provided by law. No such debt shall be contracted for a period longer than that of the probable life of the work or purpose for which the debt is to be contracted, to be determined by general laws, which determination shall be conclusive.

The money arising from any loan creating such debt or liability shall be applied only to the work or purpose specified in the act authorizing such debt or liability, or for the payment of such debt or liability, including any notes or obligations issued in anticipation of the sale of bonds evidencing such debt or liability. [Const. 1846, Art. VII, sec. 12; renumbered Art. VII, sec. 4, Const. 1894 as amend. in 1905, 1918 and 1920; amend. and renumbered Art. VII, sec. 12, 1938]

This section specifies how the state's debt shall be paid and provides the mechanism for relating the life of a bond issue to the life of the improvement for which the bond has been issued. All bond issue debt must be paid off in forty years, and no bond issue can extend to a period longer than the life of the project being financed. The first paragraph requires the issuance of serial bonds whose debt must be paid in equal annual installments starting no later than a year from the time at which the debt was contracted. Serial bonds foreclose the temptation of administrations to make improvements but relegate payment for those improvements to future administrations and taxpayers. Serial bonds enable the government to calculate costs over time, thus bringing some regularity and predictability to government finance. Forty years was chosen because it was seen as more coincident "with the life of the generation authorizing such debt."[5]

SECTION 13

Refund of state debts. The legislature may provide means and authority whereby any state debt may be refunded if, when it was contracted, the privilege to pay prior to the date payable was reserved to the state and provided that the debt as thus refunded shall be paid in equal annual installments which shall be not less in amount than the required annual installments of the debt so refunded. [1938]

Section 13 authorizes the state to insert ''call'' provisions in its bonds, enabling the state to refund bonds that may have been issued at high interest rates when the rates drop. Surplus revenues may be used for the early redemption of the debt.

SECTION 14

State debt for elimination of railroad crossings at grade; expenses; how borne; construction and reconstruction of state highways and parkways. The legislature may authorize by law the creation of a debt or debts of the state, not exceeding in the aggregate three hundred million dollars, to provide moneys for the elimination, under state supervision, of railroad crossings at grade within the state, and for incidental improvements connected therewith as authorized by this section. The provisions of this article, not inconsistent with the section, relating to the issuance of bonds for a debt or debts of the state and the maturity and payment thereof, shall apply to a state debt or debts created pursuant to this section; except that the law authorizing the contracting of such debt or debts shall take effect without submission to the people pursuant to section 11 of this article. The aggregate amount of a state debt or debts which may be created pursuant to this section shall not exceed the difference between the amount of the debt or debts heretofore created or authorized by law, under the provisions of section 14 of article VII of the constitution in force on July first, nineteen hundred thirty-eight, and the sum of three hundred million dollars. The expense of any grade cross-ing elimination the construction work for which was not commenced before January first, nineteen hundred thirty-nine, including incidental improvements connected therewith as authorized by this section, whether or not an order for such elimination shall theretofore have been made, shall be paid by the state in the first instance, but the state shall be entitled to recover from the railroad company or companies, by way of reimbursement (1) the entire amount of the railroad improvements not an essential part of elimination, and (2) the amount of the net benefit to the company or companies from the elimination exclusive of such railroad improvements, the amount of such net benefit to be adjudicated after the completion of the work in the manner to be prescribed by law, and in no event to exceed fifteen per centum of the expense of the elimination, exclusive of all incidental improvements. The reimbursement by the railroad companies shall be payable at such times, in such manner and with interest at such rate as the legislature may prescribe.

The expense of any grade crossing elimination the construction work for which was commenced before January first, nineteen hundred thirty-nine, shall be borne by the state, railroad companies, and the municipality or municipalities in the proportions formerly prescribed by section 14 of article VII of the constitution in force on July first, nineteen hundred thirty-eight, and the law or laws enacted pursuant to its provisions, applicable to such elimination, and subject to the provisions of such former section and law or laws, including advances in aid of any railroad company or municipality, although such elimination shall not be completed until after January first, nineteen hundred thirty-nine.

A grade crossing elimination the construction work for which shall be commenced after January first, nineteen hundred thirty-nine, shall include incidental improvements rendered necessary or desirable because of such elimination, and reasonably included in the engineering plans therefor.

Out of the balance of all moneys authorized to be expended under section 14 article VII of the constitution in force on July first, nineteen hundred thirty-eight, and remaining unexpended and unobligated on such date, fifty million dollars shall be deemed segregated for grade crossing eliminations and incidental improvements in the city of New York and shall be available only for such purposes until such eliminations and improvements are completed and paid for.

Notwithstanding any of the foregoing provisions of this section the legislature is hereby authorized to appropriate, out of the proceeds of bonds now or hereafter sold to provide moneys for the elimination of railroad crossing at grade and incidental improvements pursuant to this section, sums not exceeding in the aggregate sixty million dollars for the construction and reconstruction of state highways and parkways. [Const. 1894, Art. VII, sec. 14 as amend. in 1925; amend. 1927, 1938, 1941]

Prior constitutional amendments had brought little progress toward the elimination of railroad grade crossings, either because the railroads were financially unable or were simply unwilling to bear their costs of the elimination. Those costs had been set at 50 percent. This section, which some referred to as the railroad relief amendment, was based on the assumption that the railroads could not pay the 50 percent. It required the state to bear the cost of all projects begun after January 1, 1939, except that the state was permitted to seek reimbursement, not to exceed 15 percent of the expense involved, for improvements that resulted in a net benefit to the railroads.

Fifty million dollars of the $300 million authorized was earmarked for the elimination of all grade crossing in New York City. In 1942, an amendment allowed $60 million of the grade crossing bond issue funds to be used for improvements of highways and parkways. The amendment did not increase the bond indebtedness of the state; rather it changed the purpose for which part of the balance could be used.

SECTION 15

Sinking funds; how kept and invested; income therefrom and application thereof. The sinking funds provided for the payment of interest and the extinguishment of the principal of the debts of the state heretofore contracted shall be continued; they shall be separately kept and safely invested, and neither of them shall be appropriated or used in any manner other than for such payment and extinguishment as hereinafter provided. The comptroller shall each year appraise the securities held for investment in each of such funds at their fair market value not exceeding par. He shall then determine and certify to the legislature the amount of each of such funds and the amounts which, if thereafter annually contributed to each such fund, would, with the fund and with the accumulations thereon and upon the contributions thereto, computed at the rate of three per centum per annum, produce at the date of maturity the amount of the debt to retire which such fund was created, and the legislature shall thereupon appropriate as the contribution to each such fund for such year at least the amount thus certified.

If the income of any such fund in any year is more than a sum which, if annually added to such fund would, with the fund and its accumulations as aforesaid, retire the debt at maturity, the excess income may be applied to the interest on the debt for which the fund was created.

After any sinking fund shall equal in amount the debt for which it was created no further contribution shall be made thereto except to make good any losses ascertained at the annual appraisals above mentioned, and the income thereof shall be applied to the payment of the interest on such a debt. Any excess in such income not required for the payment of interest may be applied to the general fund of the state. [Const. 1846, Art. VII, sec. 13 as added in 1874; renumbered Art. VII, sec. 5, Const. 1894 as amend. in 1920; amend. and renumbered Art. VII, sec. 15, 1938]

A sinking fund is a mechanism for systematic retirement of state debt in which revenue is earmarked for a special fund to retire debt created by particular projects. The first paragraph was intended to preserve the inviolability of the sinking funds and had the effect of preventing the state from borrowing from sinking funds for current expenses. By implication, the section provides for the creation of separate sinking funds for each issue. The annual installments are to be computed on the basis of an interest earning at the rate of 3 percent annually. Any excess in the sinking fund can be used to reduce appropriations to the fund for the payment of interest on the debt for which the fund had been created. Any additional excess can be transferred to the general fund. Because sinking funds are based on the assessed value of state property in the fiscal year, any increase in these values increases the value of the sinking fund, inflating it beyond the projected need and making the tax burden higher than necessary. These latter provisions were added to overcome the rigidities of sinking funds.

SECTION 16

Payment of state debts; when comptroller to pay without appropriation. The legislature shall annually provide by appropriation for the payment of the interest upon and installments of principal of all debts created on behalf of the state except those contracted under section 9 of this article, as the same shall fall due, and for the contribution to all of the sinking funds heretofore created by law, of the amounts annually to be contributed under the provisions of section 15 of this article. If at any time the legislature shall fail to make any such appropriation, the comptroller shall set apart from the first revenues thereafter received, applicable to the general fund of the state, a sum sufficient to pay such interest, installments of principal, or contributions to such sinking fund, as the case may be, and shall so apply the moneys thus set apart. The comptroller may be required to set aside and apply such revenues as aforesaid, at the suit of any holder of such bonds. [Const. 1894, Art. VII, sec. 11 as amend. in 1920; amend. and renumbered Art. VII, sec. 16, 1938]

This section makes appropriations for the debt mandatory on the legislature. It establishes a priority on revenue funds over all other uses and, most strikingly, gives the comptroller the power to set aside such appropriations if the legislature fails to do so. With the adoption of this provisions, the state in effect surrendered its sovereign right to repudiate its debts. Bondholders are explicitly granted the right to enforce their bond contracts on the state in a judicial forum.

SECTION 17

Authorizing the legislature to establish a fund or funds for tax revenue stabilization reserves; regulating payments thereto and withdrawals therefrom. The legislature may establish a fund or funds to aid in the stabilization of the tax revenues of the state available for expenditure or distribution. Any law creating such a fund shall prescribe the method of determining the amount of revenue from any such tax or taxes which shall constitute a norm of each fiscal year. Such part as shall be prescribed by law of any revenue derived from such tax or taxes during a fiscal year in excess of such norm shall be paid into such fund. No moneys shall at any time be withdrawn from such fund unless the revenue derived from such tax or taxes during a fiscal year shall fall below the norm for such year; in which event such amount as may be prescribed by law, but in no event an amount exceeding the difference between such revenue and such norms, shall be paid from such fund into the general fund.

No law changing the method of determining a norm or prescribing the amount to be paid into such a fund or to be paid from such a fund into the general fund may become effective until three years from the date of its enactment. [1943]

This section permits the legislature to establish a tax stabilization reserve fund(s). The purpose of such a fund is to set aside part of the state's revenue in time of surplus as a reserve against depressed times. Its chief sponsor, Assemblyman Abbot Low Moffat, noted that "there is no way under the present constitution that this can be done without the danger that some subsequent legislature will raid the reserve for political purposes."[6] The amendment is entirely permissive but, if implemented, triggers the restrictions in the section. It would mean the establishment of tax norms whereby if revenue was greater than expected, the legislature could set aside the surplus as a reserve for times when tax revenues did not meet the norm. In a further attempt to prevent manipulation and misuse of fund, the section stipulates that any law changing the method of determining the norm will not be effective for three years following its adoption. The end result of such fund(s) is to lessen the likelihood of new taxes in times of recession or depression. The state has implemented this provision and created a number of these funds.

SECTION 18

Bonus on account of service of certain veterans in World War II. The legislature may authorize by law the creation of a debt or debts of the state to provide for the payment of a bonus to each male and female member of the armed forces of the United States, still in the armed forces, or separated or discharged under honorable conditions, for service while on active duty with the armed forces at any time during the period from December seventh, nineteen hundred forty-one to and including September second, nineteen hundred forty-five, who was a resident of this state for a period of at least six months immediately prior to his or her enlistment, induction or call to active duty. The law authorizing the creation of the debt shall provide for payment of such bonus to the next of kin of each male or female member of the armed forces who, having been a resident of this state for a period of six months immediately prior to his or her enlistment, induction or call to active duty, while on active duty at any time during the period from December seventh, nineteen hundred forty-one to and including September second, nineteen hundred forty-five; or who died while on active duty subsequent to September second, nineteen hundred forty-five, or after his or her separation or discharge under honorable conditions, prior to receiving payments of such bonus. An apportionment of the moneys on the basis of the periods and places of service of such members of the armed forces shall be provided by general laws. The aggregate of the debts authorized by this section shall not exceed four hundred million dollars. The provisions of this article, not consistent with this section, relating to the issuance of bonds for a debt or debts of the state and the maturity and payment thereof, shall apply to a debt or debts created pursuant to this section; except that the law authorizing the contracting of such debt or debts shall take effect without submission to the people pursuant to section eleven of this article.

Proceeds of bonds issues pursuant to law, as authorized by this section as in force prior to January first, nineteen hundred fifty shall be available and may be expended for the payment of such bonus to persons qualified therefor as now provided by this section. [1947, amend. 1949]

Section 18 provides for a cash bonus to New York State veterans of World War II and to the next of kin of deceased members of the armed forces. The actual amount was left to the legislature, but in no case could the aggregate amount exceed $400 million. Those who were residents six months prior to induction or enlistment were eligible for the bonus. Residency in the state at the time of application is not required. This provision was necessitated by People v. Westchester County National Bank (1921), which interpreted section 8 so as to cast doubt on legislative power to grant such bonuses. The provision exempts any debt created from the referendum requirement of section 11.

SECTION 19

State debt for expansion of state university. The legislature may authorize by law the creation of a debt or debts of the state, not exceeding in the aggregate two hundred fifty million dollars, to provide moneys for the construction, reconstruction, rehabilitation, improvement and equipment of facilities for the expansion and development of the program of higher education provided and to be provided at institutions now or hereafter comprised within the state university, for acquisition of real property therefore, and for payment of the state's share of the capital costs of locally sponsored institutions of higher education approved and regulated by the state university trustees. The provisions of this article, not inconsistent with this section, relating to the issuance of bonds for a debt or debts of the state and the maturity and payment thereof, shall apply to a state debt or debts created pursuant to this section; except that the law authorizing the contracting of such debt or debts shall take effect without submission to the people pursuant to section eleven of this article. [1957]

A third constitutional exception to the debt limitations of this article is created by this section. It provides for the creation of a debt of $250 million for the expansion of the State University of New York. The amendment, approved in 1957, was the first opportunity New Yorkers had to express their attitude toward the state university system. They approved the amendment by a million votes.

Article VIII

Local Finances

The local finance article contains a number of complex restrictions on debt and taxes, even more exceptions to these restrictions, and a number of special provisions for New York City. Like many other state constitution finance articles, it is a detailed list of restrictions on the debt, borrowing, and taxing powers of local governments. These limitations take the form of regulations on the methods, purposes, time period, and conditions and cumulative amount of indebtedness that can be incurred. The restrictions include: restrictions on gifts or loans of money, property, or credit (section 1); limits on total amount of debt that may be incurred, along with a clause allowing the legislature to limit that amount further (sections 4, 5); limits on the amount to be raised by real estate taxes for local purposes (sections 10, 12); and state control of the allocation of property taxes (section 12; Art. III, sec. 1; Art. XVI, sec. 1). In addition to the restrictions contained in this article, local governments are the creatures of the state as far as their taxing powers are concerned (Art. IX sec. 2c(8)); the state controls the creation of public authorities (Art. X, sec. 5); and the state prohibits local governments from guaranteeing or assuming the debt of public authorities (Art. X, sec. 5). It should be noted that while the 1938 Constitutional Convention tightened the regulation of borrowing in the local finance article, it liberalized restrictions on borrowing for housing purposes in the new housing article (Art. XVIII).

The assumption underlying the restrictions embodied in Article VIII is that local governments cannot be trusted to act responsibly, especially in incurring debt and contingent liability that will not have to be paid until future years. The state must assume primary responsibility for regulation of local finance because fiscal irresponsibility on the part of local governments implicates the financial position of the state itself. The financial crisis in New York City in the mid–

1970s is vivid evidence of the close relationship between the fiscal integrity of state and local governments.

In spite of the labyrinth of provisions, there is some doubt as to whether these restrictions have fostered sound fiscal practices in local governments.[1] One reason for this doubt has been the willingness to pile exemption on constitutional exemption when the need arises. A second reason is the creation of public benefit corporations (authorities), which enable local governments to raise their de facto debt limits to many times the constitutional limits. These and similar practices have made it difficult to determine conclusively whether debt limits have actually restricted the total amount of borrowing, and if so to what degree.

The numerous exceptions coupled with the devices used to avoid the debt and tax limits have resulted in an article that is longer than the U.S. Constitution, contains cumbersome sentences of over 150 words, and is largely ineffectual in creating a constitutional framework for sound borrowing practices. The financial crisis in New York City and a series of court decisions denying local governments power to exclude from their tax limits taxes collected to pay for public employment retirement costs (Hurd v. City of Buffalo, 1974; Bethlehem Steel Corporation v. Board of Education, 1978) forced the legislature to adopt a series of emergency measures, but they have not forced a comprehensive reexamination of the constitutional law of local finance in New York.

SECTION 1

Gift or loan of property or credit of local subdivisions prohibited; exceptions for enumerated purposes. No county, city, town, village or school district shall give or loan any money or property to or in aid of any individual, or private corporation or association, or private undertaking, or become directly or indirectly the owner of stock in, or bonds or, any private corporation or association; nor shall any county, city, town, village or school district give or loan its credit to or in aid of any individual, or public or private corporation or association, or private undertaking, except that two or more such units may join together pursuant to law in providing any municipal facility, service, activity or undertaking which each of such units has the power to provide separately. Each such unit may be authorized by the legislature to contract joint or several indebtedness, pledge its or their faith and credit for the payment of such indebtedness for such joint undertaking and levy real estate or other authorized taxes or impose charges therefore subject to the provisions of this constitution otherwise restricting the power of such units to contract indebtedness or to levy taxes on real estate. The legislature shall have power to provide by law for the manner and the proportion in which indebtedness arising out of such joint undertakings shall be incurred by such units and shall have power to provide a method by which such indebtedness shall be determined, allocated and apportioned among such units and such indebtedness treated for purposes of exclusion from applicable constitutional limitations, provided that in no event shall more than the total amount of indebtedness incurred for such joint undertaking be included in ascertaining the power of all such participating units to incur indebtedness. Such law may provide that such determination, allocation and apportionment shall be conclusive if made or approved by the comptroller. This provision shall not prevent a county from contracting indebtedness for the purpose of advancing to a town or school district, pursuant to law, the amount of unpaid taxes returned to it.

Subject to the limitations on indebtedness and taxation applying to any county, city, town or village nothing in this constitution contained shall prevent a county, city or town from making such provision for the aid, care and support of the needy as may be authorized by law, nor prevent any such county, city or town from providing for the care, support, maintenance and secular education of inmates of orphan asylums, homes for dependent children or correctional institutions and of children placed in family homes by authorized agencies, whether under public or private control, or from providing health and welfare services for all children, nor shall anything in this constitution contained prevent a county, city, town or village from increasing the pension benefits payable to retired members of a police department or fire department or to widows, dependent children or dependent parents of members or retired members of a police department or fire department; or prevent the city of New York from increasing the pension benefits payable to widows, dependent children or dependent parents of members or retired members of the relief and pension fund of the department of street cleaning of the city of New York. Payments by counties, cities or towns to charitable, eleemosynary, correctional and reformatory institutions and agencies, wholly or partly under private control, for care, support and maintenance, may be authorized, but shall not be required, by the legislature. No such payments shall be made for any person cared for by any such institution or agency, nor for a child placed in a family home, who is not received and retained therein pursuant to rules established by the state board of social welfare or other state department having the power of inspection thereof. [Const. 1846, Art. VIII, Sec. 11 as added in 1874; amend. and renumbered Art. VIII, sec. 10; amend. 1931, amend. and renumbered Art. VIII, sec. 1, 1938; amend. 1959, 1963, 1965]

The first paragraph of this section originated in the era of municipal defaults in the 1870s, when the credit of municipalities was used to aid private corporations, especially railroads and land speculators. Article VII, section 1 had prohibited the state from providing such credit to private corporations; the railroads, in response, turned to local governments. Local governments are forbidden to give or loan their property or money to any private corporation. In 1938, this prohibition was extended to public corporations as well, but local governments may give their money or property to public corporations. The distinction allows flexibility with regard to the moneys of the state while preventing any impairment of local credit on which the solvency and financial structure of local government are founded.[2] The greater danger was use of credit because it does not require taxes to be raised at the time obligations are incurred, thus passing on burdens to future generations. The gifts and loan provision of this section is an addition to and stricter than the federal and state public purpose doctrine which merely require that taxing and spending be undertaken for some valid public purpose.

The court of appeals indicated its approach to this section in Union Free School District No. 3, Town of Rye v. Town of Rye (1939). The town of Rye was mandated by statute to borrow money to pay the uncollected school taxes with no obligation on the part of the school district to repay the town. The court rejected the claim that such borrowing constituted a gift or loan of credit of the town to or in aid of the school district. The specific arrangement was not a gift or loan of credit because the town was not borrowing for the school district's purposes but for its own purposes. The state legislature had made it a town function or purpose to pay the money for the schools thus the town was borrowing for its own purposes. In *Union Free School District*, the court came close to allowing the state to define as a function of one municipality the provision of its credit to that of another municipality, thus reducing the significance of the prohibition.

The effectiveness of this restriction was further diluted in Comereski v. City of Elmira (1955). There a public corporation, a parking authority, was authorized to sell bonds and construct and operate parking lots in the city. The city was authorized to contract with the authority to pay any yearly deficits incurred by the authority up to $25,000, with revenues to be generated from parking meters on the city's streets. In sustaining the arrangement against a challenge based on this section, the court of appeals ruled that the city had not contracted its credit in aid of a public corporation but rather had contracted to make a gift to the corporation of $25,000 a year. The court majority based its decision on pragmatism: "The problems of a modern city can never be solved unless arrangements like these . . . are upheld. . . . We should not strain ourselves to find illegality in such programs" (at 254). The court failed to examine or cite Article X, section 5, which would seem to have a direct bearing on the facts of this case.

Whether this arrangement was merely an evasion of the restrictions of this section or not, the case provided an important precedent for later extensions of and variations on this arrangement. Just such an extension and variation was presented in Wein v. City of New York (1975). A Stabilization Reserve Corporation, the prototype of the Municipal Assistance Corporation, created to meet New York City's unprecedented financial crisis, was authorized to issue bonds, the proceeds of which would be paid to the city comptroller for use by the city's general fund. Although the law stated that the bonds or other obligations of the corporation were not the debt of the city or the state, the city was authorized to pay such amounts as necessary to maintain the debt service reserve fund to assure annual payment on the bonds issued by the corporation. If the city did not make such payments, the state comptroller was authorized to pay the first moneys available to the fund. Such a scheme, it was argued, amounted to a commitment of the city's credit to discharge the obligations of the corporation. A closely divided court sustained the statute by relying on the reasoning of *Comereski*. The court reasoned that the city had an absolute right following receipt of state aid to pay a portion of that aid to a public benefit corporation. The fact that this scheme involved a commitment to continue to do so in future years—a clear pledge of the city's credit—did not seem to trouble the court. The effect of this extension of *Comereski* to a non-self-sustaining public corporation is to enable local governments to circumvent the restrictions of section 1 of this article and section 5 of Article X.

The court has permitted a municipality to lease its public improvements to private concerns as long as the benefit accrues to the public and the municipalities and the facility is to be used for a public purpose, one that the municipality itself would be able to undertake (Murphy v. Erie County, 1971). The provision would not prevent a county from leasing a renovated stadium from a private investor and then in turn leasing it to a private baseball team for eighteen years if the agreements were entered into for a legitimate public purpose—in this case, public entertainment.[3]

Federal moneys received by a municipality under a program that permits loans to private entities are not subject to the loan-and-gift clause.[4]

Much litigation and numerous comptrollers' opinions have dealt with the questions of whether a disbursement is to be considered a gift or payment for consideration, which may include satisfaction of a moral or equitable obligation when it is legitimate to disburse moneys to public employees or for the improvement or maintenance of private property, and the legitimacy of gifts or loans to private organizations such as little leagues, drug abuse programs, and chambers of commerce (e.g., Antonopolulous v. Beame, 1973; People v. Prendergast, 1911; Opins. Compt. Gen., 82–255, 81–384, 78–899). The limitation on gifts to private corporations can be overcome by virtually any form of consideration because if there is consideration there is no gift.

Numerous statutes existed allowing for local intergovernmental cooperation, but constitutional authorization was required for exemptions to the prohibition on loan of credit to another public corporation or borrowing for other than a municipal purpose. The first paragraph constitutionalized the power of local governments to cooperate and also provided broad authority for cooperation among any combination of local governmental units. The goal was to encourage local governments to cooperate in providing more efficient services to their inhabitants. Section 1 supersedes the more specific exemptions for water sewage and drainage granted in section 2(A–F) of this article. Local governmental units are not permitted to cooperate for any purposes they could not constitutionally pursue on their own. This is significant because counties do not possess the full array of urban functions. In those areas, joint city-county cooperative ventures would not be permitted under this section. Joint ventures involving housing would be prohibited because housing is not a county purpose. Counties are excluded from the provision of the housing article (Art. XVIII).

The legislature determines how the indebtedness arising out of these joint ventures shall be determined, allocated, and apportioned. Generally the debt is apportioned against the debt capacity of the participating governments.

The second paragraph contains a series of exceptions to the prohibition contained in the opening of this section. They parallel those found in Article VII, section 8(a), with local additions for New York City. It allows the use of moneys for sectarian institutions meeting state requirements that operate charitable or eleemosynary institutions (cf. Art. IX, sec. 3). The list of exceptions has grown over the years, with the most recent additions being increases in the pension benefits for sanitation workers, fire fighters, and police officers and their beneficiaries. The authorized exemptions are permissive only, creating no obligation on the part of local governments.

SECTION 2

Restrictions on indebtedness of local subdivisions; contracting and payment of local indebtedness; exceptions. No county, city, town, village or school district shall contract any indebtedness except for county, city, town, village or school district purposes, respectively. No indebtedness shall be contracted for longer than the period of probable usefulness of the object or purpose for which such indebtedness is to be contracted, to be determined by or pursuant to general or special laws, which determination shall be conclusive, and in no event for longer than forty years. No indebtedness hereafter contracted or any portion thereof shall be refunded beyond such period computed from the date such indebtedness was contracted. Indebtedness heretofore contracted may be refunded only with the approval of and on terms and conditions prescribed by the state comptroller, but in no event for a period exceeding twenty years from the date of such refunding. No indebtedness shall be contracted by any county, city, town, village or school district unless such county, city, town, village or school district shall have pledged its faith and credit for the payment of the principal thereof and the interest thereon. Except for indebtedness contracted in anticipation of the collection of taxes actually levied and uncollected or to be levied for the year when such indebtedness is contracted and indebtedness contracted to be paid in one of the two fiscal years immediately succeeding the fiscal year in which such indebtedness was contracted, including any refunding therefor, shall be paid in annual installments, the first of which, except in the case of refunding of indebtedness heretofore contracted, shall be paid not more than two years after such indebtedness or portion thereof shall have been contracted, and no installment, except in the case of refunding of indebtedness heretofore contracted, shall be more than fifty per centum in excess of the smallest prior installment.

Notwithstanding the foregoing provisions, indebtedness contracted by the city of New York and each portion of any such indebtedness from time to time so contracted for the supply of water, including the acquisition of land in connection with such purpose, may be financed either by serial bonds with a maximum maturity of fifty years, in which case such indebtedness shall be paid in annual installments as hereinbefore provided, or by sinking fund bonds with a maximum maturity of fifty years, which shall be redeemed through annual contributions to sinking funds established and maintained for the purpose of amortizing the indebtedness for which such bonds are issued. Notwithstanding the foregoing provisions, indebtedness hereafter contracted by the city of New York and each portion of any such indebtedness from time to time so contracted for (a) the acquisition, construction or equipment of rapid transit railroads, or (b) the construction of docks, including the acquisition of land in connection with any of such purposes, may be financed either by serial bonds with a maximum maturity of forty years, in which case such indebtedness shall be paid in annual installments as hereinbefore provided, or by sinking fund bonds with a maximum maturity of forty years, which shall be redeemed through annual contributions to sinking funds established and maintained for the purpose of amortizing the indebtedness for which such bonds are issued.

Notwithstanding the foregoing provisions, but subject to such requirements as the legislature shall impose by general or special law, indebtedness contracted by any county, city, town, village or school district and each portion thereof from time to time contracted for any object or purpose for which indebtedness may be contracted may also be financed by sinking fund bonds with a maximum maturity of fifty years, which shall be redeemed through annual contributions to sinking funds established by such county, city, town, village or school district, provided, however, that each such annual contribution shall be at least equal to the amount required, if any, to enable the sinking fund to redeem, on the date of the contribution, the same amount of such indebtedness as would have been paid and then be payable if such indebtedness had been financed entirely by the issuance of serial bonds, except, if an issue of sinking fund bonds is combined for sale with an issue of serial bonds, for the same object or purpose, then the amount of each annual sinking fund contribution shall be at least equal to the amount required, if any, to enable the sinking fund to redeem, on the date of each such annual contribution, (i) the amount which would be required to be paid annually if such indebtedness had been issued entirely as serial bonds, less (ii) the amount of indebtedness actually issued as serial bonds. Sinking funds established on or after January first, nineteen hundred eighty-six pursuant to the preceding sentence shall be maintained and managed by the state comptroller pursuant to such requirements and procedures as the legislature shall prescribe, including provisions for reimbursement by the issuer of bonds payable from such sinking funds for the expense related to such maintenance and management.

Provision shall be made annually by appropriation by every county, city, town, village and school district for the payment of interest on all indebtedness and for the amounts required for (a) the amortization and redemption of term bonds, sinking fund bonds and serial bonds, (b) the redemption of certificates or other evidence of indebtedness (except those issues in anticipation of the collection of taxes or other revenues, or renewals thereof, and which are described in paragraph A of section five of this article and those issues in anticipation of the receipt of the proceeds of the sale of bonds theretofore authorized) contracted to be paid in such year out of the tax levy or other revenues applicable to a reduction thereof, and (c) the redemption of certificates or other evidence of indebtedness issued in anticipation of the collection of taxes or other revenues, or renewals thereof, which are not retired within five years after their date of original issue. If at any time the respective appropriating authorities shall fail to make such appropriations, a sufficient sum shall be set apart from the first revenues thereafter received and shall be applied to such purposes. The fiscal officer of any county, city, town, village or school district may be required to set apart and apply such revenues as aforesaid at the suit of any holder of obligations issued for any such indebtedness. [1938; amend. 1949, 1953, 1985]

The first paragraph contains provisions regulating local borrowing in order to ensure sound practices and preserve and strengthen local credit. Parallel provisions are found in the state finance article (VII, sec. 12). Refunding may not be used as a means of extending repayment of debt beyond the period authorized. The last sentence restricts the refunding of debts contracted prior to 1939 to a period of no more than twenty years with the approval of the comptroller.

The second paragraph requires that all indebtedness be supported by the faith and credit of the issuing locality and that all such indebtedness, except in anticipation of taxes actually levied and uncollected or to be levied for the year in which such indebtedness is contracted, shall be by serial bonds payable in annual installments. In order to avoid fractional redemptions and ballooning of debt payments, the section provides that all installments need not be equal but that no installment be more than 50 percent in excess of the smallest prior payment subsequent to the first installment. This requirement would prevent pyramiding of debt and deferring debt payment. The serial bond system of financing debt adopted earlier by the state was applied to local government for similar reasons (see Art. VII).

Because of the unique financial problems facing New York City, exceptions to these limitations were made. The city was permitted to issue either serial or sinking fund bonds with a maximum maturity of forty years for water supply, rapid transit, and dock construction.

The fourth paragraph enables cities, towns, villages, and school districts (municipalities) to issue sinking fund bonds to be repaid from sinking funds funded by the issuer for any purpose for which serial bonds may be currently sold. This authorization gives municipalities more flexibility in bond markets. New York City is the chief beneficiary of this amendment because an inability to satisfy investor demand for nonserial bonds means payment of higher interest rates to increase the marketability of serial bonds with less desirable maturities.

The final paragraph is modeled after Article VII, section 11 and was adopted for similar reasons: to safeguard the credit of local governments and thereby assume the lowest interest rates and the ability to issue bonds when necessary by granting to bondholders first claim on all available revenues and the right to initiate suit in court for enforcement of those claims.

This section has also lost some of its sting as a result of decisions like *Wein v. City* and *Comereski v. Elmira*. By diverting a source of city revenue to a public benefit corporation and enabling the corporation to borrow against that stream of revenue, with the provision that the city will not itself be liable for the debt of the public corporation, the faith-and-credit pledge is bypassed.

There are, however, limits to what the court will allow. *Flushing National Bank v. Municipal Assistance Corporation* (1976) provided one such limitation on attempts to skirt the faith-and-credit clause. The state set up the Municipal Assistance Corporation (MAC) and imposed a three-year moratorium on the city's outstanding short-term obligation on those holders who declined to accept long-term bonds issued by the MAC whose bonds were not backed by the full faith and credit of the state or the city. By depriving short-term noteholders of judicial remedies for at least three years, the Moratorium Act made meaningless the verbal pledge of faith and credit. In what can be seen as a partial repudiation of the language of *Comereski*, the court wrote: "Emergencies and the police power, although they may modify their applications, do not suspend constitutional principles" (at 740).

SECTION 2–a

Local indebtedness for water supply, sewage and drainage facilities and purposes; allocations and exclusions of indebtedness. Notwithstanding the provisions of section one of this article, the legislature by general or special law and subject to such conditions as it shall impose:

A. May authorize any county, city, town or village or any county or town on behalf of an improvement district to contract indebtedness to provide a supply of water, in excess of its own needs, for sale to any other public corporation or improvement district;

B. May authorize two or more public corporations and improvement districts to provide for a common supply of water and may authorize any such corporation, or any county or town on behalf of an improvement district, to contract joint indebtedness for such purpose or to contract indebtedness for specific proportions of the cost;

C. May authorize any county, city, town or village or any county or town on behalf of an improvement district to contract indebtedness to provide facilities, in excess of its own needs, for the conveyance, treatment and disposal of sewage from any other public corporation or improvement district;

D. May authorize two or more public corporations and improvement districts to provide for the common conveyance, treatment and disposal of sewage and may authorize any such corporation, or any county or town on behalf of an improvement district, to contract joint indebtedness for such purpose or to contract indebtedness for specific proportions of the cost;

E. May authorize any county, city, town or village or any county or town on behalf of an improvement district to contract indebtedness to provide facilities, in excess of its own needs, for drainage purposes from any other public corporation or improvement district;

F. May authorize two or more public corporations and improvement districts to provide for a common drainage system and may authorize any such corporation, or any county or town on behalf of an improvement district, to contract joint indebtedness for such purpose or to contract indebtedness for specific proportions of the cost.

Indebtedness contracted by a county, city, town or village pursuant to this section shall be for a county, city, town or village purpose, respectively. In ascertaining the power of a county, city, town or village to contract indebtedness any indebtedness contracted pursuant to paragraphs A and B of this section shall be excluded. The legislature shall provide the method by which a fair proportion of joint indebtedness contracted pursuant to paragraphs D and F of this section shall be allocated to any county, city, town or village.

The legislature by general law in terms and in effect applying alike to all counties, to all cities, to all towns and/or to all villages also may provide that all or any part of indebtedness contracted or proposed to be contracted by any county, city, town or village pursuant to paragraphs D and F of this section for a revenue producing public improvement or service may be excluded periodically in ascertaining the power of such county, city, town or village to contract indebtedness. The amount of any such exclusion shall have a reasonable relation to the extent to which such public improvement or service shall have yielded or is expected to yield revenues sufficient to provide for the payment of the interest on and amortization of or payment of indebtedness contracted or proposed to be contracted for such public improvement or service, after deducting all costs of operation, maintenance and repairs thereof. The legislature shall provide the method by which a fair proportion of joint indebtedness proposed to be contracted pursuant to paragraphs D and F of this section shall be allocated to any county, city, town or village for the purpose of determining the amount of any such exclusion. The provisions of paragraph C of section five and section ten-a of this article shall not apply to indebtedness contracted pursuant to paragraphs D and F of this section.

The legislature may provide that any allocation of indebtedness, or determination of the amount of any exclusion of indebtedness, made pursuant to this section shall be conclusive if made or approved by the state comptroller. [1953, amend. 1955]

This section allows the legislature to authorize any county, city, town, or village or any city, town, or village on behalf of an improvement district to contract indebtedness for a supply of water, or conveyance, treatment and disposal of sewage for sale to any other public corporation or improvement district. It permits two or more public corporations and improvement districts to provide a common supply of water or joint sewage and drainage facilities and to contract joint indebtedness for such purposes or to contract indebtedness for fixed proportions or the costs (see Art. IX, sec. 1(c)). The indebtedness incurred shall be excluded in ascertaining the power of the county, city, town, or village to contract indebtedness. This section removes any doubts raised by section 1 of this article as to the constitutionality of such joint ventures. The amendment encourages local governments to develop adequate water and sewage systems and to construct facilities common to several governmental units, saving money and providing more efficient delivery services. It has been superseded by the broader authority granted in section 1.

SECTION 3

Restrictions on creation and indebtedness of certain corporations. No municipal or other corporation (other than a county, city, town, village, school district or fire district, or a river improvement, river regulating, or drainage district, established by or under the supervision of the department of conservation) possessing the power (a) to contract indebtedness and (b) to levy taxes or benefit assessments upon real estate or to require the levy of such taxes or assessments, shall hereafter be established or created, but nothing herein shall prevent the creation of improvement districts in counties and towns, provided that the county or town or towns in which such districts are located shall pledge its or their faith and credit for the payment of the principal of an interest on all indebtedness to be contracted for the purposes of such districts, and in ascertaining the power of any such county or town to contract indebtedness, such indebtedness shall be included, unless such indebtedness would, under the provisions of this article, be excluded in ascertaining the power of a county or town to contract indebtedness. No such corporation now existing shall hereafter contract any indebtedness without the consent, granted in such manner as may be prescribed by general law, of the city or village within which, or of the town within any unincorporated area of which any real estate may be subject to such taxes or assessments. If the real estate subject to such taxes or assessments is wholly within a city, village or the unincorporated area of a town, in ascertaining the power of such city, village or town to contract indebtedness, there shall be included any indebtedness hereafter contracted by such corporation, unless such indebtedness would, under the provisions of this article, be excluded if contracted by such city, village or town. If only part of the real estate subject to such taxes or assessments is within a city, village or the unincorporated area of a town, in ascertaining the power of such city, village or town to contract indebtedness, there shall be included the proportion, determined as prescribed by general law, of any indebtedness hereafter contracted by such corporation, unless such indebtedness would, under the provisions of this article, be excluded if contracted by such city, village or town. [1938]

Section 2–a allows local governments to borrow jointly, but this section prevents the creation of metropolitan districts, which would be able to provide area-wide services. This proscription on the creation of new, overlapping independent districts having the power to borrow and levy taxes and assessments on real estate is an attempt to prevent the development of borrowing loopholes. Exceptions are made for school districts, fire districts, certain districts under the state department of conservation, and local improvements districts in counties and towns that would pledge their faith and credit for the debt of such districts. The last part of the article spells out how such indebtedness shall be apportioned. The section further provides that no existing taxing unit shall incur any debt without the consent of the locality any of whose property is subject to taxation or assessment by these taxing units. Finally any debt incurred is to be included in determining the debt limitation of the locality, unless such debt would otherwise have been exempt had it been undertaken by the locality itself. The method of granting consent and apportioning debt, where property within more than one locality is subject to taxation or assessment by an independent taxing unit, is left to the legislature.

This section would prevent, for example, the creation of a sanitary district unless a county or town in which the district is located is willing to pledge its faith and credit to payment of the indebtedness created by that district. If the district was in existence prior to 1939, the constitution merely provides that no such corporation can contract debt without the consent of the city, village, or town in which the district is located, and that debt is to be included in the debt service of the city village or town.

SECTION 4

Limitations on local indebtedness. Except as otherwise provided in this constitution, no county, city, town, village or school district described in this section shall be allowed to contract indebtedness for any purpose or in any manner which, including existing indebtedness, shall exceed an amount equal to the following percentages of the average full valuation of taxable real estate of such county, city, town, village or school district:

(a) the county of Nassau, for county purposes, ten per centum;

(b) any county, other than the county of Nassau, for county purposes, seven per centum;

(c) the city of New York, for city purposes, ten per centum;

(d) any city, other than the city of New York, having one hundred twenty-five thousand or more inhabitants according to the latest federal census, for city purposes, nine per centum;

(e) any city having less than one hundred twenty-five thousand inhabitants according to the latest federal census, for city purposes, excluding education purposes, seven per centum;

(f) any town, for town purposes, seven per centum;

(g) any village for village purposes, seven per centum; and

(h) any school district which is coterminous with, or partly within, or wholly within, a city having less than one hundred twenty-five thousand inhabitants according to the latest federal census, for education purposes, five per centum; provided, however, that such limitation may be increased in relation to indebtedness for specified objects or purposes with (1) the approving vote or sixty per centum or more of the duly qualified voters of such school district voting on a proposition therefor submitted at a general or special election, (2) the consent of The Regents of the University of the State of New York and (3) the consent of the state comptroller. The legislature shall prescribe by law the qualifications for voting at any such election.

Except as otherwise provided in this constitution, any indebtedness contracted in excess of the respective limitations prescribed in this section shall be void.

In ascertaining the power of any city having less than one hundred twenty-five thousand inhabitants according to the latest federal census to contract indebtedness, indebtedness heretofore contracted by such city for education purposes shall be excluded. Such indebtedness so excluded shall be included in ascertaining the power of a school district which is coterminous with, or partly within, or wholly within, such city to contract indebtedness. The legislature shall prescribe by law the manner by which the amount of such indebtedness shall be determined and allocated among such school districts. Such law may provide that such determinations and allocations shall be conclusive if made or approved by the state comptroller.

In ascertaining the power of a school district described in this section to contract indebtedness, certificates or other evidences of indebtedness described in paragraph A of section five of this article shall be excluded.

The average full valuation of taxable real estate of any such county, city, town, village or school district shall be determined in the manner prescribed in section ten of this article.

Nothing contained in this section shall be deemed to restrict the powers granted to the legislature by other provisions of this constitution to further restrict the powers of any county, city, town, village or school district to contract indebtedness. [1938; amend. 1951]

Section 4 specifies the maximum debt-incurring capacity or ceiling on non-excludable net debt for different classes of local governments. The use of variable percentages reflects the differing financial needs of the local governments in the state. New York and the county of Nassau were given a limit of 10 percent, the highest in the article. New York received a high percentage to compensate for the fact that it had to provide for county purposes within its jurisdiction and Nassau because it had adopted a form of government requiring it to undertake functions that in other counties were undertaken by smaller units of government. For all other cities over 125,000, the limit was set at 9 percent; for cities under that size and all towns and villages, it is 7 percent; and for school districts coterminous with, partly within, or wholly within a city of less than 125,000 population, 5 percent, with the added proviso that the limit could be exceeded with the approval of 60 percent of the voters and the consent of the regents and the state comptroller. The 60 percent approval referendum was added to allow for flexibility in the face of future anticipated needs for school building construction. This section makes it clear that debts of these school districts are not to be included in the city's or village's debt, but such debt is to be included in the determination of the school district's ability to contract further indebtedness. The separate debt limits for cities and school districts would permit school reorganizations in and near cities without bringing the school debt within the city's debt limit. The amendment gives school districts control over and responsibility for their fiscal affairs.

The basis for computing the debt was the assessed real estate evaluations averaged over five years. A five-year rather than a one-year base was chosen to eliminate fluctuations in borrowing capacity caused by yearly increases or decreases in assessed valuations. A five-year period provides more stability in municipal financing. Full as opposed to fractional valuation, which varies enormously from one municipality to another as a fraction of market value, was adopted because it reflects more accurately a locality's ability to pay.

The state has provided local governments with a variety of avenues to evade debt limits. In addition to the creation of special districts and public authorities, the stated debt limitations are subject to a number of exclusions and exemptions (sec. 5–7). Moreover, in all areas of the state except for New York City, borrowing jurisdictions overlap, providing them with greater borrowing and taxing power. A village with 7 percent would also include an overlapping town limit of 7 percent, and overlapping county limit of 7 percent (10 percent for Nassau), for a total debt limit of 21 percent.

The court of appeals in Robertson v. Zimmermann (1935) held that the bonded indebtedness of a sewer authority whose bonds are paid solely with revenues generated by the authority with no liability on the part of the city were debts that did not have to be included with the city's debt. The decision encouraged the creation of similar authorities.

In New York State Electric & Gas Corp. v. Plattsburgh (1939), the court of appeals sustained a bond issue by an authority that was to be paid solely from revenue derived from the electric system but voided a bond issued for construction of the proposed new electric system that was to be paid from general revenues derived from taxable property of the city. Since the amount of those bonds put the city over its debt limits—at the time 10 percent—the bonds were issued in violation of this section. In Wein v. City of New York (1975), the court sustained an arrangement whereby the city of New York, though in no way obligated for the debts of the Stabilization Reserve Corporation, would commit its funds to keep the reserve fund solvent. The dissenters saw the entire scheme as a device to facilitate evasion of the debt ceiling of this section. Such use of these public benefit corporations has enabled municipalities to fund operating deficits without encumbering their constitutional and statutory debt limits. For these reasons, the debt limitations specified in this section have not been as effective as expected.

The last paragraph explicitly allows the legislature to place further restrictions on the power of local government to incur indebtedness. The provision was added to prevent the section from being interpreted as a limitation on the legislature's power to control the fiscal affairs of local governments. Cities under 125,000 inhabitants, and presumably others as well, are permitted to reduce their debt limits provided that such a reduction is subject to a referendum.[5]

SECTION 5

Ascertainment of debt-incurring power of counties, cities, towns and villages; certain indebtedness to be excluded. In ascertaining the power of a county, city, town or village to contract indebtedness, there shall be excluded:

A. Certificates or other evidences of indebtedness (except serial bonds of an issue having a maximum maturity of more than two years) issued for purposes other than the financing of capital improvements and contracted to be redeemed in one of the two fiscal years immediately succeeding the year of their issue, and certificates or other evidences of indebtedness issued in any fiscal year in anticipation of (a) the collection of taxes on real estate for amounts theretofore actually levied and uncollected or to be levied in such year and payable out of such taxes, (b) moneys receivable from the state which have theretofore been apportioned by the state or which are to be so apportioned within one year after their issue and (c) the collection of any other taxes due and payable or to become due and payable within one year or of other revenues to be received within one year after their issue; excepting any such certificates or other evidence of indebtedness or renewals thereof which are not retired within five years after their date of original issue.

B. Indebtedness heretofore or hereafter contracted to provide for the supply of water.

C. Indebtedness heretofore or hereafter contracted by any county, city, town or village for a public improvement or part thereof, or service, owned or rendered by such county, city, town or village, annually proportionately to the extent that the same shall have yielded to such county, city, town or village net revenue; provided, however, that such net revenue shall be twenty-five per centum or more of the amount required in such year for the payment of the interest on, amortization of, or payment of, such indebtedness. Such exclusion shall be granted only if the revenues of such public improvement or part thereof, or service, are applied to and actually used for payment of all costs of operation, maintenance and repairs, and payment of the amounts required in such year for interest on and amortization of or redemption of such indebtedness, or such revenues are deposited in a special fund to be used solely for such payments. Any revenues remaining after such payments are made may be used for any lawful purpose of such county, city, town or village, respectively. Net revenue shall be determined by deducting from gross revenues of the preceding year all costs of operation, maintenance and repairs for such year, or the legislature may provide that net revenue shall be determined by deducting from the average of the gross revenues of not to exceed five of the preceding years during which the public improvement or part thereof, or service, has been in operation, the average of all costs of operation, maintenance and repairs for the same years.

A proportionate exclusion of indebtedness contracted or proposed to be contracted also may be granted for the period from the date when such indebtedness is first contracted or to be contracted for such public improvement or part thereof, or service, through the first year of operation of such public improvement or part thereof, or service. Such exclusion shall be computed in the manner provided in this section on the basis of estimated net revenue which shall be determined by deducting from the gross revenues estimated to be received during the first year of operation of such public improvement or part thereof, or service, all estimated costs of operation, maintenance and repairs for such year. The amount of any such proportionate exclusion shall not exceed seventy-five per centum of the amount which would be excluded if the computation were made on the basis of net revenue instead of estimated net revenue.

Except as otherwise provided herein, the legislature shall prescribe the method by which and the terms and conditions under which the proportionate amount of any such indebtedness to be so excluded shall be determined and no proportionate amount of such indebtedness shall be excluded except in accordance with such determination. The legislature may provide that the state comptroller shall make such determination or it may confer appropriate jurisdiction on the appellate division of the supreme court in the judicial departments in which such counties, cities, towns or villages are located for the purpose of determining the proportionate amount of any such indebtedness to be so excluded.

The provisions of this paragraph C shall not affect or impair any existing exclusions of indebtedness, or the power to exclude indebtedness, granted by any other provision of this constitution.

D. Serial bonds, issued by any county, city, town or village which now maintains a pension or retirement system or fund which is not on an actuarial reserve basis with current payments to the reserve adequate to provide for all current accruing liabilities. Such bonds shall not exceed in the aggregate an amount sufficient to provide for the payment of the liabilities of such system or fund, accrued on the date of issuing such bonds, both on account of pensioners on the pension roll on that date and prospective pensions to dependents of such pensioners and on account of prior service of active members of such system or fund on that date. Such bonds or the proceeds thereof shall be deposited in such system or fund. Each such pension or retirement system or fund thereafter shall be maintained on an actuarial reserve basis with current payments to the reserve adequate to provide for all current accruing liabilities.

E. Indebtedness contracted on or after January first, nineteen hundred sixty-two and prior to January first, nineteen hundred ninety-four, for the construction or reconstruction of facilities for the conveyance, treatment and disposal of sewage. The legislature shall prescribe the method by which and the terms and conditions under which the amount of any such indebtedness to be excluded shall be determined, and no such indebtedness shall be excluded except in accordance with such determination.

[1938; amend. 1949; 1951; 1953; 1963; 1983]

This section contains the general exemptions from the debt limitations (see Wein v. State). In subdivision (A), tax anticipation notes are exempted, as well as notes issued against delinquent taxes. Certificates of indebtedness issued for purposes other than capital improvements and serial bonds issued for not more than two years are also exempted from the debt limits.

Subdivision (B) allows exemptions from debt incurred to supply water. Most water supply projects are in fact revenue producing.

Subdivision (C) exempts from debt limits any debt from revenue-producing projects proportionate to the extent that the revenues forthcoming from these projects, after covering operating expenses, cover the debt service charged. Municipalities are permitted to obtain a proportionate exemption of debt incurred for a revenue-producing undertaking at the time when the debt was contracted instead of only at the time when the improvement was completed. The exemption at the earlier time is limited to 25 percent of the amount of debt actually expected to be self-financing. The addition makes it easier for municipalities to finance revenue-producing undertakings. The legislature is directed to act and has authorized the comptroller to determine the amount of exclusion.

The purpose of subdivision (D) is to make it possible for municipalities to place unsound pension funds on an actuarially sound basis. Because this would require the contracting of debts, exempting such debt would give local governments an incentive to take this step. Also specified are the conditions under which these bonds shall be issued, limits on the amount, and conditions for the maintenance of the fund.

Subdivision (E) excludes from a local government's constitutional debt limits indebtedness contracted for sewer purposes. It was adopted to encourage localities to develop new sewer treatment facilities and meet their sewer requirements without impairing their ability to finance other essential capital expenditures.

SECTION 6

Debt-incurring power of Buffalo, Rochester and Syracuse; certain additional indebtedness to be excluded. In ascertaining the power of the cities of Buffalo, Rochester and Syracuse to contract indebtedness, in addition to the indebtedness excluded by section 5 of this article, there shall be excluded:

Indebtedness not exceeding in the aggregate the sum of ten million dollars, heretofore or hereafter contracted by the city of Buffalo or the city of Rochester and indebtedness not exceeding in the aggregate the sum of five million dollars heretofore or hereafter contracted by the city of Syracuse for so much of the cost and expense of any public improvement as may be required by the ordinance or other local law therein assessing the same to be raised by assessment upon local property or territory.

[Const. 1894, Art. VIII, sec. 10 as amend. in 1909; amend. and renumbered Art. VIII, sec. 6, 1938]

This amendment was obtained by these three cities, the largest in the state outside New York City, to help them cope with debt ratios approaching their constitutional limits. It exempts $10 million of assessments bonds in Buffalo and Rochester and $5 million in Syracuse from the debt service charged to the cities.

SECTION 7

Debt-incurring power of New York City; certain additional indebtedness to be excluded. In ascertaining the power of the city of New York to contract indebtedness, in addition to the indebtedness excluded by section 5 of this article, there shall be excluded:

A. Indebtedness contracted prior to the first day of January, nineteen hundred ten, for dock purposes proportionately to the extent to which the current net revenues received by the city therefrom shall meet the interest on and the annual requirements for the amortization of such indebtedness. The legislature shall prescribe the method by which and the terms and conditions under which the amount of any such indebtedness to be so excluded shall be determined, and no such indebtedness shall be excluded except in accordance with such determination. The legislature may confer appropriate jurisdiction on the appellate division of the supreme court in the first judicial department for the purpose of determining the amount of any such indebtedness to be so excluded.

B. The aggregate of indebtedness initially contracted from time to time after January first, nineteen hundred twenty-eight, for the construction or equipment, or both, of new rapid transit railroads, not exceeding the sum of three hundred million dollars. Any indebtedness thereafter contracted in excess of such sum for such purposes shall not be so excluded, but this provision shall not be construed to prevent the refunding of any of the indebtedness excluded hereunder.

C. The aggregate of indebtedness initially contracted from time to time after January first, nineteen hundred fifty, for the construction, reconstruction and equipment of city hospitals, not exceeding the sum of one hundred fifty million dollars. Any indebtedness thereafter contracted in excess of such sum for such purposes, other than indebtedness contracted to refund indebtedness excluded pursuant to this paragraph, shall not be so excluded.

D. The aggregate of indebtedness initially contracted from time to time after January first, nineteen hundred fifty-two, for the construction and equipment of new rapid transit railroads, including extensions of and interconnections with and between existing rapid transit railroads or portions thereof, and reconstruction and equipment of existing rapid transit railroads, not exceeding the sum of five hundred million dollars. Any indebtedness thereafter contracted in excess of such sum for such purposes, other than indebtedness contracted to refund indebtedness excluded pursuant to this paragraph, shall not be so excluded.

E. Indebtedness contracted for school purposes, evidenced by bonds, to the extent to which state aid for common schools, not exceeding two million five hundred thousand dollars, shall meet the interest and the annual requirements for the amortization and payment of part or all of one or more issues of such bonds. Such exclusion shall be effective only during a fiscal year of the city in which its expense budget provides for the payment of such debt service from such state aid. The legislature shall prescribe by law the manner by which the amount of any such exclusion shall be determined and such indebtedness shall not be excluded hereunder except in accordance with the determination so prescribed. Such law may provide that any such determination shall be conclusive if made or approved by the state comptroller.

[Const. 1894, Art. VIII, sec. 10 as amend. in 1909, 1927; amend. and renumbered Art. VIII, sec. 7, 1938; amend. 1949, 1951]

Section 7 deals exclusively with special exemptions for New York City. Subdivision (A) is obsolete since all the bonds issued before 1910 have been paid. In the mid–1920s New York City proposed to construct and operate an independent subway system estimated to cost $600 million. Near its debt limit and with little likelihood that the transit system would be self-supporting, the city appealed to the legislature, which passed an amendment (subdivision (B)) excluding $300 million in bonds from the debt limit.

Subdivision (C) allows the city to issue $150 million in bonds for hospital purposes outside the debt limit, and subdivision (D) allows the city to borrow, outside the debt limit, $500 million for new transit lines and the modernization of existing ones. This exclusion and that in (B) are one-time debt authorizations. Subdivision (E) authorizes New York City to exclude from its debt limit an amount of bonds for school purposes to the extent that such debt service on those bonds is supported by revenues not to exceed $2.5 million of the city from state aid for education. The actual increase in debt contracting power created by this exemption depends on, among others, prevailing interest rates. In 1950, the amount of increase was $40 million; by 1990, that amount had dropped to $24 million. The exemption was meant to aid the city in financing school construction and other capital improvements.

SECTION 7–a

Debt-incurring power of New York City; certain indebtedness for railroads and transit purposes to be excluded. In ascertaining the power of the city of New York to contract indebtedness, in addition to the indebtedness excluded under any other section of this constitution, there shall be excluded:

A. The aggregate of indebtedness initially contracted from time to time by the city for the acquisition of railroads and facilities or properties used in connection therewith or rights therein or securities of corporations owning such railroads, facilities or rights, not exceeding the sum of three hundred fifteen million dollars. Provision for the amortization of such indebtedness shall be made either by the establishment and maintenance of a sinking fund therefor or by annual payment of part thereof, or by both such methods. Any indebtedness thereafter contracted in excess of such sum for such purposes shall not be so excluded, but this provision shall not be construed to prevent the refunding of any such indebtedness.

Notwithstanding any other provision of the constitution, the city is hereby authorized to contract indebtedness for such purposes and to deliver its obligations evidencing such indebtedness to the corporations owning the railroads, facilities, properties or rights acquired, to the holders of securities of such owning corporations, to the holders of securities of corporations holding the securities of such owning corporations, or to the holders of securities to which such acquired railroads, facilities, properties or rights are now subject.

B. Indebtedness contracted by the city for transit purposes, and not otherwise excluded, proportionately to the extent to which the current net revenue received by the city from all railroads and facilities and properties used in connection therewith and rights therein owned by the city and securities of corporations owning such railroads, facilities, properties or rights, owned by the city, shall meet the interest and the annual requirements for the amortization and payment of such non-excluded indebtedness. In determining whether indebtedness for transit purposes may be excluded under this paragraph of this section, there shall first be deducted from the current net revenue received by the city from such railroads and facilities and properties used in connection therewith and rights therein and securities owned by the city: (a) an amount equal to the interest and amortization requirements on indebtedness for rapid transit purposes heretofore excluded by order of the appellate division, which exclusion shall not be terminated by or under any provision of this section; (b) an amount equal to the interest on indebtedness contracted pursuant to this section and of the annual requirements for amortization on any sinking fund bonds and for redemption of any serial bonds evidencing such indebtedness; (c) an amount equal to the sum of all taxes and bridge tolls accruing to the city in the fiscal year of the city preceding the acquisition or the railroads or facilities or properties or rights therein or securities acquired by the city hereunder, from such railroads, facilities and properties; and (d) the amount of net operating revenue derived by the city from the independent subway system during such fiscal year.

The legislature shall prescribe the method by which and the terms and conditions under which the amount of any indebtedness to be excluded hereunder shall be determined, and no indebtedness shall be excluded except in accordance with the determinations prescribed. The legislature may confer appropriate jurisdiction on the appellate division of the supreme court in the first judicial department for the purpose of determining the amount of any debt to be so excluded. [1938]

This section makes provision for excluding certain self-liquidating debts contracted by the city for local transit purposes not already excluded.

Subdivision (A) extends the debt limit by $315 million for the expansion and the improvement of New York City's transit system. It is a one-time exclusion to be applied only to the transit system. Provision is made for refunding because the drafters believed the language might otherwise be read to prevent any refunding of the bonds.[6] The city is explicitly authorized to contract indebtedness for purposes of unifying the transit system by incorporating the independent private transit lines into a public independent subway system.

Subdivision (B) provides that any outstanding indebtedness contracted by the city for transit purposes and not otherwise excluded may be excluded proportionately to the extent to which the net revenue received by the city in the last fiscal year from all its transit facilities meets the interest on the annual requirements for the amortization and payment of such excluded indebtedness during the fiscal year.[7]

Before the determination of whether indebtedness for transit purposes is excluded, four deductions from current net revenues are mandated. The legislature is then to prescribe the method and conditions by which the amount shall be determined and may confer jurisdiction on the appellate division of the supreme court to make this determination.

SECTION 8

Indebtedness not to be invalidated by operation of this article. No indebtedness of a county, city, town, village or school district valid at the time of its inception shall thereafter become invalid by reason of the operation of any of the provisions of this article. [Const. 1894, Art. VIII, sec. 10 as amend. in 1909; amend. and renumbered Art. VIII, sec. 8, 1938]

This provision protects the indebtedness of a county, city, town, village, or school district valid at the time of its inception from the effects of the provisions of this article.

SECTION 9

When debt-incurring power of certain counties shall cease. Whenever the boundaries of any city are the same as those of a county, or when any city includes within its boundaries more than one county, the power of any county wholly included within such city to contract indebtedness shall cease, but the indebtedness of such county shall not, for the purpose of this article, be included as a part of the city indebtedness. [Const. 1894, Art. VIII, sec. 10, as amend. in 1899; amend. and renumbered Art. VIII, sec. 9, 1938]

Whenever the boundaries of any city are the same as those of a county or when any city shall include within its boundaries more than one county, the power of any county included within such city to become indebted shall cease. This provision arose out of the consolidation of counties into the city of New York. In spite of the consolidation, the boards of supervisors of the counties continued to operate. To prevent the "misfortune" of fiscal conflicts between parallel governments, this section cut off the counties' power to incur debt.[8]

SECTION 10

Limitations on amount to be raised by real estate taxes for local purposes; exceptions. Hereafter, in any county, city, village or school district described in this section, the amount to be raised by tax on real estate in any fiscal year, in addition to providing for the interest on and the principal of all indebtedness, shall not exceed an amount equal to the following percentages of the average full valuation of taxable real estate of such county, city, village or school district, less the amount to be raised by tax on real estate in such year for the payment of the interest on and redemption of certificates or other evidence of indebtedness described in paragraphs A and D of section five of this article, or renewals thereof:

(a) any county, for county purposes, one and one-half per centum; provided, however, that the legislature may prescribe a method by which such limitation may be increased to not to exceed two per centum;

(b) any city of one hundred twenty-five thousand or more inhabitants according to the latest federal census, for city purposes, two per centum;

(c) any city having less than one hundred twenty-five thousand inhabitants according to the latest federal census, for city purposes, two per centum;

(d) any village, for village purposes, two per centum;

(e) Notwithstanding the provisions of sub-paragraphs (a) and (b) of this section, the city of New York and the counties therein, for city and county purposes, a combined total of two and one-half per centum.

The average full valuation of taxable real estate of such county, city, village or school district shall be determined by taking the assessed valuations of taxable real estate on the last completed assessment rolls and the four preceding rolls of such county, city, village or school district, and applying thereto the ratio which such assessed valuation on each of such rolls bears to the full valuation, as determined by the state tax commission or by such other state officer or agency as the legislature shall by law direct. The legislature shall prescribe the manner by which such ratio shall be determined by the state tax commission or by such other state officer or agency.

Nothing contained in this section shall be deemed to restrict the powers granted to the legislature by other provisions of this constitution to further restrict the powers of any county, city, town, village or school district to levy taxes on real estate. [Const. 1846, Art. VIII, sec. 11 as added in 1874 and amend. in 1884; renumbered Art. VIII, sec. 10; Const. 1894; amend. 1938, 1949, 1953, 1985]

The excessive accumulation of debts by municipal governments after the Civil War, the fact that much of the borrowed money in New York City flowed through the Tweed Ring, and the growing concern that the rate of real estate taxation in the large cities was excessive led to this section. It restricts, and the legislature may further restrict, the amount to be realized by real estate taxers for local purposes. In recognition of the differences among local units, varying rates are specified. This five-year average was to be based on the full valuation of taxable real estate in order to eliminate the artificial variations in taxing authority from jurisdiction to jurisdiction because of differing local assessment practices. The substitution of full assessment adopted in 1951 had the effect of greatly expanding the amount that could be raised for taxation.

The tax limit in New York City was raised to 2½ percent in 1953 in response to a financial crisis in that city.

An attempt by the legislature to assign a probable usefulness of three years to the amounts paid for pensions and social security benefits that would have characterized those as capital expenditures, excluded from the tax limits under the "pay as you go" provision of section 11, was struck down by the court of appeals in Hurd v. City of Buffalo (1974). In response, the legislature passed the Emergency City School District Relief Act and the State Real Property Tax Act, which reenacts substantially the same legislation, with the additional finding of an emergency. The court in Bethlehem Steel Corporation v. Board of Education (1978) ruled that the legislation was "nothing more than an attempt to circumvent the constitutional limitation to the amount of revenue that may be raised by local subdivisions of the state through the taxation of real property" (at 834).

A municipality may reduce the tax limit below the 2 percent provided in this section. Since such a reduction would curtail the power of elected officials to raise taxes, a mandatory referendum would be required (Art. IX, sec. 1 (2)).[9]

SECTION 10–a

Application and use of revenues from certain public improvements. For the purpose of determining the amount of taxes which may be raised on real estate pursuant to section ten of this article, the revenues received in each fiscal year by any county, city or village from a public improvement or part thereof, or service, owned or rendered by such county, city or village for which bonds or capital notes are issued after January first, nineteen hundred fifty, shall be applied first to the payment of all costs of operation, maintenance and repairs thereof, and then to the payment of the amounts required in such fiscal year to pay the interest on and the amortization of, or payment of, indebtedness contracted for such public improvements or part thereof, or service. The provisions of this section shall not prohibit the use of excess revenues for any lawful county, city or village purpose. The provision of this section shall not be applicable to a public improvement or part thereof constructed to provide for the supply of water. [1949; amend. 1953]

Section 10–a was added to the constitution to prevent a municipality from evading the real estate tax limit by levying taxes outside that limit for debt service on an improvement and simultaneously using the revenue from the improvements for general municipal operating expenses. To accomplish this objective, the section requires the revenue of municipal improvements to be used first for the payment of operating expenses and the debt service for the improvement. Because towns are not affected by this section, they are not included in the provision. Use of excess revenue for lawful municipal purposes is permitted, but the legislature may restrict the use of that revenue if it desires.

SECTION 11

Taxes for certain capital expenditures to be excluded from tax limitation. (a) Whenever the city of New York is required by law to pay for all or any part of the cost of capital improvements by direct budgetary appropriation in any fiscal year or by the issuance of certificates or other evidence of indebtedness (except serial bonds of an issue having a maximum maturity of more than two years) to be redeemed in one of the two immediately succeeding fiscal years, taxes required for such appropriation or for the redemption of such certificates or other evidence of indebtedness may be excluded in whole or in part by such city from the tax limitation prescribed by section ten of this article, in which event the total amount so required for such appropriation and for the redemption of such certificates or other evidence of indebtedness shall be deemed to be indebtedness to the same extent and in the same manner as if such amount had been financed through indebtedness payable in equal annual installments over the period of the probable usefulness of such capital improvement, as determined by law. The fiscal officer of such city shall determine the amount to be deemed indebtedness pursuant to this section, and the legislature, in its discretion, may provide that such determination, if approved by the state comptroller, shall be conclusive. Any amounts determined to be deemed indebtedness of any county, city, other than the city of New York, village or school district in accordance with the provisions of this section as in force and effect prior to January first, nineteen hundred fifty-two, shall not be deemed to be indebtedness on and after such date.

(b) Whenever any county, city, other than the city of New York, village or school district which is coterminous with, or partly within, or wholly within, a city having less than one hundred twenty-five thousand inhabitants according to the latest federal census provides by direct budgetary appropriation for any fiscal year for the payment in such fiscal year or in any future fiscal year or years of all or any part of the cost of an object or purpose for which a period of probable usefulness has been determined by law, the taxes required for such appropriation shall be excluded from the tax limitation prescribed by section ten of this article unless the legislature otherwise provides. [1938; amend. 1949, 1951]

Section 10 allows local governments to exclude from their tax limits all taxes used for debt service. Section 11 allows the local governments specified to make appropriations for capital expenditures or improvements for which they otherwise might borrow and to exclude the taxes raised for such appropriations from the tax limits specified in section 10. This provides local governments with a significant exemption because real property taxes for capital expenditures can be raised without constitutional limit. The purpose was to encourage local governments to finance projects on a "pay as you go basis" without restriction by tax limit. Since there is no debt incurred, such limits are not subject to debt limitations. New York City is permitted to exclude taxes raised for such purposes from its tax limit, but this section requires that such appropriations be counted toward the debt limits of the city—that is, debt will be imputed. Since the amounts charged toward the debt limit have in fact been paid and are not actual obligations, they have been labeled phantom debts. No reason was given for singling out New York City for such treatment, but suspicions about the city's lack of fiscal responsibilities may have been behind this limit on how far New York City's property taxes could be raised.

SECTION 12

Powers of local governments to be restricted; further limitations on contracting local indebtedness authorized. It shall be the duty of the legislature, subject to the provisions of this constitution, to restrict the power of taxation, assessment, borrowing money, contracting indebtedness, and loaning the credit of counties, cities, towns and villages, so as to prevent abuses in taxation and assessments and in contracting of indebtedness by them. Nothing in this article shall be construed to prevent the legislature from further restricting the powers herein specified of any county, city, town, village or school district to contract indebtedness or to levy taxes on real estate for the payment of interest on or principal of indebtedness theretofore contracted. [Const. 1846 Art. VIII, sec. 9; amend. and renumbered Art. XII, sec. 1, Const. 1894; amend. and renumbered Art. IX, sec. 9, 1938; amend. (sec. revised) and renumbered Art. VIII, sec. 12]

Section 12 makes it the right and duty of the legislature to restrict the powers of local governments with respect to taxing and borrowing when such power is being abused. The legislature may further limit the power to levy taxes and contract debt. The legislature, however, is not permitted to restrict the power of local governments to impose taxes on real estate for obligations that were sold to the public with the understanding that debt service in those obligations would not be included within the tax limit.

Article IX

Local Government

This article provides the basic system of local government in New York. Adopted in 1963, it is the latest in a series of efforts by constitution makers in the state to address the contentious and complex question of the allocation of power between the state and local governments. It was meant to embody a new concept in state-local relationships by constitutionally recognizing that the "expansion of powers for effective local self-government" is a purpose of the people of the state.[1] It attempts to strike a balance between keeping local government completely dependent on the legislature and granting them complete autonomy. Deciding what powers and functions are appropriately exercised at the local level and what ones are statewide in scope is contentious because people disagree over these determinations and complex because changes in social and economic conditions require continual reassessment of established divisions.

Home rule, the discretionary authority of local governments to shape their charters and exercise local self-government, takes different forms. In guaranteeing certain powers to local governments that the state cannot alter by ordinary statute, the article creates an *imperium in imperio* (a state within a state); in granting very broad powers that the state government can preempt only by general laws, the article embraces a devolution-of-powers model. The incorporation of both approaches, it was thought, would create a "reservoir of selected significant power"[2] and prevent state interference in matters of local concern. By extending home rule powers for the first time to towns and smaller governments, the article had the effect of bringing home rule powers of cities, counties, towns, and villages much closer to parity.

Under its provisions, local governments are given the power to adopt or amend local laws relating to their "property affairs and government" that are not inconsistent with provisions of the constitution or general laws and to adopt or amend local laws not inconsistent with the constitution or general laws relating to specifically enumerated subjects, whether or not these subjects relate to the property affairs of government of local governments, subject to the power of the legislature to expressly restrict adoption of such laws. The legislature is expressly directed to confer upon local government additional powers relating to property affairs or government and to withdraw or restrict those powers. The legislature is also directed to enact a statute of local governments granting local governments additional powers. These latter powers are given quasi-constitutional status in that the powers so granted cannot be repealed except by the action of two successive legislatures with the concurrence of the governor.

Article IX was adopted, in part, to stop the judicial erosion of home rule powers. It has had the effect of providing greater judicial access to local governments. Traditionally counties were denied standing to attack the constitutionality of state legislation affecting county powers. In Black Brook v. State (1977), the court of appeals held that Article IX created a limited exemption to that rule, arguing that to deny standing to local governments would frustrate the purpose for which the article was adopted: promoting strong local government. The sections of this article should be read in conjunction with other parts of the constitution dealing with local government. These include Article V, sections 6–7; Article VI (providing the court system); Article XI (providing for the educational system); and Articles XIII, XVI–XVIII.

SECTION 1

Bill of rights for local governments. Effective local self-government and intergovernmental cooperation are purposes of the people of the state. In furtherance thereof, local governments shall have the following rights, powers, privileges and immunities in addition to those granted by the other provisions of this constitution:

(a) Every local government, except a county wholly included within a city, shall have a legislative body elective by the people thereof. Every local government shall have power to adopt local laws as provided by this article.

(b) All officers of every local government whose election or appointment is not provided for by this constitution shall be elected by the people of the local government, or of some division thereof, or appointed by such officers of the local government as may be provided by law.

(c) Local governments shall have power to agree, as authorized by act of the legislature, with the federal government, a state or one or more other governments within or without the state, to provide cooperatively, jointly or by contract any facility, service, activity or undertaking which each participating local government has the power to provide separately. Each such local government shall have power to apportion its share of the cost thereof upon such portion of its area as may be authorized by act of the legislature.

(d) No local government or any part of the territory therefore shall be annexed to another until the people, if any, of the territory proposed to be annexed shall have consented thereto by majority vote on a referendum and until the governing board of each local government, the area of which is affected, shall have consented thereto upon the basis of a determination that the annexation is in the over-all public interest. The consent of the governing board of a county shall be required only where a boundary of the county is affected. On or before July first, nineteen hundred sixty-four, the legislature shall provide, where such consent of a governing board is not granted, for adjudication and determination, on the law and the facts, in a proceeding initiated in the supreme court, of the issue of whether the annexation is in the over-all public interest.

(e) Local government shall have power to take by eminent domain private property within their boundaries for public use together with excess land or property but no more than is sufficient to provide for appropriate disposition or use of land or property which abuts on that necessary for such public use, and to sell or lease that not devoted to such use. The legislature may authorize and regulate the exercise of power of eminent domain and excess condemnation by a local government outside its boundaries.

(f) No local government shall be prohibited by the legislature (1) from making a fair return on the value of the property used and useful in its operation of a gas, electric of water public utility service, over and above costs of operation and maintenance and necessary and proper reserves, in addition to an amount equivalent to taxes which such service, if privately owned, would pay to such local government, or (2) from using such profits for payment of refunds to consumers or for any other lawful purpose.

(g) A local government shall have the power to apportion its cost of a governmental service or function upon any portion of its area, as authorized by act of the legislature.

(h)(1) Counties, other than those wholly included within a city, shall be empowered by general law, or by special law enacted upon county request pursuant to section two of this article, to adopt, amend or repeal alternative forms of county government provided by the legislature or to prepare, adopt, amend or repeal alternative forms of their own. Any such form of government or any amendment thereof, by act of the legislature or by local law, may transfer one or more functions or duties of the county or of the cities, towns, villages, districts or other units of government wholly contained in such county to each other or when authorized by the legislature to the state, or may abolish one or more offices, departments, agencies or units of government provided, however, that no such form or amendment, except as provided in paragraph (2) of this subdivision, shall become effective unless approved on a referendum by a majority of votes cast thereon in the area of the county outside of cities, and in the cities of the county, if any, considered as one unit. Where an alternative form of county government or any amendment thereof, by act of the legislature or by local law, provides for the transfer of any function or duty to or from any village or the abolition of any office, department, agency or unit of government of a village wholly contained in such county, such form or amendment shall not become effective unless it shall also be approved on the referendum by a majority of the votes cast thereon in all the villages so affected considered as one unit.

(2) After the adoption of an alternative form of county government by a county, any amendment thereof by act of the legislature or by local law which abolishes or creates an elective county office, changes the voting or veto power of or the method of removing an elective county officer during his term of office, abolishes, curtails or transfers to another county officer or agency any power of an elective county officer or changes the form or composition of the county legislative body shall be subject to a permissive referendum as provided by the legislature.

[Const. 1812 Art. IV, sec. 15; amend. and renumbered Art. X, sec. 2, Const. 1846; amend. 1899; 1927, 1929, 1935; amend. and renumbered Art. IX, secs. 1, 2, 7, 8, 14, 1938; amend. 1958; amend. (sec. revised) and renumbered Art. IX, sec. 1, 1963]

The opening paragraph declares the philosophy that guides the provisions of the article; that effective local government and intergovernmental cooperation are purposes of the people of the state. It is followed by eight items that make up what is generally known as the bill of rights for local government. Subdivisions (a) and (b) grant local governments the right to have an elective body and power to adopt local laws. The right to have local officers elected or appointed by a local electorate is the heart of local self-government. It is an important bulwark against state interference in the form of selection of local officials or the transfer and consolidation of functions among local units. While this provision has served to prevent some state intrusion, courts have permitted extensive intervention when important state interests are involved.[3]

Subdivision (c) permits local governments as authorized by the legislature to join with other governments—federal, state, or local—to provide cooperatively, jointly or by contract, any facility, service, activity, or undertaking, which each local government has the power to provide separately. By providing a constitutional basis for this cooperation, legal obstacles were removed, and local governments were encouraged to cooperate where such cooperation would reduce overlapping units of government and duplication of services. Contracting for or transferring functions would create lower costs and more efficient delivery of services.

Subdivision (c) was aimed at fostering cooperation where annexation is undesirable. Subdivision (d) encourages consolidation by annexation while providing protection for local units that do not wish it. Successful annexation requires approval by majority vote of the people in the territory to be annexed, approval of the governing boards of the annexed and annexing units upon their determinations that the annexation is in the public interest. The requirement of approval of local governing boards was added at the request of the Association of

Towns, which did not want towns to lose their best tax base without any voice in the matter.[4] A constitutional amendment was necessary to overcome the effects of Cutler v. Herman (1957), which declared a statute requiring a town board's consent a violation of Article III, section 17, which prohibits a private or local bill incorporating villages. In the event that consent of a governing board is not granted, the decision is placed in the hands of the judiciary.[5] In deciding the question, the court is performing a quasi-legislative task involving the resolution of conflicting policy determination by two local governmental units. For this reason, the court of appeals has held that it will not provide full review of facts and law. As long as the appellate court has acted pursuant to law and has not acted in a "completely irrational manner," review will not be granted (Mayor of Mt. Kisco v. Supervisor of Bedford, 1978).

Subdivision (e) grants to local governments the power of eminent domain. Local governments other than counties had been granted the power for purposes of housing in Article XVIII, sections 8–9. The section contains two limitations on that power: that no more be taken than is necessary to accomplish the public purpose intended and that exercise of that power beyond the boundaries of the local government shall be subject to regulations enacted by the legislature. The amendment authorizes cities to take excess by condemnation proceedings subject to legislative regulations. Without this excess condemnation power, a local government's ability to obtain abutting property was limited. As improvement on condemned property usually caused damage to adjoining property, extra financial burdens were imposed on the community. The power to take property in excess of its needs enables the local unit to avoid these damages and resell the surplus.

Subdivision (f) was adopted in response to the court of appeals decisions in Village of Boonville v. Maltbie (1936). Boonville, a municipal corporation, was entitled to a fair rate of return from its electricity-generating property used and useful for the public service in the same way a private utility would be. But the court went on to say that since the municipality derives its power to create and operate an electric utility from the legislature, that legislature may limit the exercise of that power as it sees fit. If the legislature sees fit to decide that a municipality running an electric utility should run it at cost and that consumers should not be charged a rate that allows the municipality to earn a profit, such an enactment would be legal and constitutional. This section responds to that possibility by assuring municipalities that they would not be treated differently than private utilities.

Subdivision (g) enables a governing unit to apportion a fair share of the cost of government functions or services to areas under its jurisdiction receiving those services, in the manner authorized by the state legislature.

Subdivision (h)(1)(2) is an amalgam of amendments that had their origins in the early twentieth-century reorganization and consolidation of county government movement. Local government structures in New York were anachronistic and inefficient: division of responsibility, duplication of services, a veritable army of local officials, and a local tax system that Governor Al Smith characterized as "a joke."[6] Transfers of functions were difficult, if not impossible. In some towns, three assessors were elected, but in order to substitute one assessor or a board of assessors in their place, a constitutional amendment was necessary. These provisions direct the legislature to authorize counties to adopt, amend, or repeal alternative forms of government, which the legislature has done in the County Charter Law.[7] That law allows county governments to choose among alternative forms of government as provided. All the alternatives contain a structure providing for executive responsibility, but other than this requirement, the law allows counties to modernize their governments and to adopt a form best suited to their particular needs and character, consistent with any other limitations the legislature by general law provides. These charters allow for the transfer of functions to the county of overlapping, small, inadequate local governments or special districts. The problem was particularly acute in the areas of health care, highways, and welfare, functions now firmly in the hands of the county governments.

The ability of counties to accomplish the goals of consolidation and transfer of functions is limited by the requirement that any such changes be approved by a majority of the voters in both the city and the area of the county outside the city or cities. Any transfer of functions involving a village would also have to be approved by a majority in the village, thus requiring a triple majority. Concern for loss of popular control and fear of being overwhelmed by other governmental units, especially cities, prompted these concurrent majority requirements. They were upheld by the U.S. Supreme Court against an equal protection of the law challenge in Town of Lockport v. Citizens for Community Action (1977).

The courts have interpreted subdivision (h)(2) strictly. In Morin v. Foster (1978), a change in the county charter abolishing the county manager's four-year term was determined to be a change that curtailed the powers of an elective county officer and thus requiring a permissive referendum. On the other hand, as noted below, courts have upheld charter provision, which differ from requirements set forth in state law.

SECTION 2

Powers and duties of legislature; home rule powers of local governments; statute of local governments. (a) The legislature shall provide for the creation and organization of local governments in such manner as shall secure to them the rights, powers, privileges and immunities granted to them by this constitution.

(b) Subject to the bill of rights of local governments and other applicable provisions of this constitution, the legislature:

(1) Shall enact, and may from time to time amend, a statute of local governments granting to local governments powers including but not limited

to those of local legislation and administration in addition to the powers vested in them by this article. A power granted in such statute may be repealed, diminished, impaired or suspended only by enactment of a statute by the legislature with the approval of the governor at its regular session in one calendar year and the re-enactment and approval of such statute in the following calendar year.

(2) Shall have the power to act in relation to property, affairs or government of any local government only by general law, or by special law only (a) on request of two-thirds of the total membership of its legislative body or on request of its chief executive officer concurred in by a majority of such membership, or (b) except in the case of the city of New York, on certificate of necessity from the governor reciting facts which in his judgment constitute an emergency requiring enactment of such law and, in such latter case, with the concurrence of two-thirds of the members elected to each house of the legislature

(3) Shall have the power to confer on local governments powers not relating to their property, affairs or government including but not limited to those of local legislation and administration, in addition to those otherwise granted by or pursuant to this article, and to withdraw or restrict such additional powers.

(c) In addition to powers granted in the statute of local governments or any other law, (i) every local government shall have the power to adopt and amend local laws not inconsistent with the provision of this constitution or any general law relating to its property, affairs or government, and, (ii) every local government shall have power to adopt and amend local laws not inconsistent with the provisions of this constitution or any general law relating to the following subjects, whether or not they relate to the property, affairs or government of such local government, except to the extent that the legislature shall restrict the adoption of such a local law relating to other than the property, affairs or government of such local government:

(1) The powers, duties, qualifications, number, mode of selection and removal, terms of office, compensation, hours of work, protection, welfare and safety of its officers and employees, except that the cities and towns shall not have such power with respect to members of the legislative body of the county in their capacities as county officers.

(2) In the case of a city, town or village, the membership and composition of its legislative body.

(3) The transaction of its business.

(4) The incurring of its obligations, except that local laws relating to financing by the issuance of evidences of indebtedness by such local government shall be consistent with laws enacted by the legislature.

(5) The presentation, ascertainment and discharge of claims against it.

(6) The acquisition, care, management and use of its highways, roads, streets, avenues and property.

(7) The acquisition of its transit facilities and the ownership and operation thereof.

(8) The levy, collection and administration of local taxes authorized by the legislature and of assessments for local improvements, consistent with laws enacted by the legislature.

(9) The wages or salaries, the hours of work or labor, and the protection, welfare and safety or persons employed by any contractor or sub-contractor performing work, labor or services for it.

(10) The government, protection, order, conduct, safety, health and well being of persons or property therein.

(d) Except in the case of a transfer of functions under an alternative form of county government, a local government shall not have power to adopt local laws which impair the powers of any other local government.

(e) The rights and powers of local governments specified in this section insofar as applicable to any county within the city of New York shall be vested in such city. [Const. 1846, Art. III, sec. 17 and sec. 22 as added in 1874; amend. in 1874; amend. and renumbered Art. III, sec. 26, Const. 1894; amend. 1923; amend. and renumbered Art. IX, secs. 1, 4, 9, 11, 12, 16; amend. 1958; 1963 (newly revised)]

Section 2 is also a revised and consolidated section based on provisions going back to the 1846 Constitution. It grants local government significant powers, empowers the exercise of state legislative power with regard to local governments, and limits the exercise of those powers. The section begins with a statement of grants of power to and limitations upon the state legislature. Subject to the provision of section 1 and other applicable provisions of the constitution, the legislature is directed to enact and, when desirable, revise a statute of local governments[8] granting certain power to local governments. Among these are the power to adopt ordinances and resolutions, power to acquire real and personal property, and power to fix, levy, and collect charges and fees. The powers granted by this statute are accorded a special status in that once granted, they cannot be repealed, impaired, or suspended except by the action of two successive legislatures with the concurrence of the governor. In enacting the statute, the legislature made certain reservations, and if state legislation affecting a power granted to local government is within the scope of those reservations, restriction on the powers granted can be achieved by ordinary legislative process.

The state legislature has the power to act in relation to the property affairs or government of any local government only by general law as defined in section 3(d)(1) and by special law as defined in section 3(d)(4) and only when requested by two-thirds of the membership of the local legislative body or the chief executive officer, with the concurrence of a majority of that body, or, except in the case of New York City, emergencies certified by the governor and concurred in by two-thirds of the legislature. The legislature is empowered to confer on local governments power not related to their property affairs or government, including but not limited to those of local legislation and administration, and the power to withdraw or restrict such additional powers.

The municipal purpose doctrine states that localities can spend money only for purposes the legislature authorizes. Although there seems to be a broad delegation of police power to localities in Article IX, such authority must be found in some legislative authorization or specific constitutional provision. Article XVIII grants cities, villages, and towns, but not counties urban renewal and housing powers. In practice this is not a significant restriction on cities as the General City Law, section 20, grants them the power to spend money for any purpose that the state may spend money. There is no counterpart in the County Law to section 20 of the General City Law. When a county wishes to engage in urban functions it must seek a specific enabling act from the legislature. Additional reservations are contained in section 3(a).

Section 2(c) enables local governments to adopt local laws relating to those government's property, affairs or government or to the specified subjects as long as those laws are consistent with the state constitution and any general state law.

SECTION 3

Existing laws to remain applicable; construction; definitions. (a) Except as expressly provided, nothing in this article shall restrict or impair any power of the legislature in relation to:

(1) The maintenance, support or administration of the public school system, as required or provided by article XI of this constitution, or any retirement system pertaining to such public school system,

(2) The courts as required or provided by article VI of this constitution, and

(3) Matters other than the property, affairs or government of a local government.

(b) The provisions of this article shall not affect any existing valid provisions of acts of the legislature or of local legislation and such provisions shall continue in force until repealed, amended, modified or superseded in accordance with the provisions of this constitution.

(c) Rights, powers, privileges and immunities granted to local governments by this article shall be liberally construed.

(d) Whenever used in this article the following terms shall mean or include:

(1) "General law." A law which in terms and in effect applies alike to all counties, all counties other than those wholly included within a city, all cities, all towns or all villages.

(2) "Local government." A county, city, town or village.

(3) "People." Persons entitled to vote as provided in section one of article two of this constitution.

(4) "Special law." A law which in terms and in effect applies to one or more, but not all, counties, counties other than those wholly included within a city, cities, town or villages.

[Const. 1894 Art. III, sec. 26; amend. 1935; amend. and renumbered Art. IX, sec. 3, 1938; amend. (sec. revised) 1963]

Section 3(a) provides that the article shall not be read to impair the legislative power in relation to the public school and retirement systems.

Subdivision (b) provides for a smooth transition from statutes and rules in effect prior to the adoption of this article. Subdivision (c) is an express repudiation of Dillon's Rule, by which powers granted local government were to be construed strictly in favor of the state (City of Clinton v. Cedar Rapids and Missouri Railroad Co., 1868). Subdivision (d) defines the significant terms used in the article. The terms *special* and *general laws* have been read by the courts in such a way as to blunt the limitation that law affecting local affairs be general in character. (See Article III, section 17.) The extent of county power under their charters has occasioned much litigation. The county charter law, found in the Municipal Home Rule Law, sets forth areas in which county charter provisions may not be inconsistent with state law, indicating that county charter provisions are not required to be consistent with state law beyond these specified areas.[9]

In a landmark case, Town of Smithtown v. Howell et al. (1972), the court of appeals upheld a locally enacted county charter provision that superseded a general state law. The decision was based on section 1(h) and its statutory implementation. In Matter of Heimbach v. Mills (1979), the court upheld a charter provision placing power to set real property tax equalization rates in the elected county executive rather than with the board of assessors as provided in the state's Real Property Law. The court, in upholding the charter provision, argued that if consistency with general state law was required, "every charter provision would have to conform to every applicable general law and there could never be such a thing as an alternative form of county government or effective home rule in the localities" (at 732). Resnick v. County of Ulster (1978) extended that ruling to noncharter counties with regard to issues covered by section 1(e) of this article. "To allow the issue of whether county legislatures may adopt provisions relating to their 'affairs of government' to turn on the existence or nonexistence of county charters would be contrary to the spirit of home rule" (at 287). Generally, the power to enact laws inconsistent with general laws does not extend to other local governments. To the extent that such power exists, it is based on statutory authority as in provisions of the Municipal Home Rule Law allowing towns and villages to supersede various general provisions of the Town Law and Village Law. These supercession statutes do grant real home rule powers to towns and villages but can be repealed by ordinary legislation. The court of appeals has also acknowledged local authority to legislate on matters defined as of local concern, meaning related to their property, affairs or government.

The fact that a local law deals with matters touched on by state law does not automatically invalidate that law (Adler v. Deegan, 1939, Cardoza, J. concurring; People v. Judiz, 1976). Generally, the courts have determined that the police power of local governments may not be exercised by local laws inconsistent with general law or when the legislature has restricted such power by preempting the area. The difference between inconsistency and preemption is not always clear. The test used by the courts is whether the legislature has "evidenced a desire that its regulations should preempt the possibility of varying local regulations,"[10] while inconsistency exists where local laws "prohibit what would be permissible under state law or impose additional restrictions on rights under state law as to inhibit the operation of the state's general laws,"[11] or whether the state specifically permits the conduct prohibited at the local level.

Under these principles, the court has held that New York City's ban on discrimination in private clubs was not preempted by the State Executive Law (New York State Club Association v. City of New York, 1987); that same city's regulation of the conversion of apartments into condominiums was not inconsistent with the General Business Law (Council for Owner Occupied Housing v. Koch, 1984); and a county's ban on the sale of cesspool additive without approval of county health commissioner was not preempted by the Environmental Conservation Law (Jancyn Manufacturing Company v. Suffolk County, 1987).

Power to appoint, alter terms of, and fill vacancies of local offices has also been the focus of court determinations of the extent of home rule powers. Nydick v. Suffolk County Legislature (1975) raised the question of whether a vacancy in the office of a county legislator was to be filled by the governor under the state's County Law or according to the Suffolk County Charter, which called for filling the vacancy by the county legislature. Since the county charter law permits charter counties to provide for appointment of any county officers, section 400 of that law was not a "general law" as defined in section 3, and the county provision was valid under section 2 of this article.

A significant affirmation of county charter power was handed down in Westchester County Civil Service Employees Association, Inc. v. Del Bello (1979). There, the court upheld a charter law that had the effect of shortening the term of the sheriff by merging the office with the Parkway Police in apparent violation of the then-specified term of three years (Art. XIII, sec. 13). The court responded that the purpose of the county home rule amendment was to change the nature of county government by allowing the voters of the counties to make decisions regarding the organization and structure of the county. By allowing counties to adopt alternative forms of government, the counties were also permitted to provide for the appointment, election, or abolition of any county officer. Article IX, section 1(h) permitted the county to abolish the office of sheriff if it so desired, freeing the county from the requirement of the three year term for the sheriff. Decisions like *Del Bello*, *Nydick*, and *Resnick* suggested a willingness on the part of the judiciary to provide an expansive reading of county charter powers under Article IX. However this suggestion was scotched in a series of decisions that, if not inconsistent with the earlier cases, have severely limited their significance. In Matter of Kelley v. McGee (1982), the court of appeals sustained state legislation mandating the salaries of district attorneys against the claim that such a mandate violated the home rule powers of the county. While declaring district attorneys to be local officers, the court ruled that the salaries of that office are a matter of state concern. District attorneys are responsible for enforcing state penal law, and adequate salaries would ensure that the best available attorneys would be doing the enforcement. In Carey v. Oswego County Legislature (1983), the court upheld the governor's exclusive right to appoint an interim district attorney under section 400(7) of the County Law. Even though *Nydick* and *Resnick* held that local laws would take precedence over this statute, the court, citing *Kelley*, held that state statute serves the significant state interest of ensuring the independence, integrity, and competence of the office. The court attempts to reconcile its holding with *Nydick* and *Resnick* by pointing to the significant difference between county legislators and district attorneys and the fact that the latter is a constitutional officer under Article XIII not subject to Article IX. As Article XIII by its own terms is made subject to Article IX, this argument loses some of its force.

Finally, in Cuomo v. Chemung County Legislature (1983), the right of the governor to fill a vacancy of the office of sheriff was sustained. The net result of these decisions is to put into question the vitality of county home rule. "If the state may freely legislate with respect to such peculiarly local concerns as the compensation of local offices and the procedure for filling vacancies in local offices one might wonder whether any local matters are secure from state interference."[12] The significance of this article has also been reduced by the court's handling of the clause "matters other than the property, affairs and government" of local governments. When the matter is adjudged one of statewide concern, the constitutionally mandated procedures specified in this article are not applicable.

In general, the court of appeals has followed court decisions handed down prior to the adoption of this article and given the phrase "matter of state concern" an expansive reading (Adler v. Deegan, 1929). It has held that the needs of the people of the state for housing were sufficient to sustain powers in the Urban Development Corporation statute, which cut into village zoning powers (Floyd v. New York State Urban Development Corp., 1973) and to sustain the power of the state by ordinary legislation to set up the Adirondack Park Agency with planning and zoning powers, against the argument that planning and zoning were powers specifically granted to local governments (Wambat Realty Corp. v. State, 1977). This was the first home rule case alleging the suspension of an enumerated power. In not requiring the double enactment procedures of section 2(b)(1), the decision severely limited the protection afforded local governments. This erosion continued in Hotel Dorset Co. v. Trust for Cultural Resources of the City of New York (1978), which held that a law that applied only to one museum was not a "special law" under the terms of this article. Stressing the serious financial problems facing cultural institutions, the court wrote, in familiar language, ''We should not strain ourselves to find illegality in such programs'' (at 370), quoting Wein v. City of New York (1975), in turn quoting Comereski v. City of Elmira (1955). In Uniformed Firefighters Association v. City of New York (1980), the court struck down a local law passed by the city requiring residence in the city as a condition of appointment to civil service positions. The city claimed authority under the power to adopt laws in relation to its property affairs and government. The state statute allowed a more permissive requirement for certain department employees, notwithstanding any local laws, charters, or codes to the contrary. The city argued that this law was not a general law because it did not affect all cities. The court struck the city enactment down, arguing that residential mobility of civil servants ''unrelated to job performance or department organization is a matter of statewide concern not subject to municipal home rule'' (at 90). In subsequent decisions, the court has continued to find state concerns in sustaining overrides of local legislation.[13]

Another significant factor restricting local autonomy is the use of state mandates or legislative requirements that local governments provide a specific service and meet minimum state standards, such as engaging in collective bargaining with employee associations or establishing terms and conditions of local public employment.[14] New York imposes more mandates on its local governments than any other state. While the state compensates local governments for mandates through generous distribution of general purpose aid, there is no question that such mandates directly affect the autonomy of local governments. In Toia v. Regan (1976), the court of appeals sustained a state mandate that local governments bear 50 percent of nonfederal costs for welfare programs although that mandate would severely limit availability of sufficient tax revenues, rendering meaningless a county's right to manage its own affairs. *Toia* illustrates the tension between state mandates and the principle of home rule.

The general direction of court decisions has been to favor the exercise of state over local authority. The adoption of Article IX has not been entirely successful in reversing an entrenched judicial doctrine stretching from Dillon's Rule to Adler v. Deegan, a doctrine that continues to undergird the court's approach to home rule.

Article X

Corporations

Between 1820 and 1860, the economy of New York was transformed by the growth of venture capitalism in transportation, manufacturing, and banking. Central to this transformation was the increasing resort to the corporate form. Because banks were the principal mechanism for pooling capital for investment in these corporations, they became the focus of state attention during the first half of the nineteenth century. This article regulates the chartering of corporations, generally barring special acts granting exclusive privilege to a particular organization, and defines their liability. A special provision regulates savings banks and loan associations. The last sections regulate public benefit corporations, more commonly known as public authorities.

SECTION 1

> **Corporations, formation of.** Corporations may be formed under general law; but shall not be created by special act, except for municipal purposes, and in cases where, in the judgment of the legislature, the objects of the corporation cannot be attained under general laws. All general laws and special acts passed pursuant to this section may be altered from time to time or repealed. [Const. 1846, Art. VIII, sec. 1; renumbered Art. X, sec. 1, 1938]

The target of this section was special incorporation laws granting special privileges to individuals and refusing them to others, thereby creating monopoly and privilege. It replaced an 1821 provision allowing special incorporation with the consent of two-thirds of the legislature. This section also was designed to reduce the sheer number of special and private laws that had begun to clog the legislative process by the mid–1840s.

The ambivalence toward the corporation is reflected in the language of sections 1 and 2. On the one hand, the corporation is given constitutional recognition; on the other, an attempt is made to ensure that it will be broadly accessible and under the regulatory power of the state. Two exceptions, one specific and the other general, were included: municipalities were excepted from the prohibition, and the legislature was permitted to resort to special laws when its object could not be obtained by general laws. The latter exception was included after the 1846 convention failed to come up with language that would encompass all possible situations. Nevertheless, the principle of general incorporation was established, and subsequent legislatures implemented the principle.[1]

The second sentence reserves the power of the state to alter or repeal corporate charters. The central point is that a corporate charter is not a contract between the corporation and the state, reaffirming a position already asserted in statute form in 1829. The sentence removed any doubts about state power raised by the U.S. Supreme Court ruling that a charter granted by the state constituted a contract irrevocable by the state (Dartmouth College v. Woodward, 1819). Subject to the limitation in the Constitution, the due process clause of the state constitution, and the bar to any legislative act that prevents subsequent legislature from changing or abolishing a charter, the legislature is free to regulate corporations as it sees fit.

Most litigation has concerned the limitations that the doctrine of vested property rights imposes on legislative regulatory power.

Patterson v. Carey (1977) illustrates these limitations. There a legislative action rescinding toll increases instituted by the Jones Beach Parkway Authority was held to violate the state due process clause and the U.S. Constitution's impairment of contract clause (Art. I, sec. 10). This contemporary case suggests the continuing tension between the last sentence of this clause and the due process clauses of each constitution and the contract clause of the national constitution.

SECTION 2

Dues of corporations. Dues from corporations shall be secured by such individual liability of the corporators and other means as may be prescribed by law. [Const. 1846, Art. VIII, sec. 2; renumbered Art. X, sec. 2, 1938]

The term *dues* means debts or liabilities, and *corporators* means shareholders. The provision began as an attempt to make stockholders personally liable for debts of the corporation in proportion to their holdings, but the inability of the 1846 convention to draft language defining those liabilities consistent with general public policy resulted in compromise wording, which essentially directs the legislature to work out the problem of corporate liability. Today that liability is fixed by statute. The section has provoked little litigation.

SECTION 3

Savings bank charters; savings and loan association charters; special charters not to be granted. The legislature shall, by general law, conform all charters of savings banks, savings and loan associations, or institutions for savings, to a uniformity of powers, rights and liabilities; and all charters hereafter granted for such corporations shall be made to conform to such general law, and to such amendments as may be made thereto. The legislature shall have no power to pass any act granting any special charter for banking purposes; but corporations or associations may be formed for such purposes under general laws. [Const. 1846, Art. VIII, sec. 4 amend. in 1874; renumbered Art. X, sec. 3, 1938; amend. 1983]

The last sentence, adopted by the 1846 convention, banned special charters for banking purposes, thus excluding banks from the clause in section 1 permitting special incorporation. Singling out banks from other corporations undoubtedly reflected the anxiety of the delegates about bank failures and the contribution of wildcat banking to the panic of 1837. There seems to be little reason for the clause today.

The first sentence directs the legislature to conform all charters of savings banks and savings and loan associations, the latter added in 1983, to the requirements of other corporate charters. The Banking Act of 1838 had already dealt with the problems addressed in this section, at least as far as banks were concerned, but the court of appeals had held that trust companies and safe deposit companies were not covered by those regulations (U.S. Trust Co. v. Brady, 1885; Pardice v. Fish, 1875), and, until this amendment in 1874, it was not applicable to savings banks.[2] Savings banks, with stock under special charters, without proper restrictions upon investment in funds, and moved by a desire for large profits, had taken risks that jeopardized their depositors' funds. This provision brought all savings institutions under stricter control.

SECTION 4

Corporations; definition; right to sue and be sued. The term corporation as used in this section, and in sections 1, 2 and 3 of this article shall be construed to include all associations and joint-stock companies having any of the powers or privileges of corporations not possessed by individuals or partnerships. And all corporations shall have the right to sue and shall be subject to be sued in all courts in like cases as natural persons. [Const. 1846, Art. VIII, sec. 3; amend. 1894; amend. and renumbered Art. X, sec. 4, 1938]

This article makes the law uniform in its operation upon corporations, associations, joint stock companies, and individuals. The definition of corporation is followed by the granting of the right to sue and be sued. The section authorizes the legislature to permit the formation of these associations under general laws, a power the legislature probably possesses independent of this clause, to limit the imposition of personal liability, and to allow suits in courts as with natural persons. This granting of the right to sue does not limit legislative power to determine what shall be a cause of action against a corporation. Counties and municipal corporations can sue and, with some limitations, be sued. Under the Fourteenth Amendment, corporations are persons, so this right to sue is also protected under the U.S. Constitution. Reasonable classifications may be made under the Fourteenth Amendment, and, it appears, classifications would also be permitted under this provision, because uniformity is required only "in all like cases." When the provision was adopted, the equal protection clause of the Fourteenth Amendment did not exist. Now it seems to do little more than track the contours of that clause.

SECTION 5

Public corporations; restrictions on creation and powers; accounts; obligations of. No public corporation (other than a county, city, town, village, school district or fire district or an improvement district established in a town or towns) possessing both the power to contract indebtedness and the power to collect rentals, charges, rates or fees for the services or facilities furnished or supplied by it shall hereafter be created except by special act of the legislature.

No such public corporation (other than a county or city) shall hereafter be given both the power to contract indebtedness and the power, within any city, to collect rentals, charges, rates or fees from the owners of real estate, or the occupants of real estate (other than the occupants of premises owned or controlled by such corporation or by the state or any civil division thereof), for services or facilities furnished or supplied in connection with such real estate, if such services or facilities are of a character or nature then or formerly furnished or supplied by the city, unless the electors of the city shall approve the granting to such corporation of such powers by a majority vote at a general or special election in such city; but this paragraph shall not apply to a corporation created pursuant to an interstate compact. The accounts of every such public corporation heretofore or hereafter created shall be subject to the supervision of the state comptroller, or, if the member or members of such public corporation are appointed by the mayor of a city, to the supervision of the comptroller of such city; provided, however, that this provision shall not apply to such a public corporation created pursuant to agreement or compact with another state or with a foreign power, except with the consent of the parties to such agreement or compact.

Neither the state nor any political subdivision thereof shall at any time be liable for payment of any obligations issued by such a public corporation heretofore or hereafter created, nor may the legislature accept, authorize

acceptance of or impose such liability upon the state or any political
subdivision thereof; but the state or a political subdivision thereof may, if
authorized by the legislature, acquire the properties of any such corporation
and pay the indebtedness thereof. [1938]

This article is the first attempt to regulate constitutionally entities known as
authorities or, more formally, public benefit corporations. These are separate,
largely autonomous corporations and not operating departments of the state.
They share certain common characteristics: they are created by special act of
the legislature; possess broad administrative autonomy; usually finance themselves through bond issues, users' fees, or tolls; and operate outside the normal
constitutional and statutory restrictions of state government. The most prominent
examples are the New York Port Authority and the New York State Thruway
Authority.

By 1938, the state had thirty-three such authorities. Their unregulated growth
prompted the adoption of this article. Its provisions reflect an ambivalence toward
these authorities: on the one hand they unquestionably were convenient and did
necessary work; on the other they created "serious dangers."[3] Governor Al
Smith, a delegate to that convention, caught one side of this ambivalence when
he said this article would "paralyze the one method we have discovered of
getting work done expeditiously without taxing our people."[4] The first paragraph
implicitly recognizes their value but requires that they originate in a special act
of the legislature, thus requiring the legislature to pass directly on the establishment of each new authority. Without state approval, it was argued, local authorities would multiply unnecessarily. The establishment of these public benefit
corporations was considered a sovereign power that should not be delegated.
The phrase *special act* was not defined.[5]

The second paragraph was a response to the blatant use of the authority to
perform what were traditionally considered municipal functions (an example was
the Buffalo Sewer Authority) and the fact that once established they were autonomous and isolated from the political process. If voters believed it necessary
to contract indebtedness in excess of debt limitations, they ought to do so by
voting. This provision was meant to overrule at least in part Robertson v. Zimmermann (1935), which had upheld the validity of authorities as separate entities
apart from the state and not subject to the normal restrictions on the creation of
debt. The fact that these boards were not responsible to the electorate or even
to the legislature in any direct way prompted the third paragraph. The comptroller
of the state would supervise their finances in ways similar to the auditing of
regular state departments but the position does not include the power to audit
all vouchers before payment, or the power to void those payments absent that
pre-audit (Smith v. Levitt, 1972). The independence of the office in exercising
this function was emphasized in Patterson v. Carey (1977) wherein a statute
requiring the comptroller to review proposed toll increases of the Jones Beach
Parkway Authority was held to violate this section. The court noted that the

provision gave the legislature no power to control the comptroller's exercise of discretion.

The last paragraph prevents the state from assuming any liability for the debts of these authorities. Every statute setting up authorities up to the 1938 convention had in fact contained a clause denying state liability for the bonds of these authorities. Despite these disclaimers, the court of appeals suggested that the state would be liable for their debts in Williamsburgh Savings Bank v. State (1926). By inserting this paragraph, the convention hoped to prevent that from happening. Towns were excepted from the limitation because they could set up water and sewer systems, and others, only by creating special districts.

Strictly interpreted, the provisions of this article, along with Article XVI, section 1 and Article VII, sections 8 and 12, would have severely limited the usefulness of public authorities. Such interpretation was not forthcoming, and resort to public authorities has increased in number and scope. Major examples include the New York Housing Finance Agency (HFA, 1960), the Urban Development Corporation (UDC, 1968), State of New York Mortgage Agency (1970), and the Stabilization Reserve Corporation (SRC, 1974). All of these authorities were only marginally self-supporting. In each case liability was denied, as required by this section, but a moral obligation to back the debts of the authorities was included. The practice by the state of assuming a "moral obligation" to make up any deficits has blunted the impact of this section.

The statute setting up the HFA pledges that the state will not impair any rights or remedies of bondholders or alter any rights invested by the statute. This provision would seem to make the statute repealable until the bonds were paid off. If so, serious questions can be raised about its compatibility with section 1 of this article, which states that all laws of public and private corporations may be altered from time to time. The constitutionality of these practices came before the court of appeals in a case involving the SRC. The statute setting up this authority had the effect of avoiding debt ceilings and committing the credit of the state to the debts of the authority. The court in Wein v. City of New York (1975) gave its blessing to these practices. In reaching its conclusion, the court held that the statutory scheme is "within the letter of the Constitution" and suggested that the court ought not to strain itself in looking for illegalities (at 619). The financial plight of the city and state was apparently the significant factor in determining the court's hands-off approach to the use of these authorities.

A second device, lease financing, has also blunted the effect of this article. The state leases a facility under a long-term contract whereupon the developer issues revenue bonds to be paid off with the rent. When the lease expires, title reverts to the state. This device evades the referendum requirement at the state level and the debt limitation at the local level. Its major advantage is that it can be used for completely non-self-supporting projects. For example, the Empire State Plaza was constructed under such an arrangement, with Albany County issuing the long-term bonds for funding.

It may be that debt limitations and the provision of this article are anachronistic straitjackets. The decisions of the courts in New York giving deferential interpretations to these sections have had the effect of saving these provisions while permitting the state to avoid addressing the tensions between financing state and local government and the constitutional limitations on this financing.

SECTION 6

Liability of state for payment of bonds of public corporation to construct state thruways; use of state canal lands and properties. Notwithstanding any provision of this or any other article of this constitution, the legislature may by law, which shall take effect without submission to the people:

(a) make or authorize making the state liable for the payment of the principal of and interest on bonds of a public corporation created to construct state thruways, in a principal amount not to exceed five hundred million dollars, maturing in not to exceed forty years after their respective dates, and for the payment of the principal of and interest on notes of such corporations issued in anticipation of such bonds, which notes and any renewals thereof shall mature within five years after the respective dates of such notes; and

(b) authorize the use of any state canal lands and properties by such public corporation for so long as the law may provide. To the extent payment is not otherwise made or provided for, the provisions of section sixteen of article seven shall apply to the liability of the state incurred pursuant to this section, but the powers conferred by this section shall not be subject to the limitations of this or any other article. [1951]

When the decision was made to resume construction on the New York Thruway after World War II, Governor Thomas E. Dewey and the legislature did not wish to burden state finances with the cost of construction and maintenance. Instead a public authority, the New York Thruway Authority, was created. It was to be self-liquidating and self-financing with power to issue bonds and impose tolls. To insure the project and keep costs at a minimum, this amendment guaranteed the full faith and credit of the state as backing for the authority's bonds.[6] It is an explicit exception to section 5 of this article.

SECTION 7

Liability of state for obligations of the port of New York authority for railroad commuter cars; limitations. Notwithstanding any provision of this or any other article of this constitution, the legislature may by law, which shall take effect without submission to the people, make or authorize making the state liable for the payment of the principal of and interest on obligations of the port of New York authority issued pursuant to legislation heretofore or hereafter enacted, to purchase or refinance the purchase of, or to repay advances from this state made for the purpose of purchasing, railroad passenger cars, including self-propelled cars, and locomotives and other rolling stock used in passenger transportation, for the purpose of leasing such cars to any railroad transporting passengers between municipalities in the portion of the port of New York district within the state, the majority of the trackage of which within the port of New York district utilized for the transportation of passengers shall be in the state; provided, however, that the total amount of obligations with respect to which the state may be made liable shall not exceed one hundred million dollars at any time, and that all of such obligations shall be due not later than thirty-five years after the effective date of this section.

To the extent payment is not otherwise made or provided for, the provisions of section sixteen of article seven shall apply to the liability of the state incurred pursuant to this section, but the powers conferred by this section shall not be subject to the limitations of this or any other article. [1961]

A special report to the governor in 1959 recommended that the New York Port Authority undertake to replace outdated commuter equipment for the New York Central, New Haven, and Long Island railroads. For the Port Authority to finance the project through a purchase-lease agreement with the railroads in weak financial condition would have adversely affected the authority's credit. To prevent this, this amendment, another exception to section 5, allows the state to guarantee the bonds.[7]

SECTION 8

Liability of state on bonds of a public corporation to finance new industrial or manufacturing plants in depressed areas. Notwithstanding any provision of this or any other article in this constitution, the legislature may by law, which shall take effect without submission to the people, make or authorize making the state liable for the payment of the principal of and interest on bonds of a public corporation to be created pursuant to and for the purposes specified in the last paragraph of section eight of article seven of this constitution, maturing in not to exceed thirty years after their respective dates, and for the principal of and interest on notes of such corporation issued in anticipation of such bonds, which notes and any renewals thereof shall mature within seven years after the respective dates of such notes, provided that the aggregate principal amount of such bonds with respect to which the state shall be so liable shall not at any one time exceed six hundred million dollars, excluding bonds issued to refund outstanding bonds. [1961; amend. and renumbered Art. X, sec. 8, 1969, amend. 1985]

The last section of this article provides the constitutional basis for the creation of a third public authority, the New York Job Development Authority. The section enabled the state to guarantee the obligations of this authority up to $50 million. By the late 1960s, that limit had been reached, and subsequent amendments increased the figure to $600 million.

Article XI

Education

This article expresses the state's commitment to the principle of universal secular education and directs the legislature to enforce and foster that principle.

SECTION 1

> **Common schools**. The legislature shall provide for the maintenance and support of a system of free common schools, wherein all the children of this state may be educated. [Const. 1894, Art. IX, sec. 1; renumbered Art. XI, sec. 1, 1938]

With the adoption of this section, New York not only recognized what had been state policy for some time—that elementary, secondary, and higher education should be maintained at state expense—but also made education a fundamental constitutional value. The scope of this clause has been shaped by legislative enactment and court decision. Because the state has granted free education for all students, courts have held that a student has a property interest protected by the due process clauses of the national Constitution (Goss v. Lopez, 1975). The clause includes the rights to education for handicapped, delinquent, neglected, and dependent children (Wiltwyck School for Boys Inc. v. Hill, 1962). On the other hand, a student who received a certificate for graduation but could not read nor write could not sue for educational malpractice because this section did not impose a duty on school districts to see that each pupil received a minimum level of education; rather they were required to provide minimal acceptable services in contrast to unsystemized delivery of instruction (Donohue v. Copiague Union Free School District, 1979).

Most controversial has been the question of school financing. The great disparities in wealth of the school districts in the state have produced a large expenditure-level gap between the wealthiest and poorest. In Levittown Union Free School District v. Nyquist (1982), the court of appeals rejected challenges based on this and the equal protection section, arguing that despite the presence of Article XI, section 1, the rational basis standard was the correct level of scrutiny for the equal protection challenge. The mere citing of education in the constitution did not make it a fundamental right. The provision is a grant of power to the legislature, and allocation of funds is a matter peculiarly appropriate for legislative bodies.

SECTION 2

> **Regents of the university.** The corporation in the year one thousand seven hundred eighty-four, under the name of The Regents of the University of the State of New York, is hereby continued under the name of The University of the State of New York. It shall be governed and its corporate powers, which may be increased, modified or diminished by the legislature, shall be exercised by not less than nine regents. [Const. 1894, Art. IX, sec. 2; renumbered Art. XI, sec. 2, 1938]

New York established the first state system of education in the country. Two authorities were established by the legislature: the regents of the University, with jurisdiction over higher education, and the Superintendent of Common Schools (public schools), later Superintendent of Public Instruction, heading a department of the same name. The division created friction and dispute between the two authorities. This section gave constitutional status to the New York Board of Regents to insulate it from capricious legislative action and partisan politics. So great was the opposition to a complete unification of the educational system, however, that the convention backed off, putting the Superintendent under regents' control. That unification was accomplished by statute in 1904. The provision does not limit the legislature's power to deal with matters of education, and, subject to the limitations in the section, it has unlimited discretion to deal with educational matters (Institute of Metropolis Inc. v. University of State of New York, 1936). The powers exercised by the regents were to be such powers as conferred by law.

SECTION 3

> **Use of public property or money in aid of denominational schools prohibited; transportation of children authorized.** Neither the state nor any subdivision thereof shall use its property or credit or any public money, or authorize or permit either to be used, directly or indirectly, in aid or maintenance, other than for examination or inspection, of any school or

institution of learning wholly or in part under the control or direction of any
religious denomination, or in which any denominational tenet or doctrine is
taught, but the legislature may provide for the transportation of children to
and from any school or institution of learning. [Const. 1894, Art. IX, sec.
4; amend. and renumbered Art. XI, sec. 3, 1938; renumbered Art. XI, sec.
3, 1962]

Prior to this amendment, it was not uncommon for religious and secular
instruction to be combined in public schools, in spite of a 1777 article (thirty-
five) abolishing the established church.

This provision, known popularly as the Blaine amendment after Congressman
James Blaine, who sponsored a similar amendment to the U.S. Constitution in
1875, was precipitated by a proposal in the 1893 legislature that parochial schools
should receive a pro rata share of state school aid. The prohibition aimed at
preventing state finances from being used for sectarian educational purposes but
was not intended to prevent Bible reading.[1] The clause has two exceptions: aid
for examinations and inspections of these schools is permitted, as is the expenditure of public funds to provide transportation for pupils to and from school.
The latter exception was added in 1938 in response to Judd v. Board of Education
(1938), which declared such aid a violation of this section. Article VII, section
1 also permits aid to secular education for orphans, whether in public or private
institutions, a clause inserted specifically to limit the scope of this section.[2] In
spite of its stricter language, the provision has not been interpreted to provide
greater protection than the establishment clause of the First Amendment.

Its presence, in conjunction with the establishment clause, has prevented
massive direct aid to sectarian educational institutions (Committee for Public
Education v. Nyquist, 1973; Aguilar v. Felton, 1985), but the two provisions
have not prevented the federal and state governments from providing various
forms of aid to sectarian education. Transportation, released time, textbooks,
remedial and testing services, free lunches, and poverty programs have all been
given constitutional sanctions (People ex rel. Lewis v. Graves, 1927; Zorach v.
Clauson, 1951; Board of Education v. Allen, 1967; Committee for Public Education v. Regan, 1980). Finally it has not been interpreted to prevent religious
denominations from using the premises and facilities of the state university.[3]
The clauses have forced the state government to resort to ingenious and costly
methods of record keeping to meet the no-excessive-entanglement rule requirement of Lemon v. Kurtzman (1971).

The clause was controversial when adopted and remains so today. The attempt
to eliminate it from the constitution proposed in 1967 contributed to the failure
to ratify.

Article XII

Defense

SECTION 1

Defense; militia. The defense and protection of the state and of the United States is an obligation of all persons within the state. The legislature shall provide for the discharge of this obligation and for the maintenance and regulation of an organized militia. [1962]

In every constitution from 1777 on, New York has provided for the militia. The detailed provisions of the earlier constitutions were eliminated by a 1962 amendment following the recommendations of the Temporary Commission on the Revision and Simplification of the Constitution. The first sentence recognizes the duty of every person in the state to defend and protect the state. The second is an implementing clause, giving the governor and the legislature, within the confines of federal law, the freedom to structure the state's military department as they see fit.

Article XIII

Public Officers

This article is the result of a complicated and circuitious set of amendments and renumbering that brought together the major provisions in the constitution dealing with public officers. Nonetheless, there is significant overlap between the provisions of this article and those of the local government article (IX).

SECTION 1

Oath of office; no other test for public office. Members of the legislature, and all officers, executive and judicial, except such inferior officers as shall be by law exempted, shall, before they enter on the duties of their respective offices, take and subscribe the following oath of affirmation: ''I do solemnly swear (or affirm) that I will support the constitution of the United States, and the constitution of the State of New York, and that I will faithfully discharge the duties of the office of _____ , according to the best of my ability;'' and no other oath, declaration or test shall be required as a qualification for any office of public trust, except that any committee of a political party may, by rule, provide for equal representation of the sexes on any such committee, and a state convention of a political party, at which candidates for public office are nominated, may, by rule, provide for equal representation of the sexes on any committee of such party. [Const. 1821, Art. VI, sec. 1; renumbered Art. XII, sec. 1, Const. 1846 as amend. in 1874; renumbered Art. XIII, sec. 1, 1894; amend. 1938]

This section contains the oath of office. Unlike the national Constitution, it requires one to take the oath and subscribe to that oath so that a permanent record remains on file. Exactly who is a public official required to take the oath depends on statute and the nature of the service rendered.[1] All other oaths or tests for public office are banned. The delegates wished to protect appointees from any political or religious tests. Thus, a law making eligibility for the office of chief of police depend on membership in a political party having the highest or next highest representation in the common council was held to violate this no-declaration-or-tests clause, as was a statute requiring any temporary justice appointed to be the same political party as the disabled justice (Rathbone v. Wirth, 1896; Schieffelin v. Goldsmith, 1930). On the other hand, reasonable residence requirements for office-holders on the board of education did not violate this provision, nor would impartial application of basic standards to ensure ethical conduct (Rogers v. Buffalo, 1890).

Just after women attained the right to vote, party organizations doubled membership on their committees for the purpose of representing women. Some county committees made the representation mandatory. This rule and a similar rule adopted by the Republican State Convention were declared violations of this clause (Burton v. Schmidt, 1926; Bacon v. Schnieding, 1930). The final "except" clause was meant to reverse these decisions and remove any doubt about the power of political parties in the state to ensure equal representation for women.

SECTION 2

Duration of term of office. When the duration of any office is not provided by this constitution it may be declared by law, and if not so declared, such office shall be held during the pleasure of the authority making the appointment. [Const. 1777, Art. XXVIII; amend. and renumbered Art. IV, sec. 16, Const. 1821; amend. and renumbered Art. 10, sec. 3, Const. 1846; amend. and renumbered Art. XIII, sec. 6, 1938; renumbered Art. XIII, sec. 2, 1962]

This provision gives elected officials and executives the power to ensure effective administration and policy control over their employees, enabling them to carry out their duties. It applies to public officers who are defined as those whose positions are created and whose powers and duties are prescribed by statute and who exercise a high degree of initiative and independent judgment. In applying this standard, an appellate court held that a housing director hired by a housing authority was not a public officer under this section (Matter of Lake v. Binghamton Housing Authority, 1987).

SECTION 3

Vacancies in office; how filled; boards of education. The legislature shall provide for filling vacancies in office, and in case of elective officers, no person appointed to fill a vacancy shall hold his office by virtue of such appointment longer than the commencement of the political year next succeeding the first annual election after the happening of the vacancy; provided, however, that nothing contained in this article shall prohibit the filling of vacancies on boards of education, including boards of education of community districts in the city school district of the city of New York, by appointment until the next regular school district election, whether or not such appointment shall extend beyond the thirty-first day of December in any year. [Const. 1846, Art. X, sec. 5; renumbered Art. XIII, sec. 8, 1938; renumbered Art. XIII, sec. 3, 1962; amend. 1977]

The necessity of filling vacancies on a temporary basis so that duties are not seriously interrupted prompted this provision. Because the electorate could not practically and conveniently provide this continuity, the legislature was delegated power to make provision in the event of such vacancies. By keeping the tenure of the temporary appointment to as short a period of time as possible, the clause balances the need for continuous authority and minimal interference with the popular will. The clause applies to all elective offices. Laws providing for automatic and instantaneous devolution of power and duties of certain elected officials do not violate this clause. When the president and president pro tem of a city council became, pursuant to statute, mayor and president of the city council, respectively, on the death of the mayor, the court held that such an arrangement was constitutional in part because no vacancy, as that word is used in this section, had occurred (Burns v. Kinley, 1983).

In Roher v. Dinkins (1972), the court of appeals held that part of the education law allowing vacancies on school boards to be filled for the unexpired terms violated the clause mandating the appointees may hold office for no longer than the commencement of the political year following the first annual election held after the occurrence of a vacancy. In response to this decision, the section was amended in 1977. Its sponsor gave as justification that "political year" was never meant to apply to the state school system.[2]

SECTION 4

Political year and legislative term. The political year and legislative term shall begin on the first day of January; and the legislature shall, every year, assemble on the first Wednesday after the first Monday in January. [Const. 1821, Art. I, sec. 14; amend. and renumbered Art. X, sec. 6, Const. 1846; amend. Const. 1894; amend. and renumbered Art. XIII, sec. 9, 1938; renumbered Art. XIII, sec. 4, 1962]

The phrase *legislative term* was added to prevent any misunderstanding as to what was meant by political year. The term was set in January to shorten the period between the election and the meeting of the legislature. Prior to the adoption of this section, the legislative term had begun in July. The day was changed from Tuesday to Wednesday so that members would not have to travel on Sunday for purposes of caucusing.

SECTION 5

Removal from office for misconduct. Provision shall be made by law for the removal for misconduct or malversation in office of all officers, except judicial, whose powers and duties are not local or legislative and who shall be elected at general elections, and also for supplying vacancies created by such removal. [Const. 1846, Art. X, sec. 7; renumbered Art. XIII, sec. 10, 1938; renumbered Art. XIII, sec. 5, 1962]

Prior to this section, public officials could be removed only by impeachment. The removal provision was given constitutional status because it was felt that any official elected by the people whose term of office was prescribed by the constitution ought to be removed only under constitutional authorization. The purpose here is not so much to punish as to improve the public service. The courts have interpreted the "misconduct malversation" clause to require an intentional disregard of duty, moral turpitude, or violation of the public trust (Matter of Smith v. Perlman, 1984). Mere oversight or technical violations without more will not generally trigger this provision (Matter of Pisciotta v. Dendievel, 1973). The section has been interpreted to prevent the legislature from removing judicial officers by statute, but the legislature may provide for removal of local officers (La Carrubba v. Klein, 1977). In Donnelly v. Roosevelt (1932), a supreme court held that the legislature, as possessor of complete lawmaking powers in the state, can regulate the affairs of local government, and matters relating to public service come within that power. Section 7 did not restrict the power in that regard but made it "a duty of the legislature to act in respect of certain officers, and to that extent it was deprived of discretionary power." The court concluded that the commands of the section "that existing power be exercised in relation to some officers did not deprive or prohibit the legislature from exercising a power which it possessed as to others" (at 529).

Other provisions for removal are found in Article VI, sections 22–24, and section 13 of this article.

SECTION 6

When office to be deemed vacant; legislature may declare. The legislature may declare the cases in which any office shall be deemed vacant when no provision is made for that purpose in this constitution. [Const. 1846; Art. X, sec. 8; renumbered Art. XIII, sec. 11, 1938; renumbered Art. XIII, sec. 6, 1962]

This section, unlike section 5, is permissive. It distinguishes between removal and declaring a position vacant. A vacancy can occur because of removal or resignation. Thus, the legislature could not under sections 5 or 6 remove a judicial officer because such removal can take place only under Article VII, sections

22–24; it can, however, determine when a judicial office is vacant (Thaler v. State, 1974).

SECTION 7

Compensation of officers. Each of the state officers named in this constitution shall, during his continuance in office, receive a compensation, to be fixed by law, which shall not be increased or diminished during the term for which he shall have been elected or appointed; nor shall he receive to his use any fees or perquisites of office or other compensation. [Const. 1846 Art. X, sec. 9 as added in 1874; amend. and renumbered Art. XIII, sec. 12, 1938; renumbered Art. XIII, sec. 7, 1962]

This provision provides state officers with a degree of independence and protection from arbitrary or politically motivated harassment. Until recently, district attorneys, for purposes of this article, were considered state officers. Adoption of Article IX, the bill of rights for local government, led the court of appeals to rule that a district attorney could no longer be considered a state officer within the meaning of this section (Matter of Kelley v. McGee, 1982). In *Kelley*, compensation adjustments that otherwise would have been a violation of this section were allowed to stand. In 1979 the attorney general, reasoning along the same lines, had made a similar ruling with regard to sheriffs.[3]

SECTION 8

Election and term of city and certain county officers. All elections of city officers, including supervisors, elected in any city or part of a city, and of county officers elected in any county wholly included in a city, except to fill vacancies, shall be held on the Tuesday succeeding the first Monday in November in an odd-numbered year, and the term of every such officer shall expire at the end of an odd-numbered year. This section shall not apply to elections of any judicial officer. [Const. 1894, Art. XII, sec. 3; amend. and renumbered Art. IX, sec. 15, 1938; renumbered Art. XIII, sec. 8, 1965 (sec. revised)]

This section was seen as a home rule measure by the 1894 convention. It separated state and national elections from municipal elections so only municipal issues would determine the outcome. The rationale was that party considerations were less relevant to the affairs of a city, which involve essentially nonpartisan questions of probity and proper management. According to two students of New York politics, the major effect in upstate cities was to increase ethnic as opposed to partisan competition.[4]

In 1926, Article VI, section 19 was amended to permit the election of judges as the legislature shall see fit. This raised the question of whether the legislature could, under section 19, authorize judicial elections in even-numbered years. When the legislature did so, the court in Matter of Adler v. Voorhees (1930) ruled that section 19 superseded the last sentence of this section. Originally the clause applied only to cities over 50,000 in population. That language was dropped in 1926. The provision requiring inferior judges to be elected only in odd-numbered years was eliminated, making this section consistent with the language in section 19 and the *Voorhees* decision.

SECTIONS 9–12

[Renumbered sections 4–7.]

SECTION 13

Law enforcement and other officers. (a) Except in counties in the city of New York and except as authorized in section one of article nine of this constitution, registers in counties having registers shall be chosen by the electors of the respective counties once in every three years and whenever the occurring of vacancies shall require; the sheriff and the clerk of each county shall be chosen by the electors once in every three or four years as the legislature shall direct. Sheriffs shall hold no other office. They may be required by law to renew their security, from time to time; and in default of giving such new security, their offices shall be deemed vacant. The governor may remove any elective sheriff, county clerk, district attorney or register within the term for which he shall have been elected; but before so doing he shall give to such officer a copy of the charges against him and an opportunity of being heard in his defense. In each county a district attorney shall be chosen by the electors once in every three or four years as the legislature shall direct. The clerk of each county in the city of New York shall be appointed, and be subject to removal, by the appellate division of the supreme court in the judicial department in which the county is located. In addition to his powers and duties as clerk of the supreme court, he shall have power to select, draw, summon and empanel grand and petit jurors in the manner and under the conditions now or hereafter prescribed by law, and shall have such other powers and duties as shall be prescribed by the city from time to time by local law.

(b) Any district attorney who shall fail faithfully to prosecute a person charged with the violation in his county of any provision of this article which may come to his knowledge, shall be removed from office by the governor, after due notice and an opportunity of being heard in his defense. The expenses which shall be incurred by any county, in investigating and prosecuting any charge of bribery or attempting to bribe any person holding office under the laws of this state, within such county, or of receiving bribes by any such person in said county, shall be a charge against the state, and their payment by the state shall be provided for by law.

(c) The city of New York is hereby vested with power from time to time to abolish by local law, as defined by the legislature, the office of any county officer within the city other than judges, clerks of counties and district attorneys, and to assign any or all functions of such officers to city officers, courts or clerks of counties, and to prescribe the powers, duties, qualifications, number, mode of selection and removal, terms of office and compensation of the persons holding such offices and the employees therein, and to assign to city officers any powers or duties of clerks of counties not assigned by this constitution. The legislature shall not pass any law affecting any such matters in relation to such offices within the city of New York except on message from the governor declaring that an emergency exists and the concurrent action of two-thirds of the members of each house, except that existing laws regarding each such office shall continue in force, and may be amended or repealed by the legislature as heretofore, until the power herein granted to the city has been exercised with respect to that office. The provisions of article nine shall not prevent the legislature from passing general or special laws prescribing or affecting powers and duties of such city officers or such courts or clerks to whom or which functions of such county officers shall have been so assigned, in so far as such powers or duties embrace subjects not relating to property, affairs or government of such city. [Const. 1821 Art. IV, secs. 8, 9; amend. and renumbered Art. X, secs. 1–4; amend. 1874; amend. and renumbered Art. X, secs. 1, 2 and Art. XIII, sec. 6, Const. 1894; amend. and renumbered Art. IX, secs. 5–8, 1938; amend. 1958, 1963 (sec. revised), 1972, 1984, 1989]

This section is divided into three distinct but related subdivisions. Subdivision (a) is a home rule provision protecting local government from legislative transfer of certain local functions to state agencies or other local jurisdictions. It fixes the terms and manner of selection of registers, sheriffs, district attorneys, and clerks of the counties in New York City, with two exceptions: one relating to the City of New York, found in subdivision (c) of this section, and the other in Article IX, section 1(h).

The constitution provides for an elective sheriff in each county outside New York City, who serves for a term of four years and may hold no other office. The section originally specified three-year terms, but an 1984 amendment allowed the legislature to set the term at four years, which it has elected to do.[5] This amendment passed at the request of counties to increase stability in the office of sheriff and reduce the time and money spent campaigning. The functions of the sheriff are spelled out in the County Law of the state rather than in this section. An amendment approved in 1989 removing a clause prohibiting a county from ever assuming responsibility for the acts of the sheriff renders the security requirements obsolete because counties will likely assume this liability in the future. A county outside New York City acting under Article IV, section 1(h), may alter or abolish upon voter approval the office of elective county sheriff. New York City under section 13(c) may abolish the office within the city without a referendum.

The district attorney is also a constitutional office. The section provides that it be an elective position with a term of three or four years. The option was given in 1972 for reasons similar to those used in amending the tenure of sheriffs. Since it is a constitutional office, the legislature cannot abolish or transfer or substantially impair its duties: "where the constitution establishes a specified office, or recognizes its existence and prescribes the manner in which it shall be filled," the legislature may not regulate the duties to the extent of "depriving them of a substantial attribute of the office" (People ex rel. Wogan v. Rafferty, 1913). Again, the county under Article IX, section 1(h) may adopt an alternative form of government if approved by the electorate. Under this new form, any local office, including that of district attorney, may be abolished. However, in Enders v. Rossi (1974), a county charter that had increased the term of district attorney to four years was found to violate this section. Although the county had the power to transfer functions or even abolish offices, it could not alter the terms of constitutional officers as long as those offices continued to exist.[6] There is some tension between this article and the provisions in Article IX, and it is not clear to what extent Article IX supersedes this section.

The governor is given the power to remove the officers mentioned in this section, but they have the right to notice of the charges and the opportunity to be heard in their defense. Traditionally courts have held that the governor possesses exclusive authority to determine the sufficiency of the reasons that justify removal. Such judgment is subject to judicial review, but that review is restricted to discovering whether the governor had jurisdiction and whether proper constitutional procedure was followed (Matter of Guden, 1902).

Subdivision (b), added in 1874, was originally part of an article dealing with bribery and other forms of official corruption. The reference to violations of this article no longer makes any sense because the violations referred to were enumerated in the bribery sections, which are no longer part of this article. It was hoped that by designating a specific officer to take action when corrupt activities came to light under pain of loss of office, "force and efficacy" would be given to the bribery section.[7] The state is required to bear the cost of prosecutions of state officials.

Subdivision (c) allows New York City to abolish by local law certain officers in counties within the city in order to eliminate duplication in officers and functions. This problem was particularly acute in New York City where the city's boundaries were coterminous with the five counties. The courts have expansively interpreted this section insofar as restructuring local government is concerned. An amendment to the New York Charter abolishing the county offices of sheriff, register, register of deeds, and registrar and replacing them with a city sheriff and city register was sustained under this section (Burke v. Kern, 1941).

Subdivision (c) contains three exceptions. The first, pertaining to officers in place at the time that the article became effective, is obsolete. The second allows the legislature to pass local or special laws when the governor delivers an emer-

New York Constitution and Commentary

gency message and two-thirds of each house approves. The third exception, the most significant, allows the legislature to pass special or general laws restricting the duties, powers, and functions of county officers insofar as such powers or duties "embrace subjects not relating to the property, affairs or government of such city." This provision, added in 1938, was meant to ensure that the state's hands would not be tied when a state function was involved. This last exception has turned on the difference between a general and special law. The court's interpretation of this distinction has gone to the heart of, if it has not cut the heart out of, the notion of home rule in New York State. This distinction is examined more closely in the comments in Article IX, section 2.

SECTION 14

Employees of, and contractors for, the state and local governments; wages, hours and other provisions to be regulated by the legislature. The legislature may regulate and fix the wages or salaries and the hours of work or labor, and make provisions for the protection, welfare and safety, of persons employed by the state or by any county, city, town, village or other civil division of the state, or by any contractor or subcontractor performing work, labor or services for the state or for any county, city, town, village or other civil division therefore. [Const. 1894, Art. XII, sec. 1; as amend. 1905; amend. and renumbered Art. XIII, sec. 9, 1938; amend. and renumbered Art. XIII, sec. 14, 1963]

This section was occasioned by the court of appeals decision in People ex rel. Rodgers v. Coler (1900) striking down legislation requiring contractors with the state to pay wages and ensure working conditions similar to those prevailing in the locality where the work was being done. This amendment was an almost immediate response to *Coler* and indicates the gap that existed between the people and the judiciary on the question of social and economic legislation. When the court heard challenges to newly enacted legislation, it continued to maintain that such legislation bore no reasonable relation to the public's health, welfare, and safety. Nevertheless in the face of the amendment, the court upheld the legislation (People ex rel. Williams Engineering and Contracting Co. v. Metz, 1908). A subsequent repudiation of the philosophy embodied in *Coler* by the New York high court makes the importance of this article contingent on the unlikely possibility that the court might readopt the narrow view of state police power repudiated by the court and public for more than fifty years.

Article XIV

Conservation

New York was the first state to provide constitutional protection for a major natural resource. The threat posed to the environment by commercial and industrial development, now an issue of international concern, was recognized by New Yorkers in the nineteenth century.

The Forest Preserve Act of 1885 eventually led to this article, which opens with the dramatic proclamation that the forest preserve of the state "shall be forever kept as wild forest land." It is one of the unique aspects of the New York Constitution.

SECTION 1

Forest preserve to be forever kept wild; certain highways and ski trails authorized; limited use for certain highways authorized; exchange of lands with the village of Saranac Lake, Town of Arietta, International Paper Company and Sagamore Institute, Inc. authorized for certain purposes. The land of the State, now owned or hereafter acquired, constituting the forest preserve as now fixed by law, shall be forever kept as wild forest lands. They shall not be leased, sold or exchanged, or be taken by any corporation, public or private, nor shall the timber thereon be sold, removed or destroyed. Nothing herein contained shall prevent the state from constructing, completing and maintaining any highway heretofore specifically authorized by constitutional amendment, nor from constructing and maintaining to federal standards federal aid interstate highway route five hundred two from a point of the vicinity of the city of Glens Falls, thence northerly to the vicinity of the villages of Lake George and Warrensburg, the hamlets of South Horicon and Pottersville and thence northerly in a generally straight line on the west side of Schroon Lake to the vicinity of the hamlet of Schroon, then continuing northerly to the vicinity of Schroon Falls, Schroon River and North Hudson, and to east of Makomis Mountain, east of the hamlet of New Russia, east of the village of Elizabethtown and continuing northerly in the vicinity of the hamlet of Towers Forge, and east of Poke-O-Moonshine Mountain and continuing northerly to the vicinity of the village of Keeseville and the city of Plattsburgh, all of the aforesaid taking not to exceed a total of three hundred acres of state forest preserve land, nor from constructing and maintaining not more than twenty miles of ski trails thirty to eighty feet wide on the north, east and northwest slopes of Whiteface Mountain in Essex County, nor from constructing and maintaining not more than twenty miles of ski trails thirty to eighty feet wide, together with appurtenances thereto, on the slopes of Belleayre Mountain in Ulster and Delaware counties and not more than thirty miles of ski trails thirty to eighty feet wide, together with appurtenances thereto, on the slopes of Gore, South and Pete Gay mountains in Warren county, nor from relocating, restructuring and maintaining a total of not more than fifty miles of existing state highways for the purpose of eliminating the hazards of dangerous curves and grades, provided a total of no more than four hundred acres of forest preserve land shall be used for such purpose and that no single relocated portion of any highway shall exceed one mile in length. Notwithstanding the foregoing provisions, the state may convey to the village of Saranac Lake ten acres of forest preserve land adjacent to the boundaries of such village for public use in providing for refuse disposal and in exchange therefore the village of Saranac Lake shall convey to the state thirty acres of certain true forest land owned by such village on Roaring Brook in the northern half of Lot 113, Township 11, Richards Survey. Notwithstanding the foregoing provisions, the state may convey to the town of Arietta twenty-eight acres of forest preserve land within such town for public use in providing for the extension of the runway and landing strip of the Piseco airport and in exchange therefor the town of Arietta shall convey to the state thirty acres of certain land owned by such town in the town of Arietta. Notwithstanding the foregoing provisions and subject to legislative approval of the tracts to be exchanged prior to the actual transfer of title, the state, in order to consolidate its land holdings for better management, may convey to International Paper Company approximately eight thousand five hundred acres of forest preserve land located in townships two and three of Totten and Crossfield's Purchase and township nine of the Moose River Tract, Hamilton county, and in exchange therefore International Paper Company shall convey to the state for incorporation into the forest preserve approximately the same number of acres of land located within such townships and such County on condition that the legislature shall determine that the lands to be received by the state are at least equal in value to the lands to be conveyed by the state. Notwithstanding the foregoing provisions and subject to legislative approval of the tracts to be exchanged prior to the actual transfer of title and the conditions herein set forth, the state, in order to facilitate the preservation of historic buildings listed on the national register of historic places by rejoining an historic grouping of buildings under unitary ownership and stewardship, may convey to Sagamore Institute, Inc. a not-for-profit educational organization, approximately ten acres of land and buildings thereon adjoining the real property of the Sagamore Institute, Inc. and located on Sagamore Road, near Racquette Lake Village, in the town of Long Lake, county of Hamilton, and in exchange therefor; Sagamore Institute, Inc. shall convey to the state for incorporation into the forest preserve approximately two hundred acres of wild forest land located within the Adirondack Park on condition that the legislature shall determine that the lands to be received by the state are at least equal in value to the lands and buildings to be conveyed by the state and that the natural and historic character of the lands and building conveyed by the state will be secured by appropriate covenants and restrictions and that the lands and buildings conveyed by the state will reasonably be available for public visits according to agreement between Sagamore Institute, Inc. and the state. [Const. 1894, Art. VII, sec. 7; amend. and renumbered, Art. XIV, sec. 1, 1938; amend. 1941, 1947, 1957, 1959, 1963, 1965, 1979, 1983, 1987]

This section, the heart of the article, provides that the "lands . . . of the state . . . constituting the forest preserve as now fixed by law shall be forever kept as wild forest lands . . . and that they not be leased, sold or exchanged . . . and no timber thereon sold, removed or destroyed." The emphatic language invites praise and inevitable modification. The rest of this rather lengthy section consists of those modifications: a series of exceptions to permit building and modernizing ski slopes, building and maintaining roads, and exchanges in land with the village of Saranac Lake, the town of Arietta, the Sagamore Institute, and the International Paper Company.

The section raises a number of questions. What are the "lands of the state"? What law fixes the forest preserve? What are the permissible uses of the forest preserve under the "forever wild" rubric?

Since the adoption of this section, constitutional conventions, courts, legislatures, and attorneys general have struggled to provide answers to these questions. The legislature has defined the forest preserve and in 1970 entrusted its care and custody to the Department of Environmental Conservation. That agency and its predecessors have basically determined the permitted uses of the preserve. In one of the few major court interpretations of this clause, Association for the Protection of the Adirondacks v. MacDonald (1930), the court of appeals held that a statute permitting construction of a bobsled in the forest preserve for the 1932 Winter Olympics violated this section. The court provided some guidance on uses permitted under the clause. Cutting for fire prevention, road repair, inspections, and recreational facilities are permitted uses as long as they do not in any material way interfere with the purpose of preserving the land. Because litigation has been sparse, the task of providing legal guidance has fallen largely on the attorney general. The numerous opinions from that office have generally given a strict construction to the clause but have permitted reasonable removals consistent with the no-destruction-to-any-material-degree standard enunciated in *MacDonald*.[1]

The Adirondack Park consists of approximately 6 million acres, of which approximately 40 percent is state owned. The public lands are strictly regulated, whereas the private lands, with the exception of the banning of billboards, were practically unregulated until 1968, when Governor Rockefeller appointed the Temporary Commission on the Future of the Adirondack Park. That commission's report led to the creation of the Adirondacks Park Agency whose task was to develop a master plan for land use zoning controls in the park.[2] In 1986 the state voters passed the $1.45 billion Environmental Bond Act, with a portion of that money earmarked for land acquisition and management.

Land acquisition has been a state policy throughout the twentieth century, but that policy is not without problems. Once land is acquired by the state within the confines of the Adirondacks or Catskill parks—called the Blue Line—its use is drastically restricted. This restriction is not always desirable because active timbering has beneficial effects, such as local employment and a better habitat for deer. A partial solution to this dilemma has been found through a conservation easement under which the land remains private but the state holds a veto on development rights,[3] thus preventing unwanted development while permitting timbering, mining, hunting, and recreation. More aggressive attempts to obtain land under the power of eminent domain clause require that "public purpose" condition (Art. I, sec. 7a). Is the acquiring of land in the preserve by eminent domain a public purpose if that purpose is just to have it? The state claims such possession would enable it to consolidate land in the parks and prevent further degradation. This question is under litigation.

SECTION 2

Reservoirs. The legislature may by general laws provide for the use of not exceeding three per centum of such lands for the construction and maintenance of reservoirs for municipal water supply, and for the canals of the state. Such reservoirs shall be constructed, owned and controlled by the state, but such work shall not be undertaken until after the boundaries and high flow lines thereof shall have been accurately surveyed and fixed, and after public notice, hearing and determination that such lands are required for such public use. The expense of any such improvements shall be apportioned on the public and private property and municipalities benefited to the extent of the benefits received. Any such reservoir shall always be operated by the state and the legislature shall provide for a charge upon the property and municipalities benefited for a reasonable return to the state upon the value of the rights and property of the state used and the services of the state rendered, which shall be fixed for terms of not exceeding ten years and be readjustable at the end of any term. Unsanitary conditions shall not be created or continued by any such public works. [Const. 1894, Art. VII, sec. 7 as amend. in 1913; renumbered Art. XIV, sec. 2, 1938; amend. 1953]

Full development of the watershed for regulating waters of the rivers and for development of power could not take place unless an exception to this article was made. This section permits the use of 3 percent of the forest preserve land for municipal water supply and canals and contains provisions regulating the construction and operation of reservoirs. A 1953 amendment revoked the state's power to regulate streams granted in the 1913 amendment.

SECTION 3

Forest and wild life conservation; use or disposition of certain lands authorized. 1. Forest and wild life conservation are hereby declared to be policies of the state. For the purpose of carrying out such policies the legislature may appropriate moneys for the acquisition by the state of land, outside the Adirondack and Catskill parks as now fixed by law, for the practice of forest or wild life conservation. The prohibitions of section 1 of this article shall not apply to any lands heretofore or hereafter acquired or dedicated for such purposes within the forest preserve counties but outside of the Adirondack and Catskill parks as now fixed by law, except that such lands shall not be leased, sold or exchanged, or be taken by any corporation, public or private.

2. As to any other lands of the state, now owned or hereafter acquired, constituting the forest preserve referred to in section one of this article, but outside of the Adirondack and Catskill parks as now fixed by law, and consisting in any case of not more than one hundred contiguous acres entirely separated from any other portion of the forest preserve, the legislature may by appropriate legislation, notwithstanding the provisions of section one of this article, authorize:

(a) the dedication thereof for the practice of forest or wild life conservation; or (b) the use thereof for public recreational or other state purposes or the sale, exchange or other disposition thereof; provided, however, that all moneys derived from the sale or other disposition of any of such lands shall be paid into a special fund of the treasury and be expended only for the acquisition of additional lands for such forest preserve within either such Adirondack or Catskill Park. [Const. 1894, Art. VII, sec. 16 as amend. in 1931; amend. and renumbered Art. XIV, sec. 3, 1938; amend. 1957, 1973]

The first paragraph declares forest and wildlife conservation to be the public policy of the state. It authorizes the state to acquire and reforest lands outside the Blue Line. Initially the section specified the amounts of money to be spent each year over an eleven-year period; the 1938 convention eliminated specific amounts but retained the general policy commitment. Land purchased under this provision in the forest preserve but outside the Blue Line was exempted from the restrictions found in section 1. This would allow for hunting, fishing, and the cutting and selling of timber if the legislature, by law, permits. However, these lands cannot be sold, leased, or exchanged.

The second paragraph allows the legislature to sell isolated parcels of forest preserve land, up to ten acres in size—later amended to one hundred acres—outside the Blue Line for purposes of purchasing land within the Blue Line or to use such isolated parcels of land for wildlife conservation and management or for recreation. These isolated patches of land had little value because of their size and location. It was thought that selling them to purchase more land within the Blue Line would enhance the forest preserve. Other uses not incompatible with conservation or reforestation have been permitted.

SECTION 4

Protection of natural resources; development of agricultural lands. The policy of the state shall be to conserve and protect its natural resources and scenic beauty and encourage the development and improvement of its agricultural lands for the production of food and other agricultural products. The legislature, in implementing this policy, shall include adequate provision for the abatement of air and water pollution and of excessive and unnecessary noise, the protection of agricultural lands, wetlands and shorelines, and the development and regulation of water resources. The legislature shall further provide for the acquisition of lands and waters, including improvements thereon and any interest therein, outside the forest preserve counties, and the dedication of properties so acquired or now owned, which because of their natural beauty, wilderness character, or geological, ecological or historical significance, shall be preserved and administered for the use and enjoyment of the people. Properties so dedicated shall constitute the state nature and historical preserve and they shall not be taken or otherwise disposed of except by law enacted by two successive regular sessions of the legislature. [1969]

This section declares it the public policy of the state to conserve, improve, and protect its natural resources and the quality of the environment. The amendment was initially proposed at the abortive 1967 Constitutional Convention, where it received unanimous praise. It is sometimes referred to as the conservation bill of rights. Its sponsors had the rather ambitious goal of making scenic beauty, unlittered land, clean waters, and unpolluted air the inalienable right of every New Yorker.[4] It establishes a state nature and historic preserve to protect the heritage of the state beyond the forest preserve. By using the adjective *scenic* rather than *natural*, the amendment probably includes buildings within its scope. Its range is not limited to large wilderness areas and includes natural areas or historical sites close to metropolitan areas where the need may be greatest. The criteria for preservation are scenic beauty, wilderness character, and geological, ecological, or historic significance. Protection of the kind envisaged by this section had already been provided by statute, at least in part. The section gives constitutional status to that protection and provides an all-inclusive preservation policy, including as it does wetlands and agricultural lands. The broad policy goals of the section were implemented by statutes in the 1970s.[5]

One interesting aspect of this article is the last sentence, which says that attempts to take or dispose of property or land designated worthy of protection should require more than ordinary legislative action but less than that required for a constitutional amendment. It is an attempt to avoid freezing public policy in the constitution while at the same time providing protection against hasty or special interest–based legislation.

SECTION 5

Violations of article; how restrained. A violation of any of the provisions of this article may be restrained at the suit of the people or, with the consent of the supreme court in appellate division, on notice to the attorney-general at the suit of any citizen. [Const. 1894, Art. VII, sec. 7 as amend. in 1913; amend. and renumbered Art. XIV, sec. 5, 1938]

Violations of this article may be restrained by suit of the people or, with the consent of the appellate division of the supreme court on notice to the attorney general, at the suit of any individual citizen. The power is vested in the first instance with the attorney general but in order to encourage enforcement and compliance, a secondary right is given to any citizen of the state to maintain the action should the attorney general default, provided that the appellate division consents. A membership corporation has a right to sue for purposes of this section (Oneida County Forest Preserve Council v. Wehle, 1955). Since the section limits suits to restrain actions, courts may not consent to applicants' resort to other remedies (People v. Systems Properties, 1953). Despite this provision, there has been little litigation under this article.

Article XV

Canals

The other natural resource protected by the constitution is the barge canal system. The first mention of canals appeared in the 1821 Constitution. With continued canal development throughout the nineteenth century, it is not surprising that regions and parties attempted to constitutionalize canal policy. The article forbids the state from disposing of the system except for unnecessary parts, prohibits charging tolls, and authorizes the legislature to make laws and regulations governing navigation and to enact appropriations for its maintenance.

SECTION 1

Disposition of canals and canal properties prohibited. The legislature shall not sell, lease, abandon or otherwise dispose of the now existing or future improved barge canal, the divisions of which are the Erie canal, the Oswego canal, the Champlain canal, and the Cayuga and Seneca canals, or of the terminals constructed as part of the barge system; nor shall it sell, lease, abandon or otherwise dispose of any portion of the canal system existing prior to the barge canal improvement which portion forms a part of, or functions as a part of, the present barge canal system; but such canals and terminals shall remain the property of the state and under its management and control forever. This prohibition shall not prevent the legislature, by appropriate laws, from authorizing the granting of revocable permits for the occupancy or use of such lands or structures. [Const. 1846, Art. VII, sec. 6 as amend. in 1874; renumbered Art. VII, sec. 8, Const. 1894; amend. and renumbered Art. XV, sec. 1, 1938]

SECTION 2

Prohibition inapplicable to lands and properties no longer useful; disposition authorized. The prohibition of sale, abandonment or other disposition contained in section 1 of this article shall not apply to barge canal lands, barge canal terminals or barge canals terminal lands which have or may become no longer necessary or useful for canal or terminal purposes; nor to any canal lands and appertaining structures constituting the canal system prior to the barge canal improvement which have or may become no longer necessary or useful in conjunction with the now existing barge canal. The legislature may by appropriate legislation authorize the sale, exchange, abandonment or other disposition of any barge canal lands, barge canal terminals, barge canal terminal lands or other canal lands and appertaining structures which have or may become no longer necessary or useful as a part of the barge canal system, as an aid to navigation thereon, or for barge canal terminal purposes.

All funds that may be derived from any sale or other disposition of any barge canal lands, barge canal terminals, barge canal terminal lands or other canal lands and appertaining structures shall be paid into the general fund of the treasury. [Const. 1846 Art. VII, sec. 6 as amend. in 1874; renumbered Art. VII, sec. 8, Const. 1894; amend. (sec. revised) and renumbered Art. XV sec. 2, 1938]

These sections commit the state to a policy of maintaining a water highway across the state and preventing its transfer to any other government agency, corporation, or individual. In 1874, the parts of the canal to be protected by this section were specified, allowing the legislature, by implication, to dispose of any canal not listed. In 1938, the Barge River Canal System, the successor to the old Erie Canal, was included in the protections of the provision; however, the movement has been away from constitutional restriction and toward legislative discretion on canal policy.

An amendment allowing revocable permits for private use of canals gave the legislature more flexibility. This latter clause merely recognized common practice and the past statutory policy of granting revocable permits as long as such permits did not interfere with the full use of the canals. A 1938 amendment enabled the legislature to dispose of lands no longer considered useful or necessary. The court of appeals has interpreted these sections to allow the use of canal waters by adjacent cities as long as waters were in excess of that needed for canal purposes (Sweet v. City of Syracuse, 1891).

SECTION 3

No tolls to be imposed; contracts for work and materials; no extra compensation. No tolls shall hereafter be imposed on persons or property transported on the canals, but all boats navigating the canals and the owners and masters thereof, shall be subject to such laws and regulations as have been or may hereafter be enacted concerning the navigation of the canals. The legislature shall annually make provision for the expenses of the superintendence and repairs of the canals, and may provide for the improvement of the canals in such a manner as shall be provided by law. All contracts for work or materials on any canal shall be made with the persons who shall offer to do or provide the same at the lowest price, with adequate security for their performance. No extra compensation shall be made to any contractor; but if, from an unforeseen cause, the terms of any contract shall prove to be unjust and oppressive, the superintendent of public works may, upon the application of the contractor, cancel such contract. [Const. 1846, Art. VII, sec. 3, as amend. in 1854, 1882; renumbered Art. VII, sec. 9; amend. and renumbered Art. XV, sec. 3, 1938]

This provision forbids tolls for the use of canals and authorizes the legislature to appropriate funds for their operation, repair and improvement. The "free canal" movement reflected the competition between railroads and canals during the nineteenth century. The last two sentences were aimed at correcting fraudulent practices such as favoritism and unreasonably low bidding.

SECTION 4

Lease or transfer to federal government of barge canal system authorized. Notwithstanding the prohibition of sale, abandonment or other disposition contained in section one of this article, the legislature may authorize by law the lease or transfer to the federal government of the barge canal, consisting of the Erie, Oswego, Champlain, Cayuga and Seneca divisions and the barge canal terminals and facilities for purpose of operation, improvement and inclusion in the national system of inland waterways. Such lease or transfer to the federal government for the purposes specified herein may be made upon such terms and conditions as the legislature may determine with or without compensation to the state. Nothing contained herein shall prevent the legislature from providing annual appropriations for the state's share, if any, of the cost of operation, maintenance and improvement of the barge canal, the divisions thereof, terminals and facilities in the event of the transfer of the barge canal in whole to the federal government whether by lease or transfer. The legislature, in determining the state's share of the annual cost of operation, maintenance and improvement of the barge canal, the several divisions, terminals and facilities, shall give consideration and evaluate the benefits derived from the barge canal for purposes of flood control, conservation and utilization of water resources.[1959]

This section allows for the transfer of the canal system to the United States and makes it part of the national system of inland waterways. The purpose was to release the state from the burden of maintenance, with the expectation that the national government would modernize the canal system. The provision is permissive only; as of 1990 no such action has been taken. Instead the state has embarked on a multimillion-dollar rehabilitation of the canal system for tourism and cultural activities.

Article XVI

Taxation

Taxes can be imposed for any constitutionally valid public purpose but not for purely private purposes. The taxing power is an attribute of sovereignty and exists apart from the constitution, though it is limited by it (Shapiro v. New York, 1973). Article III, section 1, as well as section 1 of this article, confers all taxing power granted to the legislature. This article largely declares existing statutory law and serves as a guarantee against radical legislative change in the tax system. The constitution places few limitations on the power to tax, thus facilitating the expansion and diversification of the tax system in New York.

SECTION 1

Power of taxation; exemptions from taxation. The power of taxation shall never be surrendered, suspended or contracted away, except as to securities issued for public purposes pursuant to law. Any laws which delegate the taxing power shall specify the types of taxes which may be imposed thereunder and provide for their review.

Exemptions from taxation may be granted only by general law. Exemptions may be altered or repealed except those exempting real or personal property used exclusively for religious, educational or charitable purposes as defined by law and owned by any corporation or association organized or conducted exclusively for one or more such purposes and not operating for profit. [1938]

This provision prevents tax policies from becoming contracts between states and corporations. Alterations of tax liabilities are thus not breaches of contracts. This provision also prevents the legislature from contracting preestablished limits on tax liability binding on subsequent legislatures (Roosevelt Raceway Inc. v. Monaghan, 1961). The public securities exception allows certain public corporations or entities such as the Urban Development Corporation or the Higher Education Services Corporation to issue tax-exempt bonds and other revenue-generating activities (Wein v. Beame, 1977).

The second sentence prohibits blanket enabling acts empowering cities to impose taxes at their own discretion, as occurred during the 1930s. The provision requires the state to exercise some control when delegating taxing power to cities to ensure that the taxing policies of municipalities do not conflict or compete with state policies. It also allows the legislature to specify the type of tax—sales, excise, income—and designate the use to which the proceeds may be put.[1] Since the legislature undoubtedly already had the power to protect the state tax structure, the sentence was inserted to ensure its exercise.[2] Attempts by New York City to limit taxpayer access to court for review of tax decisions led to the guarantee of administrative or judicial review.

General laws are laws that relate to persons, entities, or things as a class or operate alike on all members of a class. By limiting the legislature's power to withdraw exemptions from specific classes of nonprofit organizations, the state declared their work more important than any tax revenue lost (Diocese of Rochester v. Planning Board of Town of Brighton, 1956). There are three classes of exemptions: federal property, over which the state has no control; property exempted by constitutional provisions (mandated exemptions in this section); and property exempted by statute (permissive exemptions). The legislature has expanded the kinds of property exempted from taxation to include, among others, public authorities, credit unions, and railroad real property.[3] The constitutionally mandated exemptions have been merely restated in statutory form and not adequately defined. The judiciary's attempt to categorize organizations into the mandated or permissive class resulted in further proliferation of exemptions and an erosion of the tax base. Legislation passed in 1971 and again in 1981 attempted to address these problems and reassert the legislature's role in implementing the exemption provision.[4] The granting of such exemptions has been held not to violate the establishment clause of the First Amendment (Walz v. Tax Commissioner of the City of New York, 1970).

SECTION 2

Assessments for taxation purposes. The legislature shall provide for the supervision, review and equalization of assessments for purposes of taxation. Assessments shall in no case exceed full value.

Nothing in this constitution shall be deemed to prevent the legislature from providing for the assessment, levy and collection of village taxes by taxing authorities of those subdivisions of the state in which the lands comprising the respective villages are located, nor from providing that the respective counties of the state may loan or advance to any village located

in whole or in part within such county the amount of any tax which shall
have been levied for village purposes upon any lands located within such
county and remaining unpaid. [1938]

This provision makes it mandatory upon the legislature to provide for the
supervision, review, and equalization of assessments. The second sentence prevents the practice of assessing at higher than the full value of the property. In
practice property values have generally been underassessed in the state by a
considerable margin despite a statute mandating assessment at full value. Notwithstanding this provision and statutory requirements, inequalities in assessments continued to grow. In large measure this can be attributed to a 1777
constitutional provision providing for the local election of assessor and collectors
(Art. IX, sec. 16). The state has created the Board of Equalization and Assessment charged with the duty of establishing an equalization rate to be used in the
distribution of state financial aid,[5] but its powers to act under this provision are
limited by the home rule provisions of Article IX. Full assessment of property
values was required after the court of appeals in Hellerstein v. Assessors of the
Town of Islip (1975) ordered full value assessment, though the state has since
repealed the statute on which that decision was based.

The second paragraph of this section was necessitated to counter the effect of
People ex rel. Town of Pelham v. Village of Pelham (1915), which voided the
practice of allowing counties to advance delinquent taxes owed to villages and
then to collect those taxes themselves and disallowed the rule enabling assessment
and collection of village taxes upon tax rolls of the towns in which villages were
located. It settled the dispute between town and village assessors and collectors
as to who had priority in the levying of village taxes, as well as who should
receive advances from the county against delinquent taxes. It also appears to
allow towns to take over the assessment and collection of taxes for villages
within their jurisdictions.

It was hoped that change would allow for a more orderly and efficient system
of municipal tax collection. It is permissive and not mandatory in nature. The
provision illustrates the tension between promoting values such as efficiency and
order, which necessitate some centralization, and the home rule principle of local
control, which promotes decentralization (see Art. IX).

SECTION 3

Situs of intangible personal property; taxation of. Moneys, credits,
securities and other intangible personal property within the state not
employed in carrying on any business therein by the owner shall be deemed
to be located at the domicile of the owner for purposes of taxation, and, if
held in trust, shall not be deemed to be located in this state for purposes of
taxation because of the trustee being domiciled in this state, provided that
if no other state has jurisdiction to subject such property held in trust to

death taxation, it may be deemed property having a taxable situs within this state for purposes of death taxation. Intangible personal property shall not be taxed ad valorem nor shall any excise tax be levied solely because of the ownership or possession thereof, except that the income therefrom may be taken into consideration in computing any excise tax measured by income generally. Undistributed profits shall not be taxed. [1938]

This provision guarantees to nonresident individuals and out-of-state corporations that they can keep money and securities and other intangible personal property in the state without fear of legislative imposition of taxes on their intangibles. Income from the property, however, may be taken into account in computing any excise tax measured by income generally, and when such intangibles are put to use in trade and commerce, they are subject to excise taxes. Most cases interpreting the clause have involved whether the taxes imposed are covered by the section (Ampo Printing-Advertising Offset Corporation v. New York, 1964). A tax on mortgages does not violate this section (Franklin Society for Home Building & Savings v. Bennett, 1939), nor do filing fees paid to surrogate court (Joslin v. Regan, 1979). The last sentence was added to prohibit legislation similar to that then found in the Internal Revenue Code imposing penalties on excessive accumulation of earnings. Its proponents hoped it would stimulate new enterprise and create jobs in the state.[6]

SECTION 4

Certain corporations not to be discriminated against. Where the state has power to tax corporations incorporated under the laws of the United States there shall be no discrimination in the rates and method of taxation between such corporations and other corporations exercising substantially similar functions and engaged in substantially similar business within the state. [1938]

The provision was precipitated by proposed New York taxes on banks and banking deposits and fear that such taxes would discourage out-of-staters from placing their money in those banks, thereby eroding the status of New York City as the nation's banking capital. The possibility, a reality in some states, of taxing state banks more heavily than federal banks, thereby encouraging state banks to join the national banking association, was also behind this section. By prohibiting discrimination between state and national banking institutions, the dual system of banks would be preserved. In view of an anticipated national incorporation of industrial enterprises, it was deemed wise to extend the coverage to corporations in general.

The court of appeals has interpreted the provision to allow the state to impose taxes on state banks that would not be permitted on national banks as long as those taxes apply to a broad class in which banks are included not because they are banks but because they are employers (In re Bank of Manhattan, 1944).

SECTION 5

Compensation of public officers and employees subject to taxation. All salaries, wages and other compensation, except pensions, paid to officers and employees of the state and its subdivisions and agencies shall be subject to taxation. [1938]

By subjecting the salaries, wages, and other compensation of state employees to the income tax, this provision constitutionalized the previous tax law of the state. It was added to the constitution to remove any doubts created by limitations found in Article XIII, section 7 (public officers' compensation) and Article VI, section 25a (compensation for future judges). The word *agencies* was added because there was some doubt about whether *subdivisions* included the newly created bridge and port authorities in New York.

The court of appeals has determined that an estate tax on an annuity transferred to a widow by a deceased pensioner was not covered by this section because it was intended to exempt pensions from the income tax (In re Endemann's Estate, 1954).

SECTION 6

Public improvements or services; contract of indebtedness; creation of public corporations. Notwithstanding any provision of this or any other article of this constitution to the contrary, the legislature may by law authorize a county, city, town or village, or combination thereof acting together, to undertake the development of public improvements or services, including the acquisition of land, for the purpose of redevelopment of economically unproductive, blighted or deteriorated areas and, in furtherance thereof, to contract indebtedness. Any such indebtedness shall be contracted by any such county, city, town or village, or combination thereof acting together without the pledge of its faith and credit, or the faith and credit of the state, for the payment of the principal thereof and the interest thereon, and such indebtedness may be paid without restriction as to the amount or relative amount of annual installments. The amount of any indebtedness contracted under this section may be excluded in ascertaining the power of such county, city, town or village to contract indebtedness within the provisions of this constitution relating thereto. Any county, city, town or village contracting indebtedness pursuant to this section for redevelopment of an economically unproductive, blighted or deteriorated area shall pledge to the payment thereof that portion of the taxes raised by it on real estate in such area which, in any year, is attributed to the increase in value of taxable real estate resulting from such redevelopment. The legislature may further authorize any county, city, town or village, or combination thereof acting together, to carry out the powers and duties conferred by this section by means of a public corporation created therefor. [1938]

The local development amendment was designed to convert undeveloped areas into prosperous and revenue-generating parts of the community. The provision permits counties, cities, towns, and villages to use a technique known as tax increment financing to finance the revitalization of appropriate areas of local communities. Local bodies could issue bonds to finance projects, such as slum clearance, with the bonds repaid from tax revenues generated from the increased value of the affected area. It allows localities to contract indebtedness without the pledge of the full faith and credit of municipalities, to incur debt without restriction as to amounts or repayment installments, and to exclude debt incurred from the municipality's constitutional debt limitation. The impetus for this provision came when federal funds for urban and economic development dried up and fiscal pressures to state finances increased. It has been implemented by the Municipal Development Agency Law.

Article XVII

Social Welfare

This article, created in 1938, establishes an affirmative social right the individual may demand from the government. Along with Article XVIII (housing) and Article 1, sections 17 and 18 (rights for labor and workman's compensation), this article compares favorably with the United Nations' Declaration of Human Rights (Article 25, sec. 1) adopted a decade after these provisions were included in the New York Constitution.

SECTION 1

> **Public relief and care**. The aid, care and support of the needy are public concerns and shall be provided by the state and by such of its subdivisions, and in such manner and by such means, as the legislature may from time to time determine. [1938]

This section defines the relationship of the people to their government, requires the state to assume a major role in the field of social welfare, and removes all doubts about the validity of legislation in this area. The court of appeals has interpreted this provision as a mandate of the constitution, imposing on the state an affirmative duty to aid the needy. The court also has asserted that it was the judiciary's obligation to see that this "responsibility . . . is not shirked" (Tucker v. Toia, 1977). On the other hand, the legislature has great discretion in setting criteria for defining need and establishing programs to aid those in need (Kircher v. Perales, 1985). The clause, for example, does not mandate that public assistance be granted on an individual basis in every instance, nor does it require the state always to meet in full measure all legitimate needs of each public assistance recipient (Bernstein v. Toia, 1977).

The elaborate statutory law in New York has made public welfare an institutionalized feature of state government.[1] The Department of Social Services is largely responsible for carrying out the legislation implementing Article XVII, section 1, and the State Board of Social Welfare, designated in Article XVII, section 2, carries out the functions stated in that section and those found in Executive Law section 26-B.

SECTION 2

State board of social welfare; powers and duties. The state board of social welfare shall be continued. It shall visit and inspect, or cause to be visited or inspected by members of its staff, all public and private institutions, whether state, county, municipal, incorporated or not incorporated, which are in receipt of public funds and which are of a charitable, eleemosynary, correctional or reformatory character, including all reformatories for juveniles and institutions or agencies exercising custody of dependent, neglected or delinquent children, but excepting state institutions for the education and support of the blind, the deaf and the dumb, and excepting also such institutions as are hereinafter made subject to the visitation and inspection of the department of mental hygiene or the state commission of correction. As to institutions, whether incorporated or not incorporated, having inmates, but not in receipt of public funds, which are of a charitable, eleemosynary, correctional or reformatory character, and agencies, whether incorporated or not incorporated not in receipt of public funds, which exercise custody of dependent, neglected or delinquent children, the state board of social welfare shall make inspections, or cause inspections to be made by members of its staff, but solely as to matters directly affecting the health, safety, treatment and training of their inmates, or of the children under their custody. Subject to the control of the legislature and pursuant to the procedure prescribed by general law, the state board of social welfare may make rules and regulations, not inconsistent with this constitution, with respect to all of the functions, powers and duties with which the department and the state board of social welfare are herein or shall be charged. [Const. 1894, Art. VIII, secs. 11, 15 as amend. in 1925 and 1931; amend. and renumbered Art. XVII, sec. 2, 1938]

The 1894 convention constitutionalized the State Board of Charities, authorized it to visit and inspect institutions whether or not they received public funds, and authorized the board, within restraints set by the legislature, to issue rules and regulations.

The provision aimed mainly at the control and supervision of the large amounts of moneys being channeled into these organizations. An amendment in 1925 rationalized its jurisdiction by transferring state institutions for the education of the blind, deaf, and dumb to the more suitable Department of Education. In 1931, the name of the agency was changed to the Department of Social Welfare.

The court has interpreted the powers of the board under the provision and the police power—the power of the state to legislate to protect the health, welfare, and morals of the community—quite broadly. It upheld the powers of the board to require private, proprietary, adult homes to file financial statements, even though this class of home was not covered by the section (Katz v. Shapiro, 1978). In so ruling, the court said that as long as the statute is not inconsistent with the specific provisions of the state constitution, its reach may be broader under the police power, the "least limitable" of the essential powers of government.

SECTION 3

> **Public health**. The protection and promotion of the health of the inhabitants of the state are matters of public concern and provision therefor shall be made by the state and by such of its subdivisions and in such manner, and by such means as the legislature shall from time to time determine. [1938]

This provision gave constitutional status to the state's responsibility for promoting physical health by preventing disease and prolonging life. Fear that the activities contemplated for the Public Health Department would not be permitted under the police power was a factor in constitutionalizing its status. The court of appeals has interpreted its powers broadly, for example, Paduano v. New York, 1966).

SECTION 4

> **Care and treatment of persons suffering from mental disorder or defect; visitation of institutions for**. The care and treatment of persons suffering from mental disorder or defect and the protection of the mental health of the inhabitants of the state may be provided by state and local authorities and in such a manner as the legislature may from time to time determine. The head of the department of mental hygiene shall visit and inspect, or cause to be visited and inspected by members of his staff, all institutions either public or private used for the care and treatment of persons suffering from mental disorder or defect. [Const. 1894, Art. II, sec. 11 as amend. in 1925 and 1931; amend. and renumbered Art. XVII, sec. 4, 1938]

Prior to adoption, the state had enacted various statutes relating to mental hygiene dating back to the nineteenth century. In 1889, a commissioner of lunacy was created to inspect, enforce remedial measures, and develop ways to care for the mentally ill. The 1894 convention gave constitutional status to this office and its duties. A 1925 amendment changed the name of the office to the Department of Mental Hygiene and extended its jurisdiction. The 1938 amendment authorized staff members to make visits because it had become physically impossible for the director to inspect all the facilities personally.

SECTION 5

Institutions for detention of criminals; probation; parole; state commission of correction. The legislature may provide for the maintenance and support of institutions for the detention of persons charged with or convicted of crime and for systems of probation and parole of persons convicted of crime. There shall be a state commission of correction, which shall visit and inspect, or cause to be visited and inspected by members of its staff, all institutions used for the detention of sane adults charged with or convicted of crime. [Const. 1894, Art. VIII, Sec. 11; amend. and renumbered Art. XVII, sec. 5, 1938]

The first sentence is a general authorization to the legislature and a listing of the other components of the corrections system—probation and parole. This power seems unquestionable, but the convention felt it necessary to have each section contain a general statement concerning legislative powers.

The 1846 Constitution had provided for prison inspections. The 1894 Constitution, concerned about deplorable conditions in the prisons, provided for a state Commission of Prisons with visitation and inspection powers. In 1925, the name was changed to the Commission of Corrections, and the head of the Department of Corrections was made chair of the commission, in spite of the fact that the purpose of the commission was to oversee the work of the department. The Department of Corrections was renamed the Department of Correctional Services, and in 1973, an amendment was approved deleting the provision designating the head of the department the chair of the commission. This separation of personnel, along with the decision to transfer the commission to the executive branch, made the commission more independent.

SECTION 6

Visitation and inspection. Visitation and inspection as herein authorized, shall not be exclusive of other visitation and inspection now or hereafter authorized by the law. [Const. 1894, Art. VIII, sec. 13; amend. and renumbered Art. XVII, sec. 6, 1938]

The provision states that the legislature may provide for visits and inspections other than those mentioned in section 4. Inspections and visitations would seem to be clearly within the police power and certainly part of any statutory scheme. The pressure for placing this provision in the constitution came from judicial decisions that drastically limited visitation powers. The fact that such power is now accepted under the police power, along with a judiciary more receptive to the exercise of state power, makes the continued need for this provision questionable.

SECTION 7

> **Loans for hospital construction**. Notwithstanding any other provision of
> this constitution, the legislature may authorize the state, a municipality, or
> a public corporation acting as an instrumentality of the state or municipality
> to lend its money or credit to or in aid of any corporation or association,
> regulated by law as to its charges, profits, dividends, and disposition of its
> property or franchises, for the purpose of providing such hospital or other
> facilities for the prevention, diagnosis of treatment of human disease, pain,
> injury, disability, deformity or physical conditions, and for facilities
> incidental or appurtenant thereto as may be prescribed by law. [1969]

Acute shortages in hospital and health care facilities during the 1960s prompted
this provision, which was aimed at providing funds for the expansion and modernization of hospitals and health care facilities in the voluntary and private
sectors, as well as the public sector. This section removed doubts about such
loans deriving from constitutional provisions, such as Article VII, section 8.

Article XVIII

Housing

Prior to World War I, housing policies in New York were limited to building codes and housing regulations. After the war, housing programs were initiated to relieve housing shortages. The Great Depression intensified the twin problems of blight and shortages and forced the government to take a more active role in housing and welfare more generally. This article is the first constitutional affirmation of a public role in housing and signaled a recognition by the delegates of the importance in a constitutional democracy of decent housing and neighborhoods and the obligation of the state to aid cities in achieving that goal. Section 1 provides, in broad language, sufficient authority to enable the government to meet the housing needs of New York well into the twenty-first century. However the following nine sections are filled with detailed, cumbersome language and a series of restrictions which have blurred the clear authorization found in the first section. This cumbersome and confusing language has required the legislature and the judiciary to contort and strain the provisions to keep the article abreast of changing housing needs. The article is permissive and creates no entitlements to housing for low-income groups, but it has given impetus and constitutional legitimacy to the pursuit of the goal of decent housing for all New Yorkers. By 1965, a quarter of a century after its adoption, Article XVIII had given rise to the most sophisticated and fully developed housing program in the United States. Nevertheless the restrictions on cooperation with private enterprise and the failure to include the counties within the compass of the article have limited its flexibility and effectiveness, and more comprehensive notions of community development have made the narrow assumptions about housing embodied in the article obsolete.[1] In 1990, a resolution to amend the constitution that would have included counties among the governmental units covered by this article died in both senate and assembly committees.

SECTION 1

Housing and nursing home accommodations for persons of low income; slum clearance. Subject to the provisions of this article, the legislature may provide in such manner, by such means and upon such terms and conditions as it may prescribe for low rent housing and nursing home accommodations for persons of low income as defined by law, or for the clearance, replanning, reconstruction and rehabilitation of substandard and insanitary areas, or for both such purposes, and for recreational and other facilities incidental or appurtenant thereto. [1938; amend. 1965]

Section 1 gives the legislature almost unlimited power to accomplish the enumerated goals. There was no doubt that slum clearance and provision for low-income housing were public purposes and that eminent domain could be used to further those purposes (New York Housing Authority v. Muller, 1936). Delegates were more concerned when they drafted this article with other obstacles in the constitution. Article VII, section 8 places limits of use of state credit to public or private corporations; Article VII, section 4 places limits on local indebtedness. This section was meant to foreclose all possible constitutional objections or doubts and indicated the high importance the delegates attached to the stated goals.

The convention delegates might have stopped at this point since they made the article permissive, allowing the legislature to implement the article as it saw fit. Instead the convention proceeded to add nine more sections. These sections reflect a division of opinion among the delegates. Some delegates wished to eliminate explicitly the obstacles found in other articles; others wished to place restrictions on the power of the legislature to prevent it from rushing out and adopting a massive housing plan that would favor cities, especially New York City. This was the reason section 3 set the effective date as January 1942. The section also manifests a concern over the possibility of excessive accumulation of debt.

The legislature has adopted numerous statutes to implement this section but the words "low rent" and "low income" were not defined in the early statutes.[2] Although there is evidence from the 1938 Convention debates that these terms were meant to relate to earning levels and housing that would provide minimum tolerable standards of health and safety,[3] the courts have held that the terms do not mean the lowest possible rents or the lowest possible incomes (Neufeld v. O'Dwyer, 1948; Minkin v. New York, 1960). Low income groups are those who cannot cause unaided private enterprise to build housing to meet their limited rent-paying ability. That definition, now part of the housing law of New York, allows housing to be built for middle-income groups without violating the stipulations in section 1.

The courts interpreted this section expansively. In spite of some language to the contrary at the convention, the courts have ruled that the twin purposes of providing low-rent housing and slum clearance need not always be connected (Murray v. LaGuardia, 1943) and that neighborhoods do not have to be slums in order to come within the authority of this provision (Yonkers Community Development Agency v. Morris, 1975). Under authority provided by this section, the Urban Development Corporation has the power to override local zoning laws, and such power is not a violation of the local government bill of rights (Art. III, sec. 2(b)) (Floyd v. New York City Urban Development Corporation, 1973). In these and a long line of cases the public purpose of providing housing was sustained even though private interests were benefitted. On the other hand, an attempt to use the excess-condemnation power of section 8 to take nonblighted areas to provide housing for the elderly was held not covered under this article and therefore not a taking for a public purpose (Russin v. Town of Union of Broome County, 1987). A 1965 amendment added "nursing home accommodations" to the goals of the article.

SECTION 2

Powers of legislature in aid of the subject of section 1. For and in aid of such purposes, notwithstanding any provision in any other article of this constitution, but subject to the limitations contained in this article, the legislature may: make or contract to make or authorize to be made or contracted capital or periodic subsidies by the state to any city, town, village or public corporation, payable only with moneys appropriated therefor from the general fund of the state; authorize any city, town or village to make or contract to make such subsidies to any public corporation, payable only with moneys locally appropriated therefor from the general or other fund available for current expenses of such municipality; authorize the contracting of indebtedness for the purpose of providing moneys out of which it may make or contract to make or authorize to be made or contracted loans by the state to any city, town, village or public corporation; authorize any city, town or village to make or contract to make loans to any public corporation; authorize any city, town or village to guarantee the principal of and interest on, or only the interest on, indebtedness contracted by a public corporation; authorize and provide for loans by the state and authorize loans by any city, town or village to or in aid of corporation regulated by laws as to rents, profits, dividends and disposition of their property or franchises and engaged in providing housing facilities or nursing home accommodations; authorize any city, town or village to make loans to the owners of existing multiple dwellings for the rehabilitation and improvement thereof for occupancy by persons of low income as defined by law; grant or authorize tax exemptions in whole or in part, except that no such exemption may be granted or authorized for a period of more than sixty years; authorize cooperation with and the acceptance of aid from the United States; grant the power of eminent domain to any city, town or village, to any public corporation and to any corporation regulated by law as to rent, profits, dividends and disposition of its property or franchises and engaged in providing housing facilities.

As used in this article, the term "public corporation" shall mean any corporate governmental agency (except a county or municipal corporation) organized pursuant to law to accomplish any or all of the purposes specified in this article. [1938; amend. 1965]

This section enumerates the powers granted to the legislature to carry out the goals specified in section 1. Basically it amounts to a series of exceptions to the limitations on state and local government found in other articles of the constitution.

Article VII, section 8 prohibits the state from lending the credit or money of the state to any private corporation, association, or private undertaking; this section authorizes state loans to limited profit corporations (e.g., private housing and nursing homes). Article VIII also prevents the state from lending the state credit to aid any individual or public corporation. This section authorizes subsidies to any city, town, village, or public corporation and authorizes the contracting of state indebtedness for loans to any town, city, village, or public corporation. Article VII permits the use of state money for support of municipal, that is, public, corporations but does not allow the use of the state's credit for those same entities. This section makes an exception to that restriction "to insure the marketability of securities issued by local housing authorities."[4] This section also exempts financial measures used for the purposes found in section 1 from the prohibitions of Article X, section 5.

SECTION 3

Article VII to apply to state debts under this article, with certain exceptions; amortization of state debts; capital and periodic subsidies. The provisions of article VII, not inconsistent with this article, relating to debts of the state shall apply to all debts contracted by the state for the purpose of providing moneys out of which to make loans pursuant to this article, except (a) that any law or laws authorizing the contracting of such debt, not exceeding in the aggregate three hundred million dollars, shall take effect without submission to the people, and the contracting of a greater amount of debt may not be authorized prior to January first, nineteen hundred forty-two; (b) that any such debt and each portion thereof, except as hereinafter provided, shall be paid in equal annual installments, the first of which shall be payable not more than three years, and the last of which shall be payable not more than fifty years, after such debt or portion thereof shall have been contracted; and (c) that any law authorizing the contracting of such debt may be submitted to the people at a general election, whether or not any other law or bill shall be submitted to be voted for or against at such election.

Debts contracted by the state for the purpose of providing moneys out of which to make loans to or in aid of corporations regulated by law as to rents, profits, dividends and disposition of their property or franchises and engaged in providing housing facilities pursuant to this article may be paid in such manner that the total annual charges required for the payment of principal and interest are approximately equal and constant for the entire period in which any of the bonds issued therefor are outstanding.

Any law authorizing the making of contracts for capital or periodic subsidies to be paid with moneys currently appropriated from the general fund of the state shall take effect without submission to the people, and the amount to be paid under such contracts shall not be included in ascertaining the amount of indebtedness which may be contracted by the state under this article; provided, however, (a) that such periodic subsidies shall not be paid for a period longer than the life of the projects assisted thereby, but in any event for not more than sixty years; (b) that no contracts for periodic subsidies shall be entered into any one year requiring payments aggregating more than one million dollars in any one year; and (c) that there shall not be outstanding at any one time contracts for periodic subsidies requiring payments exceeding an aggregate of thirty-four million dollars in any one year, unless a law authorizing contracts in excess of such amounts shall have been submitted to and approved by the people at a general election; and any such law may be submitted to the people at a general election, whether or not any other law or bill shall be submitted to be voted for or against at such election. [1938; amend. 1955, 1957]

Section 3 deals with state indebtedness. The state is authorized to contract debt up to the sum of $300 million without approval of the electorate, payable over a period not to exceed fifty years. Convention delegates agreed that state debt should not swell by more than $100 million a year. The $300 million figure was arrived at by cumulating the three years between approval of the convention's work and 1942, the date that new debt could be approved by the voters.

After January 1, 1942, additional debt could be assumed with the approval of the electorate at a general election. The state is permitted to make capital or periodic (regular) subsidies from the general fund of the state not to exceed $1 million in new contracts in any given year and $34 million in accumulated payments in any one year except as authorized by popular vote. The $34 million figure was approved by the public in 1955. A statute approved by the public as required by this section now sets that figure at $44 million. The figure of $1 million has also been raised with public approval to $2,869,000.[5]

The provision for approval at the general election "whether or not any other law or bill shall be permitted to be voted for or against" is a specific exemption from section 11 of Article VII, which requires a vote at the general election "when no other law or any bill shall be submitted or voted for or against."

While this article as a whole was meant to free the legislature in this area of public policy, the specification of debt limitations and the requirement for voter approval act as limits on the ability of the legislature to carry out the mandates of the article. That ability depends on gaining approval at the polls. During the last two decades such approval has not always been forthcoming.

Other limitations of Article VII made inapplicable by this section are the amortization of debt over forty years (section 12)—this section allows fifty— and the requirement that payment must begin in not more than one year (section 12)—this section allows two years.

A 1957 amendment permits a level debt service basis for amortization of state debt arising out of loans to limited-profit housing companies. It was proposed in order to reduce carrying charges for limited-profit housing projects, which would, in turn, produce lower rentals. It exempts these loans from the equal-annual-installment requirement for the amortization of state debt found in Article VII, section 12.

SECTION 4

Powers of cities, towns and villages to contract indebtedness in aid of low rent housing and slum clearance projects; restrictions thereon. To effectuate any of the purposes of this article, the legislature may authorize any city, town or village to contract indebtedness to an amount which shall not exceed two per centum of the average assessed valuation of the real estate of such city, town or village subject to taxation, as determined by the last completed assessment roll and the four preceding assessment rolls of such city, town or village, for city, town or village taxes prior to the contracting of such indebtedness. In ascertaining the power of a city, town or village having a population of five thousand or more as determined by the last federal census, to contract indebtedness pursuant to this article there may be excluded any such indebtedness if the project or projects aided by guarantees representing such indebtedness or by loans for which such indebtedness was contracted shall have yielded during the preceding year net revenue to be determined annually by deducting from the gross revenues, including periodic subsidies therefor, received from such project or projects, all costs of operation, maintenance, repairs and replacements, and the interest on such indebtedness and the amounts required in such year for the payment of such indebtedness; provided that in the case of guarantees such interest and such amounts shall have been paid, and in the case of loans an amount equal to such interest and such amounts shall have been paid to such city or village. The legislature shall prescribe the method by which the amount of any such indebtedness to be excluded shall be determined, and no such indebtedness shall be excluded except in accordance with such determination. The legislature may confer appropriate jurisdiction on the appellate division of the supreme court in the judicial departments in which such cities or villages are located for the purpose of determining the amount of any such indebtedness to be so excluded.

The liability of a city, town or village on account of any contract for capital or periodic subsidies to be paid subsequent to the then current year shall, for the purpose of ascertaining the power of such city, town or village to contract indebtedness, be deemed indebtedness in the amount of the commuted value of the total of such capital or periodic subsidies remaining unpaid, calculated on the basis of an annual interest rate of four per centum. Such periodic subsidies shall not be contracted for a period longer than the life of the projects assisted thereby, and in no event for more than sixty years. Indebtedness contracted pursuant to this article shall be excluded in ascertaining the power of a city or such village otherwise to create indebtedness under any other section of this constitution. Notwithstanding the foregoing the legislature shall not authorize any city or village having a population of five thousand or more to contract indebtedness hereunder in excess of the limitations prescribed by any other article of this constitution unless at the same time it shall by law require such city or village to levy annually a tax or taxes other than an ad valorem tax on real estate to an extent sufficient to provide for the payment of the principal of and interest on any such indebtedness. Nothing herein contained, however, shall be construed to prevent such city or village from pledging its faith and credit for the payment of such principal and interest nor shall any such law prevent recourse to an ad valorem tax on real estate to the extent that revenue derived from such other tax or taxes in any year, together with revenues from the project or projects aided by the proceeds of such indebtedness, shall become insufficient to provide fully for payment of such principal and interest in that year. [1938; amend. 1949]

This provision has the effect of allowing cities, towns, or villages to contract indebtedness for housing purposes not to exceed 2 percent of the assessed valuation of real estate in that unit of local government averaged over the preceding five years. The convention made a distinction between cities and other local governmental units, authorizing an additional 2 percent for cities beyond the debt limits set in Article VII, section 4, but included the 2 percent for other governmental units within their general debt limits set by Article VII, section 4.

In 1949, villages of 5,000 or more in population were granted the same extra borrowing power granted the cities. The 2 percent limit is based on the average assessed valuation of real estate, whereas section 4 of Article VIII uses full valuation. This discrepancy came about when an amendment passed in 1951 changed assessed valuation to full in section 8. A similar attempt to change this section was defeated in 1966. Had full valuation been adopted the result would have been an increase in the funds available through municipal sources for housing and redevelopment. The section allows cities and villages to exclude this additional indebtedness for self-sustaining projects. The formula for determining the amount of debt excludable under this provision is left to the legislature. Bond indebtedness contracted by city housing authorities for housing projects is excluded from city debt limitations. The use of authorities has enabled cities to circumvent the 2 percent limitation of section 4.[6]

The figure of 4 percent prorated in a manner established by law over the whole period of the loan, prevents the interest from being calculated all in one year.

The second paragraph, besides specifying the liability of local government for capital and periodic subsidies, requires that where additional 2 percent indebtedness is allowed, the legislature must provide for prepayment of the principal and interest by means other than an ad valorem tax on real estate. This provision was added at the insistence of Governor Al Smith and others who did not want the burden of these programs to fall on renters and the real estate industry.[7]

SECTION 5

Liability for certain loans made by the state to certain public corporations. Any city, town or village shall be liable for the repayment of any loans and interest thereon made by the state to any public corporation, acting as an instrumentality of such city, town or village. Such liability of a city, town or village shall be excluded in ascertaining the power of such city, town or village to become indebted pursuant to the provisions of this article, except that in the event of a default in payment under the terms of any such loan, the unpaid balance thereof shall be included in ascertaining the power of such city, town or village to become so indebted. No subsidy, in addition to any capital or periodic subsidy originally contracted for in aid of any project or projects authorized under this article, shall be paid by the state to a city, town, village or public corporation, acting as an instrumentality thereof, for the purpose of enabling such city, town, village or corporation to remedy an actual default or avoid an impending default in the payment of principal or interest on a loan which has been theretofore made by the state to such city, town, village or corporation pursuant to this article. [1938; amend. 1957]

Under this section municipalities are held liable for repayment of any state loan to a public corporation, such as a housing or urban renewal agency, which acts as its agent in carrying out housing or urban renewal programs. The section prevents cities from defaulting on loans and then requesting the state legislature to make up the difference by granting a subsidy. By including the unpaid balance on a defaulted loan in the calculation of the city's debt, the city's borrowing and spending power would be curtailed. Both provisions were added to the article at the insistence of upstate delegates, who wanted to ensure that New York City could not default on any loans with impunity, forcing the rest of the state to bear the burden. For purposes of debt service, however, the contingent liability can be excluded and need only be included on actual default, and then only for the unpaid balance.

SECTION 6

Loans and subsidies; restrictions on and preference in occupancy of projects. No loan or subsidy shall be made by the state to aid any project unless such project is in conformity with a plan or undertaking for the clearance, replanning and reconstruction or rehabilitation of a substandard and insanitary area or areas and for recreational and other facilities incidental or appurtenant thereto. The legislature may provide additional conditions to the making of such loans or subsidies consistent with the purposes of this article. The occupancy of any such project shall be restricted to persons of low income as defined by law and preference shall be given to persons who live or shall have lived in such area or areas. [1938]

The meaning of this section, beyond the obvious fact that state loans and subsidies shall not be made for any other purpose except those stated in section 1, is not clear. The debate at the convention was confusing, with a number of speakers agreeing with purposes seemingly inconsistent with each other. What "conformity with a plan" appeared to mean to the delegates was that there should be some connection between every housing project and slum clearance—that before a project is built, there should be a plan for slum clearance; more specifically, for every housing unit torn down, a new one is to be built. The language is now regarded as a planning criterion: that some form of redevelopment plan must exist and that a proposed housing project not be inconsistent with that plan.

The section also contains a requirement that preference be given to persons who have lived in such areas. The purpose is readily apparent—to create as little disruption in people's lives as possible—but the requirement has been criticized as confusing:

Does "area" refer to housing project area of slum clearance area? Is it the area on which the project is being built or some other area? Who is to be preferred if one person lives or has lived in the area where the housing project is being built and another lives or has lived in some other housing or slum clearance area?[8]

SECTION 7

Liability arising from guarantees to be deemed indebtedness; method of computing. The liability arising from any guarantee of the principal of and interest on indebtedness contracted by a public corporation shall be deemed indebtedness in the amount of the face value of the principal thereof remaining unpaid. The liability arising from any guarantee of only the interest on indebtedness contracted by a public corporation shall be deemed indebtedness in the amount of the commuted value of the total interest guaranteed and remaining unpaid, calculated on the basis of an annual interest rate of four per centum. [1938]

Section 7, unlike section 5, declares all contingent liability arising from guarantees to be debt. This seems in direct conflict with clauses in section 5 unless one assumes that this section deals with the voluntary assumption of contingent liability whereas section 5 deals with involuntary liability.[9]

The last clause amounts to a computational system that permits a community under such obligations to have the interest prorated according to established tables.

SECTION 8

Excess condemnation. Any agency of the state, or any city, town, village or public corporation, which is empowered by law to take private property by eminent domain for any of the public purposes specified in section one of this article, may be empowered by the legislature to take property necessary for any such purpose but in excess of that required for public use after such purpose shall have been accomplished; and to improve and utilize such excess, wholly or partly for any other public purpose, or to lease or sell such excess with restrictions to preserve and protect such improvement or improvements. [1938]

This section, along with section 9, enables local authorities to engage in comprehensive and long-range community planning. Section 8 permits the legislature to grant the power of "excessive condemnation" to local governments, enabling them to take property in excess of that required for immediate public use. It empowers local governments or public corporations to clear and replace more than is necessary for the actual project and sell off the rest for a nonpublic or private use under effective zoning restrictions. Without this provision, local entities had the power to take only that which would be put to public use. Absent this power, little slum clearance would take place, or alternatively, cities would be forced to put whole slum clearance areas to some public use, whether that was desirable or feasible.

This provision provides the local authority with significant leeway. In re Harlem Slum Clearance Project (1952), land was condemned for rehabilitation that included stores. Subsequently some of that land was sold off at public auction, and new stores were erected on it. Such action was held not a taking for private use. The section is forward looking in that it allows housing authorities or planning agencies to purchase land for future use, enabling them to plan beyond their immediate needs.

SECTION 9

Acquisition of property for purposes of article. Subject to any limitation imposed by the legislature, the state, or any city, town, village or public corporation, may acquire by purchase, gift, eminent domain or otherwise, such property as it may deem ultimately necessary or proper to effectuate the purposes of this article, or any of them, although temporarily not required for such purposes. [1938]

Section 9 permits cities to take property not now needed as long as some future use for state housing or renewal purposes is served by such taking. It allows for the creation of a land reserve, enabling the local government to engage in long-range planning. The power is limited by the phrase *ultimately necessary*, which was added to bring the section in line with the federal due process requirements as interpreted in Cincinnati v. Vester (1929) and to prevent the state from going into the real estate speculation business.

SECTION 10

Power of legislature; construction of article. The legislature is empowered to make laws which it shall deem necessary and proper for carrying into execution the foregoing powers. This article shall be construed as extending powers which otherwise might be limited by other articles of this constitution and shall not be construed as imposing additional limitations; but nothing in this article contained shall be deemed to authorize or empower the state, or any city, town, village or public corporation, to engage in any private business or enterprise other than the building and operation of low rent dwelling houses of persons of low income as defined by law, or the loaning of money to owners of existing multiple dwellings as herein provided. [1938]

The final section of the article is a general enabling clause that makes clear that the provisions of the article supersede those sections of the constitution that otherwise might be in conflict with them. In anticipation of the possibility that a court might interpret the article in terms of the notion that the inclusion of some powers means the exclusion of others, delegates added that the article "shall not be construed as imposing additional limitations." Immediately after this expansive directive, the section concludes with a limitation that none of the powers granted in the article shall be used for any purpose "other than building and operating low income houses for persons of low income or the loaning of money to owners of existing multiple dwellings." The purpose was to make sure that the "recreational and other public facilities" mentioned in section 1 would be public and not private enterprise.

Article XIX

Amendments to the Constitution

SECTION 1

Amendments to constitution; how proposed, voted upon and ratified; failure of attorney-general to render opinion not to affect validity. Any amendment or amendments to this constitution may be proposed in the senate and assembly, whereupon such amendment or amendments shall be referred to the attorney-general whose duty it shall be within twenty days thereafter to render an opinion in writing to the senate and assembly as to the effect of such amendment or amendments upon other provisions of the constitution. Upon receiving such opinion, if the amendment or amendments as proposed or as amended shall be agreed to by a majority of the members elected to each of the two houses, such proposed amendment or amendments shall be entered on their journals, and the ayes and noes taken thereon, and referred to the next regular legislative session convening after the succeeding general election of members of the assembly, and shall be published for three months previous to the time of making such choice; and if in such legislative session, such proposed amendment or amendments shall be agreed to by a majority of all the members elected to each house, then it shall be the duty of the legislature to submit each proposed amendment or amendments to the people for approval in such manner and at such times as the legislature shall prescribe; and if the people shall approve and ratify such amendment or amendments by a majority of the electors voting thereon, such amendment or amendments shall become a part of the constitution on the first day of January next after such approval. Neither the failure of the attorney-general to render an opinion concerning such a proposed amendment nor his failure to do so timely shall affect the validity of such proposed amendment or legislative action thereon. [Const. 1821, Art. VIII, sec. 1; amend. and renumbered Art. XIII, sec. 1, Const. 1846; amend. and renumbered Art.

XIV, sec. 1, Const. 1894; amend. and renumbered Art. XIX, sec. 1, 1938; amend. 1941]

This section provides for amending the constitution by way of the legislative process. An amendment may be proposed in either the senate or the assembly and must be passed by two successive, separately elected legislatures. It is then placed on the ballot for approval or disapproval by the people. Unlike the federal amending process, New York requires only a majority vote of the legislature, and unlike the federal process, state amendments must be submitted to the people for approval. The majoritarian process makes amending the state constitution both easier and more likely in New York than in Washington.

The requirement that the attorney general's opinion be sought was added to preserve the integrity of the constitution and guard against inconsistencies that might result from such amendments. The opinion is not binding and thus not part of the legislative process of amending the constitution. A 1941 amendment adding the last sentence to this section indicates that the legislature is free to accept or ignore this advice and can pass a proposed amendment before the attorney general renders an opinion.[1] Since the legislature can also recall a proposed amendment by concurrent resolution if the attorney general finds it inconsistent with other parts of the constitution, the purpose of the provision would not be frustrated by that action.

SECTION 2

Future constitutional conventions; how called; election of delegates; compensation; quorum; submission of amendments; officers; employees; rules of vacancies. At the general election to be held in the year nineteen hundred fifty-seven, and every twentieth year thereafter, and also at such times as the legislature may by law provide, the question "Shall there be a convention to revise the constitution and amend the same?" shall be submitted to and decided by the electors of the state; and in case a majority of the electors voting thereon shall decide in favor of a convention for such purpose, the electors of every senate district of the state, as then organized, shall elect three delegates at the next ensuing general election, and the electors of the state voting at the same election shall elect fifteen delegates-at-large. The delegates so elected shall convene at the capitol on the first Tuesday of April next ensuing after their election, and shall continue their session until the business of such convention shall have been completed. Every delegate shall receive for his services the same compensation as shall then be annually payable to the members of the assembly and be reimbursed for actual traveling expenses, while the convention is in session, to the extent that a member of the assembly would then be entitled thereto in the case of a session of legislature. A majority of the convention shall constitute a quorum for the transaction of business, and no amendment to the constitution shall be submitted for approval to the electors as hereinafter provided, unless by the assent of a majority of all the delegates elected to the convention, the ayes and noes being entered on the journal to be kept. The convention shall have the power to appoint such officers, employees and assistants as it may deem necessary, and fix their compensation and to provide for the printing of its documents, journal, proceedings and other expenses of said convention. The convention shall determine the rules of its own proceedings, choose its own officers, and be the judge of the election, returns, and qualifications of its members. In case of a vacancy, by death, resignation or other cause, of any district delegate elected to the convention, such vacancy shall be filled by a vote of the remaining delegates representing the district in which such vacancy occurs. If such vacancy occurs in the office of a delegate-at-large, such vacancy shall be filled by a vote of the remaining delegates-at-large. Any proposed constitution or constitutional amendment which shall have been adopted by such convention, shall be submitted to a vote of the electors of the state at the time and in the manner provided by such convention, at an election which shall be held not less than six weeks after the adjournment of such convention. Upon the approval of such constitution or constitutional amendment, in the manner provided in the last preceding section, such constitution or constitutional amendment, shall go into effect on the first day of January next after such approval. [Const. 1846, Art. XIII, sec. 2; as amend. in 1874; amend. and renumbered Art. XIV, sec. 2, Const. 1894; amend. and renumbered Art. XIX, sec. 2, 1938]

This clause, added by the 1846 convention, is striking constitutional affirmation of popular sovereignty: that all power is inherent in the people and every twenty years they may take that power in their own hands. The provision legitimized the extraconstitutional tradition of the legislature, submitting the question of the calling of a constitutional convention to the people. It did not preclude calling additional conventions in the interim, nor did it mandate anything more than a review every twenty years. If the people were satisfied with the constitution, it would remain. The year 1957 was chosen as the start of the twenty-year cycle because if the voters chose to hold a convention, delegates would be elected in 1958, the year of statewide elections, and the aim was to insulate the delegate selection process from other elections.

The New York Court of Appeals has not played the central role in the development of the state's constitution that the Supreme Court has played at the national level; nonetheless, it has played an important role, first in denying power to the state (Wynehamer v. State, 1856; Ives v. South Buffalo Railroad Co., 1911) and later in providing expansive readings of government power (People ex rel. Durham v. LaFetra, 1921). The New York high court upheld a law allowing the fixing of maximum and minimum prices for milk, saying that statutes aimed at achieving social justice "are to be interpreted with that degree of liberality which is essential to the attainment of the end in view" (People v. Nebbia, 1933 at 271).

Of greater importance at the state as opposed to the national level are the formal opinions of the attorney general. These opinions are the only institutionalized alternative to constitutional rulings of the courts. They are not binding on courts but are entitled to due consideration. Moreover, a vast number of disputes are settled by these opinions without ever reaching the judiciary. The state attorney general is the major source of advisory opinions on the constitution. The function of those opinions is to narrow the gap between state practice and constitutional requirements.[2]

As important as the judiciary and the attorney general have been, it remains true that the primary means of altering the constitution in New York has been through constitutional conventions and constitutional amendments. This is in striking contrast to the national constitutional tradition, which, dependent as it has been on the Supreme Court, has evolved more informally and in a less democratic fashion than in New York. The detail found in the New York Constitution exists at the national level, in the nearly five hundred volumes of the Supreme Court Reports.

SECTION 3

Amendments simultaneously submitted by convention and legislature.
Any amendment proposed by a constitutional convention relating to the same subject as an amendment proposed by the legislature, coincidently submitted to the people for approval, shall, if approved, be deemed to supersede the amendment so proposed by the legislature. [Const. 1894, Art. XIV, sec. 3; amend. and renumbered Art. XIX, sec. 3, 1938]

The fact that Article XIX provides for two distinct modes of amending the constitution makes it possible for two amendments dealing with the same subject to be submitted simultaneously to the people. In that event the amendment submitted by the convention, if approved, shall supersede the amendment proposed by the legislature. This choice is consistent with the view that the convention as a constituent body chosen for the specific task of amending the constitution is closer to the sovereign will of the people than the legislature.

In 1938 the legislature proposed an amendment to Article I, section 9, dealing with pari-mutuel betting. The constitutional convention of 1938 also submitted its proposals at the November election in the same year. If the submission of the convention was considered a new constitution than the amendment concerning pari-mutuel betting submitted by the legislature would be superseded as related material—that contained in Article I, section 9, would also be before the voters. In Stoughton v. Cohen (1939), the court of appeals held that the convention intended to submit only several amendments to an otherwise unaltered and continuing constitution. Since none of these amendments related to pari-mutuel betting there was no coincident submission by the convention and legislature.

Article XX

When to Take Effect

SECTION 1

Time of taking effect. This constitution shall be in force from and including the first day of January, one thousand nine hundred thirty-nine, except as herein otherwise provided. [Const. 1894 Art. XV, sec. 1; amend. and renumbered Art. XX, sec. 1; 1938]

This article specifies the time when the constitution shall take effect. The 1894 convention, at which the constitution now in effect as amended was adopted, inserted this provision. The 1938 Constitutional Convention merely changed the date. The final exception clause was also included by the 1894 convention to provide for those parts of the constitution that could not take effect immediately, such as changes in the terms of the governor and lieutenant governor (Art. IV, sec. 1, 1894 Const.).

Notes to Part II

ARTICLE I

1. A. E. Dick Howard, "State Courts and Constitutional Rights in the Day of the Burger Court," *Virginia Law Review* 62 (1976):873; Peter Galie, "The Other Supreme Courts: Judicial Activism among State Supreme Courts," *Syracuse Law Review* 33 (1982):731.

2. The bracketed material following each section does not give a complete historical derivation for the section. It includes only those amendments, revisions, and changes which form part of the section as it currently stands. Complete historical derivations are provided in the constitution volumes of *McKinney's Consolidated Laws of New York Annotated*. Robert Allan Carter's *New York State Constitution: Sources of Legislative Intent* (Littleton, Colo.: Fred. B. Rothman & Co., 1988) provides sources for each section.

3. Matter of Luria (1970) contains an analysis of these classes of jury trials with examples of each.

4. § 30.20(1) (McKinney, 1982).

5. People v. Singer (1978). Cf. U.S. v. Birney (1982) (establishing a less demanding standard than *Singer*).

6. See Cancemi v. People (1858); People v. Cosmo (1912).

7. People ex rel. Rohrlich v. Follette (1967), and New York Criminal Procedure Law, § 320.10(2) (McKinney, 1982) codifying waiver requirements.

8. Presumably Torcaso v. Watkins (1961) would also prohibit any religious test for competency.

9. People v. Cole (1916). Even in this case, the decision to hold Christian Scientists exempt from prohibition against unlicensed practice of medicine was based on a statutory exemption, Public Health Law, § 173. The court noted that the exemption was broader than the constitutional provision in that the statute "is not confined to worship or belief but includes the practice of religious tenets." Id. 11, 174.

10. Id. at 297.

11. People v. Bohnke (1941) (ordinance regulating religious literature and solicitation upheld); People ex rel. Fish v. Sandstrom (1939) (sustaining requirement that children salute the flag); Lindenmuller v. People (1861) (upholding Sunday closing laws). Cases of blasphemy are now overruled not on free exercise grounds but on the free speech clauses of both constitutions. See Panarella v. Birenbaum (1971) (derogatory and blasphemous attacks on religion in school newspaper permitted on free speech grounds).

12. A 1784 statute noted the state's duty to "countenance and encourage virtue and religion." *Laws of New York*, 7th session, Ch. 18.

13. Temporary State Commission on the Constitutional Convention, Report 10: *Individual Freedoms* (Albany, 1967), pp. 21–22.

14. Baer v. Kolmorgen (1957); see also Diocese of Rochester v. Planning Board of Town of Brighton (1956); Smith v. Community Board of Town No. 14 (1985) (upholding right of churches and synagogues to build in residential areas). Constitutional evidence of this accommodationist approach is found in Art. XI, § 3 (permitting bus transportation to parochial students at state expense); Art. VI, § 32 (requiring where possible that agencies place children into institutions or agencies governed by persons of the same religious persuasion); Art. XVI, § 1 (which makes constitutional tax exemptions for property used for charitable, religious, or educational purposes); and Art. XVII, § 2 (state aid to charitable institutions whether religiously controlled or not).

15. Civil Practice Law and Rules, § 7010(b) (McKinney, 1980).

16. The courts have developed a distinction between a "void judgment," for which habeas corpus will give relief, and "erroneous judgment," for which it will not. The distinction is anything but clear. See People ex rel. Carr v. Martin (1941) and People v. Silberglitt (1958).

17. Fay v. Noia (1963) (state procedural rules that define how federal constitutional issues will be litigated in state courts will, for purposes of habeas corpus review, be deemed inadequate). See also Townsend v. Sain (1963); Sanders v. U.S. (1963).

18. *Rev. Rec.*, 1938, 4: 3244–3245.

19. Mental Hygiene Law, § 33.15 (McKinney, 1988); Domestic Relations Law, § 41-a (McKinney, 1988) and Debtor and Creditor Law, § 173 (McKinney, 1945).

20. People ex rel. Rothensies v. Searles (1930); People ex rel. Lobell v. McDonnell (1947).

21. People ex rel. Calloway v. Skinner (1973). For statutory provisions, New York Criminal Procedure Law, § 530, et seq. (McKinney, 1984).

22. New York Criminal Procedure Law, § 530.20 (McKinney, 1984).

23. 18 USCA 3141–56. The preventive detention section was upheld by the Supreme Court in United States v. Salerno (1987).

24. Criminal Procedure Law, § 530.60[2][a] (McKinney Suppl., 1989).

25. Carmona v. Ward, 436 F. Supp. 1153 (S.D. N.Y., 1977) (mandatory life sentence for sale of a dose of cocaine and possession of less than four ounces grossly disproportionate to offense). This was, however, federal and not state court.

26. 63 N.Y.2d 41 at 79.

27. People ex rel. Rao v. Adams (1947); People ex rel. Gross v. Sheriff of City of New York (1951).

28. Constitutional Convention of 1821, *Reports of Proceedings and Debates*, William H. Carter and William Stone, reporters (Albany, 1821), 163–66.

29. John C. Corbett, "Should the Grand Jury Be Abolished?" *Brooklyn Barrister* 25 (1974):51. See especially the excellent defense of its importance by Judge Gabrielli

in People v. Iannone (1978), id., at 594–95, and the arguments pro and con as summarized in the Temporary Commission on the Constitutional Convention, Report 7: *Individual Liberties* (Albany, 1967), 119–27.

30. People ex rel. Saunders v. Board of Supervisors, 1 Sheld. 517 (1875) at 524.

31. That right was not extended to traffic infractions: People v. Letterio (1965).

32. People v. Samuels (1980); People v. Settles (1978).

33. People v. Rogers (1979); People v. Hobson (1976); People v. Cunningham (1980); People v. Skinner (1980).

34. People ex rel. Donohoe v. Montanye (1974); cf. Morissey v. Brewer (1972); Gagnon v. Scarpelli (1973).

35. N.Y. Criminal Procedure Law, § 190.52 (McKinney, 1982).

36. Subsequently its implementation has been specified in statute. New York Criminal Procedure Law, § 40.10 et seq. (McKinney, 1981).

37. There are related doctrines that have effect in civil law, such as collateral estoppel and res judicata. Collateral estoppel was incorporated into the constitutional protection against double jeopardy in Ashe v. Swenson (1970).

38. Crim. Procedure Law, 40.20[2] a-f (McKinney, 1981). The statute prohibits separate prosecution for two offenses based on the same act or criminal transaction unless one of six exceptions is present. For court interpretation, see People v. Prescott (1985).

39. Bartkus v. Illinois (1959), affirming U.S. v. Lanza (1922).

40. People v. Bethea (1986); cf. Oregon v. Elstad (1985).

41. N.Y. Crim. Procedure Law, § 50.10(1) (McKinney, 1981). See People v. Rappaport (1979) for judicial gloss on this provision.

42. *Rev. Rec.*, 1938, 3:2586ff. The legislative committee investigating political corruption in New York City in the early 1930s was known as the Seabury investigation after its chief counsel, Samuel Seabury, who dominated the proceedings. Its investigations ultimately led to the resignation in 1932 of New York City Mayor James Walker.

43. Id., at 278. See Shales v. Leach (1986) (upholding discharge of official for refusal to answer specific and relevant questions relating to official duties).

44. The court has expanded the initial ruling to include private nonimmunized contractors, Lefkowitz v. Turley (1973), and state political party officers, Lefkowitz v. Cunningham (1977). See *Inf. Opin. A-G*, No. 83–76. Occasionally an attempt is still made to invoke the provision, Mountain v. City of Schenectady (1984) (dismissal for refusal to waive immunity is a coercive procedure in violation of Fifth Amendment).

45. *Rev. Rec.*, 1938, 3:2570–72.

46. *Ibid.*, pp. 2572–74.

47. Since the 1940s, the New York judiciary has applied a variety of tests when judging economic regulations, including rational relationship and substantial relationship. The latest full statement of the court of appeals came in Lighthouse Shore, Inc. v. Town of Islip (1976) where the court applied a rational relationship test with a strong presumption of legislative rationality.

48. Fred F. French Investing Co. v. City of New York (1976); Modjeska Sign Studios, Inc. v. Berle (1977); Vernon Park Realty Co. v. City of Mount Vernon (1954); Town of North Hemstead v. Exxon Corp. (1981).

49. 49 N.Y.2d 69, at 80.

50. Kirby v. Illinois (1972) (no right to counsel or self-incrimination protection in preindictment lineups); People v. Hawkins (1982) (same).

51. Stovall v. Denno (1967); People v. Ballot (1967). See especially People v. Adams

(1981) excluding evidence of suggestive show-up on state due process grounds, granting protection that was required by Neil v. Biggers (1982).

52. New York Session Law, Chapt. 686; New York Family Court Act, § 711 (McKinney, 1983). In re Gault (1967).

53. 45 N.Y.2d 152, at 160.

54. For further comments on due process and property rights, see Art. I, § 7.

55. City of Plattsburg v. Terrace West, Inc. (1982) (provision for jury trial for taking of private roads does not apply when taking property for public purpose).

56. First Broadcasting Corp. v. Syracuse (1981); Broome County v. Trustees of First Methodist Episcopal Church of Choconut Creek (1971).

57. Saso v. State (1960); Hallock v. State of New York (1973).

58. Central Savings Bank in New York v. City of New York (1939); Kohlasch v. New York Thruway Authority (1980).

59. Matter of Ryers (1878); People v. Henion (1892).

60. *Rev. Rec.*, 1894, 4:1050.

61. *Ibid.*, 853. See also Morton Horowitz, *The Transformation of American Law, 1780–1860* (Cambridge: Harvard University Press, 1977), chap. 3. Horowitz notes how the courts limited damages under the use of the just compensation clause.

62. New York State Constitutional Convention Committee, 1938 [Poletti Report] *Problems Related to Bill of Rights and General Welfare* (Albany: J. B. Lyons, 1938), 162. For a more cynical view of the 1919 amendment, see "Editorial," *New York Times*, October 16, 1919, 16.

63. Constitutional Convention of 1821, *Reports of the Proceedings and Debates*, N. Carter and W. L. Stone, reporters (Albany: E. & E. Hosford, 1821), 491.

64. *Ibid.*, 167–69, 487–95.

65. J. Hampden Dougherty, *Constitutional History of New York*, 2d ed. (New York: Neale Publishing, Co., 1915), 114–15.

66. Joseph Story, *Commentaries on the Constitution of the United States*, bk. III, chapt. XLIV, § 993 (abridged by the author, 1833).

67. 8 Paige 24, at 28; see Near v. Minnesota (1931).

68. New York Times v. Sullivan (1964); Gertz v. Welch (1974).

69. Chapadeau v. Utica Observer-Dispatch, Inc. (1975); Gaeta v. New York News (1984) extended the protection of *Chapadeau* by establishing a presumption that statements included in an article or broadcast do involve public concern.

70. People v. Ruggles (1811); People v. Muller (1884) (upholding prohibitions on blasphemous or obscene materials).

71. Burstyn v. Wilson (1951) (upholding Board of Regents' refusal to license film judged sacrilegious) (1952).

72. New York State Constitutional Convention Committee, 1938, *Problems Relating to the Bill of Rights and General Welfare* (Albany: J. B. Lyons, 1938), 162; People v. Most (1902) (advocacy of violence not protected); Pathe Exchange v. Cobb (1922) (motion pictures not part of press); People v. Bohnke (1941) (ordinance prohibiting distribution of material on residential property without occupants' consent upheld); People v. Feiner (1950) (disorderly conduct conviction for street speech upheld).

73. Citing to People v. P. J. Video, which cites only the recent *Bellanca* case.

74. 68 N.Y.2d 296, at 300.

75. Shad Alliance v. Smith Haven Mall, 66 N.Y.2d, at 500–501 (1985).

76. See comments on § 8.

77. Chertok v. Chertok (1924); In re Goldman's Estate (1935). This clause may have been a delayed reaction to the controversial case of Eunice Chapman. Chapman petitioned the legislature for relief after her husband sold all their property, left her, and joined the Society of Shakers. Partly out of sympathy for Ms. Chapman and partly as a punitive measure against the unpopular Shakers, the legislature in 1877 passed legislation dissolving the marriage as well as other punitive steps aimed at the Shakers. The bill was vetoed because, inter alia, it set a dangerous precedent, being the first time since 1777 that a marriage had been dissolved by the legislature, and it violated religious liberty. Frank Prescott and Joseph Zimmerman, *The Politics of the Veto of Legislation in New York* (Washington, D.C.: University Press of America, 1980), 43–45.

78. New York Penal Law § 255.05 (McKinney, 1980).

79. Debate on this issue can be found in *Rev. Rec.*, 1894, 4:1079–88, 1110–31.

80. *Opin. A–G*, 84–11, 14–16.

81. See the unpublished memorandum of Senator Saul Weprin accompanying the proposed amendment in Robert A. Carter, *The New York Constitution: Sources of Legislative Intent* (Littleton, Colo.: Fred B. Rothman & Co., 1988), p. 10.

82. *Opin. A–G*, 81–68, 84–11.

83. E.g., Matter of Esler v. Walters (1982); Under 21, Catholic Home Bureau for Dependent Children v. New York (1985).

84. *Rev. Rec.*, 1938, 4:2626.

85. Id., at 531.

86. Id., at 535.

87. *Laws of New York*, 1950, Chapt. 287. It should also be noted that the court of appeals has given broad construction to antidiscrimination legislation and to the powers of agencies charged with its implementation. See Holland v. Edwards (1954); Matter of Vetere v. Allen (1965).

88. E.g., Matter of Estate of Wilson (1983); Under 21, Catholic Home Bureau for Dependent Children v. New York (1985).

89. The three tiers are: (1) strict scrutiny of regulation when suspect category (race, alienage, national origin) or fundamental right is involved requiring government interest of the highest order. For New York application, see Phelan v. City of Buffalo (1976) (two-year residency requirement as condition for running for public offices invidious discrimination involving a fundamental right); (2) heightened scrutiny or moderate scrutiny when gender is in question requires a substantial relationship between classification and an important government purpose. People v. Whidden (1980) (unit pricing policy required in large food stores but not in drug chains sustained); (3) minimal scrutiny requiring only a rational relationship between classification and legitimate government objective. Wegman's Food Market, Inc. v. State (1980).

90. See Michael M. v. Sonoma County Superior Court (1981) (sustaining similar legislation).

91. Levittown Union Free School District v. Nyquist (1982); accord San Antonio Independent School District v. Rodriquez (1973).

92. Matter of Esler v. Walters (1982), accord Ball v. James (1981).

93. Diamond v. Cuomo (1987) (age); Board of Education of Northport, East-Northport Union Free-School District v. Ambach (1983).

94. People v. Rivera (1976); People ex rel. Cadogan v. McMann (1969).

95. Suffolk Housing Service v. Town of Brookhaven (1987); Kurzius v. Upper Brookville (1980); Asian Americans for Equality v. Koch (1988).

96. Since the adoption of this provision, the national and state government have enacted an impressive array of antidiscrimination laws, which, inter alia, have added gender, age, and handicap to the list of categories against which it is illegal to discriminate. Much of the federal legislation has preempted state efforts, but there are a variety of areas within which states continue to act—e.g., the New York City ordinance prohibiting discrimination in clubs not "distinctly private" but exempting certain religious and benevolent organizations. New York State Club Association v. New York (1987) (upholding law against due process and equal protection challenges).

97. *Revised Statutes of New York*, 1828, Pt. I, Chapt. 4 § 11.

98. *Rev. Rec.*, 1938, 1:336–40, 406–32.

99. People v. Johnson (1985).

100. People v. Ingle (1975) (invalidating individual routine traffic stops); People v. Scott (1984) (sustaining sobriety checkpoints), New York Criminal Procedure Law, § 700.15(4) (McKinney, 1984).

101. People v. Bigelow (1985) rejecting U.S. v. Leon (1984).

102. The more demanding test was set forth in Aguilar v. Texas (1964) and Spinelli v. U.S. (1969).

103. People v. P. J. Video (1986).

104. People v. Langen (1983) extends *Belton* to any part of the vehicle.

105. People v. Gokey (1983); People v. Smith (1984).

106. The New York high court has followed the federal law in a number of search and seizure areas, e.g., People v. Ponder (1981) following U.S. v. Salvucci (1980) (no automatic standing rule to challenge search); People v. Guerra (1985) following Smith v. Maryland (1979) (warrantless use of pen register approved); People v. Reynolds (1988) following California v. Ciraolo (1986) (allowing warrantless air surveillance of private property).

107. *Laws of New York*, 1958, Chapt. 676.

108. New York Criminal Procedure Law, § 700.15(4) (McKinney, 1984).

109. 18 USC § 2518[m](a) (West, 1970, suppl. 1989).

110. New York General Construction Law, §§ 70–72 (McKinney, 1951).

111. See also Waters & Co. v. Gerard (1907) (common rule that innkeeper has a lien upon all goods in rightful possession of his or her guests for the value of guest's entertainment was in force prior to 1775 and has not been altered by legislature or declared inconsistent with the constitution). *Waters* contains one of the few discussions of the historical background to this provision.

112. See Cutting v. Cutting (1881); Brookhaven v. Smith (1907); Shayne v. Evening Post Publishing Co. (1901).

113. See e.g., Woods v. Lancet (1951); Battagga v. State of New York (1961); Bing v. Thunig (1957); Gallagher v. St. Raymond's R.C. Church (1968); Millington v. Southeastern Elevator Co. (1968).

114. *Laws of New York*, 1847, Chapt. 256.

115. *Ibid.*, 1849, Chapt. 450.

116. *Rev. Rec.*, 1894 1:615. The antirailroad sentiment can be found in *ibid.*, 2:1122ff.

117. The rules and procedures governing action for recovery are found in New York Estates, Powers and Trust Laws, §§ 5-4.1–5.4.5 (McKinney, 1981); New York Public Authority Law, § 1276 (McKinney, 1982).

118. New York Estates, Powers and Trust Laws, § 5-4.3 (McKinney, 1981); Amerman v. Lizza & Sons (1974).

119. E.g., Koster v. Greenburg (1986) (excessive damage award reduced); DeCerce v. New York State Thruway Authority (1986) (contributory negligence reduces damage award by proportion of negligence).

120. New York Insurance Law, § 5104 (McKinney, 1966, 1990). The most recent comment on the nature and scope of this clause can be found in Colton v. Riccobono (1986).

121. Kilbery v. Northeast Airline Inc. (1961); Rosenthal v. Warren (1974).

122. *Laws of New York*, 1933, Chapt. 804; 1935, Chapt. 12.

123. Supreme Court decisions have contributed to the supercession, especially EEOC v. Wyoming (1983) and Garcia v. San Antonia Metro Transit Authority (1985).

124. *Laws of New York*, 1910, Chapt. 674.

125. *Ibid.*, 1914, Chapt. 41. The law was upheld against federal due process challenge in New York Central Railroad v. White (1917).

126. Governor John A. Dix in his message of support for the amendment said the principle of worker's compensation "cannot fairly be questioned." *Public Papers of John A. Dix, 1912* (Albany: J. B. Lyons, 1913), 29.

127. From the beginning, courts have given great deference to statutes adopted by legislature pursuant to this section. Shanahan v. Monarch Engineering Co. (1916); Powers v. Porcelain Insulator Corp. (1941); Helfrick v. Dahlstrom Metallic Door Co. (1931); Crosby v. State Worker's Compensation Board (1982).

128. Jensen v. Southern Pacific Railway (1915); Tallini v. Martino & Son (1983).

ARTICLE II

1. "For Absentee Voting," *New York Times*, October 5, 1919, 4:7.

2. Eber v. Board of Election (1974); in Fidell v. Board of Elections of the City of New York (1972), the Supreme Court held there is no right to an absentee ballot in a primary election.

3. New York Election Law, § 5–106(2)(5) (McKinney, 1978).

4. New York Election Law, § 5–106(6) (McKinney, 1978 and Supp. 1989).

5. Governor John T. Hoffman in his annual message to the legislature in 1892 detailed some of the practices the amendment was aimed at eliminating. Charles Z. Lincoln, ed., *Messages from the Governors* (Albany: J. B. Lyons, 1989), 6:387–91.

6. Matter of Goodman (1895); Palla v. Suffolk County Board of Elections (1972).

7. New York Election Law, § 5–104(1) (McKinney, 1978).

8. *Opin. A–G*, 39–226.

9. *Rev. Rec.*, 1894, 3:110–11.

10. *Ibid.*, 3:244–46, 4:537–45.

ARTICLE III

1. Citizens Conference on State Legislatures, *State Legislatures: An Evaluation of Their Effectiveness* (New York: Praeger, 1971), 88.

2. Joseph Zimmerman, *The Government and Policies of New York State* (New York: New York University Press, 1981), 118.

3. *Public Papers of Herbert Lehman, 1935* (Albany, n.d.), p. 23.

4. *Rev. Rec.*, 1894, 3:1002–21, 1046–54; 4:31–37, 65–96.

5. *Opin A–G*, 72–275.

6. New York State, Election Law, § 8–100–104 (McKinney, 1987 & Supp. 1990).

7. New York, Public Officer's Law, § 30 (1) (McKinney, 1988).

8. New York State, Legislative Law, § 2 (McKinney, 1952 & Supp. 1989).

9. New York (State) Constitutional Convention Committee, Reports [Poletti Report] 12 vols. (Albany, 1938), Vol. 7: *Problems Relating to Legislative Organization and Powers*, 68.

10. See Alan G. Hevesi, *Legislative Politics in New York State: A Comparative Analysis* (New York: Praeger, 1975), 9.

11. Zimmerman, *Government and Politics of New York State*, 205.

12. *New York Jurisprudence*, Statutes, §§ 8–9.

13. Constitutional Commission of 1872, *Amendments Proposed to the Constitution of the State of New York*, Sen Doc., 1873 No. 70, 30–32.

14. *Rev. Rec.*, 1938, 2:1157.

ARTICLE IV

1. *Debates and Proceedings in the New York State Constitutional Convention, 1846*, S. Croswell and R. Sutton, reporters (Albany: Argus Printer, 1846), 164.

2. 1953 *Opin. A–G*, June 3.

3. *Debates and Proceedings of the Convention of 1821* (New York: J. Seymour Printer, 1821), 173–74.

4. Joseph Zimmerman, *The Government and Politics of New York State* (New York: New York University Press, 1981), 147.

5. Ibid., 200.

6. Frank W. Prescott and Joseph F. Zimmerman, *The Politics of the Veto of Legislation in New York State* (Washington, D.C.: University Press of America, 1980), 2:1167.

7. Ibid., 1206.

8. Jones v. Smith (1985); DeZimm v. New York State Board of Parole (1988); People v. Fogerty (1966).

ARTICLE V

1. Executive Law, §§ 63, 73, 173, 174 (McKinney, 1982).

2. Agriculture and Markets Law, § 5 (McKinney, 1972).

3. Civil Service Law, § 1ff. (McKinney, 1983).

ARTICLE VI

1. Temporary Commission on the Courts, Part I: *A Recommendation for a Simplified State-wide Court System*, Leg. Doc., 1957, No. 6, 16–17.

2. David Siegel, *New York Practice* (St. Paul, Minn: West Publishing Co., 1978), § 10.

3. New York, Criminal Procedure Law, § 450.90(2)(a) (McKinney, 1983).

4. Robert MacCrate, James D. Hopkins and Maurice Rosenberg, *Appellate Justice in New York* (Chicago: American Judicature Society, 1982), 50.

5. New York, Civil Practice Laws and Rules, § 5601(a) (McKinney, 1978 & Supp., 1989).

6. New York, Civil Practice Laws and Rules, "Practice Commentaries," David Siegel, § 5601(c) (McKinney, 1978, 1989).

7. Judiciary Constitutional Convention of 1921, *Report to the Legislature*, Leg. Doc., 1922, No. 37, 15.

8. Report of Temporary Commission on Courts, 1957, Part I, 55, and *Recommendations of Judicial Conference for Reorganization of the New York State Judicial System*, Leg. Doc., 1959, No. 94, 87.

9. *Recommendations of Judicial Conference*, Report of Temporary Commission on Courts, 1958, Part I, 9.

10. Report of the Temporary Commission on the Courts, Part I, *Recommendations for the Reorganization of the Structure of the Courts of the State of New York and Their Administration*, Leg. Doc., 1958, No. 36, 12–13.

11. New York, Family Court Act, § 812 (McKinney, 1983, Supp. 1989).

12. New York, Uniform City Court Act, § 1801 (McKinney, 1963, 1989).

13. The Uniform Justice Court Act governs all these matters. Judiciary Court Acts (McKinney, 1963, 1989).

14. *Opin. A–G*, 84–57.

15. Report of the Temporary Commission on the Courts, 1957, 51.

16. *New York Rules of Court*, §§ 100.5, 100.6 (McKinney, 1988).

17. *Report on the Joint Legislative Committee on Court Reorganization*, Leg. Doc. 1973, No. 24, 17.

18. New York State Constitutional Convention, 1846, *Debates and Proceedings of the New York State Convention for the Revision of the Constitution*, S. Croswell and R. Sutton, reporters (Albany: Albany Argue Printer, 1846), 435, 582–83; *Rev. Rec.*, 1894, 2:1122–23.

19. New York, Judiciary Law, § 240 (McKinney, 1983); Public Officers Law, §§ 2, 3 (McKinney, 1988).

20. Staff Report, New York State Senate Judiciary Committee, *New York's Impeachment Law and the Trial of Governor Sulzer: A Case for Reform* (Albany, 1986), 41.

21. New York State Constitutional Convention, 1821, *Report of the Debates and Proceedings of the Convention of New York* . . . (Albany: E. and H. Hosford, 1821), 431–37.

22. *Proceedings in the Court of Impeachment in the Matter of the Impeachment of George G. Bernard, a Justice of the Supreme Court of the State of New York* (Albany: Weed Parsons and Co., 1874), 1:151–79; State of New York, *Proceedings of the Court for the Trial of Impeachments: The People of the State of New York against William Sulzer as Governor by the Assembly Thereof* (Albany: J. B. Lyons, 1913), 2:1599, 1749–50; People v. Berg (1930); Newman v. Stroebel (1932).

23. 29 USC § 621 et seq.

24. The federal law exempted elected state officials from its coverage, § 630 (f).

25. New York, Indian Law, §§ 46, 50–51 (McKinney, 1950, 1989).

ARTICLE VII

1. State of New York, *Debt Capacity and Control Analysis: An Update from the Office of the State Comptroller, Edward Regan* (Albany: September, 1989), 3–4.

2. *Report of the Debates and Proceedings of the Convention for the Revision of the Constitution of the State of New York, 1846*, William Bishop and William Attree, reporters (Albany: Evening Atlas, 1846), 723.

3. Finance Law, § 94(4) (McKinney, 1968, 1990).

4. *Seventeenth Annual Report of the Conservation Department*, Leg. Doc. 1928, No. 38, 198.

5. *Journals and Documents of the Constitutional Convention of 1938*, Doc. No. 3, 7.

6. "Legislature Gets Tax Reserve Plan," *New York Times*, February 27, 1943, 7.

ARTICLE VIII

1. New York State, Temporary State Commission on the Constitutional Convention, *Local Finance Report* (Albany, 1967), 103–4.

2. *Journals & Documents of the Constitutional Convention of 1938*, Doc.No. 6, 2.

3. *Opin. St. Compt.* 86–46.

4. *Ibid.*, 87–89.

5. *Ibid.*, 78–73.

6. *Rev. Rec.*, 1938, 3:1774.

7. *New York Jurisprudence*, Public Debt Limitations, §§ 68–69.

8. State of New York, *Report Accompanying the Proposed Greater New York Charter*, Assembly Doc. 1897, No. 53, v.

9. *Opin. St. Compt.*, 78–566.

ARTICLE IX

1. State of New York, *Public Papers of Nelson Rockefeller, 1962*, (Albany, n.d.) p. 825.

2. Memorandum of the Office for Local Government. *New York State Legislative Annual, 1963*, (New York: New York Legislative Service, 1963), 223.

3. See Article 10 for a discussion of the cases.

4. New York State, Temporary Commission on the Revision and Simplification of the Constitution, Staff Report No. 3, *Town Government* (1958), 64.

5. New York General Municipal Law, § 712(10), et seq. (McKinney, 1986 & 1990).

6. Message from the Governor Relating to the Reorganization of County Government, Leg. Doc., 1926, No. 80, 6.

7. New York State, Municipal Home Rule, § 35 (McKinney, 1969).

8. New York, Statute of Local Governments Law (McKinney, 1969).

9. James Cole, "Constitutional Home Rule in New York: 'The Ghost of Home Rule,' " *St. John's Law Review* 59 (1985):736 n. 95.

10. People v. Cook (1974), at 109.

11. Consolidated Edison Co. v. Town of Red Hood (1983), at 107–8.

12. Cole, "Constitutional Home Rule," p. 737.

13. E.g., Matter of Town of Islip v. Cuomo (1984) (state law limiting landfill in only two counties was a special law but protection of drinking water a matter of state concern); Schnapp v. Lefkowitz (1979) (public health law requiring dog owners in cities over 400,000 to remove feces by dogs not a violation of home rule as public health does not relate to property, affairs or government of local government).

14. New York State Legislative Commission on State-Local Relations, *New York State's State-Local Service Delivery System: An Interim Report* (Albany, 1987), 42.

ARTICLE X

1. L. Ray Gunn, *The Decline of Authority: Public Policy and Political Development in New York, 1800–1860* (Ithaca: Cornell University Press, 1988), 86–87.
2. Constitutional Commission of 1872, *Amendments Proposed to the Constitution of the State of New York*, Senate Doc., 1873, No. 70, 37–38.
3. *Rev. Rec.*, 1938 Conv., 3:2275.
4. Ibid., 2268.
5. See the judicial definition in City of Rye v. Metropolitan Transportation Authority (1967).
6. *First Annual Report of the State Thruway Authority* (New York, 1950), 3–8.
7. Robert W. Purcell, "Special Report to the Governor on Problems of the Railroads and Bus Lines in New York State," Mimeo., March 12, 1959, 28–33.

ARTICLE XI

1. *Rev. Rec.*, 1894, 4:861; Report of the Committee on Education and Funds Thereto, 1894 Convention, Doc. 62, 15–16.
2. *Rev. Rec.*, 1894, 3:739–41.
3. *Opin. A–G*, 69–16.

ARTICLE XIII

1. *Inf. Opin. A–G*, 77–336.
2. Introductory Memorandum of Assemblyman Robert Stavisky in Robert A. Carter, *New York Constitution: Sources of Legislative Intent* (Littleton, Colo.: Fred B. Rothman, Inc., 1988), 163.
3. *Opin. A–G*, 79–259.
4. Ralph Straetz and Frank Munger, *New York Politics* (New York: New York University Press, 1960), 48–49.
5. *County Law* § 400 (McKinney, 1977, 1989).
6. The four-year alternative was not available to the county in question because the legislature had not at the time extended the four-year alternative to that county.
7. *Debates*, 1867, 5:3820.

ARTICLE XIV

1. A list of the major opinions between 1894 and 1954 can be found in Helms v. Reid (1977).
2. *The Future of the Adirondack Park* (Albany, 1970); *Laws of New York*, 1971, Chapt. 706; as amended *Laws*, 1973, Chapt. 348; *Laws*, 1974, Chapt. 679.
3. New York Environmental Conservation Law, §§ 49–0301–0305 (McKinney, 1984).
4. *Proceedings of the Constitutional Convention of the State of New York 1967*, Vol. II, Part I, 939.

5. E.g., Conservation Bill of Rights Act, Laws, 1970, Chapt. 140; and the State Environmental Quality Review Act of 1975, which requires an environmental impact statement for any project having a "significant effect on the environment." Environmental Conservation Law, § 8–0101(2) (McKinney, 1984).

ARTICLE XVI

1. *Opin. A–G*, 83–218.
2. *Rev. Rec.*, 1938, 2:1113.
3. For full list of exemptions, see *New York Jurisprudence*, Taxation, §§ 90–196.
4. Laws of New York, 1971, Chapt. 414, Laws of New York, 1981, Chapt. 919.
5. New York, Real Property Law, §§ 200–202 (McKinney, 1968, 1990).
6. Ibid., 2249–2450.

ARTICLE XVII

1. See New York Social Service Law, §§ 1–370 (McKinney, 1983).

ARTICLE XVIII

1. For example the current article confines the state and localities to the redevelopment and clearance of blighted areas; comprehensive community development would involve programs to conserve and improve areas that are in decline but not yet slums and to do so on a community wide basis.
2. E.g. Public Housing Law, Chapt. 808, Laws of New York, 1939; Urban Redevelopment Law, Chapt. 892, Laws of New York, 1941. The latter was the first of its kind in the nation.
3. *Rev. Rec.*, 1938, 2:1532, 1561.
4. Temporary State Commission on the Constitution Convention of 1967, Report 9, *Housing, Labor and Natural Resources* (Albany, 1967), 27.
5. New York Public Housing Law, § 73 (McKinney, 1955, 1989).
6. *Opin. A–G*, 59–22.
7. *Rev. Rec.*, 1938, 4:3024–25.
8. Temporary State Commission on Constitutional Convention of 1967, Report 9, 92.
9. Ibid., 43.

ARTICLE XIX

1. *Opin. A–G*, 39–358; *Opin. A–G*, 61–52.
2. Thomas R. Morris, "State Attorneys General as Interpreters of State Constitutions," *Publius* 17 (Winter 1987):140. For legal status in New York, see *New York Jurisprudence 2d*, State of New York, § 23.

Bibliographical Essay

THE CONSTITUTIONS

The New York Constitutions through 1894 with amendments can be found in Francis Thorpe, ed., *The Federal and State Constitutions . . .* (Washington, D.C.: Government Printing Office, 1909), vol. 5. William Swindler, ed., *Sources and Documents of the United States Constitutions*, 10 vols. (Dobbs Ferry: Oceana Publications, 1978), vol. 7 contains the 1777, 1821, and 1846 Constitutions, as well as the 1897 Constitution (the 1894 Constitution, which incorporated the recommendations of the 1890 Judiciary Commission), and the proposed constitution drafted by the 1967 convention. The text of the current constitution can be found in *The Constitution of the State of New York Amended to 1988.* This publication is updated periodically by the New York secretary of state and is available from that office. Robert Allan Carter's *New York State Constitution: Sources of Legislative Intent* (Littleton, Colo.: Fred B. Rothman & Co., 1988), provides a list of sources by section for the constitution. It is an excellent research tool for locating convention debates, legislative documents, commission reports, and pertinent court decisions.

The Background

David Ellis, James A. Frost, Harold C. Syrett, and Harry Carman, *A History of New York State*, rev. ed. (Ithaca: Cornell University Press, 1967), is a good though dated one-volume history. Journals that contain relevant articles are *New York History*, *New-York Historical Society Quarterly* (ceased publication in 1980), *Empire State Reports*, and the *New York State Bar Journal*. General journals that contain pertinent materials are *State Government* and the *National Civic Review*. The latter deals with all aspects of state constitutional development and includes a yearly summary of amendments passed or rejected in the states.

For political and legal developments before the adoption of the first constitutions, see Robert C. Ritchie, *The Duke's Province: A Study of New York Politics and Society, 1664–1691* (Chapel Hill: University of North Carolina Press, 1977), and Patricia U. Bonomi, *A Factious People: Politics and Society in Colonial New York* (New York: Columbia University Press, 1971).

General Works on New York's Constitutional History

Three works treat New York's first constitution in comparative perspective. Alan Nevins, *The American State during and after the Revolution* (New York: Macmillan, 1924), is essentially descriptive. More analytical works are Willi Paul Adams, *The First American Constitutions: Republican Ideology and the Making of State Constitutions in the Revolutionary Era* (Chapel Hill: University of North Carolina Press, 1980) and Donald Lutz, *Popular Consent and Popular Control: Whig Political Theory and the Early State Constitutions* (Baton Rouge: Louisiana State University, 1980). No general work covers New York's constitutional history into the twentieth century. Charles Z. Lincoln, *The Constitutional History of New York from the Beginning of the Colonial Period to the Year 1905*, 5 vols. (Rochester: Lawyers Cooperative, 1906), the most comprehensive and reliable history, is out of print though available on microfiche from F. B. Rothman & Co., Littleton, Colorado. It includes, in addition to pertinent colonial documents, texts of the first four state constitutions and their amendments. It is a remarkable effort by a delegate to the 1894 convention and legal adviser to Governors Morton, Black, and Roosevelt. In spite of its legalistic approach, every student must depend on this work. J. Hampden Dougherty, *Constitutional History of the State of New York*, 2d ed. (New York: Neale Publishing Co., 1915), is a one-volume treatment of roughly the same period. A few articles provide broad overviews: Henry Wayland Hill, "An Analysis of Constitutional Change in New York State," in *Publications of the Buffalo Historical Society* (Buffalo: Peter Paul Book Co., 1896); Ruth Kessler, "An Analysis of Constitutional Change in New York State," *New York University Law Quarterly* 16 (November 1938); Frances D. Lyon, "The New York Constitutional Conventions," *Proceedings of the New York State Historical Association* 37 (1939):51–59; Frank Moore, "Constitutional Conventions in New York State," *New York History* 38 (1957):3–17; Franklin Feldman, "A Constitutional Convention in New York: Fundamental Law and Basic Politics," *Cornell Law Quarterly* 42 (1957):329–45; and Richard I. Nunez, "New York State Constitutional Reform—Past Political Battles in Constitutional Language," *William and Mary Law Quarterly* 10 (1968):366–77. Gerald Benjamin, "Constitutional Revision in New York: Retrospect and Prospect," in *Essays on the Genesis of the Empire State* (Albany: New York State Bicentennial Commission, 1979), provides a succinct and perspective summary of the major constitutional values that have guided constitution making in New York.

Bibliographies

The best book on constitutional history is Ernest R. Breuer, *Constitutional Developments in New York, 1777–1958: A Bibliography on Conventions and Constitutions with Selected References for Constitutional Research*, Bibliography Bulletin, 82 (Albany: New York State Library 1958). Breuer issued two updates to this work: "Constitutional Developments in New York 1958–1967, A Temporary Supplement," mimeo. (Albany,

1967), and "New York State Constitutional Convention of 1967, A Second Supplement" mimeo. (Albany, 1970); Dorothy Butch's *New York State Documents: An Introductory Manual*, Bibliography Bulletin 89 (Albany: New York State Library, 1987) provides general information about official state publications connected with the New York State constitutions, statutes, and administrative laws, as well as the legislative, executive, and judicial branches. It is an excellent starting place for students of the New York Constititution. The entries are annotated with helpful information about the location and character of the documents in question. The documents, debates, and proceedings of all the conventions held in New York between 1777 and 1967 are now available on microfiche. A guide to the use of this microfiche for the years 1777-1959 is provided by Cynthia Browne, comp., *State Constitutional Conventions: From Independence to the Completion of the Present Union, 1777-1959* (Westport, Conn.: Greenwood Press, 1973), and for the years 1959-1978 in *State Constitutional Conventions, Commissions and Amendments: An Annotated Bibliography*, 2 vols. (Washington, D.C.: Congressional Information Service, 1981).

THE CONSTITUTION OF 1777

The Sources

The proceedings of the first convention are found in the *Journal of the Provincial Congress, Provincial Convention, Committee of Safety and Council of Safety for the State of New York from 1775–1777* (Albany: T. Weed, 1842), vol. 1. The 1777 Constitution is reprinted in Lincoln, *Constitutional History of New York*, vol. 1; Thorpe, *Federal and State Constitutions*, vol. 5; and Swindler, *Sources and Documents*, vol. 7. Lincoln also reprints copies of destroyed drafts of the Constitution of 1777.

Commentaries

Earlier treatments can be found in Lincoln, *Constitutional History of New York*, 1:471–595, and Dougherty, *Constitutional History*, chap. 2. Carl Becker's *The History of Political Parties in the Province of New York, 1760–1776* (Madison: University of Wisconsin Press, 1909), a pioneering analysis of the social and economic interests that led to independence, puts the adoption of the constitution in a larger political context. Elisha Douglass, *Rebels and Democrats* (Chapel Hill: University of North Carolina Press, 1955), follows Becker's class conflict approach to constitutional change. Alfred Young's *The Democratic Republicans of New York: The Origins (1763–1797)* (Chapel Hill: University of North Carolina Press, 1967) provides useful information on the 1777 Constitution and the extent of suffrage before and after its adoption. E. Wilder Spaulding's "The State Government under the First Constitution," in *The New State*, vol. 4 of Alexander C. Flick, ed., *History of the State of New York in Ten Volumes* (New York: Columbia University Press, 1933–1937), sees the document as a triumph of the minority party of privilege. Bernard Mason's *The Road to Independence: The Revolutionary Movement in New York, 1773–1777* (Lexington: University of Kentucky Press, 1966), and his essay "New York State's First Constitution," in *Essays on the Genesis of the Empire State* (Albany: New York State Bicentennial Commission, 1979), analyze the drafts of the 1777 document, as well as the divisions among the delegates. William Polf's *1777: The*

Political Revolution and New York's First Constitution (Albany: New York Bicentennial Commission, 1977), is a pamphlet-size essay that analyzes the structure and powers of each branch of the new government and how the constitution handled the questions of rights and suffrage. It also reprints the 1777 Constitution.

Richard B. Morris, "John Jay and the New York State Constitution After Two Hundred Years," in *Essays on the Genesis of the Empire State*, reasserts the older view that John Jay was the major force in shaping the constitution. Patricia U. Bonomi's "Constitution-Making in Time of Trouble," in the same volume, focuses on the impact of the war on drafting the document. Edward Countryman, *A People in Revolution: The American Revolution and Political Society in New York, 1760–1790* (Baltimore: Johns Hopkins Press, 1981), has some evaluative comments on the character of the 1777 Constitution, which should be compared to those of Young, Douglass, and Mason. His dissertation, "Legislative Government in Revolutionary New York" (Cornell University, 1971), contains biographical information in the Provincial Congress and Provincial Convention, as well as a description of the 1777 Constitution.

THE CONVENTION OF 1801

Records

There are two available sources of the convention's work: *Journal of the Convention of the State of New York, 1801* (Albany: John Barber, Printer to the Convention, 1801), and the *Journal* as published by Catine and Leake, Printers to the State in 1821. The amendments adopted at the convention are reprinted in Lincoln, *Constitutional History of New York*, 1:189–91.

Secondary Sources

Commentary is provided by Lincoln, *Constitutional History of New York*, 1:596–612, and Dougherty, *Constitutional History*, Chap. 4. The latter treats both political and constitutional aspects of the convention. Jabez Hammond, *The History of Political Parties in the State of New York*, 3 vols. (Syracuse, N.Y.: Hall Mills & Co., 1952) is still the best general treatment of this topic. Hammond was a contemporary public figure who knew many of those he wrote about. He describes the political conflicts and events surrounding the convention. H. L. McBain, *DeWitt Clinton and the Origins of the Spoils System in New York*, Columbia Studies in Economics and Public Law, Vol. 28, No. 1 (New York: Columbia University Press, 1907), undertakes a defense of Clinton's patronage practices.

THE CONVENTION OF 1821

Records

Reports of the Proceedings and Debates of the Convention of 1821, N. H. Carter and W. L. Stone, reporters, M.T.C. Gould, Stenographer (Albany: E & E Hosford, 1821). DeCapo Press reprinted this edition in 1970. A report based on the Carter and Gould edition was published by J. Seymour Printer in 1821 and is also available on microfilm as part of the *Records of the States of the United States of America*, ed. William Sumner Jenkins (Washington, D.C.: Library of Congress and University of North Carolina, 1949). *Journal of the Convention of the State of New York, 1821* (Albany: Catine & Leake Printers to the State, 1821) is also available on microfilm. The constitution is reprinted in Thorpe, *Federal and State Constitutions*, vol. 5; Lincoln, *Constitutional and History of New York*, vol. 1; and Swindler, *Sources and Documents*, vol. 7. The *Journal of the Convention* is the daily record of the actions taken by the delegates. The *Reports*, though not verbatim transcripts, constitute the official record of the convention.

Commentaries

Lincoln, *Constitutional History of New York*, 1:613–756, and Dougherty, *Constitutional History*, chaps. 5–7, provide accounts of the convention. Merrill Peterson, ed., *Democracy Liberty, and Property: The State Constitutional Conventions of the 1820's* (Indianapolis: Bobbs-Merrill, 1966), includes excerpts from the debates of the convention and puts its work in the context of what other states were doing during the 1820s. Older studies of the political and economic forces underlying the convention's work are Dixon Ryan Fox's "New York Becomes a Democracy," in Flick, ed., vol. 6, *The Age of Reform*. This essay is based on his fuller treatment of the period entitled *The Decline of Aristocracy in the Politics of New York, 1801–1840*. (New York: Columbia University Press, 1919). Also valuable is Hammond, *History of Political Parties*, vol. 1. Donald B. Cole, *Martin Van Buren and the American Political System* (Princeton: Princeton University Press, 1984), emphasizes the role of Van Buren in leading the Bucktail majority at the convention. The two institutions abolished in 1821—the Council of Appointment and the Council of Revision—have been well studied by Alfred B. Street, *The Council of Revision of New York* (Albany: William Gould Publisher, 1859); Frank Prescott and Joseph Zimmerman, *The Council of Revision* (Albany: Graduate School of Public Affairs, University of New York at Albany, 1973); J. M. Gitterman, "The Council of Appointment in New York," *Political Science Quarterly* 7 (1892):80–115; and Hugh M. Flick, "The Council of Appointment in New York State: The First Attempt to Regulate Political Patronage, 1777–1822," *New York History* 15 (1934):353–80. The question of African American suffrage at the convention is thoroughly examined by Phyllis F. Field, *The Politics of Race in New York: The Struggle for Black Suffrage in the Civil War Era* (Ithaca: Cornell University Press, 1982). Marvin Meyers, *The Jacksonian Persuasion* (New York: Vintage Books ed., 1960), places the convention in the context of the origin and development of party alignments, as well as in the broader movement he labeled Jacksonian Persuasion. Two dissertations have focused on the convention. Helen Young, "A Study of the Constitutional Convention in 1821" (Ph.D. diss., Yale University, 1910), examines the convention's work in the light of the changes that had taken place since 1777. John Casais, "The New York Constitution Convention of 1821 and Its Aftermath" (Ph.D. diss., Columbia University, 1967), concentrates on the factional alignments and voting patterns at the convention. George P. Parkinson, "Antebellum State Constitution-Making Retention, Circumvention, Revision" (Ph.D. diss., University of Wisconsin, 1972), places the New York convention in a comparative context.

THE CONVENTION OF 1846

Sources

Report of the Debates and Proceedings of the Convention for the Revision of the Constitution of the State of New York, 1846, reported by W. G. Bishop and W. H. Attree (Albany: Evening Atlas, 1846). An alternative source is reported by S. Croswell and R. Sutton (Albany: Argus Printers, 1846). Neither of these is a verbatim transcript. *Journal of the Convention . . . 1846* (Albany: Carroll & Cook, 1846). The constitution as revised is reprinted in Lincoln, *Constitutional History of New York,* vol. 1; Thorpe, *Federal and State Constitutions,* vol. 5; and Swindler, *Sources and Documents,* vol. 7. For amendments to this constitution from 1847 to 1867, see Lincoln, 2:218–40.

Commentaries

There is no monograph on the 1846 convention. Lincoln, *Constitutional History of New York,* 2:9–217, gives it extensive treatment. Less extensive treatment is given by Dougherty, *Constitutional History,* chaps. 8–9. E. P. Cheney, "The Anti-Rent Movement and the Constitution of 1847," in Flick, ed., vol. 6, *The Age of Reform,* focuses on the connection between the antirent movement and the convention. Edna Jacobsen, "New York's Constitution: A Hundred Years Ago," *New York History* 45 (1947):191–96, summarizes the major changes made at the convention and provides some interesting social background on the delegates. A contemporary account by a prominent lawyer-politician is Benjamin Butler's "Outline of the Constitutional History of New York, An Anniversary Discourse . . . ," *Collections of the New York Historical Society,* 2d series, vol. 2 (New York, 1849), 9–75. L. Ray Gunn, *The Decline of Authority: Public Economic Policy and Political Development in New York State, 1800–1860* (Ithaca: Cornell University Press, 1988), contains the most sophisticated analysis of the convention's work (chapter 6) and is one of the few works to attempt to demonstrate a relationship between constitutional change and economic development. Meyers, *The Jacksonian Persuasion,* examines the convention's work with special attention to its treatment of the business corporation. Treatment of the African American suffrage issue is found in Field, *The Politics of Race in New York.* Francis Bergan, *The History of the New York Court of Appeals, 1847–1932* (New York: Columbia University Press, 1985), provides information on the origin of the court of appeals in the 1846 convention. Patricia McGee, "Issues and Factions: New York State Politics from the Panic of 1837 to the Election of 1848" (Ph.D. diss., St. John's University, 1970), places the convention in the context of the factionalizing and realignment of politics in New York during the 1840s. George P. Parkinson, "Antebellum State Constitution-Making: Retention, Circumvention, Revision" (Ph.D. diss., University of Wisconsin, 1972), looks at the changes effected by "radicals" in a comparative context.

FROM 1847 TO 1894

Sources

Records of the Convention of 1867: *Journal of the Convention of the State of New York, 1867* (Albany: Weed, Parsons & Co., 1867); *Proceedings and Debates of the*

Constitutional Convention of the State of New York, 1867–68, reported by Edward F. Underhill (Albany: Weed, Parsons & Co., 1868), 5 vols. The proposed constitution is available as the *Amended Constitution of the State of New York Adopted by the Convention of 1867* (Albany: Luther Caldwell, 1868). The Constitutional Commission of 1872: The record of the commission was never published, so the *Journal of the Constitutional Commission . . . 1822–1873* (Albany: Weed, Parsons & Co., 1873) is the only source of the commission's activities. The result of its work is found in *Amendments Proposed to the Constitution of the State of New York* (Albany: Argus Printer, 1873). The records of the Judiciary Commission of 1890 were never published, so the *Journal of the Constitution Commission, 1890* (Albany, 1891) is the only record of their deliberations. The commission issued reports listed in Breuer, *Constitutional Development*, 37–38.

Commentaries

Lincoln, *Constitutional History of New York*, 2:18–725 and Dougherty, *Constitutional History*, chaps. 10–14, cover the period in question thoroughly. Lincoln also reprints the proposed constitution. More recent treatment is found in Finla Crawford, "Constitutional Developments, 1867–1915" in Flick, *History*, vol. 7, *Modern Party Battles*.

THE CONVENTION OF 1894

Documents

A large number of publications accompanied the calling of the 1894 convention. The thirteen volumes of preparatory materials published for the use of the delegates are listed by title in Breuer, *Constitutional Development*, and Butch, *New York State Documents*. The convention itself produced eleven volumes of documents, records, proceedings, and journal. *The Record of the Proceedings* was published in six volumes and was revised and indexed in five volumes by William H. Steele (Albany, 1900). *The Journal of the Constitutional Convention* was published in Albany in 1894. It was also revised and indexed in two volumes (Albany: Argus Company, 1895). The 1894 Constitution is reprinted in Thorpe, *Federal and State Constitutions*, vol. 5; Lincoln, *Constitutional History of New York*, vol. 4; and Swindler, *Sources and Documents*, vol. 7. Lincoln annotates the constitution.

Commentary

Lincoln devoted an entire volume to the work of the 1894 Convention. Dougherty gives less well organized coverage in chaps. 14–18. Brief summaries of the conventions' accomplishments are found in Crawford, "Constitutional Conventions," and Frank T. Hamlin, "The New York Constitutional Convention," *Yale Law Journal* 4 (June 1895):213–22. Three recent works focus on the role of the Republican party at the convention and the impact of interest groups and regional considerations and put the convention in the larger context of New York's politics: Samuel T. McSeveney, *The Politics of Depression: Political Behavior in the Northeast, 1893–1896* (New York: Oxford University Press, 1972); Richard L. McCormick, *From Realignment to Reform:*

Political Change in New York State, 1893–1910 (Ithaca: Cornell University Press, 1981); and Robert Crosby Eager, "Governing New York State: Republicans and Reform, 1894–1900" (Ph.D. diss., Stanford University, 1977).

THE CONVENTION OF 1915

Sources

Journal of the Constitutional Convention, 1915 (Albany: J. B. Lyon Printer, 1915). The debates are in two forms: *The Record of the Constitutional Convention, 1915* (Albany: J. B. Lyon, 1915) 4 vols., and the *Revised Record of the Constitutional Convention* (Albany: J. B. Lyon, 1916), 4 vols. The large number of preliminary publications in connection with the convention is listed in Breuer, *Constitutional Developments*, and Butch, *New York State Documents*. A copy of the full text of the revised constitution was reprinted in the *New York Times*, September 12, 1915, pp. 18–21.

Commentaries

Best of the early works is Finla Crawford, "Constitutional Developments 1867–1915," in Flick, *History*, vol. 7, *Modern Party Battles*. The only monograph on the convention is Thomas Schick, *The New York State Constitutional Convention of 1915 and the Modern State Governor*, published by the National Municipal League (Sowers Printing Co., 1978). This work focuses on the convention's attempts at governmental reorganization and slights the impact of political party and political factors in general. A good corrective emphasizing the latter is Gerald McKnight, "The Perils of Reform Politics: The Abortive New York State Constitutional Reform Movement in 1915," *New York Historical Society Quarterly* 63 (July 1979):203–27. Schick provides a full bibliography of materials relating to the 1915 convention.

BETWEEN CONVENTIONS: 1916–1938

Sources

For the Judiciary Convention of 1921, Breuer, *Constitutional Developments*, and Butch, *New York State Documents*, have complete listings of proceedings, documents, and the manual. The convention's recommendations are found in *Report to the Legislature . . .*, Legislative Doc. (1922) No. 37 (Albany: J. B. Lyons, 1922). A list of amendments summarized by subject can be found in the most recent edition of the *New York State Constitution*, published by the New York secretary of state. This useful publication contains a schedule of amendments to the 1894 Constitution and the vote on all proposed amendments going back to 1821. *The New York State Constitutional Convention Committee* (Albany, 1938), whose work is popularly known as the Poletti Report after its chairman, reprints the amendments to the constitution between 1895 and 1937 in vol. 1, part 2.

Commentaries

The convention is discussed in Bergan, *The History of the New York Court of Appeals*. The way in which executive reorganization and the constitutional reforms advocated by the 1915 convention were achieved is described in Finla Crawford, "Recent Political Development, 1915–1935," in Flick, *History*, vol. 7, *Modern Party Battles*.

THE CONVENTION OF 1938

Sources

Like the 1915 convention, a mass of preparatory material was assembled. The twelve volumes, as well as other materials connected with the convention, are listed in Breuer, *Constitutional Developments*, and Butch, *New York State Documents*. The activities of the convention itself are found in *Journal of the Constitutional Convention . . . 1938* (Albany: J. B. Lyons, 1838). *Record of the Constitutional Convention . . . 1938* (Albany: J. B. Lyon, 1938), 3 vols. A *Revised Record* was issued in four volumes by the same publisher in 1938.

Commentaries

The only published monograph on the convention, Vernon O'Rourke and Douglas Campbell's, *Constitution-Making in a Democracy: Theory and Practice in New York State* (Baltimore: Johns Hopkins Press, 1943), is the first study of New York conventions to focus on interest group activity as well as partisanship. A similar approach but with more attention to the specific issues is Wilbert L. Hindman, "The New York Constitutional Convention of 1938: The Constituent Process and Interest Activity" (Ph.D. diss., University of Michigan, 1940). Frieda A. Gillette, "The New York State Constitutional Convention of 1938" (Ph.D. diss., Cornell University Press, 1944), describes the major issues and how they were handled and concludes with an analysis of partisan divisions on each of these issues. An early attempt to relate the convention decisions to public opinion is Madge McKinney, "Constitutional Amendment in New York State," *Public Opinion Quarterly* 3 (October 1939):635–45. Also useful is Arthur E. Sutherland, "Law Making by Popular Vote: Some Reflections on the New York Constitution," *Cornell Law Quarterly* 24 (1938):1–12. Articles by delegates to the convention are noted in Hindman, p. 422.

BETWEEN CONVENTIONS: 1939–1966

Sources

A list of amendments to the 1894 Constitution between 1939 and 1967 can be found in *The New York State Constitution* as published by the secretary of state of New York. The three Temporary Commissions on Constitutional Revision (1957–1961) held hearings and issued interim and topical reports on all aspects of the constitution. These, as well as the unpublished materials of the commissions, are listed and discussed in Ernest Breuer, *Constitutional Development*, and Butch, *New York State Documents*. These reports provide an excellent picture of the idea of constitutional reform in the late 1950s and early 1960s, as well as useful background information.

Commentaries

Guthrie Birkhead, Jr., *A Right to Choose: The Prospective Constitutional Convention in New York State*, prepared for the Citizenship Clearing House (Syracuse: Syracuse University Press, 1957), summarizes the pros and cons of a convention, as well as the major issues that would have faced one. Birkhead also provides a list of organizations active in constitutional reform or that had taken a position on the question of reform. Franklin Feldman, "A Constitutional Convention in New York: Fundamental Law and Basic Politics," *Cornell Law Quarterly* 42 (1957):329–45, put the upcoming vote on the 1957 convention in the context of the political limits on constitutional reform. Vol. 31 of the *St. John's Law Review* (1957) is devoted to the question of whether there ought to be a constitutional convention in 1959.

THE CONVENTION OF 1967 AND BEYOND

Sources

The Temporary Commission on the Constitutional Convention issued a series of fifteen reports on a variety of topics, which are bound in two volumes (Albany, 1966). The *Hearings of the Temporary Commission* were bound in five volumes of mimeographed transcripts in 1966. *Proceedings of the New York State Constitutional Convention* (Albany, 1968), 12 vols., contains the journal, the debates, proposed amendments, and documents of the convention. The proposed constitution can be found in *Text, Abstract and Highlights of the Proposed Constitution of the State of New York* . . . (Albany: Legislative Index Co., 1967). A list of amendments to the constitution from 1967 on is found in *The New York Constitution*, as published by the New York secretary of state.

Commentaries

Ernest R. Breuer, "New York State Constitutional Convention of 1967: A Second Supplement," mimeo. (Albany, 1970), updates his earlier bibliography and contains a list of archival material held by the New York State Library in Albany. The League of Women Voters of New York published a pamphlet, *The 1967 New York State Constitutional Convention* (New York: Foundation for Citizen Education, 1966), that provides useful background information, as well as the league's position on constitutional reform. The Citizens Union of New York City's position is presented in *New York State Constitutional Convention 1967: Complete Set of Citizens Union Position Papers* (New York: mimeograph, 1967). Two other sources of information and reform proposals are Sigmund Diamond and Nancy Lee, eds., "Modernizing State Government: The New York Constitutional Convention of 1967," *Proceedings of the Academy of Political Science* 28 (January 1967), and Columbia School of Law, "Essays on the New York Constitution," mimeo. (1966). The articles in the former are general discussions with comments by noted scholars and/or political figures; the latter is a more technical examination of constitutional problems with specific proposals for reform. Donna E. Shalala, *The City*

and the Constitution: The 1967 New York Convention's Response to the Urban Crisis
(New York: National Municipal League, 1972), examines the convention's treatment of
urban problems and analyzes the divisions among reformers. Though written from its
own perspective, League of Women Voters of New York, *Seeds of Failure: A Political
Review of New York State's 1967 Constitutional Convention* (New York: Mt. Shiver
Press, 1973), is a perceptive overview of the convention as well as the reasons for its
failure. Richard I. Nunez, "New York State Constitutional Reform—Past Political Battles
in Constitutional Language," *William and Mary Law Quarterly* 10 (1968):366–77, puts
the failure in the context of earlier conventions. Lewis B. Kaden, "The People: No!
Some Observations of the 1967 New York Constitutional Convention," *Harvard Journal
of Legislation* 5 (Summer, 1968):343–71, and William Vanden Heuval's "Reflections
on Constitutional Change," *New York State Bar Journal* 40 (June 1968):261–69, while
recognizing the inevitability of partisanship at conventions, make recommendations as to
how it can be reduced or limited. The *New York Times* is an excellent source of information
and opinion on the convention and its product.

The 1967 convention has been well covered in the dissertation literature. The fullest
treatment is Henrik N. Dullea's, "Charter Revision in the Empire State: The Politics of
New York's 1967 Constitutional Convention" (Ph.D. diss., Syracuse University, 1982).
This work examines the forces leading to the convention, plots regional, partisan, and
ideological divisions using roll call votes, provides interviews with participants, and
explores the reasons for its failure. More specific in their focus are: James A. Dunne,
"A Longitudinal Study of the Role Concepts of a Select Group of Delegates to the 1967
State Constitutional Convention" (Ph.D. diss., State University of New York at Albany,
1972); Carol S. Greenwald, "Lobbyist Perceptions of the 1967 New York State Con-
stitutional Convention" (Ph.D. diss., City University of New York, 1972); and Irving
H. Freedman, "The Issue of Public Support for Church Related Education in the 1967
Constitutional Convention: A Study in the Decision-Making Process" (Ph.D. diss., State
University of New York at Albany, 1969).

Little has been published on the need for constitutional reform since 1977. The New
York State legislature appointed a Speaker's Task Force on Constitutional Revision in
1975. That task force issued a brief report, entitled *Constitutional Revision in New York
State . . .* (Albany, 1976). Intended to be preparatory for the 1977 referendum, it reiterated
arguments of earlier commissions about the need for major constitutional reform and
called for the appointment of a new temporary commission to educate the voters on the
connection between the state government's inability to meet their needs and the defects
of the constitution. No commission was created.

No constitutional history treats the period from World War II to the present. Joseph
Zimmerman, *The Government and Politics of New York State* (New York: New York
University Press, 1981), and Peter Colby and John White, eds., *The Government and
Politics of New York State Today: Politics, Government, Public Policy*, 2d ed. (Albany:
State University of New York at Albany, 1989), are useful, balanced descriptions and
analyses of New York government and politics.

THE CURRENT CONSTITUTION

The following are selected sources on the current constitution in addition to those cited
in the notes. Regular coverage of issues concerning the New York Constitution can be

found in the *New York Times*, *Empire State Reports* (a magazine on New York government and politics), and the *New York State Bar Journal*. The law reviews of the state's law schools, especially St. John's, Albany, and SUNY at Buffalo contain articles covering various aspects of New York constitutional law. The *Syracuse Law Review* devotes one issue annually to a survey of New York State Law.

ARTICLE I

Joseph Bellacosa. "The New York Constitution: A Touch of Class." *New York State Bar Journal* 59 (April 1987):14.

James J. Bjorkman. "From Lehman to Smith Haven Mall: Evolving Federal and State Restrictions on Political Advertising." *Annual Survey of American Law* 3 (1985):713

Comment. "Privilege against Self-Incrimination—Public Employees May Not Be Dismissed for Refusal to Waive Immunity from Criminal Prosecution—*Gardner v. Broderick* (1968)." *Albany Law Review* 33 (1969):397.

———. "Article I, Section 12 of the New York State Constitution: Revised Interpretation in Wake of New Federal Standards?" *St. John's Law Review* 60 (1986):770.

———. "An Examination of the Grand Jury in New York." *Columbia Journal of Law and Social Problems* 88 (1966):2.

———. "Towards Rendering New York's Free Speech Clause Redundant: *Shad Alliance v. Smith Haven Mall*," *St. John's Law Review* 60 (1986):799.

John C. Corbett. "Shall Grand Juries Be Abolished." *Brooklin Barrister* 51 (1974):25.

Mark Christopher Dillon. "The Case for Reversing 'The Rogers Rule' on the Right to Counsel." *New York State Bar Journal* 58 (July 1986):36.

Thomas Patrick Dugan. "The Constitutionality of School Finance Systems under State Law: New York's Turn." *Syracuse Law Review* 27 (1976):573.

Peter Galie. "State Constitutional Guarantees and the Protection of Defendant's Rights: The Case of New York, 1960–1978." *Buffalo Law Review* 28 (1979):157.

———. "Recent Constitutional Developments in New York." *State Constitutional Commentaries and Notes* 1 (Fall 1989):18.

John L. Goodall. "The New York Law of Libel: Aftermath of *New York Times v. Sullivan*." *New York State Bar Journal* 58 (December 1986):11.

Judith Kaye. "Dual Constitutionalism in Practice and Principle." *Record of the Association of the Bar of the City of New York* 42 (April 1987):285.

Richard S. Mayberry and Frank A. Aloi. "Compensation for Loss of Access in Eminent Domain in New York: A Re-evaluation of the No-Compensation Rule with a Proposal for Change." *Buffalo Law Review* 16 (1967):603.

Kevin H. Moore. "Fair Comment and Music Criticism: New York Law under the Constitutional Defenses to Libel." *Syracuse Law Review* 37 (1986):79.

Note. "The Nightmare of Forcible Medication: The New York Court of Appeals Protects the Rights of Medically Ill under the State Constitution: *Rivers v. Katz*," *Brooklyn Law Review* 53 (1987):885.

———. "The Bright Lines Must Be Dimmed Once Again: Reasonable Suspicion Searches of Automobiles under the New York State Constitution." *Syracuse Law Review* 38 (1987):1251.

———. "The Effects of Gaeta v. New York Inc. on New York's Private Libel Plaintiffs." *Albany Law Review* 50 (1985):157.

Albert M. Rosenblatt and Julia C. Rosenblatt. "Six-Member Juries in Criminal Cases: Legal and Psychological Considerations." *St. John's Law Review* 47 (1973):615.

ARTICLE II

David I. Wells. "Redistricting in New York State: It's a Question of Slicing the Salami." *Empire State Reports* 4 (October–November 1978):9.

———. "The Reapportionment Game Part II." *Empire State Reports* 5 (February 1979):8.

ARTICLE III

Harold I. Abramson. "Regulating the Regulators in New York State Part I." *New York State Bar Journal* 58 (July 1986):22.

Richard A. Givens. "A Primer on the New York State Legislative Process: How It Differs from Federal Procedure." *New York State Bar Journal* 57 (April 1985):8.

ARTICLE IV

Eugene J. Gleason and Joseph Zimmerman. *Executive Dominance in New York State.* Albany: State University of New York at Albany, 1974.

Thomas O. Melia. "Settling for Second" *Empire State Reports* 12 (April 1986):39.

G. Scott Thomas. "Vacancy in Office No. 2." *Empire State Reports* 12 (April 1986):33.

ARTICLE V

Management Resources Project. *Governing the Empire State.* New York: Management Resources Project, 1988.

ARTICLE VI

Comment. "The Religious Factor in New York Adoption Proceedings." *Syracuse Law Review* 18 (1967):825.

Thomas Gleason and Salvatore Ferlazzo. "The Court of Appeals Moves towards 'Certiorari' Status." *New York State Bar Journal* 58 (May 1986).

Mendes Hershman. "The Realities of Nomination to the New York Court of Appeals." *New York State Bar Journal* 55 (November 1983):6.

Martin I. Kaminsky. "Available Compromises for Continued Judicial Selection Reform." *St. John's Law Review* 53 (1979):466.

Project. "The Appellate Division of the Supreme Court of New York: An Empirical Study of its Powers and Functions as an Intermediate State Court." *Fordham Law Review* 47 (1979):929.

C. Raymond Radigan. "Jurisdiction [of Surrogate's Court] after Piccione." *New York State Bar Journal* 56 (April 1984):12.

Alan D. Scheinkman. "The Civil Jurisdiction of the New York Court of Appeals: The Rule and Role of Finality." *St. John's Law Review* 54 (1980):443.

Carl Swidorski. "Judicial Selection Reform and the New York Court of Appeals: Illusion or Reality." *New York State Bar Journal* 55 (July 1983):10.

ARTICLES VII AND VIII

Comment. "The Future of Non-Guaranteed Bond Financing in New York." *Fordham Law Review* 45 (1977):860.
———. "Local Finance: A Brief Constitutional History." *Fordham Law Journal* 8 (1979):135.
———. "The Constitutional Debt Limit and New York City." *Fordham Law Journal* 8 (1979):185.
J. L. Hardy. "Public Authorities in New York." *Empire State Reports* 4 (March–April 1978):21.
James Leigland. "Managing Public Authorities." *Empire State Reports* 12 (May 1986):19.
Frank Macchiarola. "Local Finances under the New York State Constitution." *Fordham Law Review* 35 (1966):263.
William J. Quirk and Leon E. Wein. "A Short Constitutional History of Entities Commonly Known as Authorities." *Cornell Law Review* 56 (1971):521.
———. "Rockefeller's Constitutional Sleight of Hand." *Empire State Reports* 1 (November 1975):429.
Special Report. "Fifty Years of Executive Budgeting." *Empire State Reports* 5 (June–July 1979):19.

ARTICLE IX

Comment. "Home Rule, A Fresh Start." *Buffalo Law Review* 14 (1965):484.
———. "Abolishing Multiple Majority Referendum Requirements: Is That the Cure for Metropolitan Ills?" *Buffalo Law Review* 25 (1975):357.
Joseph F. Zimmerman. *State-Local Relations, A Partnership Approach.* New York: Praeger Publishers, 1983.

ARTICLE X

J. L. Hardy. "Public Authorities in New York" *Empire State Reports* 4 (March–April 1978):21.
James Leigland. "Managing Public Authorities: *Empire State Reports* 12 (May 1986):19.
William J. Quirk and Leon E. Wein. "A Short Constitutional History of Entities Commonly Known as Authorities" *Cornell Law Review* 56 (1971):521.
———."Rockefeller's Constitutional Sleigh of Hand" *Empire State Reports* 1 1975):421.
———.Special Report "Fifty Years of Executive Budgeting" *Empire State Reports* 5 (June–July 1979):19.

ARTICLE XI

Charles E. Rice. "The New York State Constitution and Aid to Church Related Schools." *Catholic Lawyer* 272 (1966):12.

ARTICLE XVII

Judith Kaye. "Dual Constitutionalism in Practice and Principle." *Record of the Association of the Bar of the City of New York* 42 (April 1987):285.

ARTICLE XVIII

Eugene Morris. "Housing and Urban Development Problems Facing the 1967 Constitutional Convention." *The Record of Association of the Bar of the City of New York* 21 (1966):145.

Table of Cases

314   Table of Cases

Dartmouth College v. Woodward, 4 Wheat 518 (1819), **224**

DeCerce v. New York State Thruway Authority, 120 A.D.2d 981 (1986), **289**

DeZimm v. New York State Board of Parole, 135 A.D.2d 66 (1988), **290**

Diamond v. Cuomo, 70 N.Y.2d 338, 514 N.E.2d 1356 (1987), **153, 287**

Dillon v. Nassau Civil Service, 43 N.Y.2d 574, 373 N.E.2d 1225 (1978), **115**

Diocese of Rochester v. Planning Board of Town of Brighton, 1 N.Y.2d 508, 136 N.E.2d 827 (1956), **257, 284**

District 2 Marine Engineers Beneficial Association (AFL-CIO) v. New York Shipping Association, 22 N.Y.2d 809, 239 N.E.2d 650 (1968), **65**

Donnelly v. Roosevelt, 144 Misc. 525 (1932), **239**

Donohue v. Copiague Union Free School District, 47 N.Y.2d 440, 391 N.E.2d 1352 (1979), **113, 232**

Dorsey v. Stuyvesant Town Corporation, 299 N.Y. 512, 87 N.E.2d 541 (1949), **57**

Duhan v. Milanowski, 75 Misc. 2d 1078, (1973), **63**

Dunaway v. New York, 422 U.S. 200 (1979), **59**

Duncan v. Louisiana, 391 U.S. 145 (1968), **37**

Dunham v. Dunham, 40 A.D.2d 912 (1972), **134**

Dunn v. Blumstein, 405 U.S. 330 (1972), **69**

Dworsky V. Farano, 41 N.Y.2d 780, 364 N.E.2d 827 (1977), **145**

Eber v. Board of Election, 80 Misc. 2d 334 (1974), **289**

Economic Power and Construction Co. v. Buffalo, 195 N.Y 286, 88 N.E.2d 319 (1909), **89**

EEOC v. State of New York, 266 F. Supp. 1996 (SD N.Y., 1990), **153**

EEOC v. Wyoming, 460 U.S. 226 (1983), **289**

Elrod v. Burns, 427 U.S. 347 (1976), **115**

Embury v. Connor, 3 N.Y. 511 (1850), **50**

Enders v. Rossi, 45 A.D.2d 447 (1974), **243**

Engel v. Vitale, 10 N.Y.2d 174 (1961), rev'd Engel v. Vitale, 370 U.S. 421 (1962), **31**

Esler v. Walters, 56 N.Y.2d 306, 437 N.E.2d 1090 (1982), **69**

Exempt Firemen's Benevolent Fund v. Roome, 22 A.D. 564 (1897), **95**

Fay v. Noia, 372 U.S. 391 (1963), **284**

Fidell v. Board of Elections of the City of New York, 409 U.S. 972 (1972), **289**

First Broadcasting Corp. v. Syracuse, 78 A.D.2d 490 (1981), **286**

Floyd v. New York City Urban Development Corporation, 33 N.Y.2d 1, 300 N.E.2d 704 (1973), **221, 269**

Flushing National Bank v. Municipal Assistance Corporation, 40 N.Y.2d 731, 358 N.E.2d 848 (1976), **97, 192**

Foss v. City of Rochester, 104 A.D.2d 99 (1984), aff'd & modified on other grounds, 65 N.Y.2d 247, 480 N.E.2d 717 (1984), **58**

Index

Mental health, 172
Mental Hygiene Department, 264
Mentally ill and retarded, 172
Merit System. *See* Civil Service
Message
 governor to communicate with legislature, 101–2
 objections to bill, 105–7
 of necessity, 169–70
Military. *See* Armed Forces
Militia
 governor commander-in-chief, 101
 legislature to provide for, 235
Morris, Gouverneur, 1
Municipal Assistance Corporation, 187, 192
Municipal Corporations, interpretations and powers, 192–94, 208–9, 223–24
Municipal court of the city of New York, 159–60
Municipal defaults, 186
Municipal Development Agency Law, 261
Municipal purpose doctrine, 217–18
Municipal utility plants, 212, 214
Municipal water supply, 248–49

Nassau County, 136, 196
National Constitution of 1787, 2, 5, 236
Native Americans, 157
Natural resources, 250–51
Needy, 172, 262–66
New York City, 116–17, 129–30, 137–38, 142–43, 156, 159–62, 178–79, 186–92, 201–4, 206–8, 241–44
New York Housing Finance Agency, 228
New York Port Authority, 226–27, 229–30
Non-Profit Corporations, 171–74, 230–31
Nursing home accommodations, 268

Oath, Constitutional form, 236–37
Off-budgeting, 171
Office
 duration may be declared by law, 237
 legislature may declare when vacant, 239–40
 legislature to provide for filling 237–38

oath, form, 236–37
 provision to be made for removal, 239
 qualification, no oath declaration or test required, 236–37
 terms, city and certain county offices, 240–41
 vacancies, 237–38
Officers, Public. *See* Public officers
Organize, right to, 64–65
Original jurisdiction. *See entries of specific courts*
Official referee, abolished, 161
Old age, 172
Orphan asylums, 186
Oswego Canal, 252, 254

Pardons and commutations, 102–3
Pari-mutuel betting, 53–55
Parole, 265
Parties, political, 11, 14, 236–37
Payment of state debt and interest, 180–81
Peacemaker courts, 157
Pension system. *See* Retirement system
People, definition, 218
Personal income tax, 94–95
Personal liability, stockholders and corporations, 224–25
Petition, right of guaranteed, 53, 55
Petty offenses, 43
Physically handicapped, provision for, 172
Plenary state legislative power, 77
Pocket veto, 105–7
Poletti Report, 52, 290 n.9
Police power, 76, 280
Political questions, doctrine of, 100
Political year, beginning of, 238
Pollution, 250–51
Pool-selling, 53, 55
Power of eminent domain. *See* Eminent domain
Preamble, 33
Preemptory challenges, 57
President of the Senate, 86, 104
Presidential elections, 75
Press, liberty of, 51–53
Preventive detention, 40–41

Primary elections, 35
Prison labor, 95–96
Prisons. *See* Correctional institutions
Private or local bills. *See* Laws
Private road, 49–50
Private property for public use. *See* Eminent domain and property
Probable cause, issuance of warrant and, 58–62
Probation, 265
Profits, 212, 214
Property
  compensation when taken for public use, 49–51
  dedication for state nature and historic preserve, 250–51
  deprive, due process necessary, 41, 47–48
  public, applied to local purposes, 93
  sectarian school, use restricted, 233–34
Property, personal
  intangible, not to be taxed ad valorem, 258–59
  intangible, situs for purposes of taxation, 258–59. *See also* Taxation
Property, real, *See* Taxation
Public corporations, 172–73, 192–95, 226–29, 266, 274
Public office, 35–36, 96, 236–37
Public officers
  constitutional officers to receive fixed salary, 240
  county, city, town, village, how chosen, 211, 213
  fees, 240
  refusal to testify or waive immunity, 42, 46–47
  removal for misconduct, 239
  tenure, when not fixed, 237
  terms, 216
  vacancies, 237–38
Public purpose doctrine, 49–51
  housing, urban redevelopment and, 276–77
  private property for public use, 49–50
  taxation and, 256
Punishment, cruel and unusual, 40–41

Qualifications. *See specific offices*
Quorum
  appellate division, supreme court, 125
  court of appeals, 118
  legislative, 86
  three-fifths necessary, when, 95

Racial discrimination, 36–38. *See also* Suffrage
Railroads
  commuter, 229–30
  crossings at grades, state debt for elimination, 178–79
  rapid transit debt, New York City, 201–2
Reapportionment. *See* Apportionment
Recovery of damages, 63–64
Referendum, voting on, 18, 176, 212–14, 279–80
Reforestation, 249–50
Refund, state debts, 177–78
Regents, 112–13, 196, 233
Registers in counties, 243
Registration
  armed forces, members and families, 72–73
  boards to be bipartisan, 74
  permanent system authorized, 72–73
  veterans', hospitals, inmates, and families, 72–73
Religion
  custody of children and, 157–58
  free exercise of, 37–38
Religious sect, ban on establishment of. *See* Separation of church and state
Removal
  judges, 146–51
  officers, other than judicial, local, or legislative, 239
  public officers refusing to waive immunity, 42, 46–47
Reprieves and pardons, 102–3
Reservoirs, 248–49
Residence
  presidential elections, 75
  requirements, governor, 100–101

340   Index

Vacancy, 237–38, 239–41. *See also specific offices*
Van Buren, Martin, 7, 10
Venue, change of, 90
Veterans, 31, 72, 113–14, 182–83
Veto, power of governor, 105–7
Village courts, 116–17, 131, 140–43
Villages, 211–18, 272–74
Visitations and inspections, 263–64
Voting rights. *See* Suffrage

Warrants, seach, 58–60
Water
  pollution and, 250–51
  supply, 192–93, 248–49, 189–90
Waterways, 254–55

Welfare services, 172–73, 186, 262–64
Wildlife conservation, 249–50
Wiretapping, 59, 61–62
Witness
  competency not affected by religion, 37–38
  unreasonably detained, 40
Women, rights of, 237. *See also* Suffrage, Sex Discrimination
Workers' compensation, 66–67
Wrongful death, right of action for, 63–64

Zoning, equal protection and, 48–49

About the Author

PETER J. GALIE is Professor and Chairman of the Department of Political Science at Canisius College in Buffalo, New York. He is the author of several articles on state constitutional law including "Cases and Commentaries on State Constitutions" and "State Supreme Court: The Other Constitutions."